Preparation for the

TOEFL*

Test of English as a Foreign Language

PATRICIA NOBLE SULLIVAN
GRACE YI QIU ZHONG

Macmillan · USA

*TOEFL is a registered trademark of Educational Testing Service. There is no connection between this publication and Educational Testing Service.

To our family members, who helped in innumerable ways.

John, Jesse, Mick, Rebecca, Adam

Seventh Edition

Macmillan General Reference
A Simon & Schuster Macmillan Company
1633 Broadway
New York, NY 10019

An Arco Book

MACMILLAN is a registered trademark of Macmillan, Inc.
ARCO is a registered trademark of Prentice-Hall, Inc.

Library of Congress Cataloging-in-Publication Data

ISBN 0-02-860563-2

Manufactured in the United States of America

10 9 8 7 6 5 4 3 2 1

C o n t e n t s

PART ONE
The Test of English as a Foreign Language

PART TWO
Sample Questions and Test-Taking Strategies

PART THREE
Six Practice TOEFL Tests

PART FOUR
Tapescripts for Practice Tests

Preface to the Test-Taker

Why Use This Book

This book can help you earn high scores on the TOEFL. Here are three important reasons why:

First, the practice tests in this book are very similar to those on the actual TOEFL. The practice tests were developed after a statistical analysis of questions in many recent TOEFL tests. We analyzed the frequency with which certain types of questions occurred on previous TOEFL tests and developed categories of testing points represented by each question. These testing points were then used to write practice questions that are very much like actual TOEFL questions.

Second, every practice question and every strategy relates directly to succeeding on the TOEFL. You won't waste your time or money using a book that has material that is not related to the TOEFL.

Third, this book will help you organize your study by pointing out the common testing points in each section of the TOEFL. These testing points show you what to study to score high on the TOEFL. When you focus on the testing points of the TOEFL questions as you study, you will increase your skills in answering similar questions on the actual TOEFL.

In the next few years there will be major changes in the TOEFL. The Educational Testing Service, which produces the TOEFL, is in the process of making changes that should increase the effectiveness of the test. Some sections that have been standard for many years will be removed. Other sections will change considerably. This TOEFL practice book reflects the most recent TOEFL changes, particularly in the Listening Comprehension and Reading Comprehension sections. Because of the continued revisions that will appear over the next several years, it is extremely important that you carefully read the most up-to-date TOEFL Bulletin of Information, comparing that information with what you read in this book.

How to Get the Most Out of This Book

The major part of this book consists of six practice tests. We know that practice tests help you prepare, and that is why this book gives you six of them. But it is also important for you to practice test-taking skills. We recommend the following approach to this book:

1. Use the Listening Comprehension audio cassette to get the full benefit of the Listening Comprehension practice tests.
2. Read Part One to get a general idea of the TOEFL and TWE and the general rules for taking these tests.
3. Read Part Two to learn about the types of questions, testing points, and test-taking strategies.
4. Take the complete Test 1, following the time limits exactly. First check your answers using the answer key only. If you missed a lot of questions, go back to Part Two and reread the testing points and strategies for the sections that were difficult for you. Then take the practice test again and check the answer key to see if you improved your score. After checking the answer key, read the explanatory answers to check again on the testing points of the questions you missed.
5. Take Practice Tests 2, 3, 4, 5, and 6 just as you took Test 1. Go back and forth between the practice tests and the sections in Part Two that give you information about testing points. Focus especially on the testing points in the areas that are most difficult for you.

Acknowledgments

There are several people who helped us in writing this book. Some helped by prewriting questions; others helped by taking the practice tests to test the questions. For their help in prewriting some of the test questions we would like to thank Gail Brenner, David Biggs, Karen Connor, Andrew Levandowski, and Xin Liu. Thanks also goes to Zhong Yu Ming for the many hours he spent on test questions and exercises.

For their help in pretesting the sample tests we would like to thank staff, instructors, and students at the English Language Institute at Golden Gate University in San Francisco, California: Director Karen F. McRobie; instructors Michael Smith, Tina Martin, and James J. Ives; and all the students who took the practice tests. An additional thanks goes to Gail Brenner from Santa Cruz Adult School, Santa Cruz, California, and her students for pretesting TOEFL and TWE tests. All of their comments and suggestions assisted us in producing the practice tests in this book. Any errors, however, remain ours alone.

About the Authors

GRACE YI QIU ZHONG came to the United States from Shanghai, China, in 1984. She received a Master of Arts degree in Sports Psychology from California State University, Sacramento, in 1987, and has been coaching TOEFL students since 1989.

PATRICIA NOBLE SULLIVAN is a lecturer at the University of California, Santa Cruz. She is a Ph.D. candidate in Education in Language and Literacy at the University of California, Berkeley. She has taught English and TOEFL in California, China, Taiwan, Afghanistan, and Vietnam.

PART

ONE

The Test of English as a Foreign Language

CONTENTS

A Bird's-Eye View of the TOEFL and the TWE

What Is the TOEFL?

The letters "TOEFL" stand for "Test of English as a Foreign Language." The purpose of the test is to evaluate the English proficiency of nonnative speakers of English who wish to study in colleges and universities. TOEFL scores are used by more than 2,300 institutions in the United States and Canada. For many of these institutions, you must send in your TOEFL score with your application.

The TOEFL has three sections: (1) Listening Comprehension, (2) Structure and Written Expression, and (3) Reading Comprehension. The Listening Comprehension section tests your ability to understand English as it is spoken in the United States and Canada. The Structure and Written Expression section tests your ability to recognize standard written English. The Reading Comprehension section tests your ability to understand reading passages on nontechnical subjects.

There is no single "passing score" for this test. The minimum score for admittance to an institution is set by that institution. Many universities require a score of 550 or higher for entrance, but some schools, especially if they have English language classes, may accept a person with a score below 500.

What Is the TWE?

The letters "TWE" stand for "Test of Written English." This is an essay test that is given on some scheduled TOEFL dates. If you take the TOEFL on a day that the TWE is given, you must take the test. It takes 30 minutes and is scored separately from the TOEFL score. The TOEFL and TWE scores are not combined. Even if your institution does not require the TWE, it is good practice for you, and you do not have to submit the scores to your institution.

When Are the Tests Given? How Do I Register?

The TOEFL is given almost every month on Fridays and Saturdays in many locations around the world. You can take it as many times as you wish. The applications are in a booklet called "Bulletin of Information for TOEFL and TSE." (The letters "TSE" stand for "Test of Spoken English," a test that is not described in this book.)

The Bulletin of Information is free, and it is available at many colleges, universities, and public libraries in the United States and Canada. If you cannot find one in your area, you may request one from the following agencies:

TOEFL/TSE Service   Or   TOEFL/TSE
P.O. Box 6151   Trans-Canada Educational Evaluation Services
Princeton, New Jersey 08541-6151   P.O. Box 162, Station S
USA   Toronto, ON M5M 4L7
Telephone number 609-771-7760   Canada
Fax: 609-771-7765   Telephone number 416-789-2331
Telex: 5106859596 ETSSCHO A PRIN

3

How Is the TOEFL Changing?

The Test of English as a Foreign Language is in the process of being revised in order to make it a more valid indication of your English language ability. Because of the new changes, the format of practice tests in this book is different from the format of practice tests in previous TOEFL books, especially in the Listening Comprehension and Reading Comprehension sections. The differences in the types of questions reflect new changes to the TOEFL. Be sure to read the Bulletin of Information carefully before you take the TOEFL in order to understand the latest changes to the test. Though this practice book was accurate at the time of publication, changes to the exam may have occurred since then.

How Long Are the Tests?

There is more than one form of the TOEFL, and the forms have different lengths. On some testing days, extra questions are added to the TOEFL. These questions are being tested for use in future TOEFL exams. You will not know which questions are the "test" questions, and you do not need to know, for these questions are not counted in your TOEFL score. The longer form has more questions, but it has the same value as the more common shorter TOEFL form. It does not matter which form you take; all scores are equivalent. In order to help you prepare for either form of the test, Practice Test 4 in this book is written in the longer form.

If you decide that you would rather take the shorter form of the TOEFL, sign up for the TOEFL on a day when the TWE is given. You can be fairly certain that the shorter form will be given when the TWE is given.

Summary of Test Formats

NOTE: The TOEFL is in the process of being changed. Check the latest Bulletin of Information for TOEFL to see if the summary below is accurate for the test you will take.

Test Times

	Standard (Short Form)	Long Form
Filling out forms	30 minutes (approx.)	30 minutes (approx.)
TWE	30 minutes	
TOEFL		
Listening Comprehension	30 minutes (approx.)	50 minutes (approx.)
Structure and Written Expression	25 minutes	35 minutes
Reading Comprehension	55 minutes	75 minutes
Total for TOEFL	1 hour and 50 minutes	2 hours and 40 minutes
Total Time in Testing Center	2 hours and 50 minutes	3 hours and 10 minutes
	(approx.)	(approx.)

Test Questions

	Standard (Short Form)	Long Form
Section 1: Listening Comprehension		
Part A: Short Conversations	20	30
Part B: Longer Conversations	15	25
Part C: Talks	15	25
Total	50	80
Section 2: Structure and Written Expression		
Sentence Completion	15	23
Error Identification	25	37
Total	40	60
Section 3: Reading Comprehension		
Reading Comprehension	60	90
Total	60	90
TOEFL Total Questions	150	230

General Preparation for the TOEFL

Learn the Rules of TOEFL and Apply Them to the Practice Tests

Taking the TOEFL is like playing a game. In order to play the game well, you need to know the rules of the game, and you must be able to apply the rules without spending a lot of time thinking about them. If you are very familiar with the rules, you will feel less anxious, and you will be better able to concentrate on the test itself.

Here are some of the key rules of TOEFL:

1. You can work on only one section at a time. During the time limit for one particular section, you may not turn back to the previous section or turn ahead to the next section.
2. You may not turn the page and read ahead while the Listening Comprehension directions are being read.
3. You must not make any marks in your test booklet or on your answer sheet (except for filling in the answer ovals).
4. There is no penalty for choosing the wrong answer. You should take advantage of this rule by answering every question, even if you have to guess.
5. Only one answer is allowed for each question. If you mark two answers for one question, you get no credit for that question.
6. There is no rest break during the test. If you have to leave to use the restroom or for any other reason, you may do so, but you lose valuable test time.
7. When the stop time is called, you must stop writing immediately and close your test booklet. If you do not stop writing, you risk getting no credit for the entire test and having to repeat the TOEFL at another time.

Mark Your Answer Sheet in the Correct Way

There is only one correct way to mark your answers on the answer sheet. Look at the examples below of the correct and incorrect ways of filling in the answer spaces.

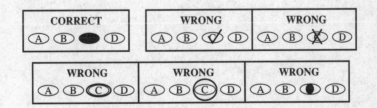

   Each time you take a practice test, use the special answer sheet to record your answers, and practice filling in the ovals correctly. Then, you will feel comfortable with this way of marking answers, and you will do it automatically at the real test.

When you take the test, you need to go back and forth between your test booklet and your answer sheet. This is sometimes difficult to do. You do not want to lose time by having to search for your place in the answer book. And you certainly do not want to make an error by marking your answer in the wrong place. To avoid these mistakes and to save time, practice using both hands to mark your place. If you are right-handed, keep your left hand on the question in your test booklet and use your right hand to mark your place on the answer sheet. After you mark an answer, keep your pencil on that place without moving it until you are ready to mark your next answer. With one hand on the question and one hand on the answer sheet, you will be able to keep track of where you are at all times. If you practice this procedure while you take the practice tests in this book, it will seem comfortable to you when you take the real test.

Eliminate Incorrect Answer Choices

On the TOEFL there is no penalty for choosing an incorrect answer; therefore, you should answer every question, even if you have to guess. If you randomly guess one answer out of four choices, your chance of getting that answer correct is 25 percent. If you randomly guess one answer out of three choices, your chance of getting that answer correct is 33 percent. If you randomly guess one answer out of two choices, your chance of getting a correct answer is 50 percent. That means if you can eliminate two of the answer choices, you increase your chance of being correct from 25 percent to 50 percent.

Ways to Eliminate Answer Choices If You Do Not Know the Correct Answer

1. First, look at all the answer choices and eliminate those that "seem" wrong even if you do not know the reason they may be wrong.
2. Second, try to figure out the testing point and think of the strategies you have learned in this book. (You will read more about testing points in Part Two of this book.)
3. Third, and last, mark one letter (A, B, C, or D) for all the remaining unanswered questions. This is not a very good strategy, but if you know you cannot finish in the time you have left, it is better to fill in the ovals than leave them blank. You may gain a point or two by pure luck.

On the Day of the Test

1. Bring your admission ticket, your passport, and two sharpened #2 pencils.
2. Get to the testing center in plenty of time to find the room and show your entry ticket.
3. Sit down and take some deep breaths to relax.

TWO

Sample Questions and Test-Taking Strategies

CONTENTS

What Are Testing Points?

A testing point is the main point of a TOEFL question. It is the specific area of English on which you are being tested. The practice tests in this book were written to reflect the testing points represented on previous TOEFL exams. Even though the questions in the real TOEFL are new for each test, many of the testing points remain the same. An understanding of the major testing points of the TOEFL, therefore, will help you organize your study time and help you prepare for the many different kinds of questions you will see on the real test. When you study with the idea of learning to recognize testing points rather than simply answering individual questions, you are using a strategy that will help you when you take the real TOEFL. The time you spend learning to recognize and understand the testing points in this book will increase your understanding of English and help you prepare for the TOEFL.

In the following practice section of this book, you will see examples of different testing points and the way they are used in the test questions. Testing points are different in each section of the TOEFL, and there may be several testing points in one question. A testing point might be a grammatical structure, a common vocabulary word, an idiom, an intonation, or a particular type of reading or listening comprehension question. When you take the practice tests in this book, you will also be testing yourself to see if you understand the testing point and the test-taking strategies to use with that testing point.

Listening Comprehension Section

The Listening Comprehension section of TOEFL tests your ability to understand spoken English. It is divided into three parts:

- *Part A: Short Conversations*
  You will listen to a brief conversation between two people and then answer a question about it.
- *Part B: Longer Conversations*
  You will listen to a longer conversation between two people and then answer approximately four or five questions about what was said.
- *Part C: Talks*
  You will listen to a single speaker giving a lecture or talk and then answer approximately four or five questions about what was said.

Sample Questions

Part A: Short Conversations

On the tape you will hear:

> *Woman:* Have you called Pete?
> *Man:* I'll call him as soon as I get home.
> *Narrator:* Question 1. What does the man mean?

Sample Answer

1. (A) ● (C) (D)

In your test book you will read:

1. (A) He will call Pete before he goes home.
   (B) He will call Pete after he gets home.
   (C) He called Pete at home.
   (D) He will call Pete tomorrow.

You learn from the conversation that the man will call Pete as soon as he gets home. Therefore, the best answer to the question is (B), "He will call Pete after he gets home." Indicate your answer by filling in answer space B for question number 1.

Part B: Longer Conversations

On the tape you will hear:

Narrator: Questions 1 and 2 are based on the following conversation between two friends at school.

   Man: Hi, Joanie. Where are you going?

Woman: Oh, hi, Paul. I'm on my way to the library.

   Man: I just wondered if you wanted to go to a movie with me.

Woman: I'd love to, but I can't. I can't believe all the work I have this semester. I only have three classes, but in all of them I have lots of reading, term papers, reports, and essay exams. It's incredible! I feel like I'll never get through everything.

   Man: That's terrible. I felt that way last year when I had term papers to write, but this semester seems much easier. I spend a lot of time in class, but most of it is in labs doing experiments. I hated writing all those term papers. Can't I talk you into going to the show anyway? I've heard that the movie over at the East Auditorium is really good. It's a murder mystery.

Woman: Oh, now I'm sure I won't go. I might go to a comedy, but I hate murder mysteries.

Narrator: Now listen to sample question number 1. Where is the woman going?

In your test booklet you will read:

1. **(A)**   To the cafeteria   Sample Answer
   (B)   To the movie theater
   (C)   To her dorm room   1. Ⓐ Ⓑ Ⓒ ⬤
   (D)   To the library

The best answer to the question "Where is the woman going?" is (D) "To the library," since the woman says, "I'm on my way to the library." Therefore, the correct choice is (D), and you should blacken the oval marked D for question number 1.

Narrator: Now listen to sample question number 2. Which of the following best describes the man's feeling about his classes?

In your test booklet you will read:

2. **(A)**   Term papers are easy for him.   Sample Answer
   (B)   He has a lot of essay exams.
   (C)   He finds lab experiments easier than writing term papers.   2. Ⓐ Ⓑ ⬤ Ⓓ
   (D)   He is busier this semester than last semester.

The best answer to the question is (C) because the man says that this semester seems much easier since he spends a lot of time in labs doing experiments. Blacken oval C for sample question 2.

Part C: Talks

On the tape you will hear:

Narrator: Questions 1 to 4 are based on the following announcement:

Woman: At this university we offer three different programs for students who have children. For those of you with very young children, we have a day care program that takes infants from 3 months to 30 months. We have another program for children between 2 and 5 years of age. And we also have an after-school program for school-aged children. This program offers sports, crafts, outings, and tutoring during after-school hours. Enrollment in these child care programs is limited and early application is essential, since our programs often have waiting lists. The fees are on an hourly basis. If any of you new students need these services, please let me know right away so I can get you an application form.

Narrator: Now listen to sample question number 1. What is the main purpose of this announcement?

In your test book you will read:

1. **(A)** To demonstrate tutoring techniques
   (B) To explain school policies
   (C) To recruit childcare workers
   (D) To explain a service

Sample Answer

1. (A) (B) (C) ●

The best answer to the question "What is the purpose of this announcement?" is (D), "To explain a service." One clue is at the end of the talk when the speaker says, "If any of you new students need these services...." Indicate your answer by blackening the oval marked D for question number 1.

Narrator: Now listen to sample question number 2. What does the speaker recommend?

In your test book you will read:

2. **(A)** Give your child extra tutoring.
   (B) Take your child to the program today.
   (C) Apply as soon as you can.
   (D) Pay next month.

Sample Answer

2. (A) (B) ● (D)

The best answer to the question "What does the speaker recommend?" is (C), "Apply as soon as you can," since the speaker says, "please let me know right away." Blacken oval C for question number 2.

Listening Strategies

The first section of the TOEFL, the Listening Comprehension section, has three different parts. The strategies for short conversations are different from the strategies for the longer conversations and talks.

Strategy for Part A, Short Conversations: The Backwards Way

The directions you hear on the Listening Comprehension section of the TOEFL tell you to listen to the question on the tape and then read the four choices and decide on the answer. This means that first you listen to the tape and next you read the answer choices. For some people this strategy works well, but other people find it helpful to read the answer choices first. The strategy of reading the answer choices first is called the Backwards Way. Here is how the Backwards Way works:

1. Turn on the tape and listen to the directions. During this time, DO NOT look at the answer choices in your test booklet or your practice test.
2. When the voice on the tape tells you to turn the page, quickly glance at the four choices printed in the test booklet. You may have only a second or two, but try to look for words that are repeated, such as names and places. This will help you understand those words if you hear them. You might even be able to make a general guess about the topic by looking at the main nouns or verbs.
3. When the speakers on the tape begin the conversation, stop reading immediately and concentrate on the conversation.
4. After the question is asked, read the four choices again, and choose your answer. If you do not immediately know the answer, try to eliminate some of the answer choices, and then pick an answer from the choices that remain.
5. Mark the answer sheet quickly but carefully. Immediately return to step 2 and glance at the answer choices for the next question, looking for repeated words, main nouns, and verbs. Repeat steps 2 through 5 for all questions in Part A.

The Backwards Way is not easy to learn because it is hard to get into the rhythm of reading the answer choices first. Many people find, however, that looking at the answer choices first helps them to understand the taped conversation better. They may recognize some of the vocabulary and possibly make a general guess about the topic before hearing the questions. Even if you cannot guess the topic, seeing the words before you hear them may help you to understand the speakers and answer the question more quickly. Try this system during your practice tests. If it helps you, then use it on the real test.

There are three major benefits of the Backwards Way:

1. You can get clues about the general topic of the questions.
2. You can use your reading ability and summarizing ability to enhance your listening skills.
3. You will have less anxiety if you can guess what the general topic is before you hear the tape. This will help you focus on specific information that you hear on the tape.

Strategies for Parts B and C, Longer Conversations and Talks

The Backwards Way is difficult to use for longer conversations and talks because each listening passage is followed by three or four sets of answer choices. If you have time, however, try to glance at some of the answer choices to help make you aware of vocabulary words and possible general topics.

The following strategies are for different levels of proficiency. The first strategy is for people who have difficulty getting even a very general idea of the conversation or talk. The second and third strategies are for people who can get the general idea of the talk but have difficulty remembering the details. Decide which level you are at and then try one of the strategies on the next page.

Strategy No. 1 (for lower proficiency levels)

As the speakers are talking, close your eyes and concentrate completely on the general topic of the conversation. Don't worry if you do not understand all the words. Try to understand what the conversation is about, where it is taking place, and who the speakers are. Answer the questions based on your general understanding of the whole conversation.

Strategy No. 2 (for higher proficiency levels)

As the speakers are talking, listen for the general topic, as described above. But also listen for more details. Pay attention to specific names, places, and activities. Think about who the speakers are. What is their relationship? Are they both students? Is one a teacher? The questions that follow these conversations are often based on the exact words of the speakers. Most of the difficulty comes from having to remember all the details without taking notes, so when you take the practice tests do not take notes.

Strategy No. 3 (for higher proficiency levels)

As the speakers are talking, look at your test booklet. Try to match the speakers' words with the possible answer choices. Often you will be able to pick out possible questions and answers as you are listening. If you feel that you are getting lost, however, stop reading immediately and concentrate on listening. You don't want to spend so much of your time looking at the answer choices that you don't hear what the speakers are saying.

General Strategies for Parts A, B, and C

General Strategy No. 1: Get Information in a Quick Glance

Though the Listening Comprehension section is designed to test your ability to understand spoken English, it is also a test of your reading ability since you are reading the answer choices and guessing the general topic. For many test-takers the main problem with reading the answers in this section is the time limit. You must read very quickly. You have only 12 seconds after each conversation to mark your answer to one question and then begin to read the next answer choices. You do not have enough time to read each answer choice slowly and carefully. So, instead of reading each sentence, just look briefly at the words in the four choices. Let your eyes travel down from answer choice to answer choice, rather than reading across the line. When you glance at the answer choices:

1. Look for words that are repeated in some of the answer choices. These words give you a clue about the topic, and may help you recognize the names you hear on the tape.
2. Look for the major differences between answer choices. You might see a different name or a different place. You might see a different verb or activity. These differences help you focus on what to listen for.

General Strategy No. 2: Eliminate Wrong Answers

If you are using the Backwards Way, you will be glancing at the answer choices first, and then guessing the topic and possible questions. Then you will focus on what the speakers say, looking for a match to your guess. After that you do not need to read the whole sentence again in order to eliminate wrong answers. Some of the answers may immediately seem wrong. Remember that even if you don't know the correct answer, it will help to eliminate at least one or two that you think are wrong.

General Strategy No. 3: Keep Up the Rhythm as You Practice

Rhythm is more important in the Listening Comprehension section than in any other section of the TOEFL. While you are practicing you may be tempted to stop the tape in order to give yourself time to get the answer. Don't do it! You cannot stop the tape during the real TOEFL, so don't do it while you are practicing. Stopping the tape will not help you prepare for the rhythm of the TOEFL. So if your goal is to pass the real TOEFL, do not stop the tape during your practice tests. Choose a place where you will not be interrupted and take each listening practice test all at one time.

General Strategy No. 4: Build Skills by Repetition

The TOEFL, like many other tests, requires both knowledge and skill. Some people have the knowledge, but get a lower score than they should because of their anxiety. Other people need more knowledge of English vocabulary and grammar to increase their score. Both knowledge and test-taking skills can be increased by taking the practice tests over and over, and this repetition may also ease your anxiety. If you understand the rules of the TOEFL, you will feel more comfortable about taking the test. The Listening Comprehension test is like a performance, and you will perform better if you do not have to think about the process you are using as you take the test.

   If the listening section is very difficult for you, do the following:

1. Take the practice test the first time without stopping the tape. Check your answers with the answer key, but DO NOT read the explanatory answers yet. Don't worry if your score is low.
2. Take the listening section of the test again without stopping the tape. Since you are repeating the test, your score does not count this time. Use this test to practice keeping up to the rhythm. Check your answers again and look at the explanatory answers in order to study the questions you missed.
3. If the test is still very difficult for you, listen to it a third time. This time stop the tape to check your understanding and to learn new words. If you stop your tape to study, you are not preparing for the rhythm of the TOEFL, but you are increasing your English skills. If you still find the Listening Comprehension section very difficult, you might try listening to the tape while you look at the tapescript in Part Four of this book.
4. Follow this procedure for each practice test. You will be increasing your skills in English, while also building your skill in keeping up to the rhythm of the TOEFL.

Testing Points

In this section you will find examples of listening comprehension questions and testing points for Part A, Part B, and Part C. The testing points for these sample questions are the testing points that are used most often on the TOEFL. Each example is followed by an explanation of the testing point.

Part A: Short Conversations

In Part A, you first hear two people speak, and then you hear a question. The question is usually about the second speaker's comment. The chart below shows common testing points for Part A. Some questions have more than one testing point and some testing points fit more than one category.

Testing Points for Part A

1. Vocabulary Word	6. Tone of Voice
2. Idiom/Phrase	7. Similar Sounds
3. Verb	8. Location
4. Order/Sequence	9. Calculation
5. Comparison	

Examples of Each Testing Point

1. Vocabulary Word

Example➤

    Woman: How do you like your literature class?
      Man: I love it; the professor is terrific.

What does the man mean?

(A) The teacher is excellent.
(B) The professor thinks the new literature book is great.
(C) He likes the subject, but he is afraid of the professor.
(D) He thinks the class would be better with another teacher.

The answer is (A). In this question the testing point is the word "terrific," which is similar in meaning to "excellent." The vocabulary words in the Listening Comprehension section are usually fairly common words, but they are difficult because you only hear the words. You do not see the words written out. When you study new words, therefore, try to listen to the way they are spoken by a native English speaker.

2. Idiom/Phrase

Example➤

> *Man:* Did you hear that Kathy just got hired as the new dean?
> *Woman:* Yes. Her effort really paid off.

What does the woman mean?

(A) Kathy will get paid more as a dean.
(B) Kathy's hard work had a positive result.
(C) Kathy could not afford what she wanted.
(D) Kathy will have more work to do as dean.

The answer is (B). The phrase that is being tested in this question is "her effort paid off." "To pay off" means to give or receive a full return or a complete benefit for something.

3. Verb

Example➤

> *Man:* Alice, I expected to see you at the party yesterday.
> *Woman:* If I had known that you were going, I would have gone.

What do we know about the woman?

(A) She didn't go to the party.
(B) She didn't remember seeing the man at the party.
(C) She left the party before the man arrived.
(D) She didn't want to see the man.

The answer is (A). The main testing point of this question is the past perfect verb and the past conditional: "if I had known...I would have...." In this type of conditional (past/unreal) you need to know that the described event did not happen. Common verb testing points include present perfect tense, passive voice, and conditionals.

4. Order/Sequence

Example➤

> *Woman:* Did you have to wait very long before the airplane left?
> *Man:* No sooner had we gotten on the airplane than the engine started.

What does the man mean?

(A) They didn't have enough time to get their seats on the plane.
(B) The pilot had trouble starting the engine.
(C) The engine started as soon as they got on the plane.
(D) They were delayed in the airport.

The answer is (C), which restates the man's comment. In this example, you must understand the order of the two things that are happening: first, "we got on the airplane," and second, "the engine started." This question also tests the past perfect verb "had gotten" and the phrases "no sooner...than..." and "as soon as." The phrase "no sooner" goes with a past tense or past perfect tense and is followed by a comparison beginning with "than."

5. Comparison

Example➤

Woman: I like to play tennis as a way to exercise.
Man: I used to feel that way too, but now I think that walking is a better way to exercise.

What can we infer about the man?

(A) He'd rather exercise by walking than by playing tennis.
(B) He doesn't like to walk as much as he likes to play tennis.
(C) His ability to play tennis has improved since he started walking.
(D) He quit playing tennis because it was not enough exercise.

The answer is (A). This question is classified as "comparison" because of the use of the word "better" and the comparison between playing tennis and walking. This question also tests the modals "used to" and "would rather," and the word "but" which introduces a contrast. When you hear the word "but," listen carefully for a change in the thought that follows.

6. Tone of Voice

Example➤

Woman: They don't know the news yet.
Man: They don't?

What does the man imply?

(A) They don't want to hear the news yet.
(B) He already told them the news.
(C) He is surprised that they don't know the news.
(D) They don't have any way to hear the news.

The answer is (C). Some TOEFL conversations require you to understand the meaning of a speaker's intonation. In the example above, the man's tone of voice would go up on the word "don't." His repetition of the woman's words indicates that he is questioning the woman and is surprised at the woman's comment. We can assume that he expected that "they" already knew the news. If his voice went down instead of up, he might be confirming the woman's comment, rather than questioning it.

7. Similar Sounds

Example➤

Woman: Why are you taking all these notes?
Man: So I can remember all the new information.

What does the man mean?

(A) He is a member of the computer information club.
(B) He doesn't want to forget what he just learned.
(C) He is organizing the information by number.
(D) He is leaving with his notes.

The answer is (B). In this sentence, the word "remember" sounds like "member." It also sounds a little like "number." Any TOEFL listening question might use words in the answer choices that sound like words in the spoken part of the question. To answer this question you must know that "remember" means the same as "not forget," so this question might also be categorized as "vocabulary." You also need to know that "taking notes" is very different from "taking something away" or "leaving."

8. Location

Example➤

     Man: I must have your receipt for this shirt in order to exchange it.
     Woman: OK. Here it is.

Where does the conversation most likely take place?

(A) In a bookstore.
(B) In a grocery store.
(C) In a department store.
(D) In a stationery store.

The answer is (C). Some TOEFL conversations require you to infer where the conversation takes place. In this example, you must be able to recognize that a shirt would most likely be exchanged in a department store. This type of question may require some cultural knowledge.

9. Calculation

Example➤

     Man: Six hundred dollars for that apartment?
     Woman: It's twice as much as the one we just saw.

What does the woman mean?

(A) The other apartment is twice as good.
(B) The rent is 60 dollars cheaper.
(C) The other apartment costs more.
(D) The other apartment costs 300 dollars a month.

The answer is (D). This type of question requires you to perform simple arithmetic. It could also be classified as "vocabulary" since, in this case, you must know the meaning of the word "twice." On other calculation questions, you may be tested on the meaning of words such as "half" or "double."

Part B: Longer Conversations

Part B consists of longer conversations between two people. After each conversation ends, you are asked three or four questions about what was said. You cannot take any notes while you listen to the conversation, so you must listen carefully for the main ideas. Some people like to look at the answer choices in the test booklet while they are listening to the conversation. Other people like to close their eyes and concentrate on the conversation, trying to imagine who is speaking and where they are. Try both of these techniques when you take the practice tests so you can find out which technique works best for you.

The five major testing points for Listening Comprehension Parts B and C are listed on the next page. Most of the questions that follow these long conversations are restatement questions. The next most common question type is inference. Only a few questions ask about the main idea, the preceding or following topics, or the location. The restatement questions often seem easy when you can read the conversation as you can in this example, but these questions are much more difficult when you only get to hear the conversation.

Testing Points for Parts B and C

1. Restatement
2. Inference
3. Main Idea
4. Preceding/Following Topic
5. Location

Examples of Each Testing Point

Conversation No. 1: Answer questions 1–4 on the basis of the following conversation between two students.

Man: Hello, Lena.

Woman: Hi, Kurt. How are you? It's been a long time since I've seen you. Don't you live in the dorm any more?

Man: No, I moved out at the beginning of last semester.

Woman: Where are you living now?

Man: I moved to the Oak Creek apartments. I'm sharing a unit with three other people, one from Brazil, one from Japan, and one from Hong Kong.

Woman: That sounds interesting. How are you getting along with your roommates?

Man: Everything is working out just fine, at least up to now. They all share the cooking and I do the shopping since I have a car.

Woman: I guess that would work out. You must have all kinds of foods from different countries.

Man: That's right. I'm really enjoying mealtime! But we've had a few other problems.

Woman: Like what?

Man: Well, one was that we got confused when the first month's telephone bill came.

Woman: What happened?

Man: We couldn't remember who had called each number, so we didn't know how much each person owed. After a lot of discussion, we each ended up paying for the calls we were sure of and dividing the rest equally. Now we all jot down the number whenever we make a call, especially the long distance calls, and we have no more telephone problems.

Woman: Hope it stays that way. I'd love to come over and meet your roommates sometime.

Man: OK. How about coming for dinner? I'll ask them about it and let you know.

Woman: Great.

1. Inference

Example➤   Where did the man live before?

(A) In Oak Creek apartments
(B) In a student dorm
(C) In a residential house
(D) In a fraternity house

The answer is (B). The woman says, "Don't you live in the dorm anymore?" From this question, we can infer that the man used to live in the dorm.

2. Restatement

Example➤   Where do two of the man's roommates come from?

(A) Italy and Japan
(B) Hong Kong and Singapore
(C) Japan and Malaysia
(D) Brazil and Japan

The answer is (D). The man says that his roommates come from Brazil, Japan, and Hong Kong.

3. Restatement

Example➤   What problem did the roommates have?

(A) They didn't know how much each person owed for telephone calls.
(B) They couldn't understand each other since they speak different languages.
(C) They had difficulty deciding who should cook.
(D) They had different lifestyles.

The answer is (A). The man says that they had a problem remembering who had made each call on their telephone bill.

4. Inference

Example➤   What can we infer about the woman?

(A) She is looking for a new house to rent.
(B) She likes to cook.
(C) She would like some new roommates.
(D) She is friendly.

The answer is (D). Although all of the other answers might be true, the best answer is that the woman is friendly since she says that she would like to meet the man's roommates.

Conversation No. 2: Answer questions 5–8 on the basis of the following conversation between two students.

> *Man:* Hi Anna. I haven't seen you around the lab lately. Are you still working here?
>
> *Woman:* Oh, hi George. I am still working for Professor Johnston, at least as much as I can. The trouble is that I'm so busy with my own classes that I don't have enough time for her lab work.
>
> *Man:* Do you have much to do?
>
> *Woman:* Well, not too much at the moment. I'm trying to pull together my data from my work last summer. Professor Johnston is giving a paper about the project in two months, and she needs to include my final results. It's not too much work, but I've got this deadline so that's why I'm here.
>
> *Man:* Are you going to continue working with Professor Johnston next semester?
>
> *Woman:* I hope so. I really like the work, and next semester I'll have more time. She has said that she'd like me to continue with the project.
>
> *Man:* Sounds good. Hey, I've got to get back to my own work now, but it was good running into you. I hope I'll see you around more often.
>
> *Woman:* OK. I hope I see you too. Bye for now.

5. Location

Example➤ Where does this conversation most likely take place?

(A) In a lecture classroom
(B) At a science conference
(C) In a science laboratory
(D) In a professor's office

The answer is (C). The first thing the man says is, "I haven't seen you around the lab lately. Are you still working here?" Since he says "working here" we infer that the speakers are in the lab as they are talking.

6. Inference

Example➤ Why has the woman come to this place?

(A) To work on a project
(B) To see the man
(C) To talk with Professor Johnston
(D) To prepare for her presentation

The answer is (A). The woman says that she is in the lab to "pull together her data" because the professor needs her results. Later she says that Professor Johnston wants her to continue working on the project. From all of this we can infer that she is in the lab to work on the project. Though she is talking to the man, we can also infer that she did not come to the lab in order to see the man, so answer (B) is incorrect. Professor Johnston, not the woman, is going to give a presentation, so (D) is wrong.

7. Restatement

Example➤   What does the woman say about her recent life?

(A)   She's been busy with her classes.
(B)   She's been working with Professor Johnston.
(C)   She's had a lot of deadlines.
(D)   She wants some time off.

The answer is (A). The woman says that she is "busy with her own classes."

8. Restatement

Example➤   What does the woman hope to do next semester?

(A)   Take another lab course
(B)   Work for Professor Johnston
(C)   Teach a lab course
(D)   Write up her project

The answer is (B). The woman says that she hopes to work for Professor Johnston next semester.

Part C: Talks

Talk No. 1: Questions 1–4 are based on this talk by a professor on the first day of a class.

I want to begin this class on the history of filmmaking with a discussion of a filmmaker who is known to people throughout the world. You've all heard of Walt Disney. No one has ever delighted more children or adults than Walt Disney, the winner of 31 Academy Awards. Almost everyone has heard of Mickey Mouse and Donald Duck, and his other popular characters like Minnie Mouse, Pluto, and Goofy.

Walt Disney started creating cartoon animations in 1920, but it was in 1928 when his best known character, Mickey Mouse, came to life. Disney also created the first sound cartoon, which he called *Steamboat Willie*. It was in this cartoon that he introduced Mickey to the public. In 1937 Walt Disney made movie history again with the first full-length cartoon film, *Snow White and the Seven Dwarfs*. In the 1950s, Walt Disney created a series of nature films. He was always planning something new. In 1955, he opened Disneyland, the "magic kingdom," in Anaheim, California. Even at his death in 1966, he was planning another massive project: Florida's Walt Disney World. Since Walt Disney's death, his film company has continued to grow and attract the public, even producing new cartoons by computer animation.

1. Main Idea

Example➤   What is the speaker mainly discussing?

(A)   The life and times of Walt Disney
(B)   Famous Disney characters
(C)   Walt Disney's work
(D)   The importance of Disney's industry

The answer is (C). The speaker continues to refer to Walt Disney's work: his cartoon characters, his nature films, and his amusement parks.

2. Restatement

Example➤   In which year did Walt Disney first begin creating cartoon animations?

(A)   1920
(B)   1928
(C)   1950
(D)   1955

The answer is (A). The speaker says that Walt Disney first started creating cartoon animation in 1920.

3. Restatement

Example➤   What was the name of Disney's first full-length cartoon film?

(A)   *Steamboat Willie*
(B)   *Snow White and the Seven Dwarfs*
(C)   *Disney World*
(D)   *Mickey Mouse*

The answer is (B). The speaker says that the name of the first full-length cartoon film was *Snow White and the Seven Dwarfs*.

4. Inference

Example➤   Which of the following was NOT planned by Walt Disney himself?

(A)   Mickey Mouse
(B)   Nature films
(C)   Disneyland
(D)   Computerized cartoons

The answer is (D). The speaker says that computerized cartoons were developed after Disney's death.

Talk No. 2: Questions 5–7 are based on this talk by an architecture instructor.

Now that you've put some time into the practical work of this course, drawing house plans, let's go back to our continuing discussion of famous architects. Today's architect is Samuel McIntire, a man from Salem, Massachusetts, who lived during the latter half of the eighteenth century, just as the United States was beginning to become a nation. McIntire had very little formal training; he learned his skill from his father, a carpenter-builder, and from architectural books. Besides doing carpentry and architectural work, McIntire became a very skilled wood sculptor, a talent that showed up in his work throughout his life.

Samuel McIntire was honored as the architect of Salem since he designed so many of the town buildings and residences. His first important commission, for the Pierce-Nichols House, came when he was only 22 years old. When this house was completed in 1782, it had more classical details than any other house in town, and it established McIntire as an up-and-coming young architect among the affluent merchants of the growing town. The exteriors of McIntire's houses were influenced by other architects of his time, but McIntire's interiors were unique. They demonstrated his love of and his skill in decorative carving.

5. Preceding Topic

Example➤   What had the students done before this lecture?

(A) Learned to do wood sculpture
(B) Designed and built houses
(C) Worked on drawing house plans
(D) Given talks about famous architects

The answer is (C). The speaker says that the students have already "put some time into" drawing house plans. Answer (D) is incorrect because it was the speaker, not the students, who gave talks on famous architects.

6. Restatement

Example➤   How did McIntire learn his skill?

(A) From affluent merchants
(B) From his father
(C) From classes at school
(D) From his co-workers

The answer is (B). The speaker says that McIntire learned his skill from his father.

7. Inference

Example➤ What was the significance of the Pierce-Nichols house?

(A) The classical design was influenced by other architects of the time.
(B) It had beautiful wood carvings in the interior.
(C) It helped establish McIntire's reputation.
(D) The exterior was unique for that time.

The answer is (C). Answers (A), (B), and (D) may be true, but they are not stated directly. We are told that the house helped to establish McIntire as an "up-and-coming" architect. That means that he was becoming well known and developing a good reputation as a professional worker.

Structure and Written Expression Section

The Structure and Written Expression section of TOEFL includes two different types of questions, Sentence Completion and Error Identification, each with its own special directions. Both question types measure your ability to recognize standard written English.

Sample Questions

Part 1: Sentence Completion Questions

The sentences in this part are not complete. One or more words are left out of each sentence. Under each sentence you will see four words or phrases marked (A), (B), (C), and (D). Choose the one word or phrase that completes the sentence correctly. Then, on your answer sheet, find the number of the question and fill in the oval that corresponds to the letter of your answer choice.

Example ➤ Birds make nests in trees ____ hide their young in the leaves and branches.

Sample Answer

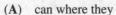

   (A) can where they
   (B) where they can
   (C) where can they
   (D) where can

The sentence should read, "Birds make nests in trees where they can hide their young in the leaves and branches." Therefore, you should choose answer (B).

Example ➤ Sleeping, resting, and ____ are the best ways to care for a cold.

Sample Answer

Ⓐ Ⓑ Ⓒ ●

   (A) to drink fluids
   (B) drank fluids
   (C) one drink fluids
   (D) drinking fluids

The sentence should read, "Sleeping, resting, and drinking fluids are the best ways to care for a cold." The three words should all be parallel; therefore, you should choose answer (D).

Part 2: Error Identification Questions

In this part each sentence has four underlined words or phrases which are marked (A), (B), (C), and (D). Choose the one word or phrase that must be changed in order for the sentence to be correct. On your answer sheet, find the number of the question and fill in the oval that corresponds to the letter of your answer choice.

Example ➤

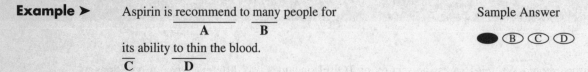

Aspirin is recommend to many people for
        A   B
its ability to thin the blood.
C   D

Sample Answer

The sentence should read, "Aspirin is recommended to many people for its ability to thin the blood." The verb in this sentence should be in the passive voice. Therefore, you should choose answer (A).

Example ➤

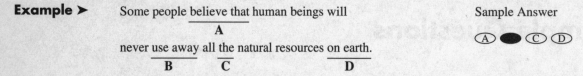

Some people believe that human beings will
              A
never use away all the natural resources on earth.
     B   C   D

Sample Answer

The sentence should read, "Some people believe that human beings will never use up all the natural resources on earth." Therefore, you should choose answer (B). The correct two-word verb "use up" is an idiom meaning "use all of something until it is gone."

Structure and Written Expression Strategies

The two parts of the Structure and Written Expression section have different test-taking strategies. These strategies are described below.

Sentence Completion Strategies

1. Look for the main subject and verb of the sentence. If there is no complete subject or verb phrase, you know that you need to find these in the answer choices. To help you see the main subject and verb, simplify the sentence by taking out the prepositional phrases (a preposition plus article, adjective, and/or noun).

   Simplifying a sentence is like taking the leaves off a tree so you can see the trunk clearly. When you simplify a sentence, you can see the testing point more clearly. You also save time, since you don't waste time trying to figure out the meanings of words that you may not need in order to find the answer.

2. Decide what kind of structure the sentence needs. Use the testing points on page 33 in this book to help you decide what is needed.

3. Read the sentence to see if it makes sense and sounds correct.

4. Mark the answer on your answer sheet.

Error Identification Strategies

1. Read the sentence through quickly to see if you recognize the error. Use the testing points listed on page 42 of this book to help you focus on possible errors.
2. If you do not see the error immediately, then simplify the sentence, focusing on the main subject, verb, and maybe the object of the sentence.
3. Look at the underlined words to see what part of speech they are and how they relate to the main subject and verb.
4. Think through the testing points listed in this book (page 42), checking each underlined word to see if it is correct.
5. Choose your answer and read the sentence to yourself to see if it sounds correct.
6. Mark your answer on the answer sheet.

Remember that you do not need to know the meaning of every word in each sentence in the Structure section in order to answer the question correctly. If you do not know the meaning of some words in the sentence, don't worry about it. Try to focus on the general meaning and the structure of the sentence.

To prepare for the TOEFL, you must do two things: you must increase your test-taking skills and you must increase your knowledge of the English language. To increase your test-taking skills, go through the practice tests as quickly and carefully as you can. To increase your knowledge of English, go back to the practice tests after you have taken them, and study the words and structures that are difficult for you.

Testing Points

This section describes the testing points for Structure and Written Expression questions. These testing points are the ones that appear most often in the two parts of the Structure and Written Expression section of the TOEFL.

Part 1: Sentence Completion

Testing Points for Sentence Completion Questions

1. Noun Phrase
2. Word Order
3. Subject + Verb
4. Verb/Verb Phrase
5. Adjective Phrase/Clause
6. Conjunction
7. Parallel Construction
8. Adverb Phrase/Clause
9. Comparison
10. Infinitive/Gerund
11. Preposition/ Prepositional Phrase
12. Superlative
13. Negative
14. Conditional
15. Pronoun

Examples of Each Testing Point

1. Noun Phrase

A noun phrase or a single noun are common testing points. The nouns may be the subject of the sentence, the object of a verb, or the object of a phrase in the sentence.

Example ➤ For people with mouth or gum problems, the dentist may prescribe _____ twice a day as partial treatment.

    (A) if irrigate
    (B) irrigates
    (C) irrigates
    (D) irrigation

The main subject is "the dentist" and the verb phrase is "may prescribe."

Take out the prepositional phrases "for people with gum and mouth problems" and "as partial treatment."

Simplify: xxxxx, the dentist may prescribe _____ twice a day xxxxx.

This sentence needs a noun phrase after the verb "prescribe." The noun tells what the dentist may prescribe. This sentence is an example of the regular pattern in English: subject, verb, object.

Example ➤ _____ the economy's performance, strengths, and weaknesses are the tables, charts, and data published by public and private agencies.

    (A) Analyzing
    (B) The tools for analyzing
    (C) The analysis of
    (D) There are tools of

The main verb is "are." This sentence needs a noun phrase to complete the subject.

Take out the prepositional phrase "by public and private agencies."

Simplify: _____ the economy's performance, strengths, and weaknesses are the tables, charts and data published xxxxx.

For this sentence, try each answer to see if it makes sense.

(A) Analyzing the xxxxx are tables, charts, and data published xxxxx.
    The word "analyzing" could be a subject, but it does not make sense.
(B) The tools for analyzing xxxxx are the tables, charts, and data xxxxx.
    This is the correct answer: tools . . . are . . . tables, charts, ...
(C) The analysis of xxxxx are tables, charts, and data xxxxx.
    This does not make sense. An analysis is not a table. An analysis is performed
    from a table or chart.
(D) The simplification of the sentence shows that it already has a main verb so this
    noun + verb is not correct.

2. Word Order

In this type of testing point, all four answer choices contain the same words, but in different order. This category of testing point also tests your knowledge of verb phrases, noun phrases, adjectives, and adverbs.

Example ➤   Duplicating the recent history of airborne achievements, the galleries of the National Air and Space Museum _____.

       (A) exhibit a collection fascinating
       (B) fascinate an exhibit collection
       (C) collection a fascinating exhibit
       (D) exhibit a fascinating collection

The main subject is "the galleries." The sentence needs a verb phrase.

Take out the phrases "duplicating the recent history of airborne achievements" and "of the National Air and Space Museum."

Simplify: xxxxx, the galleries xxxxx _____.

Try all answers to see which is correct.

(A) This answer begins with a verb, but is incorrect in the order of adjective and noun: "collection fascinating" is incorrect. The adjective should come before the noun.
(B) This choice does not make sense. Though the galleries may be fascinating, they must be fascinating to people, not to a collection.
(C) This answer does not have a verb, and this sentence needs a verb.
(D) Correct answer. xxxxx the galleries xxxxx exhibit a fascinating collection. Though the word "exhibit" is often a noun, in this sentence it is a verb.

3. Subject + Verb

In this type of testing point, the subject and the verb are in the answer choices. Both are needed to complete the sentence.

Example ➤   _____ all summer, sipping nectar and collecting pollen from flowers.

       (A) Bumblebees are the busy
       (B) Busy bumblebees are
       (C) Being busy bumblebees
       (D) Bumblebees are busy

There is no main subject or verb. The verb phrases "sipping" and "collecting" describe the main subject.

Simplify: _____ all summer, sipping xxxxx and collecting xxxxx.

Try all answers.

(A) The article "the" is incorrect in front of "busy" because there is no noun after the word "busy."
(B) This answer would need an object after "are" to describe the bees.
(C) This answer has no verb.
(D) This answer is correct. It provides a subject (bumblebees) and a verb (are).

4. Verb Phrase

There can be many different testing points in this category. You need to check the answer choices to be sure the verb is in the right tense, that it agrees with the subject in number (singular or plural), and that it is in the right voice (active or passive). When you simplify the sentence, be sure you know which verb should agree with which noun.

Example ➤   The batteries in cordless handheld vacuum cleaners _____ hundreds of times.

    (A)   can be recharged
    (B)   recharging
    (C)   recharged
    (D)   was recharged

The main subject is "batteries." There is no main verb.

Take out the prepositional phrase "in cordless handheld vacuum cleaners."

Simplify: The batteries xxxxx _____ hundreds of times.

The sentence describes a fact, and uses the passive voice and the modal "can." The answer is (A). Answer (B) is incorrect because it leaves the sentence without a verb. Answer (C) is not correct since this sentence refers to all cordless vacuum cleaners, not any specific one. Answer (D) is incorrect because the verb is singular instead of plural.

5. Adjective Phrase/Clause

The testing point in this category might be a relative pronoun, a relative clause, or an adjective participle. You can sometimes find the answer if you ask the question "what kind of?"

Example ➤   Societies must often adapt to changes _____ political or economic factors.

    (A)   which may be brought on by
    (B)   to which are brought
    (C)   for bringing on
    (D)   can be brought by

The main subject is "societies" and the verb phrase is "must often adapt." The sentence needs an adjective clause to describe the changes.

Simplify: Societies must xxxxx adapt to changes _____ xxxxx.

Try each answer.

(A)   This is the correct answer. It supplies a clause that tells what kind of changes.
(B)   This is incorrect because it means "factors are brought to changes" and this does not make sense.
(C)   It does not make sense to say "changes for bringing on political and economic factors."
(D)   The sentence needs the word "which" as a relative pronoun to refer to "changes."

6. Conjunction

Common conjunctions are the following: *and, or, but, for, both . . . and . . . , either . . . or . . . , neither . . . nor . . . .* This category also includes connective words such as *because, in order to, so . . . that,* and *however.*

Example ➤   Most libraries have general collections of reference works, such as periodicals, pamphlets _____ books.

    (A) or
    (B) yet
    (C) but
    (D) and

The subject is "libraries" and the main verb is "have."

Take out the prepositional phrase "of reference works" and the nouns in the phrase "such as periodicals, pamphlets, _____ books."

Simplify: Most libraries have general collections xxxxx, such as xxxxx, xxxxx, _____ xxxxx.

The sentence needs the conjunction "and" to indicate that all three items are included. The answer is (D).

> **Hint:** Use *and* to show addition: use *but* to show contrast; use *or* to indicate alternative(s).

7. Parallel Construction

Words or phrases used in a series should be the same part of speech. Usually a comma separates the words or phrases.

Example ➤   After you have turned over the soil, weeded, and _____ , you'll be ready to plant.

    (A) cultivating
    (B) cultivation
    (C) cultivated
    (D) cultivate

The main subject and verb are in the second clause: the subject is "you" and the verb phrase is "will be ready to plant."

Take out the second clause.

Simplify the sentence: After you have turned over the soil, weeded, and _____ , xxxxx.

This sentence has three verbs, separated by commas. This is a common clue for a parallel construction testing point. The correct answer is (C), a verb form that is in the past like "turned over" and "weeded."

8. Adverb Phrase/Clause

This category includes single adverbs or adverbial phrases or clauses. The words often answer the question *how, when, where,* or *why.*

Example ➤ Arlington National Cemetery was built _____ and other war heroes during the American Civil War.

    (A) according to honor
    (B) for honor of soldiers
    (C) in order to honor soldiers
    (D) to soldiers that were honored

The main subject is "Arlington National Cemetery" and the main verb phrase is "was built." Take out the prepositional phrase "during the American Civil War."

Simplify: Arlington National Cemetery was built _____ and other war heroes xxxxx.

The sentence needs an adverb phrase to modify the verb "built." The adverb phrase answers the question "why was it built?"

Look at each choice:

(A) This is incorrect because it makes no sense to say "to honor and other war heroes."
(B) The preposition "for" is incorrect. It is incorrect to say "was built for honor of."
(C) This is the correct answer.
(D) The word "to" is incorrect. It is incorrect to say "was built to soldiers."

9. Comparison

In a comparison question you will often see the phrases *the more* _____, *the more*; *is more* _____ *than*; *is* _____ *rather than*; or _____ *is the same as* _____.

Example ➤ Espresso coffee makers require more attention than _____.

    (A) drip coffee makers are
    (B) drip coffee makers
    (C) are other drip coffee makers
    (D) so do the other coffee makers

The main subject is "coffee makers" and the main verb is "require."

Simplify: xxxxx coffee makers require more attention than _____.

The sentence is comparing espresso coffee makers with drip coffee makers. It needs a noun phrase to be parallel with the noun phrase "espresso coffee makers." Answer (B) is correct. The other answers add an unnecessary verb.

10. Infinitive/Gerund

This category includes both infinitives and gerunds. Sometimes you are asked to choose between an infinitive, a gerund, and another verb form.

Example ➤ Walruses use their long tusks to pull themselves out of the water and _____ themselves.

    (A) protecting
    (B) to protect
    (C) protected
    (D) was protected

The main subject is "walruses" and the main verb is "use."

Take out the prepositional phrase "of the water."

Simplify: Walruses use their long tusks to pull themselves out xxxxx and _____ themselves.

The answer is (B). An infinitive must follow the verb phrase "use their tusks." The word "to" means "in order to." The two infinitives "to pull" and "to protect" must be parallel.

Hint:

Some verbs must be followed by an infinitive, others must be followed by a gerund, and others can be followed by either an infinitive or a gerund. The following table gives some examples.

- Verbs that are followed by an infinitive:

  want, wish, hope, ask, offer, promise, pretend, intend, begin, attempt, decide, learn, desire, agree, choose, expect, need

- Verbs that are followed by a gerund:

  suggest, finish, avoid, can't help, mind, enjoy, postpone, put off, delay, advise, consider, deny, miss

- Verbs that can be followed by either an infinitive or a gerund:

  like, hate, prefer, continue, try, start, forget, stop

---

11. Preposition/Prepositional Phrase

The testing points in a prepositional phrase might be the preposition, the noun, or the article.

Example ➤   President Lincoln was assassinated in Ford's Theater _____ the night of April 14, 1865.

  (A) on
  (B) at
  (C) by
  (D) in

The main subject is "President Lincoln" and the main verb is "was assassinated." Take out the prepositional phrase "in Ford's Theater."

Simplify: President Lincoln was assassinated xxxxx _____ the night of April 14.

The correct answer is (A), "on the night of April 14, 1865."

Hint:

The phrase "on the night of" means "during this particular night." The phrases "at night" or "in the night" refer to a night as compared to a day, as in "I work at night."

12. Superlative

The testing point might be the word "the" before the superlative form, or it might be the phrase "one of the xxxxx."

Example ➤   Franklin Delano Roosevelt was one of _____ Presidents in American history.

(A) such an energetic
(B) most energetic
(C) energetic
(D) the most energetic

The main subject is "Franklin Delano Roosevelt" and the verb is "was."

Take out the prepositional phrase "in American history."

Simplify : Franklin Delano Roosevelt was one of _____ Presidents xxxxx.

The phrase "one of . . ." is a clue that you need a superlative construction.

The correct form is *one of the most + adjective*. The answer is (D).

13. Negative

Common words in this testing point are *no, not, none, nothing,* and *nobody*.

Example ➤   Beer contains _____ live yeast when it leaves the brewery.

(A) no
(B) not
(C) none
(D) neither

The main subject is "beer" and the verb is "contains."

Take out the clause "when it leaves the brewery."

Simplify: Beer contains _____ live yeast xxxxx.

The answer is (A). In this sentence the word "live" is an adjective that rhymes with "alive" or "dive." It describes something that is living. The word "no" comes before the noun phrase "live yeast."

Hint:

• Use the word "no" to make a noun negative: No person can do this job alone.

• Use the word "not" to make a verb or adjective negative: He did not receive the letter.

• Use the word "none" when there is no noun after it: He and I have one, but she has none.

• Use the word "neither" with the word "nor": Neither he nor she has much money.

---

14. Conditional

There are three types of conditional sentences:
1) real (future) conditional
2) unreal (present) conditional
3) past conditional

Example ➤

_____ travelers checks, you may not need to carry money.

    (A) If you carry
    (B) To carry
    (C) If he had carried
    (D) For carrying

The main subject and verb are in the second part of the sentence. The subject is "you" and the main verb is "may not need."

Don't simplify this sentence. Read both clauses for the complete meaning.

This sentence is an example of a real (future) conditional. The correct answer is (A). The other answers make sense in the first part of the sentence, but they do not logically fit with the second half.

15. Pronoun

Any type of pronoun might be the testing point: subject, object, demonstrative, or relative pronoun.

Example ➤

The opposite of love is hate, an emotion directed toward any disturbing factor, whatever _____ may be.

    (A) that
    (B) those
    (C) them
    (D) they

The main subject is "the opposite" and the main verb is "is."

Look just at the end of the sentence for the noun that is referred to by the pronoun.

Simplify: xxxxx any disturbing factor, whatever _____ may be.

The answer is (A). The pronoun "that" refers to the single noun "factor." Answers (B) and (D) are plural so they are incorrect. Answer (C) is incorrect since it is an object pronoun, not a subject pronoun.

Part 2: Error Identification
Testing Points for Error Identification Questions

1. Word Form	9. Preposition
2. Verb	10. Reversed Words
3. Pronoun	11. Conjunction
4. Parallel Construction	12. Infinitive/ Gerund
5. Singular/Plural Noun	13. Comparative
6. Mistaken Words	14. Article
7. Unnecessary Word	15. Superlative
8. Omitted Word	

Examples of Each Testing Point

1. Word Form

Incorrect word forms are the most common testing point in this part of the test. This category refers to words that are written in the wrong form; that is, a noun might be written as an adjective or an adjective might be written as an adverb. When two or more words are written in a series they must be written in the same form. The series of words might be nouns, verbs, and/or adjectives.

Example ➤ A comfort running shoe has good arch support and enough room for toes.
               A   **B**   **C**   **D**

Simplify the sentence:

xxxxx shoe has xxxxx arch support and xxxxx room xxxxx.

The subject is "shoe" and the verb is "has."

The word "comfort " is incorrectly written as a noun, but this sentence already has a main noun. The correct word should be "comfortable," an adjective that describes the noun "shoe." The answer is (A).

Example ➤ A full-sized tripod is the most effectively way to steady a camera.
            A   **B**   **C**   **D**

Simplify the sentence:

xxxxx tripod is xxxxx.

The subject and verb are fine. The answer is (C). The word "effectively" is an adverb; it should be the adjective "effective" to modify the noun "way."

Example ➤ Oils left in a pan after cooking can turn rancid affects the food that is cooked next.
      A   **B**   **C**   **D**

Simplify the sentence:

Oils left xxxxx can turn rancid xxxxx.

The subject and verb are correct. The answer is (C). The word "affects" should be "affecting," in order to begin an adverb phrase that describes what happens after oils become rancid.

Hint:

Learn to recognize common endings of nouns, adjectives, and adverbs.

- Nouns often end in the letters: *-ion*, *-tion*, *-sion*, *-ment*, *-ness*, *-ity*, *-ence*, *-ance* (e.g., *nation*, *impression*, *kindness*, *intelligence*).

- Nouns that refer to people often end in the letters: *-er*, *-ist*, *-ian*, *-or* (e.g., *teacher*, *typist*, *beautician*, *supervisor*).

- Adjectives often end in the letters; *-ic*, *-ish*, *-ive*, *-y*, *-ous*, *-al* (e.g., *athletic*, *childish*, *native*).

- Adverbs often end in *-ly* (e.g., *happily*).

---

2. Verb

This category includes errors in verb tense, verb agreement, and voice.

Example ➤ Whether you ride your bike 30 miles a day or 30 miles a year, a helmet,
<u>A</u>

adjusted for a snug fit, should be wear on every ride.
<u>B</u>   <u>C</u>   <u>D</u>

Simplify the sentence:

xxxxx xxxxx, a helmet xxxxx, should be wear xxxxx.

The answer is (C). The subject (helmet) is receiving the action; therefore, the verb should be in the passive voice: (should be worn).

Example ➤ Laundry <u>washed</u> with soap <u>instead of</u> detergent <u>don't</u> need <u>softening</u>.
          A   B   C   D

Simplify the sentence:

Laundry xxxxx don't need xxxxx.

The subject is "laundry," and the main verb should be singular: "doesn't." The answer is (C). The phrase "washed with soap" describes the main noun, "laundry."

3. Pronoun

This category includes subject, object, possessive, or relative pronouns.

Example ➤ Never <u>use</u> a drug <u>prescribed</u> for someone else just because <u>its</u>
          A   B   C

symptoms <u>appear</u> similar.
          D

Simplify the sentence:

Never use a drug xxxxx just because its xxxxx xxxxx xxxxx.

The subject of this sentence is not written. It is the word "you," which is the unwritten subject of the verb "use." This part of the sentence is correct. The error is answer (C). The pronoun "its" refers to an object, which in this sentence would be the word "drug." This is not logical, however. The drug does not have symptoms. The correct pronoun is "your."

4. Parallel Construction

Words that are written in a series must all be the same part of speech. This type of error may also be categorized as "word form."

Example ➤

A good worker is conscientious, reliable, and efficiency.
   A   B   C   D

Simplify the sentence:

A xxxxx worker is xxxxx, xxxxx, and xxxxx.

The answer is (D). All three words describe a good worker. They must all be adjectives. The word "efficiency" is incorrect in this sentence since it is a noun. The correct word is "efficient."

Hint:

A question testing parallel construction often has three words in a row separated by commas.

---

5. Singular/Plural Noun

For this testing point, a plural noun might be written incorrectly with the letter *s* or it might have an unnecessary *s*. Mass nouns can be plural without adding an *s*.

Example ➤

Studies have shown that you can exercise in many different
          A   B

ways at a moderate paces and still gain good results.
          C   D

Simplify the sentence:

Studies have shown that xxxxx.

The subject and verb are correct in this sentence, so you need to look at the words that describe what the studies have shown. The phrase "at a moderate paces" must be incorrect because of the combination of the word "a" and a plural noun. The answer is (C).

Hint:

Whenever you see the singular "a" or "an" that is not underlined, you know the noun that follows must be singular. Look carefully at articles that are not underlined, and use them as a clue to help you decide whether the noun that comes after the article is written correctly.

---

6. Mistaken Words

This category includes words that are commonly mistaken, such as *make* instead of *do*, *little* instead of *few*, *separate* instead of *apart*, or *listen* instead of *hear*.

Example ➤   Much children like to get their faces painted with bright colors at community fairs.
　　　　　　　　　A　　　　　　　B　　　C　　　　　D

Simplify the sentence:

xxxxx children like to xxxxx

The subject and verb in this sentence are correct, but the noun "children" must be preceded by the word "many," since it is a plural form. The plural of the countable noun "child" is "children."

> **Hint:**
>
> Use the word "many" to modify a countable noun. Use the word "much" to modify an uncountable noun.

7. Unnecessary Word

Sometimes a word that should not be in a sentence is added to the sentence. This may result in a double subject, a double negative, a repeated similar adjective or adverb, or an unnecessary preposition.

Example ➤   While push-ups build your arms, shoulders and chest, sit-ups they strengthen your
　　　　　　　　　A　　　　　　　　　　　　　　　　　　　　　　　　　　B　　　　　C

abdominal muscles.
　　　D

Simplify the sentence:

xxxxx push-ups build xxxxx, xxxxx, and xxxxx, sit-ups they strengthen xxxxx.

The answer is (B). The word "they" after "sit-ups" is an unnecessary word. It results in a double subject. The correct phrase is "sit-ups strengthen your...muscles."

8. Omitted Word

In this category, a necessary word is left out of a sentence. It is often a preposition or an article.

Example ➤   Yosemite National Park is most well known its beautiful spouting geysers of all sizes.
　　　　　　　　　　　　　　　　　A　　　　B　　　C　　　　　　　　　　　　D

Simplify the sentence:

Yosemite National Park is xxxxx well known xxxxx.

The subject and verb are correct. You must look at the rest of the sentence. The answer is (B), since the word "known" in this sentence must be followed by "for."

> **Hint:**
>
> This is a very difficult category because it is harder to think of something that is missing than it is to pick out something that you can see. Read the whole sentence to yourself to see if one of the words sounds strange but seems correct. If you think a word is missing, choose the underlined word that is next to the missing word.

9. Preposition

Any preposition might be used incorrectly.

Example ➤   Surprisingly, a feeling of tiredness may result of a lack of exercise.
   A   B   C   D

Simplify the sentence:

xxxxx feeling xxxxx may result xxxxx.

The answer is (C). After the verb "result" there should be the preposition "in" or "from." Each of these words gives a different meaning to this sentence, but both could be correct in this context. With "result in" the sentence means that a person does not exercise because he or she feels tired. With "result from" a person feels tired because he or she does not exercise. Since the sentence begins with the word "surprisingly," it is probably "result from" that is the expected correct preposition.

> **Hint:**
>
> - to result in xxxxx   "Result" is a verb; xxxxx refers to the outcome of an action. (Too much rain results in flooding.)
>
> - to result from xxxxx   "Result" is a verb; xxxxx refers to the reason for an action. (Flooding results from too much rain.)
>
> - a result of xxxxx   "Result" is a noun; xxxxx refers to the reason for an action. (Flooding is the result of too much rain.)

Example ➤   When having difficulties, many people try for get help from a professional.
   A   B   C   D

Simplify the sentence:

xxxxx, many people try xxxxx.

The answer is (C). In this sentence, after the verb "try" you need the preposition "to."

10. Reversed Words

In this category two words are in the wrong order; i.e., an adjective might be written after a noun instead of before the noun.

Example ➤   Specialization in industry creates workers lack who versatility in their ability to step in to
   A   B   C   D

other jobs.

Simplify the sentence:

Specialization xxxxx creates workers xxxxx.

The subject and verb are correct. The answer is (C). The words "lack who" should be "who lack." The word "who" describes the "workers" in this sentence.

11. Conjunction

Some common conjunctions are the following: *and, or, but, both, for, neither . . . nor,* and *not only . . . but also.*

Example ➤   For challenging bicycle rides on dirt roads, the lowest gear should be 28 and less.
                      A   B   C   D

Simplify the sentence:

xxxxx, the lowest gear should be xxxxx.

The main subject and verb are correct. The answer is (D). It does not make sense to say "28 and less" in this sentence. A gear must be one or the other; therefore, the answer should be "28 or less."

Example ➤   Neither the revolution in industry and that in agriculture could have
                              A   B   C

proceeded without the progress in communication and transportation.
                          D

Simplify the sentence:

Neither xxxxx and xxxxx could have proceeded without xxxxx.

The answer is (B). The word "neither" goes with "nor." The correct sentence is "Neither the revolution in industry nor that in agriculture could have proceeded without. . . ."

12. Infinitive/Gerund

Example ➤   Except in cases of extreme emergency, police officers are required obeying all traffic laws.
                       A   B   C   D

Simplify the sentence:

xxxxx, police officers are required xxxxx.

The main subject and verb are correct. The word "required" in this sentence must be followed by an infinitive, "to obey."

13. Comparative

The specific testing points might be the ending *-er* or the phrase *more . . . than* or a construction like *as . . . as.*

Example ➤   Disneyland was Walt Disney's special dream for more as 20 years before it became a reality.
                          A   B   C   D

Simplify the sentence:

Disneyland was xxxxx.

The main subject and verb are correct. The answer is (C). The word "more" should be followed by "than."

14. Article

The words *a, an,* and *the* are often used incorrectly.

Example ➤   Scientists have gained the great deal of information about the large animals called dinosaurs
                        $\overline{\text{A}}$ $\overline{\text{B}}$

that lived millions of years ago.
$\overline{\text{C}}$ $\overline{\text{D}}$

Simplify the sentence:

Scientists have gained xxxxx information about xxxxx.

The answer is (A). The phrase "a great deal of " means "a lot" or "much."

15. Superlative

In this category you may be tested on the word *the* or *most* or the ending *-est* in a superlative phrase.

Example ➤   The staff is often the costly and most important of all the resources committed to the
                        $\overline{\text{A}}$ $\overline{\text{B}}$ $\overline{\text{C}}$

working of an institution or a business.
$\overline{\text{D}}$

Simplify the sentence:

The staff is the xxxxx and xxxxx of xxxxx.

The subject and verb are correct. The answer is (B). There are two superlative phrases in this sentence: *the most costly* and *the most important*.

Both "costly" and "important" should be preceded by "most."

Prepositional Idioms

The use of many prepositions in English is purely idiomatic: There is no logical reason that one preposition is wrong and another correct in a given expression. There are no rules for choosing the correct preposition; you must simply learn the idioms.

accede **to**	We cannot *accede to* the request for an extension of time.
accommodate **to**	Some people find it hard to *accommodate to* new situations.
accommodate **with**	We *accommodated* him *with* a loan of five dollars.
accompany **by**	The defendant was *accompanied by* a lawyer. (a person)
accompany **with**	The letter was *accompanied with* a gift. (a thing)
accused **by**	He was *accused by* the plaintiff of having filed a false statement.
accused **of**	The mechanic was *accused of* overcharging.
acquiesce **in**	The dean *acquiesced in* the decision.
acquit **of**	He was *acquitted of* the crime.
acquit **with**	The police officer *aquitted* herself *with* honor.
adapt **for**	The work simplification guide was *adapted for* our use.
adapt **from**	The movie was *adapted from* the book.
adapt **to**	They find it difficult to *adapt to* new procedures.

adequate **for**	His salary was not *adequate for* his needs.
adequate **to**	Her ability was *adequate to* the job.
advise **of**	The employees were *advised of* the new regulations.
affix **to**	A stamp was *affixed to* the letter.
agree **in**	We *agree in* principle with those who favor the plan.
agree **on**	They cannot *agree on* a plan of action.
agree **to**	They *agree to* the compromise.
agree **with**	I *agree with* the doctor.
amenable **to**	They were *amenable to* our argument.
analogous **to**	This situation is *analogous to* the one we faced last year.
annoy **by**	The clerk was *annoyed by* the frequent interruptions.
annoy **with**	The teacher was *annoyed with* the careless student.
apparent **in**	His attitude is *apparent in* his actions.
apparent **to**	The trouble is *apparent to* everyone in the office.
append **to**	A rider was *appended to* the bill.
appreciation **for**	The student had a real *appreciation for* the arts.
appreciation **of**	She expressed *appreciation of* their hard work.
appreciative **of**	We are *appreciative of* their efforts.
authority **in**	Dr. X is an *authority in* her field.
authority **on**	Mr. X is an *authority on* linear programming.
averse **to**	He was not *averse to* hard work.
basis **for**	They had a sound *basis for* agreement.
basis **in**	That argument has no *basis in* fact.
coincide **with**	Your wishes *coincide with* mine in this situation.
commensurate **with**	His salary was *commensurate with* his abilities.
comply **with**	We must *comply with* the request.
concur **in**	We *concur in* the decision of the survey committee.
concur **with**	One member did not *concur with* the others.
conform **to**	All employees must *conform to* the regulations.
consist **in**	His value *consists in* his ability to work with others.
consist **of**	The handbook *consists of* grammar rules.
consistent **in**	We should be *consistent in* applying the law.
consistent **with**	His actions are not *consistent with* his statements.
correspond **to**	Her description of the incident *corresponds to* what we believe to be the case.
correspond **with**	We have been *corresponding with* our new friends abroad.
demand **from**	What did the store owner *demand from* them in payment?
demand **of**	They had *demanded* an accounting *of* the company funds.
differ **from**	My estimate of the amount due *differs from* yours.
differ **in**	We *differ in* our opinions on the matter.
differ **on**	They *differ on* the amount owed.

differ **with**	I *differ with* your view of the situation.
discrepancy **between**	There is a *discrepancy between* the two accounts.
discrepancy **in**	There is a *discrepancy in* his account.
displeased **at**	The supervisor was *displeased at* the employee's conduct.
displeased **with**	The supervisor was *displeased with* the employee.
eligible **for**	He is *eligible for* the job.
equivalent **in**	The two offices are *equivalent in* size.
equivalent **of**	This is the *equivalent of* a full payment.
equivalent **to**	Each payment is *equivalent to* a week's salary.
excepted **from**	He was *excepted from* further responsibility.
excluded **from**	This item may be *excluded from* gross income.
exempt **from**	This type of income is *exempt from* tax.
expect **from**	What return do you *expect from* your investment?
expect **of**	What do you *expect of* your assistant?
familiar **to**	The name is *familiar to* me.
familiar **with**	He is quite *familiar with* the proceedings.
furnish **to**	Adequate supplies were *furnished to* them.
furnish **with**	Please *furnish* us *with* background information on this matter.
habit **of**	The student made a *habit of* waiting until the report was due before beginning to write it.
identical **to**	That case is *identical to* the one I am working on.
identify **by**	The dog was *identified by* its unusual markings.
identify **with**	He was *identified with* the opposing members.
ignorant **of**	She was *ignorant of* her rights.
improvement **in**	The *improvement in* the weather was a welcome change.
improvement **on**	The second draft was an *improvement on* the first.
inconsistent **in**	The judge was *inconsistent in* making the awards.
inconsistent **with**	This is *inconsistent with* established policy.
infer **from**	We *infer from* this statement that the decision has been made.
influence **by**	We were all *influenced by* the director's statements.
influence **of**	The *influence of* French words in the English language has been great.
influence **on (upon)**	The rumor of an organizational change had an *influence on (upon)* production.
influence **over**	The supervisor had a strong *influence over* his staff.
influence **with**	He referred frequently to his *influence with* those in authority.
inform **of**	Instructors should keep their students *informed of* any changes in procedure.
inherent **in**	A capacity for growth is *inherent in* all people.
insert **in**	This phrase should be *inserted in* the draft.

intercede **for**	My lawyer *interceded for* me.
intercede **with**	The professor *interceded with* the review board in my behalf.
invest **in**	The money was *invested in* stocks.
invest **with**	She was *invested with* full power to act.
irrelevant **to**	This statement is *irrelevant to* the topic.
irrespective **of**	They decided to implement the plan *irrespective of* the criticism that might result.
liable **for**	The tenant is *liable for* damages.
liable **to**	The employee is *liable to* his employer.
necessary **to**	Your help is *necessary to* the success of the project.
necessity **for**	There is no *necessity for* a reduction in force.
necessity **of**	We are faced with the *necessity of* reducing expenses.
oblivious **of (to)**	The teacher was *oblivious of* the noise outside the room.
pertinent **to**	Your comment is not really *pertinent to* the discussion.
recompense **for**	We were fully *recompensed for* the time we spent on the work.
reconcile **to**	We have become *reconciled to* our fate.
reconcile **with**	Our views cannot be *reconciled with* theirs.
similarity **in**	I agree that there is much *similarity in* their appearance.
similarity **of**	The *similarity of* the cases caused confusion.
similarity **to**	This time-saving device shows a *similarity to* one I have.
talk **of**	The traveler *talked* long *of* his experiences.
talk **to**	The lecturer *talked to* a large audience.
talk **with**	The students *talked with* the instructor.
transfer **from**	He has been *transferred from* his former position.
transfer **to**	They *transferred* him *to* another department.
unequal **in**	The contestants were *unequal in* strength.
unequal **to**	She was *unequal to* the demands placed on her.
use **for**	He had no *use for* the extra table.
use **of**	She made good *use of* her opportunity.
wait **at**	I will *wait at* the back of the room until the lecture is over.
wait **for**	The children were *waiting for* their parents to return.
wait **on (upon)**	This matter must *wait on (upon)* my leisure.

Reading Comprehension Section

This section of the TOEFL measures your comprehension of standard written English. It includes approximately five reading passages, each of which is followed by twelve questions.

Sample Questions

In the Reading Comprehension section you will read several passages. Each passage is followed by questions about it. You are to choose the best answer to the questions based on what is stated or implied in the reading passage. Mark your answer by filling in the oval that corresponds to the letter of your answer choice.

Sample Passage

A new hearing device is now available for some hearing-impaired people. This device uses a magnet to hold the detachable sound-processing portion in place. Like other aids, it converts sound into vibrations. But it is unique in that it can transmit the vibrations directly to the magnet, and then to the inner ear. This produces a clearer sound. The new device will not help all hearing-impaired people, only those with a hearing loss caused by infection or some other problem in the middle ear. It will probably help no more than 20 percent of all people with hearing problems. Those people, however, who have persistent ear infections should find relief and restored hearing with this device.

Example➤ What is the author's main purpose in writing this passage?

Sample Answer

(A) To describe a new cure for ear infections.

(B) To inform the reader of a new device.

(C) To urge doctors to use a new device.

(D) To explain the use of a magnet.

The author's main purpose is to inform the reader of a new device for hearing-impaired people. Therefore, you should choose answer (B).

Example➤ The word "relief" in the last sentence means

Sample Answer

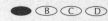

(A) less distress

(B) assistance

(C) distraction

(D) relaxation

The phrase "less distress" is similar in meaning to "relief" in this sentence. Therefore, you should choose answer (A).

53

Reading Comprehension Strategies

TOEFL reading passages can be on any topic, but you are not being tested on your knowledge of that topic. You are only being tested on your reading skills. All the answers you need are in the passage. You will be able to read more quickly, however, if you are familiar with the topic. The best way to prepare is to read as much as you can on a wide variety of topics.

There are two general strategies for the reading comprehension questions. Try both of them on the practice tests to see which works best for you. The second general strategy might work better if you are familiar with the topic of the passage.

General Strategy I

1. Read the passage through carefully, noting the major ideas.
2. Read each question and the answer choices, looking back to the passage to check your answers.
3. Mark your answer for each question as soon as you choose it.

General Strategy II

1. Skim the passage, looking for the main people, places, times, and events.
2. Skim over all the questions, answering those you know first.
3. Go back to the questions that are more difficult. Read them carefully, and look back in the passage, reading carefully to find the answers.
4. Double check your answer choices and mark each one on your answer sheet.

Vocabulary Strategies[1]

There is no separate vocabulary section, but there are many vocabulary questions included in the Reading section. The best way to prepare for vocabulary questions is to increase your vocabulary by reading in English. Read as much as you can, whenever you can. This will also help you increase your knowledge of grammar and your reading comprehension skills. As you read, write down new words and look them up later in your dictionary. Make vocabulary cards with the word and a sentence on one side and the definition and part of speech on the other. Keep these cards with you to practice whenever you have time.

At the end of this section there is a list of vocabulary words that have been on recent TOEFL exams. Study the words, making up sentences of your own to help you remember the meanings.

---

[1] For additional help in studying vocabulary, you may want to use the Vocabulary Practice audio cassette designed to accompany this book and *TOEFL SuperCourse* by Zhong and Sullivan. You can order the tape by using the coupon at the beginning of this book.

Testing Points

Reading Comprehension

In this section you will find examples of topics and types of questions that are common in TOEFL reading comprehension passages.

Topics

Though reading comprehension passages can be on any topic, many of them focus on some aspect of science. Common general topics are listed below:

1. Science
2. North American history, government, or geography
3. Art and literature, including biographies of famous people

Types of Questions

The following types of questions have appeared frequently on previous TOEFL exams. Examples of each question type are given in this section.

Reading Comprehension Question Types

1. Main Idea
2. Inference
3. Restatement
4. Vocabulary
5. Negative Question
6. Referent
7. Author's Attitude/Opinion/Purpose
8. Organization
9. Preceding/Following Topic
10. Support
11. Analogy

Vocabulary

TOEFL vocabulary questions test your ability to choose a synonym for a word as it is used in a particular sentence. The vocabulary words may be nouns, verbs, adjectives, or adverbs. They may be a single word or a phrase. If you do not know the meaning of a word, sometimes it helps to know the prefix or the root word. Below are listed a few examples of prefixes and root words. Many dictionaries give you the meanings of roots and prefixes for words. Use the information in your dictionary to increase your knowledge of new words.

Examples of Prefixes

Prefix	Meaning	Example
a, an	no, not, or without	anesthesia (without feeling), asymptomatic (without symptoms)
ante	before	antedate (come before)
anti	against, opposite	antiwar (against war)
circum	around	circumvent (circle around)
intra	within	intrastate (within the state)
inter	between	interstate (between states)

Examples of Roots

Root	Meaning	Example
chronos	time	chronology (arrangement of events in time order)
lingua	tongue, language	multilingual (speaking many languages)
phon, phone	sound	symphony (harmony of sounds)
struct	build	construction (process of building)
therm	heat	thermometer (instrument for measuring heat)
ten	hold	tenacious (holding firmly)

Examples of Each Question Type

Sample questions 1–7 are based on the following passage.

Reading Passage 1

Not much is known about the early history of printing with movable type. There is evidence, however, that hand-set printing with movable type was first invented in China and Korea. At a later time it was developed in Europe. In the 1400s, Laurens Janszoon Koster of Holland and Pamfilo Castaldi of
(5)   Italy are thought to have made the first European use of printing with movable type. It is Johann Gutenberg's name, however, that is now associated with the invention of the movable type printing press. Although the separate elements of printing (the type, the ink, the press, and the paper) were not Gutenberg's own invention, his contribution was that he printed a large quantity of work
(10) of high quality.

Born in Mainz, Germany, in about 1397, Gutenberg was trained as a goldsmith, but he became a partner in a printing office in about 1436. It was in his home town of Mainz that he began the project he is most famous for: the printing of the Mazarin Bible. To finance this great project, he borrowed
(15) money from a lawyer named Johann Fust and from a printer. He was unable to pay back the money, however, and as a result lost both his printing press and the types to Fust, who carried on Gutenberg's work.

Gutenberg's method dominated the printing industry for almost 400 years. It required hand-setting particular pieces of type, locking them into place, and
(20) then printing on wooden flatbed handpresses. The rate was slow compared to modern printing; 300 to 500 sheets a day printed on a single side was considered a good rate of production. Though not much is known about Gutenberg's life, his name lives on as a person who contributed significantly to the technology of human communication.

1. Main Idea

Example➤ Almost every passage begins with a main idea question. The main idea is the main message that the passage conveys. The beginning and the end of a passage often give clues to the main idea.

What is the main topic of this passage?

(A) a history of early printing
(B) Gutenberg's contribution to printing
(C) the printing of the Mainz Bible
(D) Gutenberg's life in Germany

The answer is (B). Although this passage begins as though it might be a history of printing, the main focus is on Gutenberg's contributions to printing. This is evident in the last sentence of the first paragraph and the final sentence of the passage.

2. Inference

In inference-type questions, the answer is not stated directly in the text. Usually you must read several sentences to understand the inference.

Example➤   The author infers that the most significant aspect of Gutenberg's work in developing the art of printing is

    (A)   the large number and quality of copies that he printed
    (B)   the printing of the Mazarin Bible
    (C)   the fact that he developed a new technique using known elements
    (D)   his inventive spirit and tenacious approach to his work

The answer is (A). Though all of the above are significant in some ways, the author states that Gutenberg's contribution to printing was that he printed a large quantity of work of high quality (lines 9-10). From this we can infer the author considers this the most significant aspect of Gutenberg's work.

3. Restatement

In restatement-type questions, the answer might be found directly in the text, or it might use synonyms or a restructuring of the grammar in the text.

Example➤   Why did Gutenberg borrow money from Fust?

    (A)   in order to fund his printing of the Bible
    (B)   in order to pay back loans for buying movable type
    (C)   in order to expand his printing ability
    (D)   in order to go into partnership with another printer

The answer is (A). Often a restatement question will use the exact words in the passage. In this restatement question, you must know that the phrase "this great project" (line 14) refers to the Mazarin Bible.

4. Vocabulary

Vocabulary questions test your ability to choose a synonym for a word or phrase as it is used in a passage.

Example➤   The word "types" in line 17 could best be replaced by which of the following?

    (A)   representative species
    (B)   sets of equivalent forms
    (C)   styles
    (D)   metal pieces

The answer is (D). All of the above words could in some instances be used as synonyms for "type." In this passage, however, the word "types" refers to the metal pieces with raised letters or figures that were inked and then pressed against paper.

5. Negative Question

A negative question asks for something that is not in the passage. There will be three answers that are right, but you are to choose the one that is *wrong*.

Example➤ According to the author, which of the following did NOT precede Gutenberg in the use of movable type printing?

    (A) Fust
    (B) Koster
    (C) Castaldi
    (D) The Chinese

The answer is (A). The passage implies that Koster, Castaldi, and the Chinese preceded Gutenberg. It does not specifically state that Fust did not precede Gutenberg, but it states that Fust "carried on" Gutenberg's work. The phrase "carried on" implies that his work followed Gutenberg's.

6. Referent

The word "referent" comes from the verb "to refer." For this type of question you must decide which word or phrase a pronoun is referring to. Usually you look to the previous noun or phrase for the answer.

Example➤ In line 19, what does the word "it" refer to?

    (A) pieces of type
    (B) four hundred years
    (C) the printing industry
    (D) Gutenberg's method

The answer is (D). For a referent question, you must look for the closest preceding (or sometimes following) phrase that means the same as the referring preposition. In this case, the word "it" refers to whatever "required hand-setting particular pieces of type." It is Gutenberg's method that required the hand-setting of particular pieces of type.

7. Author's Attitude/Opinion/Purpose

In this type of question you are not looking for a specific answer in the passage. Instead, you read to find what the author might be implying. How does the author seem to feel about the passage? What is the author trying to do?

Example➤ Why does the author mention Koster and Costaldi?

    (A) To bring out the superiority of previous inventors
    (B) To show that Gutenberg had rivals
    (C) To demonstrate that historians disagree
    (D) To broaden the scope of this discussion

The answer is (D). There is no evidence in this passage that the author wanted to discuss the superiority of previous inventors or that these inventors were rivals who were competing with Gutenberg. Answer (C) is possible, but there is no emphasis on whether historians agree or disagree on the facts. The best answer is that the addition of the names of previous inventors adds a broader perspective to the discussion of Gutenberg's work.

Sample questions 8–11 are based on the following passage.

Reading Passage 2

Scarce diamonds are more valuable than the clusters of smaller crystals known as bort and carbonado. These diamonds are large single crystals of genuine crystalline carbon.

(5) Diamonds are found in diamantiferous earth that is located in both open-air pits and underground mines. To retrieve the diamonds, the earth is crushed and concentrated. The concentrated material is then sorted by passing it over streams of water on greased tables. Since diamonds are water repellent they will stick to the grease, while the other minerals will absorb water and pass over the grease. The diamonds are then removed from the grease and cleaned,

(10) examined, sorted, and graded. The best diamonds are noted for their cleavage, their translucence, and their color.

All diamonds have a natural line of cleavage along which they may be split, and it is essential to split them before they are cut and polished. Before they are cut and polished, they look like tiny blue-grey stones; they do not twinkle

(15) or shine yet. A perfectly cut and polished diamond has 58 faces arranged regularly over its surface. It will be translucent and colorless, blue, white, green, or yellow. The value of a jewel diamond depends largely on its color, or "water," as it is called professionally. A stone of the finest water is blue-white.

8. Organization

Organization questions ask either about the general organization of the passage or the location of specific information in the passage.

Example► Which of the following statements best describes the organization of this passage?

    (A) comparison and contrast
    (B) chronological order
    (C) statement and illustration
    (D) cause and result

The answer is (C). When reading the first sentence, it may seem that this passage will compare valuable diamonds with less valuable diamonds; however, the rest of the passage does not continue the comparison. Rather, it gives more information about valuable diamonds.

9. Preceding/Following Topic

For this type of question you must infer what may have come just before the passage or what might come after the passage. Use the clues in the beginning or end of the passage to help you guess the topic.

Example➤ Which of the following most probably was the subject of the paragraph preceding the passage?

      (A) a discussion of scarce diamonds
      (B) a discussion of bort and carbonado
      (C) a discussion of the various colors of diamonds
      (D) a discussion of means of mining diamonds

The answer is (B). Since the first sentence compares scarce diamonds to bort and carbonado without defining either bort or carbonado, it is most likely that the preceding paragraph described these other types of diamond material.

10. Support

This type of question is similar to a main idea question except that it asks about a detail instead of the whole passage.

Example➤ Which of the following statements is best supported by this passage?

      (A) The value of a diamond is in large part dependent on the way it is prepared.
      (B) The natural cleavage will determine the value of a diamond.
      (C) Translucent and transparent diamonds are considered the most valuable.
      (D) Diamonds have been valued by people ever since they were discovered.

The answer is (A). Though all the statements may be true, the one that is most discussed in this passage is the importance of the preparation of the diamond.

11. Analogy

There are very few questions like this on the TOEFL. For this type of question you need to understand the relationship between two things mentioned in the passage and two other things.

Example➤ The relationship between the cleavage and translucence of a diamond is most similar to the relationship between the style of an automobile and its

      (A) color
      (B) size
      (C) price
      (D) speed

The answer is (A). The word "translucence" means the ability to see through an object when that object is partially transparent. Though this is not the same as "color," it is something that is visible in a similar way as color.

TOEFL Word List

Most of the words on the following list have been used in past versions of the TOEFL. Some of them have been the selected words in vocabulary questions and others have been used as answer choices. All of them represent the typical level of words used on the TOEFL.

abhor *(verb)* to hate or think of with disgust
The man abhorred the feel of snakes.

accelerate *(verb)* to increase the speed
This car accelerates quickly.

accessible *(adj.)* able to be reached; convenient
Elevators in tall buildings make the top floors accessible to everyone.

accurate, accuracy *(adj./noun)* exact; correct
In order to get 100 percent on the test, you must be accurate.

adjacent to *(adj.)* next to; near, but not necessarily touching
Our garage is adjacent to our house.

advantageous *(adj.)* profitable; helpful
Sometimes it is advantageous to own a car.

advocate *(noun/verb)* a person who supports or speaks in favor of something; to support
Our group is an advocate of equal opportunity for men and women.

aforementioned *(adj.)* said or written before
The aforementioned topic is one of great interest.

alert, alertly *(adj./adv.)* fully awake and ready to act; in an alert manner
The guard watched alertly as the people appeared.

amass *(verb)* to collect or pile up
The rich man had amassed his fortune over several years.

ambrosia *(noun)* food that has a delightful taste or smell; "food of the gods"
This fantastic dish tastes like ambrosia.

anomaly *(noun)* something abnormal or unusual
A bird that cannot fly is an anomaly.

anxiety *(noun)* an emotional condition of fear and uncertainty
Her family waited with anxiety for the news of her safe arrival.

appall, apalling *(verb/adj.)* to fill with fear; shocking
The number of people who starved in the famine was appalling.

appear *(verb)* to come into view; to become visible
At dawn the sun appears on the horizon.

appropriate *(adj.)* suitable; proper
A wedding dress is not appropriate to wear to a beach party.

apt *(adj.)* likely; appropriate; relevant
The mischievous child is apt to get into trouble.
Your statement is not apt to this conversation.

arouse *(verb)* to awaken; to cause to become active
My father used to arouse us at 6 A.M.

as of late *(conj. + adj.)* recently
I've been feeling tired as of late.

astute *(adj.)* clever, quick
The astute student answered all the questions correctly.

attribute *(verb)* to consider something as the result of something else
I attribute my success to my hard work.

authoritative *(adj.)* having authority; commanding
The authoritative manner of the general made us respect him.

back and forth *(adv.)* movement: first one way and then the other
The anxious man walked back and forth across the room.

barely *(adv.)* only a bit; hardly
I barely know my new neighbors; they just moved in.

barter *(verb)* to exchange goods or property for other goods or property
Ancient societies bartered food before they had money.

behold *(verb)* to look at; to observe
The clear blue-green lake is a lovely sight to behold.

beneficial *(adj.)* helpful
Fresh air and good food are beneficial to your health.

bind *(verb)* to tie or fasten; to hold to an agreement
If you bind the package with rope, it will be easier to carry.

bizarre *(adj.)* very odd or unusual
The costumes for this play are bizarre.

blunder *(verb)* to move with uncertainty; to make foolish mistakes
The candidate for president was careful not to blunder in his speech.

border *(noun)* the edge; the line or the boundary between two places
The lake is on the border of two countries.

breach *(noun)* a breaking or neglect of a rule or agreement
Fighting in the streets is a breach of the peace.

bump *(noun/verb)* a swelling; to move with a jerking motion
I have a bump on my arm from the bee sting.
The old car bumped down the dirt road.

bush *(noun)* low-growing plant with many stems
The trees, bushes, and flowers in the park are beautiful.

by degrees *(adv.)* gradually
Their friendship grew by degrees.

by rights *(adv.)* if justice were done
This property is mine by rights.

candid *(adj.)* frank, straightforward, truthful
I'll be candid with you; you did a poor job.

care *(verb)* to feel interest or sorrow; to be willing; to look after someone by providing food, medical assistance, etc.
He doesn't seem to care whether he passes or fails.

carve *(verb)* to form something by cutting away wood or stone
The statues by Michelangelo were carved from granite.

celebrate *(verb)* to do something to show that a day or event is special
We celebrated my birthday by having a party.

chart *(noun)* a map; a paper with diagrams, tables or visual information
The sailors looked at their charts to find out where they were.

circulate *(verb)* to move from place to place freely
The teacher circulated around the room as the students studied.

classify *(verb)* to arrange in classes or groups
One of the secretary's jobs is to classify the new information.

colleague *(noun)* a partner or associate working in the same profession
Her colleagues assisted her when she needed help.

collusion *(noun)* a secret agreement or discussion for a dishonest reason
The robbers were in collusion before the robbery.

command *(noun)* a position of power
The general was in command of the army.

commonplace *(adj./noun)* normal, ordinary, obvious, not interesting
It is a commonplace event to eat dinner in the evening.

compromise *(noun/verb)* a settlement of a dispute by which each side gives up something it
wants; an agreement; to make concessions
This hotel is a good compromise; it's near the lake for me and near the mountains for you.
To settle the argument, each person compromised a bit.

conceal *(verb)* to hide; to keep secret
The robber concealed a weapon under his coat.

confidential *(adj.)* secret
Some military information is confidential.

conform *(verb)* to stay in agreement with rules
People who don't conform will be discharged from the group.

congregate *(verb)* to come together
After the speech, the audience congregated around the speaker.

conserve *(verb)* to save, or to keep from destruction
During a drought, everyone needs to conserve water.

considerably *(adv.)* much, a great deal
I have considerably more work this year than I did last year.

conspicuous *(adj.)* easily seen
You look conspicuous in that large purple hat.

contemporary *(noun/adj.)* belonging to the same time; of the present time, or modern
George Washington and Benjamin Franklin were contemporaries.
I live in a contemporary house.

contrast *(verb)* to compare so that differences are made clear
Her words contrast with her actions.

convenient *(adj.)* easy to use, easy to get to, or easy to do
It is convenient to have a washing machine in your house.

counter *(noun/verb)* a table surface on which goods are shown or food prepared; to oppose; to
return an attack
You can pick up your food from the counter.
My argument was countered by my friend's argument.

craggy *(adj.)* with high, steep, or sharp rocks
The mountain climbers slowly ascended the craggy slopes.

critic *(noun)* a person who gives judgment, usually about literature, art, or music
After his new play was performed, he was anxious to read what the critics said about it.

crush *(verb)* to press so that there is breaking or injury
His leg was crushed in an automobile accident.

curious *(adj.)* eager to learn and to know; having an interest in something
Children are usually curious about the world.

cut *(noun/verb)* a reduction in size, amount or length; a style of clothes or hair; a remark that hurts a person's feelings; to remove from something larger, to stay away from or be absent from class
I don't like the cut of that dress. *(style)*
He cut the dead limb from the tree.

damage *(noun/verb)* harm or injury; to harm or injure
The insurance company will pay for the damages to your car.

decay *(verb)* to go bad; to lose power or health
Fruit decays quickly in hot weather.

defeat *(noun/verb)* loss; to cause to fail
After five victories, the soccer team suffered its first defeat.

deficit *(noun)* a condition of spending more than you have
The only way to decrease the deficit is to increase taxes.

den *(noun)* a secret place; an animal's hidden place; a room for studying
The fox's den is in the bushes.

desolate *(adj.)* ruined, barren, neglected, lonely, or sad
The small town looked desolate after the storm.

detachable *(adj.)* able to be removed, unfastened, or taken apart
The legs of this table are detachable.

deter *(verb)* to discourage
A locked door will deter thieves.

dig *(verb)* to use a tool to move earth
To get ready to plant the tree, you must dig a hole.

dim *(adj.)* not bright, not seen clearly
A small light is too dim for reading.

discerning *(adj.)* able to see clearly
A discerning eye can tell the difference between planets and stars.

discord *(noun)* disagreement, conflict
Quarrels over money have brought discord into the family.

disseminate *(verb)* to distribute; to spread widely
The news of the new king was disseminated over the whole country.

distinct *(adj.)* easily seen or heard, clearly marked, separate
She has a distinct accent.

draft *(noun/verb)* an outline of something to be done; a current of air in a room; to select a person for the armed forces
Before I submit an essay, I always write a first draft.
My brother was drafted into the army.

due to *(prep.)* because of, caused by, attributed to
The accident was due to slippery streets.

duplicate *(noun/verb/adj.)* a copy; to copy exactly; to make exactly alike
Please make a duplicate of this letter for me.

earmark *(verb/noun)* to set aside for a special purpose; an identification mark to show ownership
The boss has earmarked this money for Christmas decorations.

elaborate *(verb/adj.)* to work out with much care; worked in detail
We have made elaborate plans for New Year's Day.

eligible *(adj.)* suitable, having the right qualifications
You must pass the TOEFL in order to be eligible for entrance into many Canadian and American colleges.

emancipate *(verb)* to set free
Abraham Lincoln is famous for having emancipated people from slavery.

embrace *(verb/noun)* to take someone into one's arms to show affection; to include
When the soldier saw his family after the war he embraced his mother and father.
This speech embraces all the major ideas of the president.

emit *(verb)* to give or to send out
A volcano emits fire from the earth.

encourage *(verb)* to give hope, confidence, or support
I encourage all my children to study hard in school.

enhance *(verb)* to add to the value or importance of something
Keeping your house clean and well-cared for enhances its value.

entangle *(verb)* to become caught or involved in something so that escape is difficult
The kitten cried when it got entangled in a ball of string.

entitle *(verb)* to give a right to something
As a student here, you are entitled to use the services at the health center.

epoch *(noun)* a period of time in history
Henry Ford's automobile began a new epoch in the history of transportation.

erode, erosion *(verb/noun)* to wear away, usually by rain, wind, or acid; a wearing away
Acid eroded the metal under my car.
Water erosion from the heavy rains has caused damage to the land.

essential *(adj.)* necessary
To enter many colleges, it is essential that you get 550 on the TOEFL exam.

evacuate *(verb)* to leave empty; to withdraw
If there is a fire, evacuate the building quickly.

exceed *(verb)* to do more than enough; to go beyond; to be greater than
His success has exceeded all our hopes.

excerpt *(noun)* a part of a book or article
In the magazine, you can read an excerpt of his latest book.

exhilarating *(adj.)* filled with high spirits, lively, exciting
I have some exhilarating news: We won the national game!

expanse *(noun)* a wide open area
To raise cattle, you need a large expanse of land.

extend *(verb)* to make longer
The teacher extended the deadline for our essays for another week.

extravagant *(adj.)* wasteful; excessive
   Rich people are sometimes extravagant with their money; they spend a lot.

face *(verb)* to meet confidently; to recognize; to turn in a certain direction
   I don't want to face my friend after what I did to her.
   Please face the front of the room.

fame *(noun)* the condition of being known or talked about; good reputation
   Unfortunately, his fame as a composer did not come until after his death.

fancy *(adj.)* very decorated, not plain
   For the party, you should wear fancy clothes.

faucet *(noun)* a device for controlling the flow of liquid (usually water) from a pipe or tank
   To make the water come out, you must turn on the faucet.

feature *(noun/verb)* the appearance of something; distinct or outstanding parts; an attraction or main part; to emphasize the main part
   One of the main features of Yellowstone National Park is Old Faithful.

fellow *(adj.)* having the same ideas or position; in the same condition; associated
   My fellow workers and I are all going on a picnic together.

fictitious *(adj.)* untrue or invented
   The writer published under a fictitious name.

final analysis *(adj. + noun)* at the end, in conclusion
   In the final analysis, the Northern team won the prize for "Team of the Year."

fizz *(verb/noun)* to make a bubbling hissing sound, as when gas escapes from a liquid; a bubbling sound
   Soft drinks like Coca-Cola fizz when they are poured into a glass.

flaw *(noun)* a fault, an imperfection
   The store is selling clothes that have flaws at half price.

flicker *(verb)* to burn or shine unsteadily
   The candle flickered in the wind and then went out.

forbidden *(adj.)* prohibited; ordered not to be done
   It is forbidden to enter the compound after dark.

foster *(verb)* to help to grow or develop; to bring up with care
   A relaxed environment can foster creative ideas.

fragrance *(noun)* a pleasing smell
   I like perfume with the fragrance of fresh flowers.

frightening *(adj.)* filled with fear and alarm
   A frightening nightmare can cause a child to wake up and cry.

fuel *(noun)* a material that produces energy or heat
   Some cars run on diesel fuel and some on gasoline.

fund *(noun/verb)* a supply of necessary things, money; to provide money for support
   Our group raised money for the scholarship fund.

gain *(noun/verb)* an increase in power or wealth; to obtain something
   The boss is only interested in gain. He wants to gain power.

gemstones *(noun)* precious, valuable stones or jewels
   Some people keep gemstones in a safe.

glistening *(adj.)* shining brightly, sparkling
   In the morning, the flowers are glistening with the dewdrops.

goods *(noun)* things that have worth or are valuable
  After you count the goods, lock them in the warehouse.

graphic *(adj.)* described in clear images
  The man gave a graphic account of the fight.

grave *(adj.)* serious, requiring careful consideration
  Her illness is grave.

grumpy *(adj.)* bad-tempered
  Grandpa is always grumpy when he first wakes up.

hardly *(adv.)* only just, scarcely
  When I was sick I could hardly talk.

hatch *(verb)* to break out of an egg; to produce a plan
  The chicks are hatching today.

hearty *(adj.)* strong, in good health
  After a good breakfast, I feel hearty.

hostile *(adj.)* unfriendly
  The enemies were hostile toward each other.

huge *(adj.)* very large
  I just ate a huge dinner; I can't eat anything more.

hybrid *(noun)* an animal or plant that is the offspring of two different parents or species
  The mule is a hybrid animal, a cross between a donkey and a horse.

ignore *(verb)* to refuse to notice someone or something
  When people are angry at each other, they sometimes ignore each other.

imitate *(verb)* to copy something or use it as an example
  By imitating great artists, young artists can learn good techniques.

imperceptible *(adv.)* slight, gradual, unnoticeable
  The improvement, though imperceptible, was still there.

increase *(verb/noun)* to make larger; growth
  There is an increase in the number of students in school this year.

indefinite *(adj.)* not fixed; vague
  The factory will be closed for an indefinite period of time.

indicative *(adj.)* an indication or sign of something to come
  The blossoms on the fruit trees are indicative of spring weather.

induce *(verb)* to cause; to produce; to influence
  Her illness was induced by a poor diet and overwork.

ingenious *(adj.)* very clever and skillful
  The professor was ingenious at solving problems.

inhibit *(verb)* to restrain or suppress; to hinder
  Being very tired inhibits studying.

insatiable *(adj.)* something that cannot be satisfied
  My father has an insatiable desire for candy.

inspiring *(adj.)* uplifting; stimulating
  After the inspiring speech, the audience was filled with confidence.

insult *(verb)* to speak to in a way that is intended to hurt a person's feelings
  When the child was insulted, he cried.

intense *(adj.)* deeply felt, high in degree
   The explosion from the bomb caused intense heat for several miles.

intricate *(adj.)* complicated, difficult
   The beauty of the painting is its intricate design.

inundated *(verb)* flooded
   The rains inundated the fields, washing away the crops.

invent *(verb)* to create or design something not already existing
   The brilliant man invented a new technique to speed up his work.

landmark *(noun)* an object that marks the boundary of a piece of land; an object that is easily
   seen and can be used as a guide; an event that marks a turning point
   The first hotel built in our city is still a landmark to progress.

lateral *(adj.)* from or at the sides of something, from side to side
   Earthquakes usually cause a lateral movement in buildings.

legendary *(adj.)* from an old story told to people from generation to generation
   The legendary travels of ancient Greeks are well known in literature.

liberate *(verb)* to free
   The victorious army liberated the prisoners.

limited *(adj.)* restricted, narrow
   There is a limited number of books on this topic for sale.

literally *(adv.)* exactly, corresponding word for word to the original, lacking in imagination
   If you translate an idiom literally, you probably will not get the correct meaning.

locale *(noun)* an area, the scene of an event
   This is the locale of the accident.

ludicrous *(adj.)* ridiculous, absurd
   It is ludicrous to say that it is easy to become fluent in all languages.

lyrical *(adj.)* full of emotion, like a song
   The lyrical words of the poem made me feel almost like crying.

magnificence *(noun)* splendor, imposing beauty
   The palace is famous for its magnificence.

mandatory *(adj.)* required
   It is mandatory that you take basic science courses before entering college.

mar *(verb)* to injure or damage
   Nothing could mar the happiness of the newly wed couple.

mature *(verb/adj.)* to be fully grown, to be ready for use; perfected
   A ten-year-old child is not mature enough to leave her family.

merchandise *(noun)* things to buy or sell
   The ships brought new merchandise in to the city.

minuscule *(adj.)* a tiny bit
   There was a minuscule amount of iron in the chemical solution.

misleading *(adj.)* causing a wrong impression; deceiving
   The police were given misleading information about the crime.

moderately *(adv.)* reasonably; to a limited degree
   It is relaxing to swim in moderately warm water.

motionless *(adv.)* still, having no movement
   The bird stood motionless so that it could hardly be seen.

muscular *(adj.)* having many muscles, strong
The lifeguards on the beach were all muscular.

mutation *(noun)* a change, an alteration in the genes of a plant or animal that can be passed on to its offspring
The strong X-rays caused a mutation in the plant.

naked *(adj.)* without clothes, bare; without protection
Babies are all born naked.
I can see it with my naked eye (without a microscope or telescope).

nominal *(adj.)* very small
A nominal fee is charged to enter the museum.

nourishment *(noun)* a source of strength and support, food
Food is nourishment for my body, but love is nourishment for my heart.

now and then *(adv.)* occasionally
Now and then I like to take a nap.

oath *(noun)* a promise or vow to tell the truth
Before giving evidence before the court, you must take an oath.

obstacle *(noun)* a hindrance, something that prevents you from doing something
Arguments and fighting between nations are obstacles to world peace.

ominous *(adj.)* threatening
Ominous black clouds on the horizon indicate a rainstorm.

on the spot *(prep.)* immediately, at the place one is needed
He was killed on the spot.

operation *(noun)* a process of doing something; a surgical procedure
My father had an operation to remove his appendix.

option *(noun)* choice
You have the option of taking biology or chemistry.

outlawed *(verb)* made illegal
Guns are outlawed in many countries.

overlap, overlapping *(verb/adj.)* to cover part of something else; covering part of another thing
The roof consists of overlapping tiles.
When building a roof, you overlap the tiles.

overwhelm *(verb)* to defeat; to exhaust; to cover completely
All the work I had to do overwhelmed me.

panacea *(noun)* a remedy for all troubles
There is no panacea that will bring everlasting happiness.

particle *(noun)* a small piece, a part
Chew carefully so that you don't get a particle stuck in your throat.

passing *(adj.)* not lasting, going by
The passing years are becoming more difficult for the sick old man.

path *(noun)* a place made for walking
There is a path through the woods.

penetrate *(verb)* to go into or through; to spread
The terrible smell penetrated the whole house.

perennial *(adv.)* continuing through the whole year; lasting; perpetual
I like perennial plants because they don't die in the winter.

perjury *(noun)* a false statement after giving an oath to tell the truth
 The woman was put in jail for perjury.

perplexing *(adj.)* confusing, complicated
 It is perplexing to read the laws of the nation.

phenomenon *(noun)* something that can be perceived by the senses, something remarkable or unusual
 If you are interested in a phenomenon like how mountains are made, take a class in earth science.

plot *(verb/noun)* to plan secretly; the main story of a book or play; a small piece of ground
 The enemies of the government plotted to overthrow the government.
 I don't understand the plot of the play.
 I planted my vegetable garden on a small plot of land by my house.

point out *(verb)* to show or call attention to something
 The teacher pointed out my mistakes so that I could correct them.

poll *(noun)* a survey of public opinion made by questioning people
 The people took a poll to see which candidate might win.

posthumously *(adv.)* after one's death
 The poet was awarded the honor of "Best Poet" posthumously.

praise *(noun/verb)* an expression of approval or esteem; to give approval, admiration, honor, or glory to someone
 A teacher should praise students who do well.
 We give praise to God.

precision *(noun)* the state of being exact, correct, accurate
 A skilled engineer works with precision.

predominantly *(adv.)* most frequently or most noticeably
 The students in our school are predominantly from the North.

prevail *(verb)* to gain victory over something; to be the usual thing, commonly seen or done.
 The South prevailed over the North in the last war.
 The prevailing winds are from the West. *(adj. form)*

primitive *(adj.)* of early times; of an early culture, pretechnical culture
 In primitive times; human beings lived in caves.

private *(adj.)* concerning one person or group rather than for people in general; secret; secluded; isolated
 I don't want my boss to know my private affairs.

profitable *(adj.)* useful; bringing in money or gain
 We made a deal that was profitable to everyone.

promotion *(noun)* advancement to a higher rank or position
 After working for two years in my company, I was given a promotion.

propagate *(verb)* to increase the number of plants or animals by natural means; to spread information
 Some farmers and botanists propagate plants.

prospect *(noun)* something hoped for or looked forward to
 The prospect of getting a new job excites me.

pulp *(noun)* the soft part of fruit; a mass of soft material such as wood fiber
 To make paper, wood is soaked and mashed to a pulp.

puzzling *(adv.)* hard to understand or answer
It is puzzling that my friend quit his job.

range *(noun/verb)* a row of things; a large area; maximum distance; the limit; a stove with an oven; to travel over or roam
The Himalayas consist of a large range of mountains.
The cows feed on the range.
The range of colors in the rainbow is limited.
I bought a new range when I rebuilt my kitchen.
The deer ranged in the woods in search of food.

reach *(verb)* to stretch; to extend; to come to
The government wanted the new tax information to reach all citizens.

rebel *(verb)* to act against something; to show resistance; to fight
The child rebelled against his parents' demands by running away.

recipient *(noun)* someone who receives something
I was a recipient of the award for best singer.

recycle *(verb)* to treat waste materials like paper, glass, or metal so they can be used again
We save all our old newspapers and take them downtown to be recycled.

refrain *(verb)* to hold back; to keep oneself from doing something
Please refrain from smoking while in the elevator.

regrettably *(adv.)* sadly
Regrettably, I won't be able to come to your wedding next month.

relate *(verb)* to tell a story; to have a connection with something
Grandfather likes to relate stories from his childhood.
Scientists are trying to relate the illness to possible causes.

release *(verb)* to let go; to set free
The prisoners were released from jail.

reluctantly *(adv.)* unwillingly
The man reluctantly admitted that he was guilty.

remote *(adj.)* far away, distant
This new robot is operated by a remote switch.

repair *(verb)* to restore to a good condition
When my bicycle broke, I repaired it.

research *(noun)* an investigation to discover new facts or information
As a graduate student you are expected to do research.

resort *(noun/verb)* a place one goes to for fun, relaxation, or health; to turn to something for help to gain one's purpose
I'd like to visit a health resort on my vacation.
The teacher resorted to threatening the unruly students with additional homework.

restore *(verb)* to bring back to the original condition; to repair; to make well
A good carpenter can restore old furniture.

revere *(verb)* to have a deep respect for; to regard highly
Some people revere their grandparents.

rewarding *(adj.)* satisfying; giving pleasure in return for something
It was rewarding to see the smiles on the children's faces when they received their gifts.

rise *(verb)* to appear; to get up; to come to life; to become greater in intensity or volume
After a heavy rainstorm, a river might rise several feet.

rudimentary *(adj.)* elementary, undeveloped
In ages past, humans had rudimentary ideas of economics.

run-down *(adj.)* not cared for; weak and exhausted; fallen into disrepair
That old vacant house has become run-down.
My watch is running down; it needs a new battery.

scarcely *(adv.)* hardly, barely, almost not
We have scarcely any money left this month.

scenery *(noun)* the general appearance of a place; features of the landscape
It's nice to stop while driving and look at the scenery.

scrupulously *(adv.)* done very carefully, paying attention to detail
He does his work scrupulously.

secretly *(adv.)* not known to others
My friend secretly told me that he was going to get married.

seek *(verb)* to look for
When it started to rain, the hikers began to seek shelter.

sensible *(adj.)* reasonable, practical
It is sensible to dress warmly in cold weather.

shade *(noun/verb)* something that cuts off the sunlight; a screen or curtain; to protect from light or heat
It's cooler to sit in the shade.
On hot days I often close the shades.
An umbrella will shade you from the sun.

sheer *(adj.)* complete or absolute; of transparent cloth
It is sheer nonsense to listen for an echo in a crowded noisy place.
For her bridal veil, the woman chose a sheer lace.

shield *(verb/noun)* to protect; a piece of metal, plastic, or other material that protects
Motorcycle riders wear leather jackets to shield themselves from the wind.

silently *(adv.)* making no sound
If you sit silently, you can hear the birds sing.

single-story *(adj.)* having one floor
My friends live in a tall apartment building, but I live in a single-story house.

site *(noun)* a place where something was or will be
This looks like a good site for a picnic lunch.

sketch *(noun/verb)* a rough plan; to make a rough, quick drawing or outline
The artist made a sketch of the mountain so that he could paint it later.

slim *(adj.)* small, insufficient; slender
She has slim hopes of getting the new job.
She should become slim if she eats less.

socket *(noun)* a hole or space into which something fits
Before you can turn on the lamp, you must plug it into the socket.

solitary *(adj.)* living alone; without companions; seldom visited; lonely
The prisoner was put in solitary confinement.
Sometimes I like to take a solitary walk.

sophisticated *(adj.)* a lack of simplicity or naturalness; cultured; with the latest improvements
After living in a big city, she became quite sophisticated.

spacious *(adj.)* having a lot of space
   In our new house we have a very spacious living room.

split *(verb)* to break into two or more parts; to divide
   In order to eat a coconut, first you must split it.

stain *(noun/verb)* a mark that doesn't wash out; to permanently change the color of something
   Blood can stain your clothes if you don't wash it out.
   In my house, I stained the wooden doors light brown.

static *(adj.)* in a state of balance, not increasing or decreasing; electric charges in the atmosphere; crackling noise in radio or television
   We could not listen to the radio because of all the static.

strengthen *(verb)* to make something stronger
   If you add an introduction, it will strengthen your essay.

strict *(adj.)* demanding obedience; clearly and exactly defined; precise
   My boss is very strict; we have many rules to follow.

stripe *(noun)* a band of material of a different color, pattern, or material
   My socks have three red stripes on them.

stubborn *(adj.)* obstinate; difficult to deal with; determined
   The stubborn mule would not pull the farmer's plow.

style *(noun)* a manner of writing, speaking; a quality of being superior; a general appearance
   I like Hemingway's writing style.
   The fashionable woman always bought her clothes in the latest style.

subtle *(adj.)* difficult to perceive or describe
   The subtle effects of the artist's use of color make her work fascinating.

supernatural *(adj.)* spiritual; unexplainable by physical laws
   Ghosts and angels are supernatural.

surpass *(verb)* to do better than someone or something else
   On the last test, I surpassed my previous score.

suspicious *(adj.)* having an idea that something bad is about to happen; thinking someone may be guilty
   I have a suspicious feeling that he may be telling a lie.

swift *(adj.)* fast, quick
   The swift runner won the race.

symphony *(noun)* a long musical composition
   Beethoven's symphonies are well known throughout the world.

take place *(verb)* happen
   The first scene of the play takes place before the hero and heroine have met.
   The party will take place at my house.

temperature *(noun)* a degree of hot or cold; a body fever
   The child has a high temperature; she should stay in bed.

tension *(noun)* strain
   When my parents are angry with each other, there is a lot of tension in the house.

terrifying *(adj.)* frightening
   I had bad dreams after seeing that terrifying ghost movie.

theory *(noun)* an explanation of a general principle; an opinion, not necessarily based on logical reasoning

Darwin's theory of evolution is important in the study of botany.

My friend has a theory that rubbing the scalp will cause hair to grow.

timid *(adj.)* shy, easily frightened

The timid child hid behind his mother's skirt.

tolerate *(verb)* to put up with; to allow without protest

I can't tolerate loud, angry people.

touching *(adj.)* causing sympathy

It was very touching to receive letters from all my friends when I was in the hospital.

trace *(noun/verb)* a very small amount; a mark showing someone has been in a place; to draw or sketch; to copy; to follow a line

There is only a trace of iodine in the water.

The archaeologists found traces of an ancient civilization.

By tracing the line in the sand, we could follow the path of the insect.

transplant *(verb)* to transfer; to move to a new place

The tiny plants were transplanted from little pots in the kitchen to a sunny place in the yard.

treasured *(adj.)* valued, loved

I keep my treasured jewels in the bank.

trickle *(verb/noun)* to flow slowly; to move little by little; a slow, small flow

The accident on the highway caused traffic to slow to a trickle.

tropical *(adj.)* of the part of the earth around the equator

Many people like to spend their vacations on tropical islands where the weather is always warm.

turbulence *(noun)* the state of being violent, uncontrolled, disorderly

After the rainstorms, the turbulence of the water in the river caused damage to the farmer's fields.

unaccustomed *(adj.)* not used to something

I am unaccustomed to eating dinner at midnight.

unbearable *(adj.)* not tolerable; causing much sadness

It is unbearable for me to see you go away for a year.

uncalled-for *(adj.)* undesirable, unnecessary, not justified

That remark was rude and uncalled-for.

unquenchable *(adj.)* not able to be satisfied

I have an unquenchable thirst.

vacillate *(verb)* to waver; to be uncertain

I have a difficult time making decisions; I vacillate among all the options.

vandalism *(noun)* deliberate destruction of a work of art or private property

Because of possible vandalism, guards have been posted at the doors of the museum.

verify *(verb)* to test the truth or accuracy of something

Can you verify this answer?

vigorous *(adj.)* having strength or energy

He works in a vigorous way.

vivid *(adj.)* lively; intense; bright; clear and distinct

I had a vivid dream last night about my parents.

warn *(verb)* to inform someone of possible danger
Fire alarms warn people that something is burning.

wed *(verb)* to marry
He will be wed next June.

widespread *(adj.)* occurring over a large area
Widespread damage was caused by the earthquake.

willing *(adj.)* ready; agreeable
I am willing to help you finish your work.

withhold *(verb)* to keep or refuse to give
Don't try to withhold the truth from me.

Test of Written English (TWE)

The TWE is not given on every test day. Look in the current Bulletin of Information to see the dates on which the TWE is given. If it is given on the day you sign up for the TOEFL, you must write the TWE essay. The TWE essay is written first, before you begin the TOEFL. You have 30 minutes to plan and write your essay, which should be about 200 to 300 words. Usually the questions ask you to compare two or more things.

Sample Questions

Example 1➤ Some people prefer work or activities that mainly involve working with people. Others choose work or activities that mainly involve working with objects or machines. Compare these types of activities. Which of them do you prefer? Give reasons to support your answer.

Example 2➤ There are advantages and disadvantages to different seasons of the year, such as rainy or dry weather. Pick any two seasons that you are familiar with and compare the two. Describe what makes you prefer one over the other. What activities do you engage in? What feelings do you have during this season?

Example 3➤ Public transportation includes buses, subways, trains, and taxis. Private transportation usually refers to private cars, bicycles, or motorcycles. Compare these two kinds of transportation, and discuss the advantages and disadvantages of each. Decide which is better, giving details to support your decision.

Example 4➤ There are both advantages and disadvantages to going to school in another country. Describe the good points and bad points about going to school in another country, and come to a conclusion about whether it is better or not to study abroad or stay at home. Give support for your opinion.

Example 5➤ Some families have many children, while others have only one child. Think about the positive and negative aspects of being in a family with several children. What size of family seems best? Why?

Example 6➤ We can be educated in many ways. Though much education happens in a classroom, we are also educated in our daily life through doing activities and listening to our friends and our family members. Which is a better way to learn: in a classroom with a teacher, or outside a classroom by doing things? Support your answer with examples and details.

Example 7➤ Some people usually cook and eat their meals in their homes, while others often eat their meals in restaurants, stores, or sidewalk cafes. What are some differences between these two ways of getting food? Which is better? Why? Give reasons to support your opinion.

Example 8➤ People have different ways of relaxing. Some people like to go out walking. Others like to read, sleep, eat, listen to music, or watch television. Some people play sports or watch sports, while others dance and sing. What are some good ways to relax when you are not working? Describe some ways to relax that you are familiar with. Why are they good ways to relax? Explain your answer by giving examples.

TWE Strategies

To prepare for the TWE, use the sample topics previously given, and practice writing an essay in 30 minutes. This is the amount of time you will have to read the question, think about the topic, plan what you will say, and write your essay.

Follow this plan of attack:

1. Read the question very carefully.
   a. Put a line under the main topic.
   b. Put a line under the main words that tell you what you need to write. The following verbs are important:
      discuss, explain, state, describe, support, compare, contrast
2. Make brief notes of the examples you want to write about or the opinions you are giving.
3. Look at your notes and organize them. What should you say first, what next? How will you conclude?
4. Check back to the words you underlined in the topic. Do you have an answer, example, or opinion for each part of the question?
5. Begin writing. Begin with a clear statement that answers the main question. Give details and specific examples to support your opinion. Write clearly so your paper can be read easily. End with a summary statement that reinforces your point of view. Remember that the readers do not know what you are saying. You must make everything clear to them.
6. Check over your writing briefly to be sure it is clear and that it answers the question. For some people it helps to read the essay out loud (very quietly) to check the sentences.

Watch the clock and plan your time. As you practice, try the suggested time plan below, and adjust it to your own way of writing.

6–8 minutes—read the question and take notes to organize your answer

18–20 minutes—write your essay

2–4 minutes—check your writing

TWE Testing Points

The TWE essay is scored by readers who read the whole essay and judge it according to the description below. The best essay receives a "6." Scores of "4," "5," and "6" are considered "passing" by many schools.

Essay Scores

6 = **Clearly competent**. An essay in this category is clear and well-organized, has many details, and uses a wide variety of vocabulary words.

5 = **Competent**. An essay in this category is well organized, but does not have as many details as a level-6 essay. The vocabulary is not as varied, and it may have a few grammatical errors.

4 = **Minimal competence**. An essay in this category is adequately organized, but may not answer all parts of the question. There may be grammatical errors that confuse the reader.

3 = **Developing competence**. An essay in this category may be poorly organized so that it is difficult for the reader to understand. It may have few details supporting the statements. There may be many grammatical errors and incorrect words.

2 = **Possibly incompetent.** An essay in this category is not well organized. There may be no detail, and it is not focused on the question.

1 = **Incompetent**. An essay in this category has serious errors in organization and sentence structure.

Transition Words

From the scoring description, you can see that it is very important for you to organize your essay carefully so that the reader can understand it. The following words and phrases may help you state your ideas clearly.

1. To indicate a time or frequency or amount:

in general	every	some	after
on the whole	usually	most	at other times
in most cases	frequently	main	finally
as a rule	rarely	before	meanwhile

2. To indicate an addition:

additionally	as well as	just as
again	along with	also
further	furthermore	likewise
in the same manner	in the same way	in addition to

3. To introduce an example:

for example	namely	for instance
as an example	that is	

4. To indicate a contrast or difference:

although	instead	rather than
but	nevertheless	though
however	on the other hand	otherwise

5. To indicate a conclusion:

all in all	in consequence	in brief
as a result	the point is	in conclusion
therefore	hence	in sum

Sample TWE Essays

This section provides examples of student essays. These essays would probably receive high scores on the TWE. Next to each essay there are notes indicating the organization of the essay. Use these notes as guidelines to practice your own TWE essays.

Sample Student Essay 1

Question:

Some people prefer work or activities that mainly involve working with people. Others choose work or activities that mainly involve working with objects or machines. Compare these types of activities. Which of them do you prefer? Give reasons to support your answer.

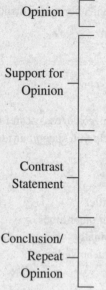

Opinion —

Of these two ways of working, either with people or with objects or machines, I prefer working with people.

Support for Opinion —

When I work with people, I can work more efficiently than when I work with machines or objects. My work then becomes interesting and productive. The reason, in my opinion, is that working with people gives us power and competition. Rivalry is a very effective motive in improving one's ability. In addition, when we talk and have conferences, we can get better ideas than we can with only one person's idea.

Contrast Statement —

On the other hand, working with machines or objects makes me bored and it takes a lot of time to complete the work I am given. You can become inhuman if you spend most of your time only handling machines. Though they are very accurate, they don't have hearts. In other words, it is hard to feel love toward machines.

Conclusion/ Repeat Opinion —

The reason I like working with people is because of companionship. We can learn something from everybody even if we don't like them. If there is companionship, people will love working with people, and we can expect progress in our lives.

Sample Student Essay 2

Question:

There are advantages and disadvantages to different seasons of the year such as rainy or dry. Pick any two seasons that you are familiar with and compare the two. Describe what it is that makes you prefer one over the other. What activities do you engage in? What feelings do you have during this season?

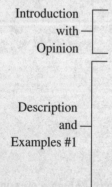

Introduction with Opinion —

Summer and winter are two seasons that I like the most among the four seasons. I like diversity in my life, and these two seasons provide me with just that.

Description and Examples #1 —

In the hot summer season, the world is full of life. Flowers are blooming, birds are singing, and I feel energetic about different kinds of outdoor activities, such as jogging, bicycling, and swimming. Swimming is one of my favorite sports. In the water, both body and mind have to work together either to move forward or simply float. It is good stress reduction for the intensive modern life that many of us have. Summer also enables us to have more fresh fruits and vegetables. I like to go to the farmers' market where I can enjoy the good prices, the availability of fresh produce, and the farmers' smiles.

Description
and
Examples #2

In winter, on the other hand, the world is quiet. Many animals stay inside, some of them even sleep inside. There is a nice warmth inside the house, while outside the world is beautiful with a white covering of snow. It's fun to watch children play in the snow. It's also fun to meet friends and relatives during winter holidays to exchange experiences and joy.

Conclusion/
Repeat Opinon

Summer and winter are so different; they offer us good feelings and a variety of opportunities to do all kinds of activities. I like all seasons, but I like summer and winter the best.

Sample Student Essay 3

Question:

Public transporation includes buses, subways, trains, and taxis. Private transportation usually refers to private cars, bicycles, or motorcycles. Compare these two kinds of transportation, and discuss the advantages of each. Decide which is better, giving details to support your decision.

Introduction
and
Opinion

In many places people have the freedom to choose whether they want to commute to work by public transportation or by private transportation. Both ways of commuting have advantages and disadvantages. In comparing the two, I prefer to use as much public transportation as possible. I only use my car when excessive inconvenience exists.

Support for
Opinion and
Examples

I like public transportation because I feel relaxed on the bus or subway. I don't have to concentrate on my driving. I can even get some reading and studying done during the commute time. Moreover, I don't have to worry about finding a parking place. In addition, when we use public transportation, we help lessen air pollution and traffic jams. A problem, however, is that the bus system in my town does not provide frequent enough stops and the location of the bus stops is not too convenient. These two problems prevent people from using public transportation.

Contrast
Examples

Private cars, on the other hand, are a more convenient way to get any place at any time. But, unfortunately, cars have many disadvantages. They produce pollution. It is hard to find a parking place in the city. They produce traffic jams, and it takes energy to drive.

Conclusion/
Repeat Opinion

If more and more people used public transportation air pollution would be better controlled and expenses would be reduced. That in turn would attract more people to use it. The more people that used it, the more money transportation businesses would get to improve their facilities and provide more locations and frequencies. I hope some day that the public transportation system will be able to provide the convenience that a private car provides.

P A R T

THREE

Six Practice TOEFL Tests

C O N T E N T S

How to Score Your Practice Tests

The following conversions give you an approximate TOEFL score. Your score on the actual TOEFL will be different since a new conversion table is prepared to reflect each TOEFL test.

To calculate your approximate score for the practice tests in this book:
1. Count the total number correct for each section.
2. Find your score range for each section on the table below in the left column under "Number Correct."
3. Look across the column to find the converted score range for each section.
4. Multiply each of the converted score range numbers by 10.
5. Divide each of the converted score numbers by 3.
6. Add the columns of numbers to get your total approximate TOEFL score.

Example (using the Short Form Conversion Table):

	Number Correct	Raw Score Range	Converted Score Range	Approximate Score
Listening Comprehension	30	30–32	50–51 × 10 = 500–510 ÷ 3 =	166–170
Structure and Written Expression	25	24–26	48–50 × 10 = 480–500 ÷ 3 =	160–166
Reading Comprehension	25	24–26	42–43 × 10 = 420–430 ÷ 3 =	140–143

Total Approximate Score Range = 466–479

Score Conversion Table: Standard (Short) Form

Use the following table to convert your score for Practice Tests 1, 2, 3, 5, and 6.

Raw Score (Number Correct)	Converted Score Range		
	Section 1	Section 2	Section 3
60			68
57–59			66–67
54–56			62–64
51–53			60–61
48–50	65–68		57–59
45–47	62–64		55–56
42–44	59–61		53–54
39–41	56–58		51–53
36–38	54–55	62–68	50–51
33–35	52–53	57–60	48–49
30–32	50–51	54–56	46–47
27–29	48–50	51–53	44–45
24–26	47–48	48–50	42–43
21–23	45–46	45–47	40–41
18–20	43–44	42–44	37–39
15–17	41–43	38–41	35–36
12–14	39–40	36–38	31–33
9–11	35–38	33–35	28–30
6–8	31–34	29–32	26–27
3–5	28–30	25–28	23–25
0–2	25–27	21–24	21–22

Score Conversion Table: Long Form

Use the following table to convert your score for Practice Test 4.

Raw Score (Number Correct)	Converted Score Range		
	Section 1	Section 2	Section 3
90			68
86–89			66–67
81–85			62–64
77–80	65–68		60–61
72–76	62–64		57–59
68–71	59–61		55–56
63–67	56–58		53–54
59–62	54–55	66–68	51–53
54–58	52–53	62–65	50–51
50–53	50–51	57–61	48–49
45–49	49–50	54–56	46–47
41–44	47–48	51–53	44–45
36–40	45–46	48–50	42–43
32–35	43–44	45–47	40–41
27–31	41–43	42–44	37–39
23–26	39–41	38–41	35–36
18–22	35–38	36–38	31–33
14–17	31–34	33–35	28–30
9–13	28–30	29–32	26–27
5–8	25–27	25–28	23–25
0–4	21–24	21–24	21–22

ANSWER SHEET FOR PRACTICE TEST 1

Section 1: Listening Comprehension

	1	2	3	4	5	6	7	8	9	10	11	12	13	14	15	16	17	18	19	20	21	22	23	24	25	26	27	28	29	30	31	32	33	34	35	36	37	38	39	40	41	42	43	44	45	46	47	48	49	50
A	Ⓐ	Ⓐ	Ⓐ	Ⓐ	Ⓐ	Ⓐ	Ⓐ	Ⓐ	Ⓐ	Ⓐ	Ⓐ	Ⓐ	Ⓐ	Ⓐ	Ⓐ	Ⓐ	Ⓐ	Ⓐ	Ⓐ	Ⓐ	Ⓐ	Ⓐ	Ⓐ	Ⓐ	Ⓐ	Ⓐ	Ⓐ	Ⓐ	Ⓐ	Ⓐ	Ⓐ	Ⓐ	Ⓐ	Ⓐ	Ⓐ	Ⓐ	Ⓐ	Ⓐ	Ⓐ	Ⓐ	Ⓐ	Ⓐ	Ⓐ	Ⓐ	Ⓐ	Ⓐ	Ⓐ	Ⓐ	Ⓐ	Ⓐ
B	Ⓑ	Ⓑ	Ⓑ	Ⓑ	Ⓑ	Ⓑ	Ⓑ	Ⓑ	Ⓑ	Ⓑ	Ⓑ	Ⓑ	Ⓑ	Ⓑ	Ⓑ	Ⓑ	Ⓑ	Ⓑ	Ⓑ	Ⓑ	Ⓑ	Ⓑ	Ⓑ	Ⓑ	Ⓑ	Ⓑ	Ⓑ	Ⓑ	Ⓑ	Ⓑ	Ⓑ	Ⓑ	Ⓑ	Ⓑ	Ⓑ	Ⓑ	Ⓑ	Ⓑ	Ⓑ	Ⓑ	Ⓑ	Ⓑ	Ⓑ	Ⓑ	Ⓑ	Ⓑ	Ⓑ	Ⓑ	Ⓑ	Ⓑ
C	Ⓒ	Ⓒ	Ⓒ	Ⓒ	Ⓒ	Ⓒ	Ⓒ	Ⓒ	Ⓒ	Ⓒ	Ⓒ	Ⓒ	Ⓒ	Ⓒ	Ⓒ	Ⓒ	Ⓒ	Ⓒ	Ⓒ	Ⓒ	Ⓒ	Ⓒ	Ⓒ	Ⓒ	Ⓒ	Ⓒ	Ⓒ	Ⓒ	Ⓒ	Ⓒ	Ⓒ	Ⓒ	Ⓒ	Ⓒ	Ⓒ	Ⓒ	Ⓒ	Ⓒ	Ⓒ	Ⓒ	Ⓒ	Ⓒ	Ⓒ	Ⓒ	Ⓒ	Ⓒ	Ⓒ	Ⓒ	Ⓒ	Ⓒ
D	Ⓓ	Ⓓ	Ⓓ	Ⓓ	Ⓓ	Ⓓ	Ⓓ	Ⓓ	Ⓓ	Ⓓ	Ⓓ	Ⓓ	Ⓓ	Ⓓ	Ⓓ	Ⓓ	Ⓓ	Ⓓ	Ⓓ	Ⓓ	Ⓓ	Ⓓ	Ⓓ	Ⓓ	Ⓓ	Ⓓ	Ⓓ	Ⓓ	Ⓓ	Ⓓ	Ⓓ	Ⓓ	Ⓓ	Ⓓ	Ⓓ	Ⓓ	Ⓓ	Ⓓ	Ⓓ	Ⓓ	Ⓓ	Ⓓ	Ⓓ	Ⓓ	Ⓓ	Ⓓ	Ⓓ	Ⓓ	Ⓓ	Ⓓ

Section 2: Structure and Written Expression

	1	2	3	4	5	6	7	8	9	10	11	12	13	14	15	16	17	18	19	20	21	22	23	24	25	26	27	28	29	30	31	32	33	34	35	36	37	38	39	40
A	Ⓐ	Ⓐ	Ⓐ	Ⓐ	Ⓐ	Ⓐ	Ⓐ	Ⓐ	Ⓐ	Ⓐ	Ⓐ	Ⓐ	Ⓐ	Ⓐ	Ⓐ	Ⓐ	Ⓐ	Ⓐ	Ⓐ	Ⓐ	Ⓐ	Ⓐ	Ⓐ	Ⓐ	Ⓐ	Ⓐ	Ⓐ	Ⓐ	Ⓐ	Ⓐ	Ⓐ	Ⓐ	Ⓐ	Ⓐ	Ⓐ	Ⓐ	Ⓐ	Ⓐ	Ⓐ	Ⓐ
B	Ⓑ	Ⓑ	Ⓑ	Ⓑ	Ⓑ	Ⓑ	Ⓑ	Ⓑ	Ⓑ	Ⓑ	Ⓑ	Ⓑ	Ⓑ	Ⓑ	Ⓑ	Ⓑ	Ⓑ	Ⓑ	Ⓑ	Ⓑ	Ⓑ	Ⓑ	Ⓑ	Ⓑ	Ⓑ	Ⓑ	Ⓑ	Ⓑ	Ⓑ	Ⓑ	Ⓑ	Ⓑ	Ⓑ	Ⓑ	Ⓑ	Ⓑ	Ⓑ	Ⓑ	Ⓑ	Ⓑ
C	Ⓒ	Ⓒ	Ⓒ	Ⓒ	Ⓒ	Ⓒ	Ⓒ	Ⓒ	Ⓒ	Ⓒ	Ⓒ	Ⓒ	Ⓒ	Ⓒ	Ⓒ	Ⓒ	Ⓒ	Ⓒ	Ⓒ	Ⓒ	Ⓒ	Ⓒ	Ⓒ	Ⓒ	Ⓒ	Ⓒ	Ⓒ	Ⓒ	Ⓒ	Ⓒ	Ⓒ	Ⓒ	Ⓒ	Ⓒ	Ⓒ	Ⓒ	Ⓒ	Ⓒ	Ⓒ	Ⓒ
D	Ⓓ	Ⓓ	Ⓓ	Ⓓ	Ⓓ	Ⓓ	Ⓓ	Ⓓ	Ⓓ	Ⓓ	Ⓓ	Ⓓ	Ⓓ	Ⓓ	Ⓓ	Ⓓ	Ⓓ	Ⓓ	Ⓓ	Ⓓ	Ⓓ	Ⓓ	Ⓓ	Ⓓ	Ⓓ	Ⓓ	Ⓓ	Ⓓ	Ⓓ	Ⓓ	Ⓓ	Ⓓ	Ⓓ	Ⓓ	Ⓓ	Ⓓ	Ⓓ	Ⓓ	Ⓓ	Ⓓ

Section 3: Reading Comprehension

	1	2	3	4	5	6	7	8	9	10	11	12	13	14	15	16	17	18	19	20	21	22	23	24	25	26	27	28	29	30	31	32	33	34	35	36	37	38	39	40	41	42	43	44	45	46	47	48	49	50	51	52	53	54	55	56	57	58	59	60
A	Ⓐ	Ⓐ	Ⓐ	Ⓐ	Ⓐ	Ⓐ	Ⓐ	Ⓐ	Ⓐ	Ⓐ	Ⓐ	Ⓐ	Ⓐ	Ⓐ	Ⓐ	Ⓐ	Ⓐ	Ⓐ	Ⓐ	Ⓐ	Ⓐ	Ⓐ	Ⓐ	Ⓐ	Ⓐ	Ⓐ	Ⓐ	Ⓐ	Ⓐ	Ⓐ	Ⓐ	Ⓐ	Ⓐ	Ⓐ	Ⓐ	Ⓐ	Ⓐ	Ⓐ	Ⓐ	Ⓐ	Ⓐ	Ⓐ	Ⓐ	Ⓐ	Ⓐ	Ⓐ	Ⓐ	Ⓐ	Ⓐ	Ⓐ	Ⓐ	Ⓐ	Ⓐ	Ⓐ	Ⓐ	Ⓐ	Ⓐ	Ⓐ	Ⓐ	Ⓐ
B	Ⓑ	Ⓑ	Ⓑ	Ⓑ	Ⓑ	Ⓑ	Ⓑ	Ⓑ	Ⓑ	Ⓑ	Ⓑ	Ⓑ	Ⓑ	Ⓑ	Ⓑ	Ⓑ	Ⓑ	Ⓑ	Ⓑ	Ⓑ	Ⓑ	Ⓑ	Ⓑ	Ⓑ	Ⓑ	Ⓑ	Ⓑ	Ⓑ	Ⓑ	Ⓑ	Ⓑ	Ⓑ	Ⓑ	Ⓑ	Ⓑ	Ⓑ	Ⓑ	Ⓑ	Ⓑ	Ⓑ	Ⓑ	Ⓑ	Ⓑ	Ⓑ	Ⓑ	Ⓑ	Ⓑ	Ⓑ	Ⓑ	Ⓑ	Ⓑ	Ⓑ	Ⓑ	Ⓑ	Ⓑ	Ⓑ	Ⓑ	Ⓑ	Ⓑ	Ⓑ
C	Ⓒ	Ⓒ	Ⓒ	Ⓒ	Ⓒ	Ⓒ	Ⓒ	Ⓒ	Ⓒ	Ⓒ	Ⓒ	Ⓒ	Ⓒ	Ⓒ	Ⓒ	Ⓒ	Ⓒ	Ⓒ	Ⓒ	Ⓒ	Ⓒ	Ⓒ	Ⓒ	Ⓒ	Ⓒ	Ⓒ	Ⓒ	Ⓒ	Ⓒ	Ⓒ	Ⓒ	Ⓒ	Ⓒ	Ⓒ	Ⓒ	Ⓒ	Ⓒ	Ⓒ	Ⓒ	Ⓒ	Ⓒ	Ⓒ	Ⓒ	Ⓒ	Ⓒ	Ⓒ	Ⓒ	Ⓒ	Ⓒ	Ⓒ	Ⓒ	Ⓒ	Ⓒ	Ⓒ	Ⓒ	Ⓒ	Ⓒ	Ⓒ	Ⓒ	Ⓒ
D	Ⓓ	Ⓓ	Ⓓ	Ⓓ	Ⓓ	Ⓓ	Ⓓ	Ⓓ	Ⓓ	Ⓓ	Ⓓ	Ⓓ	Ⓓ	Ⓓ	Ⓓ	Ⓓ	Ⓓ	Ⓓ	Ⓓ	Ⓓ	Ⓓ	Ⓓ	Ⓓ	Ⓓ	Ⓓ	Ⓓ	Ⓓ	Ⓓ	Ⓓ	Ⓓ	Ⓓ	Ⓓ	Ⓓ	Ⓓ	Ⓓ	Ⓓ	Ⓓ	Ⓓ	Ⓓ	Ⓓ	Ⓓ	Ⓓ	Ⓓ	Ⓓ	Ⓓ	Ⓓ	Ⓓ	Ⓓ	Ⓓ	Ⓓ	Ⓓ	Ⓓ	Ⓓ	Ⓓ	Ⓓ	Ⓓ	Ⓓ	Ⓓ	Ⓓ	Ⓓ

Date Taken _____

Number Correct

Section 1 _____
Section 2 _____
Section 3 _____

Practice Test 1

SECTION 1

Listening Comprehension

Time—approximately 30 minutes

Note: You can simulate actual TOEFL conditions by using the Listening Comprehension Cassettes that accompany this book. (See the first page of this book for information about how to buy the tape.) If you do not wish to purchase the tape, ask a friend to read the tapescript for Listening Comprehension Test 1, which is in Part Four, pages 379–86 of this book.

Part A

Directions: In Part A you will hear short conversations between two people. After each conversation a third person will ask a question about what was said. You will hear the conversation only one time, so you must listen carefully to what each speaker says. After you hear the conversation and the question, read the four possible answers in your test booklet and pick the one that best answers the question. Then, look on the answer sheet for the number of the question and fill in the oval that corresponds to the letter of your answer choice.

Listen to an example:

You will hear: Sample Answer

You will read:

    (A) He will call Pete before he goes home.
    (B) He will call Pete after he gets home.
    (C) He called Pete at home.
    (D) He will call Pete tomorrow.

You learn from the conversation that the man will call Pete as soon as he gets home. The best answer to the question "What does the man mean?" is (B), "He will call Pete after he gets home." Therefore, the correct answer is (B).

Now continue listening to the tape, Test 1, Section 1, Listening Comprehension Part A.

1. (A) She enjoys summer the most.
   (B) She's too busy to go traveling.
   (C) She gets bored staying home too long.
   (D) She doesn't like to travel.

2. (A) Building houses is very complicated.
   (B) He lent his other book to a friend.
   (C) This book doesn't have enough details.
   (D) He needs the information in this book.

3. (A) He left his lab and went on vacation.
   (B) He locked his lab.
   (C) He came back to work early.
   (D) He went to give a lecture.

4. (A) Connie and David have changed.
   (B) David wants to talk to Connie.
   (C) Connie and David are planning a trip together.
   (D) Connie and David have many friends.

5. (A) She used to work for the city.
   (B) She enjoys sightseeing in the city.
   (C) She thinks there are two buildings.
   (D) She has visited the museum more than once.

6. (A) She is unhappy with her work.
   (B) She wonders what job the man does.
   (C) She doesn't know what the man means.
   (D) She agrees to work on another day.

7. (A) He thinks Greg is too young.
   (B) He thinks it's a good decision.
   (C) He is surprised.
   (D) He is angry.

8. (A) Sandy wants to room with the woman.
   (B) Sandy is a very interesting person.
   (C) Sandy doesn't want to bother anyone.
   (D) Sandy is the woman's roommate.

9. (A) The complete movie was not shown.
   (B) She went to sleep during the movie.
   (C) The end surprised everyone.
   (D) She wants to see the movie again tonight.

10. (A) She already has tickets for both of them.
    (B) She's trying to fool him.
    (C) She thinks it's going to be hard to get tickets.
    (D) She doesn't want to get tickets, because they might have to stay home.

11. (A) Come back again to apply for the job.
    (B) Think about whether he really wants to resign.
    (C) Get some training before he quits his job.
    (D) Apply for an additional part-time job.

12. (A) Alex wants to change his major.
    (B) Alex is still too young to make his own decision.
    (C) Alex should not change his major without consent from his parents.
    (D) Alex is capable of making his own decision.

13. (A) He'll make an effort to go tonight.
    (B) He doesn't like commitments.
    (C) He remembered he had to go to the group meeting.
    (D) He has to go somewhere else.

14. (A) There is nothing that worries him.
    (B) He didn't do any studying.
    (C) He studied very hard.
    (D) He was bored.

15. (A) Laura doesn't understand the proposal.
    (B) Laura will not like the proposal.
    (C) Laura accepted this proposal.
    (D) Laura's proposal is excellent.

16. (A) She doesn't want a long drive to the airport.
    (B) She will hang her luggage in the closet.
    (C) She won't use the same airline again this time.
    (D) She isn't used to traveling very much.

17. (A) You can't eat the fruit whole.
    (B) You can't eat the pit.
    (C) You can't eat the fruit raw.
    (D) You can't eat the skin of the fruit.

18. (A) He is the best student in the class.
    (B) He'll have to take the exam again.
    (C) He passed the exam with the grade he expected.
    (D) His grade was not as high as he had hoped.

19. (A) They are studying hard for their finals.
    (B) The school year seemed to go by very quickly.
    (C) They've been in school a few weeks.
    (D) Even though finals are over, they still have to study for a few weeks.

20. (A) His shoulder hurts.
    (B) His eyes are dim.
    (C) He likes the ice in the lake.
    (D) He wants another cold drink.

GO ON TO THE NEXT PAGE

Part B

Directions: In Part B you will hear longer conversations between two people. After each conversation you will be asked some questions. You will hear the conversations and the questions only once, so listen carefully to what is said. After you hear a question, read the four possible answers in your test book and decide which one is the best answer to the question you heard. Then, on your answer sheet, find the number of the question and fill in the oval that corresponds to the letter of the answer you have chosen. Answer all questions based on what is stated or implied by the speakers.

Listen to the example on the tape.

You will hear:

Now listen to sample question number 1.   Sample Answer

You will read: Ⓐ Ⓑ Ⓒ ●

    (A) to the cafeteria
    (B) to the movie theater
    (C) to her dorm room
    (D) to the library

The best answer to the question "Where is the woman going?" is (D), "to the library." Therefore, the correct choice is (D).

Now listen to sample question number 2.   Sample Answer

You will hear: Ⓐ Ⓑ ● Ⓓ

You will read:

    (A) Term papers are easy for him.
    (B) He has a lot of essay exams.
    (C) He finds lab experiments easier than writing term papers.
    (D) He is busier this semester than last semester.

The best answer to the question "Which best describes the man's feelings about his classes?" is (C), "He finds lab experiments easier than writing term papers." Therefore, the correct answer is (C).

Now listen to the test. Remember, you are not allowed to take any notes or write in your test book.

GO ON TO THE NEXT PAGE >

21. **(A)** finding books in the library
    (B) an exam in a class
    (C) a student's research project
    (D) asking directions to a class

22. **(A)** in the mountains
    (B) in the Southwest desert
    (C) in New York
    (D) on the Atlantic coast

23. **(A)** the southwestern desert
    (B) the end of the Anasazi civilization
    (C) native American history
    (D) desert climates

24. **(A)** There is another person studying a similar topic.
    (B) There are no books in the library about this particular topic.
    (C) She thinks the student should change his focus.
    (D) She has a lot of books on this topic for the student.

25. **(A)** Boston
    (B) San Francisco
    (C) New York
    (D) Milwaukee

26. **(A)** It is going to the wrong destination.
    (B) The departure times are not appropriate.
    (C) The train will arrive too late.
    (D) The ticket is too expensive.

27. **(A)** because it goes on to Boston
    (B) because it is slower
    (C) because there is no place to sleep
    (D) because it arrives in the middle of the night

28. **(A)** friends
    (B) sea birds
    (C) a trip
    (D) Fridays

29. **(A)** They are friends.
    (B) They have just met.
    (C) They are brother and sister.
    (D) They have a class together.

30. **(A)** to sit in the sun
    (B) to watch the waves
    (C) to observe sea birds
    (D) to have picnics

31. **(A)** Saturday
    (B) one year later
    (C) Friday
    (D) after the summer

32. **(A)** taking a vacation
    (B) going to sleep
    (C) seeing a movie
    (D) traveling to New York City

33. **(A)** in a restaurant
    (B) in an office
    (C) in a classroom
    (D) in a house

34. **(A)** She enjoys hiking.
    (B) Her cousin has a cabin in Canada.
    (C) She wants to get away from the city.
    (D) She can't afford to stay in a hotel.

35. **(A)** The car needs to be fixed.
    (B) They need to work the next day.
    (C) Their flight doesn't leave until the next day.
    (D) The weather is very bad that night.

GO ON TO THE NEXT PAGE

Part C

Directions: In this part of the test, you will hear talks by a single person. After each talk, you will be asked some questions. You will hear the talks and the questions only once, so listen carefully to what is said. After you hear a question, read the four possible answers in your test book and decide which one is the best answer to the question you heard. Then find the number of the question on your answer sheet and fill in the oval that corresponds to the letter of the answer you have chosen. Answer all questions based on what is stated or implied in the talk.

Listen to the example on the tape.

You will hear:

Now listen to sample question number 1.

Sample Answer

You will read:

(A) to demonstrate tutoring techniques
(B) to explain school policies
(C) to recruit childcare workers
(D) to explain a service

The best answer to the question "What is the purpose of this announcement?" is (D), "to explain a service." Therefore, the correct choice is (D).

Now listen to sample question number 2.

Sample Answer

You will hear:

You will read:

(A) Give your child extra tutoring.
(B) Take your child to the program today.
(C) Apply as soon as you can.
(D) Pay next month.

The best answer to the question "What does the speaker recommend?" is (C), "Apply as soon as you can." Therefore the correct choice is (C).

Now begin. Remember, you are not allowed to write any notes in your test book.

GO ON TO THE NEXT PAGE

36. (A) a magazine
    (B) a neighborhood
    (C) a period of time
    (D) a political issue

37. (A) before World War I
    (B) in the 1950s
    (C) in the 1970s
    (D) after 1985

38. (A) new viral discoveries
    (B) a brief history of 19th-century France
    (C) a movement toward world peace
    (D) the life and times of Shakespeare

39. (A) American Revolutionary period
    (B) world history
    (C) journalism
    (D) economics

40. (A) to inform people of the zoo show times
    (B) to announce the zoo will close soon
    (C) to advertise goods sold at the gift shop
    (D) to promote a restaurant serving lunch at the zoo

41. (A) lions and tigers
    (B) elephants and giraffes
    (C) sharks and rays
    (D) apes and monkeys

42. (A) the giant bird cage
    (B) the tiger house
    (C) the monkey and ape habitat
    (D) the tropical rainforest exhibit

43. (A) at the main entrance
    (B) in the gift shop
    (C) from Dr. Smith
    (D) at the primate center

44. (A) American history
    (B) twentieth-century poets
    (C) Shakespeare
    (D) Abraham Lincoln

45. (A) the date when the Civil War ended
    (B) the date when the first exam will take place
    (C) the date when the paper is due
    (D) the date when Abraham Lincoln died

46. (A) the end of the Civil War
    (B) the speech by Abraham Lincoln
    (C) the conditions in the southern states
    (D) the beginning of the war between the states

47. (A) music
    (B) literature
    (C) dance
    (D) painting

48. (A) Handel
    (B) the *Messiah*
    (C) the London Philharmonic
    (D) the symphony

49. (A) the educational level of artists has increased.
    (B) the size of the audience has grown.
    (C) the number of voices and instruments has changed.
    (D) the types of visitors have changed.

50. (A) Christmas
    (B) New Year's Day
    (C) Easter
    (D) the summer solstice

THIS IS THE END OF SECTION 1.
DO NOT READ OR WORK ON ANY OTHER SECTION OF THE TEST UNTIL TIME IS UP

STOP   STOP   STOP   STOP   STOP

SECTION 2
Structure and Written Expression

Time—25 minutes

There are two types of questions in this next section. Both types are designed to measure your ability to recognize standard written English.

Part 1: Sentence Completion

Directions: Questions 1–15 are not complete sentences. One or more words are left out of each sentence. Under each sentence, you will see four words or phrases, marked (A), (B), (C), and (D). Choose the one word or phrase that completes the sentence correctly. Then, on your answer sheet, find the number of the question and fill in the oval that corresponds to the letter of your answer choice.

Example I▶   Birds make nests in trees _____ hide their young in the leaves and branches.

      Sample Answer

    (A) can where they
    (B) where they can
    (C) where can they
    (D) where can

The sentence should read, "Birds make nests in trees where they can hide their young in the leaves and branches." Therefore, you should choose answer (B).

Example II▶   Sleeping, resting, and _____ are the best ways to care for a cold.

      Sample Answer

    (A) to drink fluids
    (B) drank fluids
    (C) one drink fluids
    (D) drinking fluids

The sentence should read, "Sleeping, resting, and drinking fluids are the best ways to care for a cold." Therefore, you should choose answer (D).

Now begin work on the questions.

GO ON TO THE NEXT PAGE ⟩

1. America's first globe maker was James Wilson, who _____ and blacksmith in his earlier life.
   - (A) a farmer had been
   - (B) had been a farmer
   - (C) farming
   - (D) being a farmer

2. Napoleon _____ the West Indian island of Santo Domingo in 1801.
   - (A) attacked
   - (B) is attacking
   - (C) has attated
   - (D) attacking

3. Modern industrial methods have supplanted individual crafts, _____ stonecarvers, coopers, and cobblers virtually extinct.
   - (A) make blacksmiths,
   - (B) made blacksmiths,
   - (C) making them blacksmiths,
   - (D) making blacksmiths,

4. Not only knowledge and skills, but also attitudes _____ in school for students' future adjustment to society.
   - (A) when cultivated
   - (B) cultivated
   - (C) which need to be cultivated
   - (D) need to be cultivated

5. On Mercator's maps, the far northern and southern polar regions are _____.
   - (A) greatly exaggerated in area.
   - (B) exaggerating greatly in area.
   - (C) greatly exaggerate in area.
   - (D) great exaggeration in area.

6. On the slope of Long's Peak in Colorado _____ the ruin of a gigantic tree.
   - (A) that lies
   - (B) lies
   - (C) where lies
   - (D) lie

7. _____ in Shanghai than in any other city in China.
   - (A) More people live
   - (B) More people living
   - (C) It has more people
   - (D) More living people

8. The earth spins on its axis and _____ 23 hours, 56 minutes and 4.09 seconds for one complete rotation.
   - (A) need
   - (B) needed
   - (C) needing
   - (D) needs

9. _____ on the environment for the gratification of its needs.
   - (A) Each organism to depend
   - (B) Every organism depends
   - (C) All organisms depending
   - (D) Many organisms can depend

10. Of Charles Dickens' many novels, *Great Expectations* is perhaps _____ to many readers.
    - (A) the most satisfying one
    - (B) most satisfying one
    - (C) more than satisfying one
    - (D) the more satisfying than

11. _____, the nation's capital remained in Philadelphia, Pennsylvania.
    - (A) While designing Washington, D.C.
    - (B) Washington, D.C., was designed
    - (C) While Washington, D.C., was being designed
    - (D) Washington, D.C., designed

12. Children learn primarily by _____ the world around them.
    - (A) experiencing directly of
    - (B) experience direct
    - (C) directly physical experience
    - (D) direct physical experience of

13. It is earth's gravity that _____ people their weight.
    - (A) gives
    - (B) give
    - (C) giving
    - (D) given

14. Generally speaking, people should have _____ as their desires will allow.
    - (A) much education
    - (B) as much education
    - (C) education
    - (D) for education

 GO ON TO THE NEXT PAGE

15. A dolphin six _____ length can move as
    fast as most ships.
    (A) foot in
    (B) feet in
    (C) foot of
    (D) feet of

Part 2: Error Identification

Directions: In questions 16–40 each sentence has four underlined words or phrases marked (A), (B), (C), and (D). Choose the one word or phrase that must be changed in order for the sentence to be correct. Then, on your answer sheet find the number of the question and fill in the oval that corresponds to the letter of your answer choice.

Example I▷   Aspirin is <u>recommend</u> to <u>many</u> people for <u>its</u>   Sample Answer
                          A   B   C
                                                                                ● Ⓑ Ⓒ Ⓓ

<u>ability</u> to thin the blood.
   D

The sentence should read, "Aspirin is recommended to many people for its ability to thin the blood." Therefore, you should choose answer (A).

Example II▷   Some people <u>believe</u> that human beings will never <u>use away</u> all   Sample Answer
                                   A   B
                                                                                    Ⓐ ● Ⓒ Ⓓ

<u>the</u> natural resources <u>on earth.</u>
   C   D

The sentence should read, "Some people believe that human beings will never use up all the natural resources on earth." Therefore, you should choose answer (B).

Now begin work on the questions.

16. <u>Cotton</u> used to <u>rank</u> first <u>between</u> Alabama's crops, but it <u>represents only</u> a fraction of the
    A   B   C   D

agricultural production now.

17. Salmon <u>lay</u> their eggs and die in freshwater, <u>although</u> they live in salt water <u>when</u> most of their
             A   B   C

<u>adult lives.</u>
   D

18. To <u>building</u> their <u>nests</u>, tailorbirds <u>use</u> their <u>bills</u> as needles.
        A   B   C   D

19. Fountain pens <u>first</u> became <u>commercial</u> available <u>about</u> a hundred years <u>ago.</u>
                    A   B   C   D

20. With <u>its</u> strong claws and its many <u>protruding</u> tooth a gopher <u>is</u> an excellent digger.
          A   B   C   D

21. Drug addiction <u>has resulted of</u> many <u>destroyed</u> careers, and <u>expulsions</u> from school or college.
                    A   B   C

GO ON TO THE NEXT PAGE

22. Because of the Lewis and Clark Expedition, the United States begin to realize the true value of the
    <u>A</u>   <u>B</u>   <u>C</u>
    Louisiana territory.
    <u>D</u>

23. Americans annually import more than $3 billion worthy of Italian clothing, jewelry, and shoes.
    <u>A</u>   <u>B</u>   <u>C</u>   <u>D</u>

24. Akuce Ganuktibm, she spent her life working with the health and welfare of the families of workers.
                      <u>A</u>   <u>B</u>   <u>C</u>   <u>D</u>

25. There are many different ways of comparing the economy of one nation with those of another.
    <u>A</u>   <u>B</u>   <u>C</u>   <u>D</u>

26. Male guppies, like many other male fish, are more color than females.
    <u>A</u>   <u>B</u>   <u>C</u>   <u>D</u>

27. When rhinos take mud baths, the mud create a barrier to biting insects.
    <u>A</u>   <u>B</u>   <u>C</u>   <u>D</u>

28. Benjamin Franklin, as an inventor, he had broad interests, mechanical skills, persistence, and a
                      <u>A</u>   <u>B</u>   <u>C</u>
    practical view of life.
    <u>D</u>

29. In the stock market, the fluctuations in Standard and Poor's 500 Index does not always conform to
    <u>A</u>   <u>B</u>   <u>C</u>   <u>D</u>
    Dow Jones Averages.

30. A jellyfish, which isn't really a fish, it has no brain, no bones, and no face.
                  <u>A</u>   <u>B</u> <u>C</u>   <u>D</u>

31. International trade, going traveling, and television have lain the groundwork for modern global life
                        <u>A</u>   <u>B</u>   <u>C</u>
    styles.
    <u>D</u>

32. The most visible remind of the close relationship between the United States and France is the
                    <u>A</u>   <u>B</u>   <u>C</u>
    famous Statue of Liberty, which stands in New York harbor.
                          <u>D</u>

33. Until diamonds are cut and polished, they just like look small blue-grey stones.
    <u>A</u>   <u>B</u>   <u>C</u>   <u>D</u>

34. Jackie Robinson, whose joined the Brooklyn Dodgers in 1947, was the first black American to play
                      <u>A</u>   <u>B</u>   <u>C</u>
    baseball in the major leagues.
            <u>D</u>

35. Laser technology is the heart of a new generation of high-speed copiers and printer.
    <u>A</u>   <u>B</u>   <u>C</u>   <u>D</u>

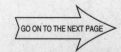
GO ON TO THE NEXT PAGE

36. Fertilize farmland is one of the biggest natural resources in the Central States.
      A   B   C   D

37. The symptoms of diabetes in the early stages are too slight that people don't notice them.
          A   B   C   D

38. *Gone with the Wind* written after Margaret Mitchell quit her job as a reporter because of an ankle
                A   B   C   D

injury.

39. With a policy of eminent domain, the state has control ultimate of all real property.
        A   B   C   D

40. Hay fever symptoms, ranged from mild to severe, differ in degree according to the individual.
          A   B   C   D

THIS IS THE END OF SECTION 2.
DO NOT READ AHEAD OR WORK ON ANY OTHER SECTION UNTIL TIME IS UP.

STOP STOP STOP STOP STOP

SECTION 3

Reading Comprehension

Time—55 minutes

Directions: In this section you will read several passages. Each passage is followed by questions about it. Choose the one best answer, (A), (B), (C), or (D), for each question. Then, on your answer sheet, find the number of the question and fill in the oval that corresponds to the letter of your answer choice. Answer all questions based on what is stated or implied in the passage.

Read the following passage:

A new hearing device is now available for some hearing-impaired people. This device uses a magnet to hold the detachable sound-processing portion in place. Like other aids, it converts sound into vibrations. But it is unique in that it can transmit the vibrations directly to the magnet, and then to the inner ear. This produces a clearer sound. The new device will not help all hearing-impaired people, only those with a hearing loss caused by infection or other problem in the middle ear. It will probably help no more than 20 percent of all people with hearing problems. Those people, however, who have persistent ear infections should find relief and restored hearing with the new device.

Example I▶

What is the author's main purpose?

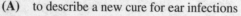 

Sample Answer

(A) to describe a new cure for ear infections
(B) to inform the reader of a new device
(C) to urge doctors to use a new device
(D) to explain the use of a magnet

The author's main purpose is to inform the reader of a new device for hearing-impaired people. Therefore, you should choose answer (B).

Example II▶

The word "relief" in the last sentence means

Sample Answer

(A) less distress
(B) assistance
(C) distraction
(D) relaxation

The phrase "less distress" is similar in meaning to "relief" in this sentence. Therefore, you should choose answer (A).

Now begin with the questions.

GO ON TO THE NEXT PAGE >

Questions 1 to 12 are based on the following passage:

(1)   Martin Luther King, Jr., is well known for his work in civil rights and for his many famous speeches, among them his moving "I Have A Dream" speech. But fewer people know much about King's childhood. M.L., as he was called, was born in 1929 in Atlanta, Georgia, at the home of his maternal grandfather. M.L.'s grandfather, the Reverend A.D. Williams, purchased their home on Auburn Avenue in 1909,

(5)   twenty years before M.L. was born. The Reverend Williams, an eloquent speaker, played an important role in the community since so many people's lives centered around the church. He allowed his church and his home to be used as a meeting place for a number of organizations dedicated to the education and social advancement of blacks. M.L. grew up in this atmosphere, with his home being used as a community gathering place, and was no doubt influenced by it.

(10)   M.L.'s childhood was not especially eventful. His father was a minister and his mother was a musician. He was the second of three children, and he attended all-black schools in a black neighborhood. The neighborhood was not poor, however. Auburn Avenue was the main artery through a prosperous neighborhood that had come to symbolize achievement for Atlanta's black people. It was an area of banks, insurance companies, builders, jewelers, tailors, doctors, lawyers, and other black-owned or black-

(15)   operated businesses and services. Even in the face of Atlanta's segregation, the district thrived. Dr. King never forgot the community spirit he had known as a child, nor did he forget the racial prejudice that was a seemingly insurmountable barrier that kept black Atlantans from mingling with whites.

1. What is this passage mainly about?
    (A) the prejudice that existed in Atlanta
    (B) Martin Luther King's childhood
    (C) M.L.'s grandfather
    (D) the neighborhood King grew up in

2. The word "eloquent" in line 5 means most nearly
    (A) powerful
    (B) active
    (C) romantic
    (D) fascinating

3. The word "gathering" in line 9 could best be replaced by
    (A) picking
    (B) learning
    (C) exciting
    (D) meeting

4. As used in line 10, the word "eventful" is closest in meaning to which of the following?
    (A) valued
    (B) memorable
    (C) admirable
    (D) emotional

5. In line 13, the word "it" refers to which of the following?
    (A) achievement
    (B) neighborhood
    (C) segregation
    (D) services

6. According to the author, blacks in King's neighborhood were involved in all the following businesses and services EXCEPT
    (A) dentistry
    (B) medicine
    (C) law
    (D) banking

7. The word "tailors" in line 14 describes people who are associated with which of the following trades?
    (A) flower arranging
    (B) shoe making
    (C) garment making
    (D) book binding

8. According to the author, King was influenced by
    (A) community spirit
    (B) black lawyers
    (C) his mother
    (D) his speeches

9. The word "thrived" in line 15 refers to which of the following?
    (A) achieved
    (B) surrendered
    (C) flourished
    (D) held

GO ON TO THE NEXT PAGE

10. As used in line 17, which of the following is closest in meaning to the word "seemingly"?
    (A) apparently
    (B) inevitably
    (C) inexplicably
    (D) hastily

11. The word "mingling" in line 17 could best be replaced by which of the following?
    (A) interfering
    (B) gargling
    (C) consuming
    (D) associating

12. According to the author, M.L.
    (A) had a difficult childhood
    (B) was a good musician as a child
    (C) loved to listen to his grandfather speak
    (D) grew up in a relatively rich area of Atlanta

GO ON TO THE NEXT PAGE

Questions 13 to 24 are based on the following passage:

(1)   Carbohydrates, which are sugars, are an essential part of a healthy diet. They provide the main source of energy for the body, and they also function to flavor and sweeten foods. Carbohydrates range from simple sugars like glucose to complex sugars such as amylose and amylopectin. Nutritionists estimate that carbohydrates should make up about one-fourth to one-fifth of a person's diet. This translates to about
(5)   75–100 grams of carbohydrates per day.

A diet that is deficient in carbohydrates can have an adverse effect on a person's health. When the body lacks a sufficient amount of carbohydrates it must then use its protein supplies for energy, a process called gluconeogenesis. This, however, results in a lack of necessary protein, and further health difficulties may occur. A lack of carbohydrates can also lead to ketosis, a build-up of ketones in the body
(10)   that causes fatigue, lethargy, and bad breath.

13. What is the main idea of this passage?
(A) Carbohydrates are needed for good health.
(B) Carbohydrates prevent a build-up of proteins.
(C) Carbohydrates can lead to ketosis.
(D) Carbohydrates are an expendable part of a good diet.

14. The word "function" as used in line 2 refers to which of the following?
(A) neglect
(B) serve
(C) dissolve
(D) profess

15. The word "range" as used in line 2 is closest in meaning to which of the following?
(A) probe
(B) proceed
(C) hail
(D) extend

16. In line 3, the word "estimate" could best be replaced by
(A) disbelieve
(B) declare
(C) calculate
(D) wonder

17. According to the passage, what do most nutritionists suggest?
(A) Sufficient carbohydrates will prevent gluconeogenesis.
(B) Carbohydrates are simple sugars called glucose.
(C) Carbohydrates should make up about a quarter of a person's daily diet.
(D) Carbohydrates should be eaten in very small quantities.

18. Which of the following do carbohydrates NOT do?
(A) prevent ketosis
(B) cause gluconeogenesis
(C) provide energy for the body
(D) flavor and sweeten food

19. Which of the following words could best replace "deficient" as used in line 6?
(A) outstanding
(B) abundant
(C) insufficient
(D) unequal

20. What does the word "this" refer to in line 8?
(A) using protein supplies for energy
(B) converting carbohydrates to energy
(C) having a deficiency in carbohydrates
(D) having an insufficient amount of protein

21. According to the passage, which of the following does NOT describe carbohydrates?
(A) a protein supply
(B) a necessity
(C) a range of sugars
(D) an energy source

22. The word "lack" in line 9 is most similar to which of the following?
(A) plethora
(B) shortage
(C) derivation
(D) commission

 GO ON TO THE NEXT PAGE

23. Which of the following best describes the author's tone?
    (A) sensitive
    (B) emotional
    (C) informative
    (D) regretful

24. Which of the following best describes the organization of this passage?
    (A) cause and result
    (B) comparison and contrast
    (C) specific to general
    (D) definition and example

GO ON TO THE NEXT PAGE

Questions 25 to 36 are based on the following passage:

(1)   After two decades of growing student enrollments and economic prosperity, business schools in the United States have started to face harder times. Only Harvard's MBA School has shown a substantial increase in enrollment in recent years. Both Princeton and Stanford have seen decreases in their enrollments. Since 1990, the number of people receiving Masters in Business Administration (MBA)
(5)   degrees, has dropped about 3 percent to 75,000, and the trend of lower enrollment rates is expected to continue.

There are two factors causing this decrease in students seeking an MBA degree. The first one is that many graduates of four-year colleges are finding that an MBA degree does not guarantee a plush job on Wall Street, or in other financial districts of major American cities. Many of the entry-level management
(10)   jobs are going to students graduating with Master of Arts degrees in English and the humanities as well as those holding MBA degrees. Students have asked the question, "Is an MBA degree really what I need to be best prepared for getting a good job?" The second major factor has been the cutting of American payrolls and the lower number of entry-level jobs being offered. Business needs are changing, and MBA schools are struggling to meet the new demands.

25. What is the main focus of this passage?
(A) jobs on Wall Street
(B) types of graduate degrees
(C) changes in enrollment for MBA schools
(D) how schools are changing to reflect the economy

26. The phrase "two decades" in line 1 refers to a period of
(A) 10 years
(B) 20 years
(C) 50 years
(D) 100 years

27. The word "prosperity" in line 1 could best be replaced by which of the following?
(A) success
(B) surplus
(C) nurturing
(D) education

28. Which of the following business schools has NOT shown a decrease in enrollment?
(A) Princeton
(B) Harvard
(C) Stanford
(D) Yale

29. The phrase "trend of" in line 5 is closest in meaning to which of the following?
(A) reluctance of
(B) drawback to
(C) movement toward
(D) extraction from

30. As used in line 7, the word "seeking" could best be replaced by which of the following?
(A) examining
(B) avoiding
(C) seizing
(D) pursuing

31. Which of the following descriptions most likely applies to Wall Street?
(A) a center for international affairs
(B) a major financial center
(C) a shopping district
(D) a neighborhood in New York

32. The word "plush" in line 8 most probably means
(A) legal
(B) satisfactory
(C) fancy
(D) dependable

33. According to the passage, what are two causes of declining business school enrollments?
(A) lack of necessity for an MBA and an economic recession
(B) low salary and foreign competition
(C) fewer MBA schools and fewer entry-level jobs
(D) declining population and economic prosperity

34. The word "cutting" in line 12 could best be replaced by which of the following?
(A) wounding
(B) reducing
(C) dividing
(D) carving

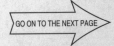
GO ON TO THE NEXT PAGE

35. As used in line 14, the word "struggling" is closest in meaning to
  (A) evolving
  (B) plunging
  (C) starting
  (D) striving

36. Which of the following might be the topic of the next paragraph?
  (A) MBA schools' efforts to change
  (B) future economic predictions
  (C) a history of the recent economic changes
  (D) descriptions of non-MBA graduate programs

GO ON TO THE NEXT PAGE

Questions 37 to 48 are based on the following passage:

(1)   A pilot cannot fly a plane by sight alone. In many conditions, such as flying at night and landing in dense fog, a pilot must use radar, an alternative way of navigating. Since human eyes are not very good at determining speeds of approaching objects, radar can show a pilot how fast nearby planes are moving. The basic principle of radar is exemplified by what happens when one shouts in a cave. The echo of the
(5)   sounds against the walls helps a person determine the size of the cave. With radar, however, the waves are radio waves instead of sound waves. Radio waves travel at the speed of light, about 300,000 kilometers in one second. A radar set sends out a short burst of radion waves. Then it receives the echoes produced when the waves bounce off objects. By determining the time it takes for the echoes to return to the radar set, a trained technician can determine the distance between the radar set and other objects. The word
(10)   "radar," in fact, gets its name from the term "radio detection and ranging." "Ranging" is the term for detection of the distance between an object and the radar set. Besides being of critical importance to pilots, radar is essential for air traffic control, tracking ships at sea, and for tracking weather systems and storms.

37. What is the main topic of this passage?
    (A) the nature of radar
    (B) types of ranging
    (C) alternatives to radar
    (D) history of radar

38. In line 1, the word "dense" could be replaced by
    (A) cold
    (B) wet
    (C) dark
    (D) thick

39. According to the passage, what can radar detect besides location of objects?
    (A) size
    (B) weight
    (C) speed
    (D) shape

40. The word "shouts" in line 4 is most similar in meaning to which of the following?
    (A) eavesdrops
    (B) yells
    (C) confesses
    (D) whispers

41. Which of the following words best describes the tone of this passage?
    (A) argumentative
    (B) imaginative
    (C) explanatory
    (D) humorous

42. The phrase "a burst" in line 7 is closest in meaning in which of the following?
    (A) an attachment
    (B) a discharge
    (C) a stream
    (D) a ray

43. The word "it" in line 7 refers to which of the following?
    (A) a radar set
    (B) a short burst
    (C) a radion wave
    (D) light

44. Which of the following could best replace the word "bounce" in line 8?
    (A) overturn
    (B) groove
    (C) extend
    (D) rebound

45. Which type of waves does radar use?
    (A) sound
    (B) heat
    (C) radio
    (D) light

46. The word "tracking" in line 12 is closest in meaning to which of the following?
    (A) repairing
    (B) searching for
    (C) glancing at
    (D) fighting

GO ON TO THE NEXT PAGE

47. Which of the following would most likely be the topic of the next paragraph?
(A) other uses of radar
(B) uses of sonar technology
(C) other technology used by pilots
(D) a history of flying

48. What might be inferred about radar?
(A) It takes the place of a radio.
(B) It gave birth to the invention of the airplane.
(C) It developed from a study of sound waves.
(D) It has improved navigational safety.

GO ON TO THE NEXT PAGE

Questions 49 to 60 are based on the following passage:

(1)   Langston Hughes was one of the greatest American writers of the twentieth century. He was born in Joplin, Missouri, and moved to Cleveland at the age of fourteen. Several years later he spent one year in Mexico before attending Columbia University in New York. For a few years after that he roamed the world as a seaman, visiting ports around the world and writing some poetry. He returned to the United

(5)   States and attended Lincoln University, where he won the Witter Bynner Prize for undergraduate poetry. After graduating in 1928, he traveled to Spain and to Russia with the help of a Guggenheim fellowship. His novels include *Not Without Laughter* (1930) and *The Big Sea* (1940). He wrote an autobiography in 1956 and also published several collections of poetry. The collections include *The Weary Blues* (1926), *The Dream Keeper* (1932), *Shakespeare in Harlem* (1942), *Fields of Wonder* (1947), *One Way Ticket*

(10)   (1947), and *Selected Poems* (1959). A man of many talents, Hughes was also a lyricist, librettist, and a journalist. As an older man in the 1960s he spent much of his time collecting poems from Africa and from African-Americans to popularize black writers. Hughes is one of the most accomplished writers in American literary history, and he is seen as one of the artistic leaders of the Harlem Renaissance, the period when a neighborhood that was predominantly black produced a flood of great literature, music,

(15)   and other art forms depicting daily city life for African-Americans.

49. What is the main topic of this passage?
(A) the life of Langston Hughes
(B) the Harlem Renaissance
(C) African-American writers
(D) American twentieth-century writers

50. Where was Langston Hughes born?
(A) Spain
(B) New York
(C) Missouri
(D) North Carolina

51. The word "roamed" as used in line 3 is closest in meaning to which of the following?
(A) traveled
(B) soared
(C) floated
(D) walked

52. As used in line 4, which of the following words could best replace the word "ports"?
(A) islands
(B) ships
(C) friends
(D) harbors

53. To which of the following movements might *Shakespeare in Harlem* refer?
(A) the Civil War
(B) the Harlem Riots
(C) the Harlem Renaissance
(D) the Civil Rights Movement

54. What provided Hughes with assistance for his travel to Spain and Russia?
(A) his job as a reporter
(B) his career as a soldier
(C) a literary fellowship
(D) a college study program

55. The word "talents" in line 10 could be be replaced by which of the following?
(A) desires
(B) abilities
(C) strategies
(D) careers

56. According to the author, what did Hughes do during the later years of his life?
(A) write short stories
(B) popularize African-American writers
(C) advocate racial equality
(D) write about life in Harlem

57. Which of the following could best replace the word "accomplished" as used in line 12?
(A) successful
(B) prolific
(C) brilliant
(D) imaginative

58. The author uses the word "flood" in line 14 to refer to
(A) a drought
(B) an outpouring
(C) a cloudburst
(D) a streak

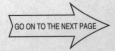 GO ON TO THE NEXT PAGE

59. Which of the following can best substitute for the word "depicting" in line 15?
    (A) congratulating
    (B) blessing
    (C) screening
    (D) portraying

60. According to the passage, Langston Hughes was all of the following EXCEPT
    (A) a novelist
    (B) a poet
    (C) an historian
    (D) a journalist

THIS IS THE END OF TEST 1

Practice Test 1
Answer Key

Section 1: Listening Comprehension

Part A

1. D	5. D	9. A	13. D	17. D
2. D	6. D	10. C	14. C	18. D
3. C	7. C	11. B	15. B	19. B
4. A	8. A	12. D	16. A	20. A

Part B

21. C	24. A	27. D	30. C	33. D
22. B	25. C	28. C	31. C	34. C
23. B	26. D	29. A	32. A	35. A

Part C

36. A	39. C	42. A	45. C	48. B
37. A	40. A	43. A	46. B	49. C
38. C	41. D	44. A	47. A	50. C

Section 2: Structure and Written Expression

Part 1: Sentence Completion

1. B	4. D	7. A	10. A	13. A
2. A	5. A	8. D	11. C	14. B
3. D	6. B	9. B	12. D	15. B

Part 2: Error Identification

16. C	21. B	26. D	31. A	36. A
17. C	22. B	27. C	32. A	37. C
18. A	23. C	28. B	33. C	38. A
19. B	24. A	29. B	34. A	39. C
20. C	25. C	30. C	35. D	40. C

Section 3: Reading Comprehension

1. B	13. A	25. C	37. A	49. A
2. A	14. B	26. B	38. D	50. C
3. D	15. D	27. A	39. C	51. A
4. B	16. C	28. B	40. B	52. D
5. B	17. C	29. C	41. C	53. C
6. A	18. B	30. D	42. B	54. C
7. C	19. C	31. B	43. A	55. B
8. A	20. A	32. C	44. D	56. B
9. C	21. A	33. A	45. C	57. A
10. A	22. B	34. B	46. B	58. B
11. D	23. C	35. D	47. A	59. D
12. D	24. D	36. A	48. D	60. C

Practice Test 1
Explanatory Answers

SECTION 1

Listening Comprehension

Part A

1. Woman: Didn't Kathleen go traveling with you last summer?

Man: Are you kidding? Even if it didn't cost anything, she'd rather stay home.

What does the man imply about Kathleen?
(A) She enjoys summer the most.
(B) She's too busy to go traveling.
(C) She gets bored staying home too long.
(D) She doesn't like to travel.

(D) The man says that Kathleen would rather stay home, even if traveling were free. Therefore, we can assume that Kathleen does not like to travel.

2. Woman: You bought another book on architecture?

Man: This book has some details I need.

What does the man mean?
(A) Building houses is very complicated.
(B) He lent his other book to a friend.
(C) This book doesn't have enough details.
(D) He needs the information in this book.

(D) The word "details" refers to bits of information that the man says he needs.

3. Man: Professor Benson is working in his lab this afternoon.

Woman: But his vacation isn't over until next week.

What did Professor Benson probably do?
(A) He left his lab and went on vacation.
(B) He locked his lab.
(C) He came back to work early.
(D) He went to give a lecture.

(C) Since Professor Benson is working even though his vacation is not over yet, we can assume that he came back to work before he needed to.

4. Man: I was surprised when you told me that Connie and David have become good friends.

Woman: I know. They didn't used to get along well, did they?

What does the woman mean?
(A) Connie and David have changed.
(B) David wants to talk to Connie.
(C) Connie and David are planning a trip together.
(D) Connie and David have many friends.

(A) Since Connie and David didn't use to get along and they are now good friends, we can assume that they have changed their feelings toward each other. "To get along" means to be able to work or play together without fighting or arguing.

113

5. Man: Have you been to the city museum?

Woman: Twice, I believe.

What does the woman mean?

(A) She used to work for the city.

(B) She enjoys sightseeing in the city.

(C) She thinks there are two buildings.

(D) She has visited the museum more than once.

(D) The word "twice" means "two times." The best answer, therefore is "more than once."

6. Man: Excuse me, Amy, is it possible for us to switch our shifts this week?

Woman: Which day do you want to switch to?

What does the woman imply?

(A) She is unhappy with her work.

(B) She wonders what job the man does.

(C) She doesn't know what the man means.

(D) She agrees to work on another day.

(D) We can assume that the woman agrees to exchange work days since she asks about the day. If she did not agree to exchange work days she would probably give a reason why she could not.

7. Woman: Greg says he's going to take three extra classes.

Man: He's got to be kidding.

What does the man mean?

(A) He thinks Greg is too young.

(B) He thinks it's a good decision.

(C) He is surprised.

(D) He is angry.

(C) The expression "you've got to be kidding" is said when someone is surprised at what he or she hears. It is similar to saying, "I don't believe it!"

8. Woman: I need to advertise for another roommate for next semester.

Man: Why bother? Sandy is interested.

What does the man mean?

(A) Sandy wants to room with the woman.

(B) Sandy is a very interesting person.

(C) Sandy doesn't want to bother anyone.

(D) Sandy is the woman's roommate.

(A) The man's question means, "Why take the time and effort to advertise, since I know that Sandy would like to room with you."

9. Man: How did the movie end?

Woman: I don't know, it'll be continued tonight.

What does the woman mean?

(A) The compete movie was not shown.

(B) She went to sleep during the movie.

(C) The end surprised everyone.

(D) She wants to see the movie again tonight.

(A) When the woman says the movie will be continued, she means that the end of the movie has not been shown yet.

10. Man: Do you want to see if I can get tickets to the football game next week?

Woman: I don't think we stand a chance, but try anyway.

What does the woman mean?

(A) She already has tickets for both of them.

(B) She's trying to fool him.

(C) She thinks it's going to be hard to get tickets

(D) She doesn't want to get tickets, because they might have to stay home.

(C) The phrase "we don't stand a chance" means that something will be very difficult to do.

11. Woman: Do you really mean you want to quit this job?

    Man: Well, maybe I'd better give it a second thought.

    What is the man going to do?
    (A) Come back again to apply for the job
    (B) Think about whether he really wants to resign
    (C) Get some training before he quits his job
    (D) Apply for an additional part-time job

    (B) To give something a "second thought" means to think it over again and possibly change your mind.

12. Man: You should persuade Alex to change his major.

    Woman: Why? He's mature enough to make up his own mind.

    What does the woman mean?
    (A) Alex wants to change his major.
    (B) Alex is still too young to make his own decision.
    (C) Alex should not change his major without consent from his parents.
    (D) Alex is capable of making his own decision.

    (D) The phrase "to make up one's own mind" means to make a decision without being told by others what to do.

13. Woman: Are you going to the group meeting tonight?

    Man: I can't, I have another commitment.

    What does the man mean?
    (A) He'll make an effort to go tonight.
    (B) He doesn't like commitments.
    (C) He remembered he had to go to the group meeting.
    (D) He has to go somewhere else.

    (D) When the man says he has another commitment, it means that he has agreed to be at another place or activity.

14. Woman: Hey, Jim, how was your vacation?

    Man: Oh, I did nothing but study.

    What does the man mean?
    (A) There is nothing that worries him.
    (B) He didn't do any studying.
    (C) He studied very hard.
    (D) He was bored.

    (C) If the man did nothing except study all during his vacation, we can assume that he was studying very hard.

15. Woman: Do you think Laura will accept this proposal?

    Man: No way.

    What does the man mean?
    (A) Laura doesn't understand the proposal.
    (B) Laura will not like the proposal.
    (C) Laura accepted this proposal.
    (D) Laura's proposal is excellent.

    (B) The phrase "no way" means that the man is certain that Laura will not accept the proposal. We can infer that if she will not accept it, she does not like it.

16. Man: Why did Sue change her schedule?

    Woman: So she could leave from a closer airport.

    What does the woman imply about Sue?
    (A) She doesn't want a long drive to the airport.
    (B) She will hang her luggage in the closet.
    (C) She won't use the same airline again this time.
    (D) She isn't used to traveling very much.

    (A) If the airport is closer it means that Sue will not have to drive such a long way to get there.

17.   Man: Can I eat this fruit as it is?
Woman: No, you have to peel it first.

What does the woman mean?
(A) You can't eat the fruit whole.
(B) You can't eat the pit.
(C) You can't eat the fruit raw.
(D) You can't eat the skin of the fruit.

(D) The outside skin of fruit is called a "peel." The verb "to peel" means to take off the skin.

18.   Woman: Marcus didn't get the score he
                wanted.
       Man: But he did pass the test.

What are they saying about Marcus?
(A) He is the best student in the class.
(B) He'll have to take the exam again.
(C) He passed the exam with the grade he
     expected.
(D) His grade was not as high as he had hoped.

(D) Answer (D) is the only one that refers to Marcus not getting the grade he wanted.

19.   Woman: I feel like it's only been a few
                weeks since school started.
       Man: And it's already almost time for
                our final exams!

What do the speakers imply?
(A) They are studying hard for finals.
(B) The school year seemed to go by very
     quickly.
(C) They've been in school a few weeks.
(D) Even though finals are over, they still have
     to study for a few weeks.

(B) When the woman says that it feels like school started only a few weeks ago, the man shows his agreement by stating that it is almost time for final exams. We can assume, therefore, that it seems to them that the school year has gone by very fast.

20.   Woman: What does Rich want?
       Man: He wants some ice for his sore
                shoulder.

What does the man imply about Rich?
(A) His shoulder hurts.
(B) His eyes are dim.
(C) He likes the ice in the lake.
(D) He wants another cold drink.

(A) When a part of the body is sore, it means that it hurts.

Part B

21. What is this conversation mainly about?
    (A) finding books in the library
    (B) an exam in a class
    (C) a student's research project
    (D) asking directions to a class

(C) This is a main idea question. The man and woman are discussing the man's plans for a research project about the Anasazi civilization.

22. Where was the Anasazi civilization located in the United States?
    (A) in the mountains
    (B) in the Southwest desert
    (C) in New York
    (D) on the Atlantic coast

(B) This is a restatement question. The man states that the Anasazi Indians lived in the southwest desert area of the United States.

23. What subject is the student going to focus on?
    (A) the southwestern desert
    (B) the end of the Anasazi civilization
    (C) Native American history
    (D) desert climates

(B) This is a restatement question. The student says he will focus on why the Anasazi civilization suddenly ended. Answer (A) is mentioned, but it is not the topic of the research project. Answer (C) is too general.

24. Which of the following things does the woman say?
    (A) There is another person studying a similar topic.
    (B) There are no books in the library about this particular topic.
    (C) She thinks the student should change his focus.
    (D) She has a lot of books on this topic for the student.

(A) This is a restatement question. The woman mentions that another student named Eddy is also studying the Anasazi.

25. Where is the woman interested in going?
    (A) Boston
    (B) San Francisco
    (C) New York
    (D) Milwaukee

(C) This is a restatement question. In several places in the conversation, both speakers mention the destination as New York.

26. What is the woman's response to the first train mentioned?
    (A) It is going to the wrong destination.
    (B) The departure times are not appropriate.
    (C) The train will arrive too late.
    (D) The ticket is too expensive.

(D) This is a restatement question. The woman buys the second ticket because she says the first one is too expensive.

27. Why is one ticket cheaper?
    (A) because it goes on to Boston
    (B) because it is slower
    (C) because there is no place to sleep
    (D) because it arrives in the middle of the night

(D) This is an inference question. The ticket seller says that the train arrives in New York at midnight and then waits until morning to continue its journey. We can assume that this is why the price is lower.

28. What is the main topic of this conversation?
    (A) friends
    (B) sea birds
    (C) a trip
    (D) Fridays

(C) This is a main idea question. The conversation is centered on the destination and the arrangements for leaving for the beach.

29. What can you infer about these two speakers?
    (A) They are friends.
    (B) They have just met.
    (C) They are brother and sister.
    (D) They have a class together.

(A) This is an inference question. Because the two speakers are planning to take a trip with some friends to the beach, it is most likely that the two speakers are friends.

30. Why does the woman like going to Grover's Beach?
    (A) to sit in the sun
    (B) to watch the waves
    (C) to observe sea birds
    (D) to have picnics

(C) This is a restatement question. The woman says that she likes to go to Grover's Beach to watch the sea birds.

31. When do they plan to meet again?
    (A) Saturday
    (B) one year later
    (C) Friday
    (D) after the summer

(C) This is a restatement question. The woman tells the man that the group will meet at four o'clock on Friday to leave for the beach.

32. What are the two speakers talking about doing?
    (A) taking a vacation
    (B) going to sleep
    (C) seeing a movie
    (D) traveling to New York City

(A) This is a main idea question. The conversation between the two speakers is about taking a two-week vacation.

33. Where is this conversation most likely taking place?
    (A) in a restaurant
    (B) in an office
    (C) in a classroom
    (D) in a house

(D) This is a location question. The man talks about going into the garage to fix the car, and the woman talks about going to the attic to find some camping things. Since a garage is a place where a car is parked, and an attic is the space in a house above the ceilings and below the roof, the conversation is taking place in a house.

34. Why does the woman want to spend her vacation camping?
    (A) She enjoys hiking.
    (B) Her cousin has a cabin in Canada.
    (C) She wants to get away from the city.
    (D) She can't afford to stay in a hotel.

(C) This is a restatement question. She says that she is tired of the traffic and congestion in New York City where she presumably lives.

35. Why can't they leave that night for their vacation?
    (A) The car needs to be fixed.
    (B) They need to work the next day.
    (C) Their flight doesn't leave until the next day.
    (D) The weather is very bad that night.

(A) This is a restatement question. The man says that he has to fix the car before it will be ready for a trip.

Part C

36. What is the main subject of this lecture?
    (A) a magazine
    (B) a neighborhood
    (C) a period of time
    (D) a political issue

(A) This is a restatement question. The lecture is about *The Masses*, which is described as a magazine.

37. When was *The Masses* first published?
    (A) before World War I
    (B) in the 1950s
    (C) in the 1970s
    (D) after 1985

(A) This is a restatement question. The lecturer says that the magazine was printed before World War I.

38. Which of the following topics would most likely be printed in *The Masses*?
    (A) new viral discoveries
    (B) a brief history of nineteenth-century France
    (C) a movement toward world peace
    (D) the life and time of Shakespeare

(C) This is a restatement question. The speaker says that there were articles such as growing political movements for peace in World War I.

39. What class would this lecture most likely be a part of?
    (A) American Revolutionary Period
    (B) world history
    (C) journalism
    (D) economics

(C) Journalism is the most likely answer choice because the discussion is about a magazine, which is a form of journalism. The speaker begins with the statement, "while we are talking about media. . . ."

40. What is the purpose of this announcement?
    (A) to inform people of the zoo show times
    (B) to announce the zoo will close soon
    (C) to advertise goods sold at the gift shop
    (D) to promote a restaurant serving lunch at the zoo

(A) This is a main idea question. The anouncement is about three animal shows at the zoo that day.

41. Which of the following kinds of animals is one of the shows featuring?
    (A) lions and tigers
    (B) elephants and giraffes
    (C) sharks and rays
    (D) apes and monkeys

(D) This is a restatement question. The second show features a feeding of the apes and monkeys.

42. What will Dr. Smith give a guided tour of?
    (A) the giant bird cage
    (B) the tiger house
    (C) the monkey and ape habitat
    (D) the tropical rainforest exhibit

(A) This is a restatement question. The announcer says that Dr. Smith will guide a tour of the giant bird cage.

43. Where does the announcer say that a person can get information about the animal show times?
    (A) at the main entrance
    (B) in the gift shop
    (C) from Dr. Smith
    (D) at the primate center

(A) This is a restatement question. The speaker says that a person can get information at the information booth at the main entrance.

44. What subject is this introduction mainly about?
    (A) American history
    (B) twentieth-century poets
    (C) Shakespeare
    (D) Abraham Lincoln

(A) This is a main idea question. The lecturer is introducing a course on the history of the American South after the Civil War.

45. What is the significance of December 15th?
    (A) the date when the Civil War ended
    (B) the date when the first exam will take place
    (C) the date when the paper is due
    (D) the date when Abraham Lincoln died

(C) This is a restatement question. The lecturer states that December 15th will be the date when the paper will be due.

46. What will the speaker probably discuss next?
    (A) the end of the Civil War
    (B) the speech by Abraham Lincoln
    (C) the conditions in the southern states
    (D) the beginning of the war between the states

(B) This is a following topic question. The speaker states that the first topic he will discuss will be the speech given by Abraham Lincoln after the battle at Gettysburg, Pennsylvania. The next part of this introduction would most likely cover this event.

47. What is this lecture about?
    (A) music
    (B) literature
    (C) dance
    (D) painting

(A) This is an inference question. The lecture is about one of the "greatest musical pieces. . . ."

48. What is the name of the musical piece the speaker describes?
    (A) Handel
    (B) the *Messiah*
    (C) the London Philharmonic
    (D) The Symphony

(B) This is a restatement question. The speaker continues to refer to the piece known as the *Messiah*.

49. How have the versions of this work varied throughout the years?
    (A) The educational level of artists has increased.
    (B) The size of the audience has grown.
    (C) The number of voices and instruments has changed.
    (D) The types of visitors have changed.

(C) This is a restatement question. The speaker says that at one time there were 50 instruments and 70 voices, but later there were at least 10,000 voices and 500 instruments.

50. What celebration was this work intended for?
    (A) Christmas
    (B) New Year's Day
    (C) Easter
    (D) the summer solstice

(C) This is a restatement question. It was intended for Easter.

SECTION 2

Structure and Written Expression

Part 1: Sentence Completion

1. America's first globe maker was James Wilson, who _____ and blacksmith in his earlier life.
    (A) a farmer had been
    (B) had been a farmer
    (C) farming
    (D) being a farmer

(B) Verb tense. The past perfect tense is needed as part of the clause "who had been a farmer and blacksmith. . . . "

2. Napoleon _____ the West Indian island of Santo Domingo in 1801.
    (A) attacked
    (B) is attacking
    (C) has attacted
    (D) attacking

(A) Verb tense. The past tense describes an action completed in the past.

3. Modern industrial methods have supplanted individual crafts, _____ stonecarvers, coopers, and cobblers virtually extinct.
    (A) make blacksmiths,
    (B) made blacksmiths,
    (C) making them blacksmiths,
    (D) making blacksmiths,

(D) This sentence means that individual artists like blacksmiths are not common now because of modern methods of industry. The word "making" is part of the phrase "making [something] extinct."

4. Not only knowledge and skills, but also attitudes _____ in school for students' future adjustment to society.
    (A) when cultivated
    (B) cultivated
    (C) which need to be cultivated
    (D) need to be cultivated

(D) Verb. The noun "attitudes" needs the verb "need" to complete the sentence. The meaning is that attitudes, knowledge, and skills all need to be developed (cultivated).

5. On Mercator's maps, the far northern and southern polar regions are _____.
    (A) greatly exaggerated in area
    (B) exaggerating greatly in area
    (C) greatly exaggerate in area
    (D) great exaggeration in area

(A) Word order. The word "greatly" modifies "exaggerated," which is a passive contruction.

6. On the slope of Long's Peak in Colorado _____ the ruin of a gigantic tree.
    (A) that lies
    (B) lies
    (C) where lies
    (D) lie

(B) Verb. This is a reversed order sentence. The standard order would be "The ruins of a tree lies on the slope of Long's Peak."

7. _____ in Shanghai than in any other city in China.
    (A) More people live
    (B) More people living
    (C) It has more people
    (D) More living people

(A) Comparison/ subject +verb. The word "than" is a clue that this is a comparison: "more people in Shanghai than. . . . "

8.   The earth spins on its axis and _____ 23 hours, 56 minutes and 4.09 seconds for one complete rotation.
     (A) need
     (B) needed
     (C) needing
     (D) needs

(D) Verb. The sentence needs a present tense verb. The verb "needs" is parallel to "spins."

9.   _____ on the environment for the gratification of its needs.
     (A) Each organism to depend
     (B) Every organism depends
     (C) All organisms depending
     (D) Many organisms can depend

(B) Subject + verb. This is a present tense singular sentence that states a fact.

10. Of Charles Dickens' many novels, *Great Expectations* is perhaps _____ to many readers.
     (A) the most satisfying one
     (B) most satisfying one
     (C) more than satisfying one
     (D) the more satisfying than

(A) Superlative. The superlative must use the word "the" before "most."

11. _____, the nation's capital remained in Philadelphia, Pennsylvania.
     (A) While designing Washington, D.C.,
     (B) Washington, D.C., was designed,
     (C) While Washington, D.C., was being designed
     (D) Washington, D.C., designed

(C) Adjective clause/word order. This clause uses a passive form of the verb "was being designed."

12. Children learn primarily by _____ the world around them.
     (A) experiencing directly of
     (B) experience direct
     (C) directly physical experience
     (D) direct physical experience of

(D) Adverb phrase. The main phrase is "children learn . . . by experience." The word "experience" in this sentence is a noun. It would also be possible to say, "children learn by experiencing the world," but in this case there would be no preposition "of."

13. It is earth's gravity which _____ people their weight.
     (A) gives
     (B) give
     (C) giving
     (D) given

(A) Verb. The verb is in the present tense, a part of the adjective clause "which gives people. . . ."

14. Generally speaking, people should have _____ as their desires will allow.
     (A) much education
     (B) as much education
     (C) education
     (D) for education

(B) Comparative. This is an example of the comparison "as much as" which compares two ideas. In this case the comparison is between education and desire.

15. A dolphin six _____ length can move as fast as most ships.
     (A) foot in
     (B) feet in
     (C) foot of
     (D) feet of

(B) Preposition. Since the number is six (which is more than one), the noun must be plural ("feet"). The preposition "in" is used with the noun "length." In other situations other prepositions are used, for instance, you could say, "I'd like six feet of rope."

Part 2: Error Identification

16. Cotton used to rank first between
     <u>A</u>   <u>B</u>   <u>C</u>

     Alabama's crops, but it <u>represents only a</u>
                                      <u>D</u>

     fraction of the agricultural production now.

(C) Preposition. The word "between" is used to compare only two things. In this sentence the plural form of "crops" implies that there are more than two crops being compared. The correct word is "among."

17. Salmon <u>lay</u> their eggs and die in fresh
             <u>A</u>

     water, <u>although</u> they live in salt water
             <u>B</u>

     <u>when</u> most of their adult <u>lives.</u>
     <u>C</u>   <u>D</u>

(C) Preposition. The correct word is "during," which refers to the period of time that salmon live.

18. <u>To building</u> their <u>nests,</u> tailorbirds use
     <u>A</u>   <u>B</u>

     <u>their</u> bills <u>as</u> needles.
     <u>C</u>   <u>D</u>

(A) Infinitive/gerund. The correct word is "build." This refers to a future action: "in order to build their nests. . . ."

19. Fountain pens <u>first</u> became <u>commercial</u>
                     <u>A</u>   <u>B</u>

     <u>available</u> about a hundred years <u>ago.</u>
     <u>C</u>   <u>D</u>

(B) Word form. The correct word is "commercially," which modifies "available."

20. With <u>its</u> strong claws and <u>its</u> many
          <u>A</u>   <u>B</u>

     <u>protruding tooth</u> a gopher is <u>an excellent</u>
     <u>C</u>   <u>D</u>

     digger.

(C) Singular/plural noun. The word should be "teeth," the plural form of "tooth," since a gopher has more than one tooth.

21. Drug addiction has <u>resulted of</u> many
                         <u>A</u>   <u>B</u>

     <u>destroyed</u> careers, and <u>expulsions</u> from
     <u>C</u>   <u>D</u>

     school or college.

(B) Preposition. After the verb "result" should be the preposition "in." The prepostion "of" can follow the noun "result," but not the verb.

22. Because of the Lewis and Clark <u>Expedi-</u>
                                     <u>A</u>

     tion, the United States <u>begin to realize</u>
                              <u>B</u>

     <u>the true value</u> of the Louisiana <u>territory.</u>
     <u>C</u>   <u>D</u>

(B) Verb. The correct word is "began," the past tense form of the verb. It would also be grammatically correct to write "has begun," "begins," or "will begin" in this type of sentence. The word "begin" is incorrect since it must follow a plural word. The United States is considered singular since it is the name of one country.

23. Americans annually <u>import</u> <u>more than</u>
                         <u>A</u>   <u>B</u>

     $3 billion <u>worthy</u> of Italian <u>clothing,</u>
                <u>C</u>   <u>D</u>

     jewelry, and shoes.

(C) Word form. The correct word is "worth." We say "$2 dollars' worth of goods," which means you are buying something that costs the equivalent of $2.00. The word "worthy" is an adjective that means "having value or worth," or "deserving."

24. Akuce Ganuktibm, <u>she</u> spent her <u>life</u>
                       <u>A</u>   <u>B</u>

     working with the health and <u>welfare</u> of
                                  <u>C</u>

     the families of <u>workers.</u>
     <u>D</u>

(A) Unnecessary word. The word "she" is not needed in this sentence. It makes a double subject.

25. There are many different ways
   <u>   </u>
        A
   of comparing the economy of one nation
   <u>   </u>
                B
   with those of another.
   <u>   </u> <u>   </u>
     C   D

(C) Pronoun. The correct word is "that" since it refers to "economy," a singular noun.

26. Male guppies, like many other male fish,
   <u>   </u>   <u>   </u>
      A   B
   are more color than females.
   <u>   </u> <u>   </u>
      C   D

(D) Word form. The correct word is the adjective "colorful," not the noun "color," since this is a description of the fish.

27. When rhinos take mud baths, the mud
   <u>   </u>   <u>   </u>
      A   B
   create a barrier to biting insects.
   <u>   </u>   <u>   </u>
       C   D

(C) Verb. The correct word is "creates," a present tense verb form that goes with the singular noun, "mud."

28. Benjamin Franklin, as an inventor, he had
                    <u>   </u> <u>   </u>
                          A   B
   broad interests, mechanical skills,

   persistence, and a practical view of life.
   <u>   </u>   <u>   </u>
       C   D

(B) Unnecessary word. The word "he" is incorrect since it adds a double subject.

29. In the stock market, the fluctuations in
   <u> </u>
    A
   Standard and Poor's 500 Index does not
                            <u>   </u>
                               B
   always conform to Dow Jones Averages.
   <u>   </u> <u>   </u>
      C   D

(B) Verb. The correct form of the verb is "do," to go with the plural noun, "fluctuations." To answer this question you do not have to understand the phrase "Standard and Poor's 500 Index" which refers to a service that provides ratings for people interested in investing money.

30. A jellyfish, which isn't really a fish, it
              <u>   </u> <u>   </u> <u> </u>
                    A   B   C
   has no brain, no bones and no face.
   <u>   </u>
            D

(C) Unnecessary word. The word "it" adds a double subject and is therefore incorrect.

31. International trade, going traveling, and
                      <u>   </u>
                            A
   television have lain the groundwork for
   <u>   </u> <u>   </u>   <u> </u>
       B   C
   modern global life styles.
   <u>   </u>
        D

(A) Parallel construction. The correct word is "traveling," a noun that is parallel to "trade" and "television."

32. The most visible remind of the close
                  <u>   </u>
                     A
   relationship between the United States
   <u>   </u>
        B
   and France is the famous Statue of
       <u> </u>
        C
   Liberty, which stands in New York
         <u>   </u>
          D
   harbor.

(A) Word form. The correct word is "reminder," a noun and the subject of this sentence. The word "remind" is a verb.

33. Until diamonds are cut and polished, they
   <u>   </u>   <u>   </u>
     A   B
   just like look small blue-grey stones.
   <u>   </u>   <u>   </u>
        C   D

(C) Reversed order. The correct words are "they just look like small blue-grey stones."

34. Jackie Robinson, whose joined the
                       A
    Brooklyn Dodgers in 1947, was the first
                                      B
    black American to play baseball in the
                    C   D
    major leagues.

(A) Pronoun. The correct word is "who," which begins a description of Jackie Robinson. The pronoun "whose" is associated with something belonging to someone.

35. Laser technology is the heart of a new
                      A   B
    generation of high-speed copiers and
              C
    printer.
      D

(D) Singular/plural Noun. The correct word is "printers," a plural form that goes with copiers.

36. Fertilize farmland is one of the biggest
        A   B   C
    natural resources in the Central States.
                                D

(A) Word form. The correct word is "fertilized," an adjective that describes the type of farmland.

37. The symptoms of diabetes in the early
          A   B
    stages are too slight that people don't
                  C
    notice them.
          D

(C) Adverb. The correct word is "so." A good clue in this sentence is the word "that," which often follows "so."

38. *Gone with the Wind* written after Marga-
                        A
    ret Mitchell quit her job as a reporter
              B   C
    because of an ankle injury.
            D

(A) Verb. The correct verb is "was written," a passive form of the verb.

39. With a policy of eminent domain, the
             A   B
    state has control ultimate of all real
               C   D
    property.

(C) Reversed words. The correct answer is, "the state has ultimate control of all real property." The word "ultimate" is an adjective that modifies the noun "control."

40. Hay fever symptoms, ranged from mild
                          A
    to severe, differ in degree according to
    B   C   D
    the individual.

(C) Word form. The correct word is "ranging," which begins the adjective phrase that describes the noun "symptoms."

SECTION 3
Reading Comprehension

1.   What is this passage mainly about?
     (A) the prejudice that existed in Atlanta
     (B) Martin Luther King's childhood
     (C) M.L.'s grandfather
     (D) the neighborhood King grew up in

(B) This is a main idea question. Though all of the answer choices are mentioned in the passage, only (B) covers them all.

2.   The word "eloquent" in line 5 means most nearly
     (A) powerful
     (B) active
     (C) romantic
     (D) fascinating

(A) The word "eloquent" means to speak in a way that is powerful to the listeners. Other words that describe an eloquent speaker are "fluent," "persuasive," "moving," or "stirring."

3.   The word "gathering" in line 9 could best be replaced by
     (A) picking
     (B) learning
     (C) exciting
     (D) meeting

(D) In this context, "gathering" refers to a group of people who come together. In other contexts, "gathering" could mean "picking."

4.   As used in line 10, the word "eventful" is closest in meaning to which of the following?
     (A) valued
     (B) memorable
     (C) admirable
     (D) emotional

(B) If a period of time is "eventful" or "memorable," it means that many things happened during that time that a person remembers. These happenings may be positive or negative. They may be valued or not, admirable or not, or emotional or not.

5.   In line 13, the word "it" refers to which of the following?
     (A) achievement
     (B) neighborhood
     (C) segregation
     (D) services

(B) Though the closest nouns preceding the word "it" are "people," "Atlanta," and "achievement," the word "it" stands for none of these. Instead, "it" refers to the "neighborhood" around Auburn Avenue. The word "achievement" describes the neighborhood. "People" is plural, so it cannot be referred to by "it," a singular prepostion.

6.   According to the author, blacks in King's neighborhood were involved in all of the following businesses and services EXCEPT
     (A) dentistry
     (B) medicine
     (C) law
     (D) banking

(A) There is no mention of dentistry in the passage. The others are all listed in the second paragraph.

7.   The word "tailors" in line 14 describes people who are associated with which of the following trades?
     (A) flower arranging
     (B) shoe making
     (C) garment making
     (D) book binding

(C) A tailor is a person who makes clothes for men or women. "Garment making" also refers to making clothes.

8.   According to the author, King was influenced by
     (A) community spirit
     (B) black lawyers
     (C) his mother
     (D) his speeches

(A) The last sentence refers to a community spirit that influenced King. The community spirit is also inferred at the end of the first paragraph.

9. The word "thrived" in line 15 refers to which of the following?
   (A) achieved
   (B) surrendered
   (C) flourished
   (D) held

(C) The words "to thrive" and "to flourish" both mean "to grow," "to prosper," or "to be healthy."

10. As used in line 17, which of the following is closest in meaning to the word "seemingly"?
    (A) apparently
    (B) inevitably
    (C) inexplicably
    (D) hastily

(A) The words "seemingly" and "apparently" both refer to something that one thinks is true or that appears to be true.

11. The word "mingling" in line 17 could best be replaced by which of the following?
    (A) interfering
    (B) gargling
    (C) consuming
    (D) associating

(D) The verb "to mingle" refers to an activity whereby people associate and mix freely among each other in a group.

12. According to the author, M.L.
    (A) had a difficult childhood
    (B) was a good musician as a child
    (C) loved to listen to his grandfather speak
    (D) grew up in a relatively rich area of Atlanta

(D) The neighborhood is described as "prosperous" and "thriving." Both of these imply that the neighborhood was relatively rich.

13. What is the main idea of this passage?
    (A) Carbohydrates are needed for good health.
    (B) Carbohydrates prevent a build-up of proteins.
    (C) Carbohydrates can lead to ketosis.
    (D) Carbohydrates are an expendable part of a good diet.

(A) This is a main idea question. The first and last lines of the passage both refer to carbohydrates as a necesary part of a good diet and good health.

14. The word "function" as used in line 2 refers to which of the following?
    (A) neglect
    (B) serve
    (C) dissolve
    (D) profess

(B) The verbs "to serve" and "to function" both refer to an action of providing for or supplying, acting in a certain way, or being of a certain type of use. Answer (A) means to ignore or disregard something. Answer (C) means to become liquid or to soften. Answer (D) means to declare or to acknowledge something.

15. The word "range" as used in line 2 is closest in meaning to which of the following?
    (A) probe
    (B) proceed
    (C) hail
    (D) extend

(D) The words "range" and "extend" in this sentence refer to the action of encompassing a certain number or type of items. Answer (A) means to inspect or examine something. Answer (B) means to go ahead. Answer (C) means to call, to greet, or to salute.

16. In line 3, the word "estimate" could best be replaced by
(A) disbelieve
(B) declare
(C) calculate
(D) wonder

(C) The verb "to estimate" means "to guess" or "to calculate to the best of one's ability."

17. According to the passage, what do most nutritionists suggest?
(A) Sufficient carbohydrates will prevent gluconeogenesis.
(B) Carbohydrates are simple sugars called glucose.
(C) Carbohydrates should make up about a quarter of a person's daily diet.
(D) Carbohydrates should be eaten in very small quantities.

(C) This is a restatement question. In line 3 of the first paragraph, the passage states that nutritionists recommend that carbohydrates should make up about one-fourth to one-fifth of a person's diet. Though answers (A) and (B) are also stated in the passage, they are not "what nutritionists suggest."

18. Which of the following do carbohydrates NOT do?
(A) prevent ketosis
(B) cause gluconeogenesis
(C) provide energy for the body
(D) flavor and sweeten food

(B) This is a negative question. From the second paragraph you can infer that eating a sufficient amount of carbohydrates will prevent the body from using its protein for energy, so carbohydrate intake will PREVENT, not cause, gluconeogenesis.

19. Which of the following words could best replace "deficient" as used in line 6?
(A) outstanding
(B) abundant
(C) insufficient
(D) unequal

(C) Both "deficient" and "insufficient" are adjectives that refer to something that is lacking.

20. What does the word "this" refer to in line 8?
(A) using protein supplies for energy
(B) converting carbohydrates to energy
(C) having a deficiency in carbohydrates
(D) having an insufficient amount of protein

(A) This is a referent question. The word "this" refers directly to the previous word, "gluconeogenesis," which is explained as "using the body's protein supplies for energy."

21. According to the passage, which of the following does NOT describe carbohydrates?
(A) a protein supply
(B) a necessity
(C) a range of sugars
(D) an energy source

(A) This is a negative question. The passage describes carbohydrates as all of the above except (A). Carbohydrates are distinct from proteins, and there is nothing in the passage that says that carbohydrates supply protein.

22. The word "lack" in line 9 is most similar to which of the following?
(A) plethora
(B) shortage
(C) derivation
(D) commission

(B) The words "lack" and "shortage" both refer to an insufficiency of something. Answer (A) is the opposite. Answer (C) refers to the origin or source of something, or the act of obtaining something. Answer (D) refers to an appointment, an authorization, or a charge.

23. Which of the following best describes the author's tone?
(A) sensitive
(B) emotional
(C) informative
(D) regretful

(C) This is a question about the author's tone. The author is attempting to give the reader some information regarding carbohydrates, and therefore "informative" is the best answer.

24. Which of the following best describes the organization of this passage?
    (A) cause and result
    (B) comparison and contrast
    (C) specific to general
    (D) definition and example

(D) This is an organization question. The first paragraph of the passage is a definition and description of carbohydrates. The second paragraph gives an example of what happens when the body does not have enough carbohydrates.

25. What is the main focus of this passage?
    (A) jobs on Wall Street
    (B) types of graduate degrees
    (C) changes in enrollment for MBA schools
    (D) how schools are changing to reflect the economy

(C) This is a main idea question. The passage discusses causes for drops in enrollment at MBA schools. The word "drop" refers to a decrease in the number of people enrolling in school.

26. The phrase "two decades" in line 1 refers to a period of
    (A) 10 years
    (B) 20 years
    (C) 50 years
    (D) 100 years

(B) A decade is a period of 10 years, so two decades means 20 years.

27. The word "prosperity" in line 1 could be best replaced by which of the following?
    (A) success
    (B) surplus
    (C) nurturing
    (D) education

(A) The word "prosperity" refers to success, wealth, or high growth. Answer (B) refers to an overabundance of something. Answer (C) refers to the caring of someone or something.

28. Which of the following business schools has NOT shown a decrease in enrollment?
    (A) Princeton
    (B) Harvard
    (C) Stanford
    (D) Yale

(B) This is a restatement question. In lines 2–3, it is stated that Harvard has not seen a drop in enrollment.

29. The phrase "trend of" in line 5 is closest in meaning to which of the following?
    (A) reluctance of
    (B) drawback to
    (C) movement toward
    (D) extraction from

(C) A "trend" is an inclination or leaning toward an idea or an action. In this sentence the word "movement" expresses the same idea.

30. As used in line 7, the word "seeking" could be best replaced by which of the following?
    (A) examining
    (B) avoiding
    (C) seizing
    (D) pursuing

(D) Students who are seeking an MBA are enrolled in a program of study. The verb "to pursue" a degree means the same as "to seek" a degree.

31. Which of the following descriptions most likely applies to Wall Street?
    (A) a center for international affairs
    (B) a major financial center
    (C) a shopping district
    (D) a neighborhood in New York

(B) This is an inference question. Since Wall Street is compared to "other financial districts," it can be inferred that Wall Street is also a financial center.

32. The word "plush" in line 8 most probably means
(A) legal
(B) satisfactory
(C) fancy
(D) dependable

(C) A "plush" job is one that is especially nice. There may be many benefits included in the job. The words "deluxe," "grand," or "luxurious" also express the meaning of "plush."

33. According to the passage, what are two causes of declining business school enrollments?
(A) lack of necessity for an MBA and an economic recession
(B) low salary and foreign competition
(C) fewer MBA schools and fewer entry-level jobs
(D) declining population and economic prosperity

(A) This is a restatement question. The second paragraph describes the acceptance of non-MBA graduates into management jobs and the cutting of salaries and jobs, both of which are signs of an economic recession. The first sentence of the passage also mentions "harder times," another indication of an economic recession.

34. The word "cutting" in line 12 could best be replaced by which of the following?
(A) wounding
(B) reducing
(C) dividing
(D) carving

(B) This is a vocabulary question. The word "cutting" can mean all of the above, but in this context it means "reducing."

35. As used in line 14, the word "struggling" is closest in meaning to
(A) evolving
(B) plunging
(C) starting
(D) striving

(D) The words "struggling" and "striving" both refer to working hard to accomplish a goal.

36. Which of the following might be the topic of the next paragraph?
(A) MBA schools' efforts to change
(B) future economic predictions
(C) a history of the recent economic changes
(D) descriptions of non-MBA graduate programs

(A) This is a question of the following topic. Since the final sentence of the passage talks about the struggle of MBA schools to meet new demands, we can infer that the next paragraph will go into more detail about the schools' efforts to meet these new demands.

37. What is the main topic of this passage?
(A) the nature of radar
(B) types of ranging
(C) alternatives to radar
(D) history of radar

(A) This is a main idea question. The passage discusses the basic concepts of radar technology.

38. In line 1, the word "dense" could best be replaced by
(A) cold
(B) wet
(C) dark
(D) thick

(D) The words "dense" and "thick" in this sentence mean "concentrated." In other words, there is so much fog that it is difficult to see anything.

39. According to the passage, what can radar detect besides location of objects?
(A) size
(B) weight
(C) speed
(D) shape

(C) This is a restatement question. Line 3 states that radar can show how fast other planes are moving.

40. The word "shouts" in line 4 is most similar in meaning to which of the following?
    (A) eavesdrops
    (B) yells
    (C) confesses
    (D) whispers

(B) The words "shout" and "yell" both mean to speak very loudly or to call out. The verb "to eavesdrop" means to listen to someone else surreptitiously. "To confess" is to admit something or reveal something. "To whisper" is to speak very softly.

41. Which of the following words best describes the tone of this passage?
    (A) argumentative
    (B) imaginative
    (C) explanatory
    (D) humorous

(C) This is a question of the author's tone. The passage is written with no opinions, just the facts and definitions of radar. It is written in an informative or explanatory style.

42. The phrase "a burst" in line 7 is closest in meaning to which of the following?
    (A) an attachment
    (B) a discharge
    (C) a stream
    (D) a ray

(B) The word "burst" refers to a type of discharge that is short and possibly explosive. It is the opposite of an attachment. The words "stream" and "ray" could also be discharges, but they are longer and more flowing, such as a stream of light or a ray of light.

43. The word "it" in line 7 refers to which of the following?
    (A) a radar set
    (B) a short burst
    (C) a radion wave
    (D) light

(A) This is a referent question. The noun that is referred to by the word "it" is not the closest previously mentioned noun (radion waves), but is the main topic of that previous sentence, which is "radar set." It is the radar set that receives the echoes.

44. Which of the following could best replace the word "bounce" in line 8?
    (A) overturn
    (B) groove
    (C) extend
    (D) rebound

(D) The words "bounce" and "rebound" refer to the action of recoiling or jumping back, such as a ball does when it hits the floor. Answer (A) means to upset or turn over. Answer (B) refers to a small cut, rut, or channel. Answer (C) means to make something longer.

45. Which type of waves does radar use?
    (A) sound
    (B) heat
    (C) radio
    (D) light

(C) This is a restatement question. In line 6 it is stated that radar uses radio waves.

46. The word "tracking" in line 12 is closest in meaning to which of the following?
    (A) repairing
    (B) searching for
    (C) glancing at
    (D) fighting

(B) The verb "to track" means to follow, trace, seek, or look for something.

47. Which of the following would most likely be the topic of the next paragraph?
    (A) other uses of radar
    (B) uses of sonar technology
    (C) other technology used by pilots
    (D) a history of flying

(A) This is a question about the following topic. In the last sentence the author mentions other uses of radar. A more detailed discussion of these other uses would be the most likely next topic.

48. What might be inferred about radar?
    (A) It takes the place of a radio.
    (B) It gave birth to the invention of the jet plane.
    (C) It developed from a study of sound waves.
    (D) It has improved navigational safety.

(D) This is an inference question. The passage begins by stating how difficult it is to fly an airplane by sight alone, thus implying that the use of radar makes it safer to fly planes.

49. What is the main topic of this passage?
    (A) the life of Langston Hughes
    (B) the Harlem Renaissance
    (C) African-American writers
    (D) American twentieth-century writers

(A) This is a main idea question. The passage is mainly about Langston Hughes. Choices (B), (C), and (D) are all too general to cover the narrower focus of this passage on just one writer.

50. Where was Langston Hughes born?
    (A) Spain
    (B) New York
    (C) Missouri
    (D) North Carolina

(C) This is a restatement question. The author states that Hughes was born in Missouri.

51. The word "roamed" as used in line 3 is closest in meaning to which of the following?
    (A) traveled
    (B) soared
    (C) floated
    (D) walked

(A) Though "roam" in some cases might refer to the act of walking as in choice (D), here "roam" means to travel. Since as a seaman Hughes would have been on a ship most of the time, we would not assume that he was walking around the world. Answer (B) refers to the act of flying. Though answer (C) is correct in that Hughes was floating on water in a ship, it does not give the same meaning as moving around the world. The word "roam" infers movement from one place to another, whereas the word "float" just refers to the act of staying on top of water.

52. As used in line 4, which of the following words could best replace the word "ports?"
    (A) islands
    (B) ships
    (C) friends
    (D) harbor

(D) The word "port" can refer to a harbor or bay where ships can dock. The port is also an entrance to a seaport, a city or town next to the harbor or dock. Hughes may have visited ports on islands, but this answer is too narrow.

53. Which of the following movements might *Shakespeare in Harlem* refer to?
    (A) the Civil War
    (B) the Harlem Riots
    (C) the Harlem Renaissance
    (D) the Civil Rights Movement

(C) This is an inference question. The passage states that Hughes was one of the leading artists in the movement known as the Harlem Renaissance. Thus, it can be inferred that *Shakespeare in Harlem* would most likely be about the Harlem Renaissance.

54. What provided Hughes with assistance for his travel to Spain and Russia?
    (A) his job as a reporter
    (B) his career as a soldier
    (C) a literary fellowship
    (D) a college study program

(C) This is an inference question. The author states that Hughes traveled to Spain and Russia with the help of a Guggenheim Fellowship. Since the passage has been discussing Hughes' literary work, we can assume that the Guggenheim Fellowship is a literary fellowship. The word "fellowship" means a grant of money given to a scholar for advanced study in his or her field.

55. The word "talents" in line 10 could best be replaced by which of the following?
    (A) desires
    (B) abilities
    (C) strategies
    (D) careers

(B) The words "talents" and "abilities" refer to special aptitudes of a person. Answer (A) refers to things that a person wants, not things that he or she can do. Answer (C) refers to plans or schemes for doing something. Answer (D) refers to a person's profession or occupation.

56. According to the author, what did Hughes do during the later years of his life?
(A) write short stories
(B) popularize African-American writers
(C) advocate racial equality
(D) write about life in Harlem

(B) This is a restatement question. Near the end of the passage the author states that as an older man Hughes spent time collecting poems from Africa and from African-Americans to popularize other black writers. The phrase "the later years" refers to the same period of time as "older man."

57. Which of the following could best replace the word "accomplished" as used in line 12?

(A) successful
(B) prolific
(C) brilliant
(D) imaginative

(A) An "accomplished" person is one who has achieved success. Answer (B) refers to someone who has produced an abundant amount of material. Answer (C) refers to someone who is very intelligent. Answer (D) refers to someone who is very creative or innovative. Though answers (B), (C), and (D) might be true of Hughes and might also be a part of being "accomplished," answer (A) is closest to the meaning of the word.

58. The author uses the word "flood" in line 14 to refer to
(A) a drought
(B) an outpouring
(C) a cloudburst
(D) a streak

(B) The word "flood" in this sentence refers to an abundant production of works of art. The word "outpouring" has a similar meaning. Answer (A) is the opposite. Answer (C) refers to a sudden, brief rainstorm. Answer (D) can refer to a thin line or strip of something.

59. Which of the following can best substitute for the word "depicting" in line 15?
(A) congratulating
(B) blessing
(C) screening
(D) portraying

(D) The verbs "to depict" and "to portray" both refer to representing something or someone, often by drawing, painting, or acting. Answer (A) means "saluting" or "giving best wishes." Answer (B) means "giving approval, consent, or permission." Answer (C) means "filtering," "concealing," or "protecting."

60. According to the passage, Langston Hughes was all of the following EXCEPT
(A) a novelist
(B) a poet
(C) an historian
(D) a journalist

(C) This is a negative question. The other three choices are all mentioned as occupations of Hughes.

Test 1 • Answers

ANSWER SHEET FOR PRACTICE TEST 2

Section 1: Listening Comprehension

Section 2: Structure and Written Expression

Section 3: Reading Comprehension

Date Taken _____

Number Correct

Section 1 _____

Section 2 _____

Section 3 _____

Practice Test 2

SECTION 1
Listening Comprehension

Time—approximately 30 minutes

NOTE: You can simulate actual TOEFL conditions by using the Listening Comprehension cassettes that accompany this book. If you do not have the tape, ask a friend to read the tapescript for Listening Comprehension Test 2, which is in Part Four, pages 387–94 of this book.

Part A

Directions: In Part A you will hear short conversations between two people. After each conversation a third person will ask a question about what was said. You will hear the conversation only one time, so you must listen carefully to what each speaker says. After you hear the conversation and the question, read the four possible answers in your test booklet and pick the one which best answers the question. Then look on the answer sheet for the number of the question and fill in the oval that corresponds to the letter of your answer choice.

Listen to an example:

You will hear:

You will read:

    Sample Answer

    (A) He will call Pete before he goes home.
    (B) He will call Pete after he gets home.
    (C) He called Pete at home.
    (D) He will call Pete tomorrow.

You learn from the conversation that the man will call Pete as soon as he gets home. The best answer to the question "What does the man mean?" is (B), "He will call Pete after he gets home." Therefore, the correct answer is (B).

Now listen to the tape: Practice Test 2, Section 1, Listening Comprehension Part A.

137

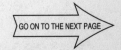

1. (A) The salesperson says they will fit.
    (B) His nephew already has a pair of gloves.
    (C) Only one size will fit.
    (D) The gloves are all the same size.

2. (A) Test the new computer.
    (B) Start writing another section of the paper.
    (C) Go to another lab.
    (D) Change his project.

3. (A) She needs to buckle her safety belt.
    (B) The safety belt is in the back seat.
    (C) He is waiting for somebody to arrive.
    (D) The car has no seat belts.

4. (A) Change lines.
    (B) Go to another theater.
    (C) Follow the map.
    (D) Go back home.

5. (A) A good presentation needs a lot of preparation.
    (B) The presentation was very good.
    (C) He can always turn to her for help.
    (D) He should get some sleep.

6. (A) Cook an egg for Dan.
    (B) Go buy some eggs.
    (C) Plan food for Dan's dinner.
    (D) Eat eggs.

7. (A) She is on a plane.
    (B) She needs to be picked up at school.
    (C) She is often late.
    (D) She has been delayed at work.

8. (A) His cousin's name is Jack.
    (B) Jack is coming to see him.
    (C) His cousin knows Jack very well.
    (D) Jack doesn't know the woman.

9. (A) Stand still.
    (B) Get some exercise.
    (C) Sit down.
    (D) Change his residence.

10. (A) He doesn't want the woman to go away on a trip.
    (B) He is cautioning the woman to be careful.
    (C) He is guiding the woman step by step.
    (D) He wants to borrow the woman's watch.

11. (A) School begins later this year.
    (B) School will be easy this year.
    (C) She'd better start her work early.
    (D) He wants her to relax.

12. (A) Since the weather is nice, she wants to go boating.
    (B) She thinks the park is too far away.
    (C) She suggests they go to the park.
    (D) She's not a very fast walker.

13. (A) How much will the book cost?
    (B) Which book store did she go to?
    (C) Whom did she talk to?
    (D) What library has the book he needs?

14. (A) It has been a good day.
    (B) That's the place we're going.
    (C) We've finished our day's work.
    (D) The store is closed for the day.

15. (A) She owes money to the landlord.
    (B) She is checking out Bill's telephone number.
    (C) She wants to take a rest.
    (D) She will pay her portion of the telephone bill.

16. (A) These bananas are on sale and ready to eat.
    (B) These are the best bananas in the state.
    (C) These bananas are already overripe.
    (D) These bananas are not ripe.

17. (A) She did not like all the rain.
    (B) The rain is good for the crops.
    (C) Part of each day was clear.
    (D) She hopes the drought is over.

18. (A) She began to like it more after learning more.
    (B) She will major in organic chemistry.
    (C) It was hard to learn everything.
    (D) She got better grades at the end of the class.

19. (A) She canceled the room.
    (B) She enjoyed their trip to the reservoir.
    (C) She is sure that he made the right decision.
    (D) She reserved a table in a restaurant.

20. (A) Penny goes to Smith College.
    (B) Penny stopped going to Smith College.
    (C) Penny has just begun school at Smith College.
    (D) Penny likes Smith College the best.

GO ON TO THE NEXT PAGE

Part B

Directions: In Part B you will hear longer conversations between two people. After each conversation you will be asked some questions. You will hear the conversations and the questions only once, so listen carefully to what is said. After you hear a question, read the four possible answers in your test book and decide which one is the best answer to the question you heard. Then, on your answer sheet, find the number of the question and fill in the oval that corresponds to the letter of the answer you have chosen. Answer all questions based on what is stated or implied by the speakers.

Listen to the example on the tape.

> *You will hear:*

Now listen to sample question number 1.

> *You will read:*

Sample Answer

Ⓐ Ⓑ Ⓒ ⬤

(A) to the cafeteria
(B) to the movie theater
(C) to her dorm room
(D) to the library

The best answer to the question "Where is the woman going?" is (D), "to the library." Therefore, the correct choice is (D).

Now listen to sample question number 2.

> *You will hear:*

> *You will read:*

Sample Answer

Ⓐ Ⓑ ⬤ Ⓓ

(A) Term papers are easy for him.
(B) He has a lot of essay exams.
(C) He finds lab experiments easier than writing term papers.
(D) He is busier this semester than last semester.

The best answer to the question "Which best describes this man's feelings about his classes?" is (C), "He finds lab experiments easier than writing term papers." Therefore, the correct answer is (C).

Now listen to the test. Remember, you are not allowed to take any notes or write in your test book.

GO ON TO THE NEXT PAGE

21. (A) teaching English classes
    (B) summer vacation
    (C) other teachers
    (D) students in history classes

22. (A) two
    (B) three
    (C) four
    (D) five

23. (A) English
    (B) economics
    (C) history
    (D) computer science

24. (A) morning
    (B) afternoon
    (C) evening
    (D) late night

25. (A) Carolina Tradition
    (B) Carolina Bakery
    (C) Carolina Coffee Shop
    (D) Carolina Basketball

26. (A) eggs and bacon
    (B) cereal
    (C) fresh fruit
    (D) French toast

27. (A) 6 days
    (B) 10 years
    (C) 60 years
    (D) 100 years

28. (A) by car
    (B) by train
    (C) by plane
    (D) by boat

29. (A) Los Angeles
    (B) San Jose
    (C) Sacramento
    (D) San Francisco

30. (A) that they may have taken a wrong road
    (B) that they cannot find a gas station
    (C) that it is getting dark
    (D) that there is no service attendant

31. (A) to use the bathroom
    (B) to rest
    (C) to ask directions
    (D) to get fuel

32. (A) in a classroom
    (B) in a bedroom
    (C) in a pool
    (D) on a baseball field

33. (A) 6
    (B) 10
    (C) 50
    (D) 60

34. (A) to eat breakfast
    (B) to eat dinner
    (C) to go to class
    (D) to see a movie

35. (A) morning
    (B) evening
    (C) midnight
    (D) noon

GO ON TO THE NEXT PAGE

Part C

Directions: In this part of the test, you will hear talks by a single person. After each talk, you will be asked some questions. You will hear the talks and the questions only once, so listen carefully to what is said. After you hear a question, read the four possible answers in your test book and decide which one is the best answer to the question you heard. Then find the number of the question on your answer sheet, and fill in the oval that corresponds to the letter of the answer you have chosen. Answer all questions based on what is stated or implied in the talk.

Listen to this sample talk.

You will hear:

Now listen to sample question number 1.   Sample Answer

You will read:

    (A) to demonstrate tutoring techniques
    (B) to explain school policies
    (C) to recruit childcare workers
    (D) to explain a service

The best answer to the question "What is the purpose of this announcement?" is (D), "to explain a service." Therefore, the correct choice is (D).

Now listen to sample question number 2.   Sample Answer

You will hear:

You will read:

    (A) give your child extra tutoring.
    (B) Take your child to the program today.
    (C) Apply as soon as you can.
    (D) Pay next month.

The best answer to the question "What does the speaker recommend?" is (C), "Apply as soon as you can." Therefore, the correct choice is (C).

Now begin. Remember, you are not allowed to write any notes in your test book.

GO ON TO THE NEXT PAGE

36. (A) to advertise a new film *To Be or Not to Be?*
    (B) to inform people that a film will not be shown
    (C) to critique the characters in *To Be or Not to Be?*
    (D) to discuss William Shakespeare's life

37. (A) Shakespeare may not have been the actual writer.
    (B) The ceiling of the theater is leaking.
    (C) The comedy is not very funny.
    (D) The film has been misplaced.

38. (A) John F. Kennedy
    (B) William Shakespeare
    (C) Queen Victoria
    (D) Madonna

39. (A) humorous
    (B) tragic
    (C) sad
    (D) dark

40. (A) a class in stilt walking
    (B) a stilt walking performance
    (C) a formal dance
    (D) a trip to Kenya

41. (A) a dance club
    (B) a student arts committee
    (C) a group of professors
    (D) a sports team

42. (A) Sunday
    (B) Tuesday
    (C) Friday
    (D) Saturday

43. (A) tax reform
    (B) judges' pensions
    (C) electing a political candidate
    (D) electing a judge

44. (A) The program needs to be changed.
    (B) The laws are working well.
    (C) There should be a new governor.
    (D) There should be less spending in education.

45. (A) 20 percent of his or her salary
    (B) 30 percent of his or her salary
    (C) 50 percent of his or her salary
    (D) 60 percent of his or her salary

46. (A) vote for her candidate
    (B) call their state representatives
    (C) march in protest of the governor
    (D) not listen to other opinions

47. (A) economics of South America
    (B) Latin American history
    (C) United States history
    (D) political science

48. (A) the Oscar Award
    (B) the Pulitzer Prize
    (C) the Medal of Honor
    (D) the Nobel Peace Prize

49. (A) 1400s
    (B) 1700s
    (C) 1800s
    (D) 1900s

50. (A) Spanish and French
    (B) English and German
    (C) French and German
    (D) Spanish and English

THIS IS THE END OF SECTION 1.
DO NOT READ OR WORK ON ANY OTHER SECTION OF THE TEST UNTIL TIME IS UP.

STOP STOP STOP STOP STOP

SECTION 2

Structure and Written Expression

Time—25 minutes

Part 1: Sentence Completion

Directions: Questions 1–15 are not complete sentences. One or more words are left out of each sentence. Under each sentence, you will see four words or phrases, marked (A), (B), (C), and (D). Choose the one word or phrase that completes the sentence correctly. Then, on your answer sheet, find the number of the question and fill in the oval that corresponds to the letter of your answer choice.

Example I▶

Birds make nests in trees _____ hide their young in the leaves and branches.

Sample Answer

Ⓐ ● Ⓒ Ⓓ

(A) can where they
(B) where they can
(C) where can they
(D) where can

The sentence should read, "Birds make nests in trees where they can hide their young in the leaves and branches." Therefore, you should choose answer (B).

Example II▶

Sleeping, resting, and _____ are the best ways to care for a cold.

Sample Answer

Ⓐ Ⓑ Ⓒ ●

(A) to drink fluids
(B) drank fluids
(C) one drink fluids
(D) drinking fluids

The sentence should read, "Sleeping, resting, and drinking fluids are the best ways to care for a cold." Therefore, you should choose answer (D).

Now begin work on the questions.

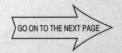

1. With new technology, cameras can take pictures of underwater valleys _____ color.
   (A) within
   (B) for
   (C) in
   (D) by

2. _____ the fifth largest among the nine planets that make up our solar system.
   (A) The Earth is
   (B) The Earth being
   (C) That the Earth is
   (D) Being the Earth

3. In mathematics, a variable is a symbol _____ some element of a set.
   (A) and representing
   (B) represents
   (C) that represents
   (D) represents that

4. _____ actress's life is in many ways unlike that of other women.
   (A) An
   (B) A
   (C) As the
   (D) That the

5. About 20 miles from Boston, _____ a little town named Concord that has a rich history.
   (A) has
   (B) there is
   (C) there are
   (D) where is

6. An advisor to both Franklin Delano Roosevelt and Harry Truman, _____ of Bethune-Cookman College.
   (A) Dr. Mary Mcleod Bethune was the founder
   (B) Dr. Mary Mcleod Bethune, who was the founder
   (C) the founder was Dr. Mary Mcleod Bethune
   (D) did the founder Dr. Mary Mcleod Bethune

7. Warmth, moisture, and oxygen are three necessary requirements _____ most seedlings.
   (A) for cultivating
   (B) for cultivate
   (C) as cultivating
   (D) can cultivate

8. In the west the birth of a girl is welcomed with an enthusiam _____ to that of a boy.
   (A) equally
   (B) equal
   (C) they are equal
   (D) and equal

9. A well-known large natural lake is Lake Tahoe, _____ straddles the California-Nevada border.
   (A) and
   (B) which
   (C) since
   (D) for

10. Before _____, they used horse-drawn wooden carts.
    (A) farmers have had tractors
    (B) tractors owned by farmers
    (C) having tractors farmers
    (D) farmers had tractors

11. Tuna, _____, may weigh up to 1,000 pounds.
    (A) is the sea giant
    (B) can be giants of the sea
    (C) one of the sea giants
    (D) the sea of the giant

12. Physical fitness exercises can cause injuries _____ the participants are not careful.
    (A) that
    (B) to
    (C) if
    (D) with

13. Total weight of all the ants in the world is much greater than _____.
    (A) to all human beings
    (B) all human beings is that
    (C) that of all human beings
    (D) is of all human beings

14. _____ for overall health.
    (A) Extra fiber in one's diet is helpful
    (B) Extra fiber is one's helpful diet
    (C) Helpful one's diet is extra fiber
    (D) One's diet is helpful in extra fiber

15. Elephants scratch themselves with sticks _____.
    (A) holding in their trunks
    (B) in their trunks holding
    (C) hold in their trunks
    (D) held in their trunks

GO ON TO THE NEXT PAGE ➤

Part 2: Error Identification

Directions: In questions 16–40 each sentence has four underlined words or phrases, marked (A), (B), (C), and (D). Choose the one word or phrase that must be changed in order for the sentence to be correct. Then, on your answer sheet find the number of the question and fill in the oval that corresponds to the letter of your answer choice.

Example I▶

Aspirin is recommend to many people for its
          A   B   C

ability to thin the blood.
      D

Sample Answer

● Ⓑ Ⓒ Ⓓ

The sentence should read, "Aspirin is recommended to many people for its ability to thin the blood." Therefore, you should choose answer (A).

Example II▶

Some people believe that human beings will never use away all
                        A   B

the natural resources on earth.
    C   D

Sample Answer

Ⓐ ● Ⓒ Ⓓ

The sentence should read, "Some people believe that humans will never use up all the natural resources on earth." Therefore, you should choose answer (B).

Now begin work on the questions.

16. In order to survive, trees rely to the amount of annual rainfall they receive, as well as the
                            A   B   C

seasonal distribution of the rain.
          D

17. The purchased of Louisiana was one of the biggest events in the history of the United States.
          A   B   C   D

18. A future system of solid waste managements should begin with reduction in the amount of waste.
                      A   B   C   D

19. The tongue is the principle organ of taste, and is crucial for chewing, swallowed, and speaking.
                        A   B   C   D

20. The members of both the House of Representatives and the Senate are election by the citizens of the
              A   B   C   D

United States.

21. The human ear cannot hear a sound that vibrates less than 16 times the second.
                  A   B   C   D

22. Some tree frogs can alter their colors in order to blend to their environment.
          A   B   C   D

23. If one is invited out to a dinner, it is perfectly proper to go either with or without no a gift.
              A   B   C   D

24. Some birds, such as quails, can move instant from a resting position to full flight.
                                          A   B   C   D

25. In 1961 America's first manned spacecraft launched.
    A   B   C   D

GO ON TO THE NEXT PAGE

26. Geochemistry includes the study of the movement of elements from one place to another as a result
    <u>A</u>   <u>B</u>   <u>C</u>

    of processes chemical.
    <u>D</u>

27. Fireflies product light through a complex chemical reaction that takes place within their abdominal
    <u>A</u>   <u>B</u>   <u>C</u>   <u>D</u>

    cells.

28. Wind is the motion that occurs when lighter air rises and cools heavier air replaces it.
    <u>A</u>   <u>B</u>   <u>C</u>   <u>D</u>

29. Under the crust of the Earth are bubbling hot liquids that sometime rise to the surface.
    <u>A</u>   <u>B</u>   <u>C</u>   <u>D</u>

30. Oceans of the world exerts strong influences on the weather over the Earth's surface.
    <u>A</u>   <u>B</u>   <u>C</u>   <u>D</u>

31. The Columbine flower can survive in almost any type of gardens condition in the United States.
    <u>A</u>   <u>B</u>   <u>C</u>   <u>D</u>

32. Kiwi birds search the ground with the bills for insects, worms, and snails to eat.
    <u>A</u>   <u>B</u>   <u>C</u>   <u>D</u>

33. If protect, a solar cell lasts for a long time and is a good source of energy.
    <u>A</u>   <u>B</u>   <u>C</u>   <u>D</u>

34. The growth rate of the Pacific Rim countries is five times fast as comparable areas during the Industrial
    <u>A</u>   <u>B</u>   <u>C</u>   <u>D</u>

    Revolution.

35. Drug abuse have become one of America's most serious social problems.
    <u>A</u>   <u>B</u>   <u>C</u>   <u>D</u>

36. The Commitments of Traders Report is released by the Commodity Futures Trading Commission
    <u>A</u>

    on eleventh day of each month.
    <u>B</u>   <u>C</u>   <u>D</u>

37. Heartburn can best be understood as a symptom causing by acid reflux due to a weak lower
    <u>A</u>   <u>B</u>   <u>C</u>   <u>D</u>

    esophageal sphincter.

38. In 1903, when the Wright brothers announced they had invented a flying machine, his news was
    <u>A</u>   <u>B</u>   <u>C</u>

    generally ignored.
    <u>D</u>

39. Lasers are indispensable tools for delicate eyes surgery.
    <u>A</u>   <u>B</u> <u>C</u>   <u>D</u>

40. Alexander Calder, who was originally interested in mechanical engineering, later became a sculpture.
    <u>A</u>   <u>B</u>   <u>C</u>   <u>D</u>

THIS IS THE END OF SECTION 2.
DO NOT READ OR WORK ON ANY OTHER SECTION OF THE TEST UNTIL TIME IS UP.
STOP   STOP   STOP   STOP   STOP

SECTION 3
Reading Comprehension

Time—55 minutes

Directions: In this section you will read several passages. Each passage is followed by questions about it. Choose the one best answer, (A), (B), (C), or (D), for each question. Then, on your answer sheet, find the number of the question and fill in the oval that corresponds to the letter of your answer choice. Answer all questions based on what is stated or implied in the passage.

Read the following passage:

A new hearing device is now available for some hearing-impaired people. This device uses a magnet to hold the detachable sound-processing portion in place. Like other aids, it converts sound into vibrations. But it is unique in that it can transmit the vibrations directly to the magnet, and then to the inner ear. This produces a clearer sound. The new device will not help all hearing-impaired people, only those with a hearing loss caused by infection or some other problem in the middle ear. It will probably help no more than 20 percent of all people with hearing problems. Those people, however, who have persistent ear infections should find relief and restored hearing with the new device.

◀Example I▶

What is the author's main purpose?

(A) to describe a new cure for ear infections
(B) to inform the reader of a new device
(C) to urge doctors to use a new device
(D) to explain the use of a magnet

Sample Answer

Ⓐ ● Ⓒ Ⓓ

The author's main purpose is to inform the reader of a new device for hearing-impaired people. Therefore, you should choose answer (B).

◀Example II▶

The word "relief" in the last sentence means

(A) less distress
(B) assistance
(C) distraction
(D) relaxation

Sample Answer

● Ⓑ Ⓒ Ⓓ

The phrase "less distress" is similar in meaning to "relief" in this sentence. Therefore, you should choose answer (A).

Now begin with the questions.

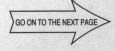 GO ON TO THE NEXT PAGE

Questions 1 to 12 are based on the following passage:

(1)   Surrealism was a movement in graphic art and literature that was founded in Paris, in 1924, by André Breton. Inspired by another movement in art called Dadaism, the Surrealist movement has been one of the most influential art movements in the 20th century. It eventually had a worldwide audience, flourishing notably in the United States during World War II. Surrealism focused on the role of the

(5)   unconscious in the creative process. In a nihilistic protest, it rejected all aspects of Western culture. Surrealist writers, such as Aragon and Soupalt, believed in directly transcribing onto paper anything their unconscious mind wished them to. They never altered or revised what they wrote because that would have interfered with the purity of their creation. Surrealist painters, a group that included such famous names as Miro, Dali, and Ernst, displayed a wide variety of style and content. Though Breton was the founder

(10)   of this movement, his strong leadership style brought about dissent, which resulted in several of the painters officially breaking away from the movement.

1. With what topic is this passage primarily concerned?
   (A) influential painters such as Miro, Dali, and Ernst
   (B) the Surrealist movement in graphic art and literature
   (C) nihilism as an aspect of the Surrealist movement
   (D) André Breton's leadership style

2. As used in line 1, which of the following is the closest in meaning to the phrase "a movement"?
   (A) a trend
   (B) an action
   (C) an exercise
   (D) a gesture

3. Which of the following is closest in meaning to the word "inspired" in line 2?
   (A) excited
   (B) influenced
   (C) stifled
   (D) created

4. Why does the author mention Dadaism?
   (A) to demonstrate the importance of Surrealism
   (B) to give background information about Surrealism
   (C) to show the lack of influence of Dadaism
   (D) to infer that André Breton rejected Dadaism

5. What does "it" refer to in line 5?
   (A) a protest
   (B) the unconscious
   (C) Surrealism
   (D) the creative process

6. The word "altered" in line 7 means
   (A) changed
   (B) forgot
   (C) believed
   (D) allowed

7. Which of the following is closest to the meaning of "purity" in line 8?
   (A) integrity
   (B) fragility
   (C) dignity
   (D) simplicity

8. According to the passage, all of the following are true of Surrealism EXCEPT?
   (A) Surrealism was influenced by Dadaism.
   (B) Surrealists believed that the unconscious played an important role in the creative process.
   (C) Some Surrealist painters quit the official movement because of André Breton.
   (D) Surrealism embraced Western culture.

9. The word "displayed" in line 9 is closest in meaning to which of the following?
   (A) neglected
   (B) replaced
   (C) exhibited
   (D) condemned

 GO ON TO THE NEXT PAGE

10. The word "dissent" in line 10 is closest in meaning to which of the following?
    (A) disagreement
    (B) distress
    (C) distraction
    (D) discouragement

11. The phrase "breaking away" in line 11 means
    (A) escaping
    (B) separating
    (C) defecting
    (D) passing

12. Which of the following statements is best supported by this passage?
    (A) André Breton founded art and literature in Paris.
    (B) André Breton rejected Dadaism because of Nihilism.
    (C) André Breton supported Miro in his painting.
    (D) André Breton was a vital part of the Surrealist movement.

GO ON TO THE NEXT PAGE

Questions 13 to 24 are based on the following passage:

(1)   Footracing is a popular activity in the United States. It is seen not only as a competitive sport but also as a way to exercise, to enjoy the cameraderie of like-minded people, and to donate money to a good cause. Though serious runners may spend months training to compete, other runners and walkers might not train at all. Those not competing to win might run in an effort to beat their own time or simply to enjoy the fun

(5)   and exercise. People of all ages, from those of less than one year (who may be pushed in strollers) to those in their eighties, enter into this sport. The races are held on city streets, on college campuses, through parks, and in suburban areas, and they are commonly 5 to 10 kilometers in length.

        The largest footrace in the world is the 12-kilometer Bay to Breakers race that is held in San Francisco every spring. This race begins on the east side of the city near San Francisco Bay and ends on

(10) the west side at the Pacific Ocean. There may be 80,000 or more people running in this race through the streets and hills of San Francisco. In the front are the serious runners who compete to win and who might finish in as little as 34 minutes. Behind them are the thousands who take several hours to finish. In the back of the race are those who dress in costumes and come just for fun. One year there was a group of men who dressed like Elvis Presley, and another group consisted of firefighters who were tied together

(15) in a long line and who were carrying a firehose. There was even a bridal party, in which the bride was dressed in a long white gown and the groom wore a tuxedo. The bride and groom threw flowers to bystanders, and they were actually married at some point along the route.

13. The main purpose of this passage is to
    (A) encourage people to exercise
    (B) describe a popular activity
    (C) make fun of runners in costume
    (D) give reasons for the popularity of footraces

14. As used in line 1, the word "activity" is most similar to which of the following?
    (A) pursuit
    (B) motion
    (C) pilgrimage
    (D) expectation

15. The word "cameraderie" as used in line 2 could be best replaced by which of the following?
    (A) games
    (B) companionship
    (C) jokes
    (D) views

16. The phrase "to a good cause" in line 2 could be best replaced by which of the following?
    (A) for an award
    (B) to reward the winner
    (C) for a good purpose
    (D) to protect a wise investment

17. Which of the following is NOT implied by the author?
    (A) Footraces appeal to a variety of people.
    (B) Walkers can compete for prizes.
    (C) Entering a race is a way to give support to an organization.
    (D) Running is a good way to strengthen the heart.

18. The word "beat" as used in line 4 could be best replaced by which of the following?
    (A) incline
    (B) overturn
    (C) outdo
    (D) undermine

19. As used in line 5, the word "strollers" refers to
    (A) cribs
    (B) wheelchairs
    (C) wagons
    (D) carriages

20. In what lines does the author give reasons for why people enter footraces?
    (A) lines 1–5
    (B) lines 6–9
    (C) lines 10–13
    (D) lines 13–15

GO ON TO THE NEXT PAGE

21. The word "costumes" as used in line 13 most likely refers to
    (A) outfits
    (B) uniforms
    (C) cloaks
    (D) suits

22. Which of the following is NOT mentioned in this passage?
    (A) Some runners looked like Elvis Presley.
    (B) Some runners were ready to put out a fire.
    (C) Some runners were participating in a wedding.
    (D) Some runners were serious about winning.

23. A "bystander" as used in line 17 refers to which of the following?
    (A) a walker
    (B) a participant
    (C) a spectator
    (D) a judge

24. Which of the following best describes the organization of this passage?
    (A) chronological order
    (B) specific to general
    (C) cause and result
    (D) statement and example

GO ON TO THE NEXT PAGE

Questions 25 to 36 are based on the following passage:

(1)   May 7, 1840, was the birthday of one of the most famous Russian composers of the nineteenth century: Peter Illich Tchaikovsky. The son of a mining inspector, Tchaikovsky studied music as a child and later studied composition at the St. Petersburg Conservatory. His greatest period of productivity occurred between 1876 and 1890, during which time he enjoyed the patronage of Madame von Meck, a woman

(5)   he never met, who gave him a living stipend of about $1,000.00 a year. Madame von Meck later terminated her friendship with Tchaikovsky, as well as his living allowance, when she, herself, was facing financial difficulties. It was during the time of Madame von Meck's patronage, however, that Tchaikovsky created the music for which he is most famous, including the music for the ballets of *Swan Lake* and *The Sleeping Beauty*. Tchaikovsky's music, well known for its rich melodic and sometimes melancholy passages, was

(10)   one of the first that brought serious dramatic music to dance. Before this, little attention had been given to the music behind the dance. Tchaikovsky died on November 6, 1893, ostensibly of cholera, though there are now some scholars who argue that he committed suicide.

25. With what topic is the passage primarily concerned?
    (A) the life and music of Tchaikovsky
    (B) development of Tchaikovsky's music for ballets
    (C) Tchaikovsky's relationship with Madame Von Meck
    (D) the cause of Tchaikovsky's death

26. Tchaikovsky's father was most probably
    (A) a musician
    (B) a supervisor
    (C) a composer
    (D) a soldier

27. Which of the following is closest in meaning to the word "productivity" in line 3?
    (A) fertility
    (B) affinity
    (C) creativity
    (D) maturity

28. In line 4, the phrase "enjoyed the patronage of" probably means
    (A) liked the company of
    (B) was mentally attached to
    (C) solicited the advice of
    (D) was financially dependent upon

29. Which of the following could best replace the word "terminated" in line 5?
    (A) discontinued
    (B) resolved
    (C) exploited
    (D) hated

30. According to the passage, all of the following describe Madame von Meck EXCEPT:
    (A) She had economic troubles.
    (B) She was generous.
    (C) She was never introduced to Tchaikovsky.
    (D) She enjoyed Tchaikovsky's music.

31. Where in the passage does the author mention Tchaikovsky's influence on dance?
    (A) lines 1–3
    (B) lines 5–7
    (C) lines 7–9
    (D) lines 9–12

32. According to the passage, for what is Tchaikovsky's music most well known?
    (A) its repetitive and monotonous tones
    (B) the ballet-like quality of the music
    (C) the richness and melodic drama of the music
    (D) its lively, capricious melodies

33. According to the passage, *Swan Lake* and *The Sleeping Beauty* are
    (A) dances
    (B) songs
    (C) operas
    (D) plays

34. Which of the following is NOT mentioned in the passage?
    (A) Tchaikovsky's influence on ballet music
    (B) Tchaikovsky's unhappiness leading to suicide
    (C) the patronage of Madame von Meck
    (D) Tchaikovsky's productivity in composing

35. Which of the following is closest in meaning to the word "behind" as used in line 11?

(A) supporting

(B) in back of

(C) going beyond

(D) concealing

36. In line 11, the word "ostensibly" could be best replaced by

(A) regretfully

(B) assuredly

(C) tragically

(D) apparently

GO ON TO THE NEXT PAGE

Questions 37 to 48 are based on the following passage:

(1)   Since the world has become industrialized, there has been an increase in the number of animal species that have either become extinct or have neared extinction. Bengal tigers, for instance, which once roamed the jungles in vast numbers, now number only about 2,300, and by the year 2025 their population is estimated to be down to zero. What is alarming about the case of the Bengal tiger is that this extinction

(5)   will have been caused almost entirely by poachers who, according to some sources, are not interested in material gain but in personal gratification. This is an example of the callousness that is part of what is causing the problem of extinction. Animals like the Bengal tiger, as well as other endangered species, are a valuable part of the world's ecosystem. International laws protecting these animals must be enacted to ensure their survival, and the survival of our planet.

(10)   Countries around the world have begun to deal with the problem in various ways. Some countries, in order to circumvent the problem, have allocated large amounts of land to animal reserves. They then charge admission to help defray the costs of maintaining the parks, and they often must also depend on world organizations for support. With the money they get, they can invest in equipment and patrols to protect the animals. Another solution that is an attempt to stem the tide of animal extinction is an

(15)   international boycott of products made from endangered species. This seems fairly effective, but it will not, by itself, prevent animals from being hunted and killed.

37. What is the main topic of the passage?
    (A) the Bengal tiger
    (B) international boycotts
    (C) endangered species
    (D) problems with industrialization

38. Which of the following is closest in meaning to the word "alarming" in line 4?
    (A) dangerous
    (B) serious
    (C) gripping
    (D) distressing

39. Which of the following could best replace the word "case" as used in line 4?
    (A) act
    (B) situation
    (C) contrast
    (D) trade

40. The word "poachers" as used in line 5 could be best replaced by which of the following?
    (A) illegal hunters
    (B) enterprising researchers
    (C) concerned scientists
    (D) trained hunters

41. The word "callousness" in line 6 could best be replaced by which of the following?
    (A) indirectness
    (B) independence
    (C) incompetence
    (D) insensitivity

42. The above passage is divided into two paragraphs in order to contrast
    (A) a problem and a solution
    (B) a statement and an illustration
    (C) a comparison and a contrast
    (D) specific and general information

43. What does the word "this" refer to in line 6?
    (A) endangered species that are increasing
    (B) Bengal tigers that are decreasing
    (C) poachers who seek personal gratification
    (D) sources that may not be accurate

44. Where in the passage does the author discuss a cause of extinction?
    (A) lines 1–3
    (B) lines 4–6
    (C) lines 10–12
    (D) lines 13–15

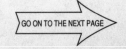GO ON TO THE NEXT PAGE

45. Which of the following could best replace the word "allocated" in line 11?
(A) set aside
(B) combined
(C) organized
(D) taken off

46. The word "defray" in line 12 is closest in meaning to which of the following?
(A) lower
(B) raise
(C) make a payment on
(D) make an investment toward

47. The author uses the phrase "stem the tide" in line 14 to mean
(A) touch
(B) stop
(C) tax
(D) save

48. Which of the following best describes the author's attitude?
(A) forgiving
(B) concerned
(C) vindictive
(D) surprised

GO ON TO THE NEXT PAGE

Questions 49 to 60 are based on the following passage:

(1)   A balanced diet contains proteins, which are composed of complex amino acids. There are 20 types of amino acids, comprising about 16 percent of the body weight in a lean individual. A body needs all 20 to be healthy. Amino acids can be divided into two groups: essential and nonessential. There are 9 essential amino acids. These are the proteins that the body cannot produce by itself, so a healthy individual

(5)   must ingest them. The 11 nonessential amino acids, on the other hand, are produced by the body, so it is not necessary to ingest them. Proteins are described as being either high-quality or low-quality, depending on how many of the 9 essential amino acids the food contains. High-quality proteins, typically found in animal meats, are proteins that have ample amounts of the essential amino acids. Low-quality proteins are mainly plant proteins and usually lack one or more of the essential amino acids. Since people

(10)   who follow a strict vegetarian diet are ingesting only low-quality proteins, they must make sure that their diets contain a variety of proteins, in order to ensure that what is lacking in one food is available in another. This process of selecting a variety of the essential proteins is called protein complementation. Since an insufficient amount of protein in the diet can be crippling, and prolonged absence of proteins can cause death, it is imperative that a vegetarian diet contains an ample amount of the essential proteins.

49. With what topic is this passage primarily concerned?
    (A) the 20 types of amino acids
    (B) high- and low-quality proteins
    (C) the process of complementation
    (D) healthy diets for vegetarians

50. The word "lean" in line 2 could be best replaced by
    (A) thin
    (B) fat
    (C) tall
    (D) short

51. The word "ingest" in line 5 is closest in meaning to which of the following?
    (A) chew
    (B) swallow
    (C) suck
    (D) drink

52. The word "ample" in line 8 is closest in meaning to which of the following?
    (A) meager
    (B) frequent
    (C) substantial
    (D) harmful

53. Which of the following would NOT be an example of a low-quality protein?
    (A) legumes
    (B) apples
    (C) grains
    (D) tuna

54. As used in line 10, which of the following words is closest in meaning to "strict"?
    (A) responsible
    (B) casual
    (C) harmonious
    (D) rigid

55. According to the passage, a vegetarian could die from insufficient protein ingestion if he or she
    (A) did not follow a varied and properly protein-complemented diet.
    (B) ate too many animal proteins, and could not digest them properly.
    (C) did not follow a diet in which nonessential proteins were ingested.
    (D) ate too many low-quality proteins.

56. Which of the following is closest in meaning to the word "crippling" as used in line 13?
    (A) discouraging
    (B) betraying
    (C) incapacitating
    (D) amazing

57. Which of the following words could best replace the word "prolonged" in line 13?
    (A) narrow
    (B) hollow
    (C) hard-hearted
    (D) extended

GO ON TO THE NEXT PAGE

58. In line 14, the word "imperative" can be best replaced by
(A) crucial
(B) impossible
(C) wonderful
(D) satisfying

59. Which of the following best describes the author's tone in this passage?
(A) forceful
(B) light
(C) casual
(D) argumentative

60. Which statement best describes the organization of this passage?
(A) Contrasting views concerning proteins are compared.
(B) The author moves from a general comment to a specific argument.
(C) A statement is given and its cause is then discussed.
(D) Items are discussed in their order of importance.

THIS IS THE END OF TEST 2

Practice Test 2
Answer Key

Section 1: Listening Comprehension

Part A

1. D	5. B	9. D	13. B	17. A
2. B	6. A	10. B	14. C	18. A
3. A	7. A	11. D	15. D	19. D
4. A	8. A	12. C	16. D	20. B

Part B

21. A	24. A	27. C	30. A	33. C
22. D	25. C	28. A	31. C	34. A
23. C	26. D	29. D	32. C	35. A

Part C

36. B	39. A	42. D	45. C	48. D
37. B	40. A	43. B	46. B	49. B
38. B	41. A	44. A	47. B	50. D

Section 2: Structure and Written Expression

Part 1: Sentence Completion

1. C	4. A	7. A	10. D	13. C
2. A	5. B	8. B	11. C	14. A
3. C	6. A	9. B	12. C	15. D

Part 2: Error Identification

16. A	21. D	26. D	31. D	36. B
17. A	22. D	27. A	32. B	37. B
18. B	23. D	28. C	33. A	38. C
19. D	24. A	29. C	34. B	39. D
20. C	25. D	30. A	35. A	40. D

Section 3: Reading Comprehension

1. B	13. B	25. A	37. C	49. D
2. A	14. A	26. B	38. D	50. A
3. B	15. B	27. C	39. B	51. B
4. B	16. C	28. D	40. A	52. C
5. C	17. D	29. A	41. D	53. D
6. A	18. C	30. D	42. A	54. D
7. A	19. D	31. D	43. C	55. A
8. D	20. A	32. C	44. B	56. C
9. C	21. A	33. A	45. A	57. D
10. A	22. B	34. B	46. C	58. A
11. B	23. C	35. A	47. B	59. A
12. D	24. D	36. D	48. B	60. B

Practice Test 2
Explanatory Answers

SECTION 1

Listening Comprehension

Part A

1.   Man: These gloves look good as a gift for my nephew, but I don't know if they will fit.
   Woman: Look, it says one size fits all.

What does the woman mean?
(A) The salesperson says they will fit.
(B) His nephew already has a pair of gloves.
(C) Only one size will fit.
(D) The gloves are all the same size.

(D) The phrase "one size fits all" means that there is only one size of some article of clothing, and it is supposed to fit all people.

2.   Man: Oh no, I can't use the computer to test my experiment; I'll never get my paper finished in time.
   Woman: Why don't you begin with the library research part?

What does the woman suggest the man do?
(A) Test the new computer.
(B) Start writing another section of the paper.
(C) Go to another lab.
(D) Change his project.

(B) The woman is suggesting that the man begins the part of the paper that he can do in the library since he cannot do the part for which he needs a computer.

3.   Woman: Come on, what are we waiting for?
   Man: I can't start until you put your seat belt on.

What does the man mean?
(A) She needs to buckle her safety belt.
(B) The safety belt is in the back seat.
(C) He is waiting for somebody to arrive.
(D) The car has no seat belts.

(A) The words "seat belt" and "safety belt" refer to the same thing. The two speakers are in a car, and the man will not begin driving until the woman puts on her seat belt.

4.   Woman: Oh, this line is for tickets to the wrong show.
   Man: We'd better move to the other line.

What are the people going to do?
(A) Change lines.
(B) Go to another theater.
(C) Follow the map.
(D) Go back home.

(A) The two speakers are waiting in a line for tickets, but there is more than one line and they are waiting in the wrong line. The man suggests that they move to a different line.

5.   Man: I was really worried about doing well at my presentation this afternoon.
   Woman: But it turned out well, didn't it?

What does the woman mean?
(A) A good presentation needs a lot of preparation.
(B) The presentation was very good.
(C) He can always turn to her for help.
(D) He should get some sleep.

(B) The woman is reassuring the man that his presentation went well, even though he was worried. The phrase "turned out well" means the same as "was very good."

6.   Woman: Dan, how would you like your egg cooked?
   Man: Medium, please.

What is the woman probably going to do?
(A) Cook an egg for Dan.
(B) Go buy some eggs.
(C) Plan food for Dan's dinner.
(D) Eat eggs.

(A) We can assume that the woman is going to cook an egg for Dan since she asks him how he would like it cooked.

7.   Woman: I'm glad I called to check on the time for picking Sue up.
      Man: Was the plane delayed again?

What does the man imply about Sue?
(A) She is on a plane.
(B) She needs to be picked up at school.
(C) She is often late.
(D) She has been delayed at work.

(A) We can assume that Sue is on a plane since the woman is going to pick her up, and the man mentions an airplane being delayed.

8.   Woman: Do you know Jack?
      Man: Yes, I do; in fact he's my cousin.

What does the man mean?
(A) His cousin's name is Jack.
(B) Jack is coming to see him.
(C) His cousin knows Jack very well.
(D) Jack doesn't know the woman.

(A) The man says that Jack is his cousin.

9.   Man: I can't stand living in this place anymore.
      Woman: Well, why don't you move then?

What does the woman suggest the man do?
(A) Stand still.
(B) Get some exercise.
(C) Sit down.
(D) Change his residence.

(D) The phrase "can't stand [something]" means "dislike very much." The verb "to move" in this sentence means to move to a new place to live.

10.   Woman: It's really rocky here.
      Man: Yes, watch your step so you don't trip.

What does the man mean?
(A) He doesn't want the woman to go away on a trip.
(B) He is cautioning the woman to be careful.
(C) He is guiding the woman step by step.
(D) He wants to borrow the woman's watch.

(B) The phrase "watch your step" means "be careful." The verb "to trip" means to stumble and fall. Answer (C) is close, but we cannot be sure that the man is guiding every one of her steps. Therefore, (B) is a better answer.

11.   Woman: I have so much to do!
      Man: Take it easy, school doesn't start until next week.

What does the man mean?
(A) School begins later this year.
(B) School will be easy this year.
(C) She'd better start her work early.
(D) He wants her to relax.

(D) The phrase "take it easy" means "relax."

12.   Man: I feel like taking a walk; it's so nice outside.
      Woman: Great, let's walk around the lake in the park.

What does the woman mean?
(A) Since the weather is nice, she wants to go boating.
(B) She thinks the park is too far away.
(C) She suggests they go to the park.
(D) She's not a very fast walker.

(C) The word "let's" refers to a suggestion to do something, so "let's walk . . . " is a suggestion to go for a walk. In this conversation she suggests a walk around a lake in the park.

13.   Woman: I happened to find the book you were looking for when I was in the book store.
      Man: Oh, which one?

What does the man mean?
(A) How much will the book cost?
(B) Which book store did she go to?
(C) Whom did she talk to?
(D) What library has the book he needs?

(B) In a conversation like this, the question word "which" usually refers to the most recent noun. In this case the closest noun is "book store."

14.   Man: Is that it for today?
      Woman: That's it.

What does the woman mean?
(A) It has been a good day.
(B) That's the place we're going.
(C) We've finished our day's work.
(D) The store is closed for the day.

(C) The phrase "that's it" means "that is all" or "I am finished."

15.   Man: Here's our telephone bill.

   Woman: Good, why don't you figure out your calls, and I'll pay the rest.

What does the woman mean?
(A) She owes money to the landlord.
(B) She is checking out Bill's telephone number.
(C) She wants to take a rest.
(D) She will pay her portion of the telephone bill.

(D) The woman says that she will pay the rest of the bill so we can infer that the two people are sharing one telephone. The bill gives a list of the calls made by each person, so after the man figures out how much his phone calls are, the rest of the bill will be the woman's share.

16.   Man: Can I eat one of these bananas?
   Woman: They're not ready to eat yet.

What does the woman mean?
(A) These bananas are on sale and ready to eat.
(B) These are the best bananas in the state.
(C) These bananas are already overripe.
(D) These bananas are not ripe.

(D) If the fruit is not yet ready to eat, it must not be ripe. Answer (C) is incorrect because the word "yet" means that the bananas will be ready to eat soon, and "over-ripe" means that they are getting bad.

17.   Man: We were on vacation for two weeks.
   Woman: And half the time it was rainy.

What does the woman imply?
(A) She did not like all the rain.
(B) The rain is good for the crops.
(C) Part of each day was clear.
(D) She hopes the drought is over.

(A) We can infer that the woman did not like the rain, in part from her tone of voice. Answer (C) is incorrect because it is too specific. We know that half the time was rainy, but that could mean that one whole week was clear or that portions of each day were clear.

18.   Man: Kathleen, how did you like your organic chemistry class?
   Woman: The more I learned, the better it got.

What does the woman mean?
(A) She began to like it more after learning more.
(B) She will major in organic chemistry.
(C) It was hard to learn everything.
(D) She got better grades at the end of the class.

(A) Since the man is asking about whether the woman liked her class, the answer most likely also refers to how much she liked it. Answer (D) might be true, but we don't know for sure since the woman does not mention the grades she got.

19.   Man: You made a reservation for ten, right?
   Woman: I sure did.

What does the woman mean?
(A) She canceled the room.
(B) She enjoyed their trip to the reservoir.
(C) She is sure that he made the right decision.
(D) She reserved a table in a restaurant.

(D) The woman responds that she did make a reservation. We can infer that this is for dinner at a restaurant. It could also possibly refer to a hotel, but this is not one of the answer choices.

20.   Man: Penny's still going to Smith College, isn't she?
   Woman: No, she tranferred to Yale.

What do they say about Penny?
(A) Penny goes to Smith College.
(B) Penny stopped going to Smith College.
(C) Penny has just begun school at Smith College.
(D) Penny likes Smith College the best.

(B) "To transfer" means to move from one place to another, or one thing to another. Penny was at Smith, but now is at Yale. She does not go to Smith College anymore.

Part B

21. What is this conversation mainly about?
- (A) teaching English classes
- (B) summer vacation
- (C) other teachers
- (D) students in history classes

(A) This is a main idea question. Both speakers talk at length about their enjoyment in teaching English classes.

22. How many classes does the man say he is teaching?
- (A) two
- (B) three
- (C) four
- (D) five

(D) This is a restatement question. The man says he is teaching five classes.

23. What subject does the man teach now?
- (A) English
- (B) economics
- (C) history
- (D) computer science

(C) This is a restatement question. The speaker comments that he teaches history classes.

24. What time of day is this conversation taking place?
- (A) morning
- (B) afternoon
- (C) evening
- (D) late night

(A) This is an inference question. Since the two speakers are ordering breakfast, they are most likely eating in the morning.

25. What is the name of the restaurant?
- (A) Carolina Tradition
- (B) Carolina Bakery
- (C) Carolina Coffee Shop
- (D) Carolina Basketball

(C) This is a restatement question. The name of the restaurant is stated by the man who describes it as a traditional place attended by visitors to the university.

26. What does the man recommend the woman get?
- (A) eggs and bacon
- (B) cereal
- (C) fresh fruit
- (D) French toast

(D) This is a restatement question. The man describes how the French toast is made and the woman speaker decides to order it.

27. About how long has the restaurant been open?
- (A) 6 days
- (B) 10 years
- (C) 60 years
- (D) 100 years

(C) This is a restatement question. The man says that the restaurant has been operating for about sixty years.

28. How are the two speakers traveling?
- (A) by car
- (B) by train
- (C) by plane
- (D) by boat

(A) This is an inference question. There are several clues to infer that they are traveling by car, such as stopping at a "gas station," "road signs," and "highway signs."

29. What is the destination of the two travelers?
- (A) Los Angeles
- (B) San Jose
- (C) Sacramento
- (D) San Francisco

(D) This is a restatement question. The man first asks if there are any signs for San Francisco.

30. What are the man and woman mainly concerned about?
- (A) that they may have taken a wrong road
- (B) that they cannot find a gas station
- (C) that it is getting dark
- (D) that there is no service attendant

(A) The main topic of conversation is about being lost. We can assume that they may have taken a wrong road and are lost.

31. Why are the speakers going to the gas station?
- (A) to use the bathroom
- (B) to rest
- (C) to ask directions
- (D) to get fuel

(C) This is a restatement question. Because the two speakers are lost, they decide to go to a gas station to ask for directions.

32. Where is this conversation taking place?
  (A) in a classroom
  (B) in a bedroom
  (C) in a pool
  (D) on a baseball field

(C) This is an inference question. Since the speakers are talking about swimming, it is inferred that they are in a pool.

33. How many laps had the man completed by 6 A.M.?
  (A) 6
  (B) 10
  (C) 50
  (D) 60

(C) This is a restatement question. The man speaker says that he swam 50 laps before 6 A.M.

34. Where will the speakers probably go after they meet outside the locker rooms?
  (A) to eat breakfast
  (B) to eat dinner
  (C) to go to class
  (D) to see a movie

(A) This is a restatement question. They discuss their plans to have breakfast together.

35. What time of day is the conversation taking place?
  (A) morning
  (B) evening
  (C) midnight
  (D) noon

(A) This is an inference question. Since the two speakers discuss breakfast and the times six o'clock and five o'clock are mentioned, it can be inferred that the time of day is morning.

Part C

36. What is the purpose of the announcement?
    (A) to advertise a new film *To Be or Not to Be?*
    (B) to inform people that a film will not be shown
    (C) to critique the characters in *To Be or Not to Be?*
    (D) to discuss William Shakespeare's life

(B) This is a main idea question. Although the announcer describes the movie, the main purpose of the announcement is to inform people of the canceled showings.

37. What is the problem?
    (A) Shakespeare may not have been the actual writer.
    (B) The ceiling of the theater is leaking.
    (C) The comedy is not very funny.
    (D) The film has been misplaced.

(B) This is a restatement question. The announcer begins by saying that the movie is canceled because of a leak in the ceiling.

38. What famous person is the subject of *To Be or Not to Be?*
    (A) John F. Kennedy
    (B) William Shakespeare
    (C) Queen Victoria
    (D) Madonna

(B) This is a restatement question. Only Shakespeare is mentioned in this talk.

39. How could *To Be or Not to Be?* best be described?
    (A) humorous
    (B) tragic
    (C) sad
    (D) dark

(A) This is an inference question. The announcer describes the movie to be mostly a comedy, which is a humorous form of theater and movies.

40. What is the main topic of this announcement?
    (A) a class in stilt walking
    (B) a stilt walking performance
    (C) a formal dance
    (D) a trip to Kenya

(A) This is a main idea question. The announcement is for a class.

41. What organization is offering the event?
    (A) a dance club
    (B) a student arts committee
    (C) a group of professors
    (D) a sports team

(A) This is a restatement question. The speaker begins by announcing that the class is offered by the university dance club.

42. On what day of the week is the event to be held?
    (A) Sunday
    (B) Tuesday
    (C) Friday
    (D) Saturday

(D) This is a restatement question. The speaker mentions several times that the classes will be held on Saturdays.

43. What issue is the speaker talking about?
    (A) tax reform
    (B) judges' pensions
    (C) electing a political candidate
    (D) electing a judge

(B) This is a main idea question. The speech is about the Judicial Retirement System.

44. What is the speaker's opinion?
    (A) The program needs to be changed.
    (B) The laws are working well.
    (C) There should be a new governor.
    (D) There should be less spending in education.

(A) This is an inference question. The speaker does not think it is right that the judges are not paying as much for their benefits as other employees do. Based on this knowledge, the most likely answer is that the program needs to be changed.

45. According to the speaker, how much money can a judge get when he or she retires?
    (A) 20 percent of his or her salary
    (B) 30 percent of his or her salary
    (C) 50 percent of his or her salary
    (D) 60 percent of his or her salary

(C) This is a restatement question. The speaker says that the judge over 60 years old can receive fifty percent of his or her salary at retirement.

46. What does the speaker urge listeners to do?
    (A) vote for her candidate
    (B) call their state representatives
    (C) march in protest of the governor
    (D) not listen to other opinions

(B) This is a restatement question. At the end of the speech the speaker urges all listeners to call their state representatives.

47. In what department would this class most likely be offered?
    (A) economics of South America
    (B) Latin American history
    (C) United States history
    (D) political science

(B) This is an inference question. Since the novel is set in South America we can infer that the novel could be used in a Latin American history class.

48. What was Gabriel Garcia Márquez awarded?
    (A) the Oscar Award
    (B) the Pulitzer Prize
    (C) the Medal of Honor
    (D) the Nobel Peace Prize

(D) This is a restatement question. The speaker says that he was the winner of the Nobel Peace Prize in 1982.

49. During what period of time does the novel take place?
    (A) 1400s
    (B) 1700s
    (C) 1800s
    (D) 1900s

(B) This is a restatement question. The speaker says that the story is set in the 1700s in South America.

50. The novel is most commonly published in which two languages?
    (A) Spanish and French
    (B) English and German
    (C) French and German
    (D) Spanish and English

(D) This is a restatement question. The speaker says that these two languages are the most common for the novel.

SECTION 2

Structure and Written Expression

Part 1: Sentence Completion

1. With new technology, cameras can take pictures of underwater valleys _____ color.
   (A) within
   (B) for
   (C) in
   (D) by

(C) Preposition. The phrase "in color" describes the quality of having color in pictures.

2. _____ the fifth largest among the nine planets that make up our solar system.
   (A) The Earth is
   (B) The Earth being
   (C) That the Earth is
   (D) Being the Earth

(A) Subject + verb. The phrase begins with the main subject "The Earth," and is a statement of fact that takes a present tense verb.

3. In mathematics, a variable is a symbol _____ some element of a set.
   (A) and representing
   (B) represents
   (C) that represents
   (D) represents that

(C) Adjective clause. The clause "that represents some element . . . " describes the noun "symbol."

4. _____ actress's life is in many ways unlike that of other women.
   (A) An
   (B) A
   (C) As the
   (D) That the

(A) Article. The word "actress" must be preceded by the word "an." The word "actress" is the main noun of the sentence. "A" precedes a noun that starts with a consonant; "an" precedes a noun that starts with a vowel.

5. About 20 miles from Boston, _____ a little town named Concord that has a rich history.
   (A) has
   (B) there is
   (C) there are
   (D) where is

(B) Subject + verb. The main subject of the sentence is the singular expletive "there." (There is a little town. . . .)

6. An advisor to both Franklin Delano Roosevelt and Harry Truman, _____ of Bethune-Cookman College.
   (A) Dr. Mary Mcleod Bethune was the founder
   (B) Dr. Mary Mcleod Bethune, who was the founder
   (C) the founder was Dr. Mary Mcleod Bethune
   (D) did the founder Dr. Mary Mcleod Bethune

(A) Subject + verb. The correct answer follows the regular pattern of subject/verb. The first half of the sentence is a phrase that describes the subject, Dr. Mary Mcleod Bethune.

7. Warmth, moisture and oxygen are three necessary requirements _____ most seedlings.
   (A) for cultivating
   (B) for cultivate
   (C) as cultivating
   (D) can cultivate

(A) After the preposition "for" there must be an *-ing* form of the verb. Answer (D) is incorrect since "can cultivate" is a verb and this sentence already has a main verb.

8. In the west the birth of a girl is welcomed with an enthusiasm _____ to that of a boy.
   (A) equally
   (B) equal
   (C) they are equal
   (D) and equal

(B) Adjective. The preposition "to" follows the word "equal." Answer (A) is incorrect since it is an adverb. Answer (C) is incorrect since it makes another sentence, and answer (D) is incorrect since the word "and" does not connect two of the same parts of speech.

9. A well-known large natural lake is Lake Tahoe, _____ straddles the California-Nevada border.
   (A) and
   (B) which
   (C) since
   (D) for

(B) Preposition. The preposition "which" begins an adjective phrase that describes the position of the lake.

10. Before _____, they used horse-drawn wooden carts.
    (A) farmers have had tractors
    (B) tractors owned by farmers
    (C) having tractors farmers
    (D) farmers had tractors

(D) Verb. In this adverb clause, the verb refers to a past tense activity, so it must be past tense.

11. Tuna, _____, may weigh up to 1,000 pounds.
    (A) is the sea giant
    (B) can be giants of the sea
    (C) one of the sea giants
    (D) the sea of the giant

(C) The phrase "one of the sea giants" describes the tuna (a fish). Answer (D) does not make sense. Answers (A) and (B) are incorrect since they add a verb.

12. Physical fitness exercises can cause injuries _____ the participants are not careful.
    (A) that
    (B) to
    (C) if
    (D) with

(C) Conditional. The word "if" begins the conditional part of this sentence, "if the participants are not careful."

13. The total weight of all the ants in the world is much greater than _____.
    (A) to all human beings
    (B) all human beings is that
    (C) that of all human beings
    (D) is of all human beings

(C) Comparative. The word "that" begins the comparative phrase. "That" could be replaced by "the weight."

14. _____ for overall health.
    (A) Extra fiber in one's diet is helpful
    (B) Extra fiber is one's helpful diet
    (C) Helpful one's diet is extra fiber
    (D) One's diet is helpful in extra fiber

(A) Subject + verb. The main subject of the sentence is "fiber." The main verb is "is."

15. Elephants scratch themselves with sticks _____.
    (A) holding in their trunks
    (B) in their trunks holding
    (C) hold in their trunks
    (D) held in their trunks

(D) Adverb clause. The sentence could also be "sticks that are held in their trunks." The adverb clause "held in their trunks" describes the way the stick is held.

Part 2: Error Identification

16. In order to survive, trees rely to the amount of
<u>A</u>   <u>B</u>

annual rainfall they receive, as well as the
<u>C</u>

seasonal distribution of the rain.
<u>D</u>

(A) Preposition. The preposition "on" follows the word "rely."

17. The <u>purchased</u> of Louisiana was <u>one</u> of the
<u>A</u>   <u>B</u>

biggest events in the <u>history</u> of the <u>United States.</u>
<u>C</u>   <u>D</u>

(A) Word form. The word "purchase" is a noun in this sentence, so it cannot end in "-ed".

18. A future system of solid waste <u>managements</u>
<u>A</u>   <u>B</u>

should begin with <u>reduction</u> in the <u>amount of</u>
<u>C</u>   <u>D</u>

waste.

(B) Singular/plural noun. The noun "management" is a mass noun, and thus does not end in "s." It refers to a group of managers collectively. This sentence refers to one system of management.

19. The tongue is the <u>principle</u> <u>organ</u> of taste, <u>and</u> <u>is</u>
<u>A</u>   <u>B</u>   <u>C</u>

crucial for chewing, <u>swallowed</u>, and speaking.
<u>D</u>

(D) Parallel construction/word form. The correct word is "swallowing," which is similar in form to "chewing" and "speaking."

20. The <u>members</u> of <u>both</u> the House of Representa-
<u>A</u>   <u>B</u>

tives and the Senate are <u>election</u> by the <u>citizens</u>
<u>C</u>   <u>D</u>

of the United States.

(C) Verb. The main verb of the sentence is "to elect." In this sentence the verb is written in the passive voice; it should be "are elected."

21. The human ear <u>cannot hear</u> a sound that <u>vibrates</u>
<u>A</u>   <u>B</u>

<u>less than</u> 16 times <u>the</u> second.
<u>C</u>   <u>D</u>

(D) Article. The correct answer is "sixteen times a second." The article "a" refers to any second.

22. Some <u>tree frogs</u> can <u>alter</u> their colors <u>in order to</u>
<u>A</u>   <u>B</u>   <u>C</u>

blend <u>to</u> their environment.
<u>D</u>

(D) Preposition. The correct word is "into," which gives the meaning of two substances merging together.

23. If one is <u>invited out</u> to a dinner, it is <u>perfectly</u>
<u>A</u>   <u>B</u>

proper <u>to go</u> either with or without <u>no a</u> gift.
<u>C</u>   <u>D</u>

(D) Unnecessary word. The word "no" is not necessary since "without" implies "no." You can say "without a gift," or "with no gift."

24. Some birds, such as quails, can move <u>instant</u>
<u>A</u>

from a <u>resting</u> position <u>to</u> full <u>flight</u>.
<u>B</u>   <u>C</u>   <u>D</u>

(A) Word form. The correct answer is "instantly," an adverb that describes how the quails move.

25. In <u>1961</u> America's first <u>manned</u> <u>spacecraft</u>
<u>A</u>   <u>B</u>   <u>C</u>

<u>launched</u>.
<u>D</u>

(D) Verb. The verb in this sentence should be in the passive voice. The correct answer is "spacecraft was launched." The active form would be "Someone launched America's first manned spacecraft in 1961."

26. Geochemistry includes the study of the move-
                              A

ment of elements from one place to another
            B

as a result of processes chemical.
   C   D

(D) Reversed words. The correct answer is "as a result of chemical processes." The word "chemical" describes the type of processes.

27. Fireflies product light through a complex
             A   B

chemical reaction that takes place within
                  C

their abdominal cells.
  D

(A) Word form. The correct word is a verb, "produce," the main verb of the sentence.

28. Wind is the motion that occurs when lighter
                        A   B

air rises and cools heavier air replaces it.
            C   D

(C) Comparative. The correct answer is "cooler." The sentence is comparing and discussing air that is lighter (than other air) and air that is cooler and heavier.

29. Under the crust of the Earth are bubbling
                                 A

hot liquids that sometime rise to the surface.
   B   C   D

(C) Word form. The correct word is "sometimes," which means "on some occasions" or "occasionally." The word "sometime" means at some unspecified time in the future.

30. Oceans of the world exerts strong influences
                        A

on the weather over the Earth's surface.
  B   C   D

(A) Verb. The correct answer is "exert," a plural form of the verb that goes with the noun "oceans."

31. The Columbine flower can survive in almost
                             A   B

any type of gardens condition in the United States.
         C   D

(D) Word form. Though the word "garden" is a noun, in this sentence it is used as an adjective that describes the type of condition (a garden condition). As an adjective it cannot have a plural form.

32. Kiwi birds search the ground with the bills
              A   B

for insects, worms, and snails to eat.
   C   D

(B) Pronoun. The correct word is "their," a pronoun that indicates that the bills (beaks) belong to the birds.

33. If protect, a solar cell lasts for a long time and
       A   B   C

is a good source of energy.
            D

(A) Word form. The correct answer is "protected." The phrase could also be "if they are protected . . . ," which uses the complete form of the verb.

34. The growth rate of the Pacific Rim countries is
          A

five times fast as comparable areas during the
       B   C   D

Industrial Revolution.

(B) Omitted word. The correct answer is "five times as fast as. . . . " The word "as" needs to appear two times, once before the adjective and once after it.

35. Drug abuse have become one of America's
              A   B

most serious social problems.
   C   D

(A) Verb. The correct answer is "has," a singular verb that goes with the noun "abuse."

36. The Commitments of Traders Report is

released by the Commodity Futures Trading
‾‾‾‾‾‾‾‾‾‾‾‾‾‾‾‾‾‾‾‾‾‾‾‾‾‾‾‾‾
       A

Commission on eleventh day of each month.
            ‾‾‾‾‾‾‾‾   ‾‾‾‾‾ ‾‾‾‾‾
              B   **C**   **D**

(B) Omitted word. The correct answer is "on the eleventh day. . . ." The word "the" must be used before the word "eleventh," since "day" is singular.

37. Heartburn can best be understood as a symptom
                  ‾‾‾‾
                  A

causing by acid reflux due to a weak lower
‾‾‾‾‾‾‾   ‾‾‾   ‾‾‾‾‾‾‾‾‾
  B   **C**   **D**

esophageal sphincter.

(B) Word form. The correct answer is "caused by," which begins a phrase that describes the noun "heartburn."

38. In 1903, when the Wright brothers announced
              ‾‾‾‾
              A

they had invented a flying machine his news was
‾‾‾‾‾‾‾‾‾‾‾‾‾   ‾‾‾
     B   **C**

generally ignored.
‾‾‾‾‾‾‾‾‾
   D

(C) Pronoun. The correct answer is "their," a plural pronoun that refers to the two brothers.

39. Lasers are indispensable tools for delicate
                        ‾‾‾‾‾   ‾‾‾‾‾ ‾‾‾
                          A   **B** **C**

eyes surgery.
‾‾‾‾
  D

(D) Singular/plural noun. The correct word is "eye," a noun used as an adjective that describes the type of surgery.

40. Alexander Calder, who was originally
                              ‾‾‾‾‾‾‾‾‾
                                  A

interested in mechanical engineering, later
‾‾‾‾‾‾‾‾‾   ‾‾‾‾
   B   **C**

became a sculpture.
       ‾‾‾‾‾‾‾‾‾
          D

(D) Word form. The correct answer is "sculptor," which refers to a person. The word "sculpture" refers to an object that has been sculpted or carved.

SECTION 3
Reading Comprehension

1. With what topic is this passage primarily concerned?
   (A) influential painters such as Miro, Dali, and Ernst
   (B) the Surrealist movement in graphic art and literature
   (C) Nihilism as an aspect of the Surrealist movement
   (D) André Breton's leadership style

(B) The first sentence gives the answer to this question. It opens with "Surrealism was a movement in graphic art and literature. . . ." The paragraph then goes on to discuss Surrealism, its founder, and its followers.

2. As used in line 1, which of the following is the closest in meaning to the phrase "a movement?"
   (A) a trend
   (B) an action
   (C) an exercise
   (D) a gesture

(A) A "movement" in art means a new development or a new trend that people follow.

3. Which of the following is closest in meaning to the word "inspired" in line 2?
   (A) excited
   (B) influenced
   (C) stifled
   (D) created

(B) The words "inspire" and "influence" both mean to "stimulate." The artists were stimulated and influenced by Dadism. They may have been excited, as in answer (A), and they did create, as in answer (D), but each of these words has a different meaning. Answer (C) has the opposite meaning.

4. Why does the author mention Dadaism?
   (A) to demonstrate the importance of Surrealism
   (B) to give background information about Surrealism
   (C) to show the lack of influence of Dadaism
   (D) to infer that André Breton rejected Dadaism

(B) This is an author's purpose question. The answer can be found in part of the first sentence, ". . . the movement [Surrealism] was inspired by another movement in art called Dadaism. . . . " Dadaism directly influenced Surrealism and is therefore important background information for learning about Surrealism.

5. What does "it" refer to in line 5?
   (A) a protest
   (B) the unconscious
   (C) Surrealism
   (D) the creative process

(C) The word "it" refers to the subject of the previous sentence, "Surrealism."

6. The word "altered" in line 7 means
   (A) changed
   (B) forgot
   (C) believed
   (D) allowed

(A) "To alter" is "to change" something.

7. Which of the following is closest to the meaning of "purity" in line 8?
   (A) integrity
   (B) fragility
   (C) dignity
   (D) simplicity

(A) The words "purity" and "integrity" both refer to something being whole or untouched.

8. According to the passage, all of the following are true of Surrealism EXCEPT?
   (A) Surrealism was influenced by Dadaism.
   (B) Surrealists believed that the unconscious played an important role in the creative process.
   (C) Some Surrealist painters quit the official movement because of André Breton.
   (D) Surrealism embraced Western culture.

(D) The passage states that Surrealism rejected Western culture. This is the opposite of "embracing" Western culture. Answer (A) is mentioned in lines 2–3; answer (B) in lines 4–5; and answer (C) in lines 10–11.

9. The word "displayed" in line 9 is closest in meaning to which of the following?
   (A) neglected
   (B) replaced
   (C) exhibited
   (D) condemned

(C) The words "display" and "exhibit" both mean "to show" or "to demonstrate."

10. The word "dissent" in line 10 is closest in meaning to which of the following?
    (A) disagreement
    (B) distress
    (C) distraction
    (D) discouragement

(A) The words "dissent" and "disagreement" both mean "opposition" or "protest."

11. The phrase "breaking away" in line 11 means
    (A) escaping
    (B) separating
    (C) defecting
    (D) passing

(B) "To break away" and "to separate" both mean "to detach" oneself from another.

12. Which of the following statements is best supported by this passage?
    (A) André Breton founded art and literature in Paris.
    (B) André Breton rejected Dadaism because of Nihilism.
    (C) André Breton supported Miro in his painting.
    (D) André Breton was a vital part of the Surrealist movement.

(D) This is a support question. André Breton is mentioned several times as the leader of the Surrealist movement. In the first line he is mentioned as the founder of the movement. As the founder and leader, he was definitely an integral or vital part of the movement. Answer (A) is incorrect because André Breton did not bring all art and literature to Paris. Answer (B) is wrong because the passage does not say that Breton rejected Dadism. Answer (C) is wrong because the passage does not state this, even though it may be true.

13. The main purpose of this passage is to
    (A) encourage people to exercise
    (B) describe a popular activity
    (C) make fun of runners in costume
    (D) give reasons for the popularity of footraces

(B) The overall passage is a description of this activity. The passage is explaining the activity; it does not use words that imply that people should exercise more, nor does it give reasons for the popularity of racing. The author does mention runners in costume, and may even imply ridicule, but this is only a small part of the passage and not the main purpose.

14. As used in line 1, the word "activity" is most similar to which of the following?
    (A) pursuit
    (B) motion
    (C) pilgrimage
    (D) expectation

(A) An "activity" refers to something that a person pursues or does. The question, "What activities interest you?" means the same as "What kinds of things do you like to do?" "Activity" does not always infer motion (answer B). A "pilgrimage" (answer C) is a religious journey or a trip to a sacred place. "Expectation" (answer D) means anticipation or looking forward to something.

15. The word "cameraderie" as used in line 2 could best be replaced by which of the following?
   (A) games
   (B) companionship
   (C) jokes
   (D) views

(B) The words "cameraderie" and "companionship" both refer to fellowship, friendliness, or congeniality among people.

16. The phrase "to a good cause" in line 2 could be best replaced by which of the following?
   (A) for an award
   (B) to reward the winner
   (C) for a good purpose
   (D) to protect a wise investment

(C) The word "cause" in this sentence refers to an activity that a number of people are involved in that has the purpose of bringing about a change. For example, a group of people might work together for the cause of improving the quality of air in our environment. Answer (C) is the best answer since the word "purpose" implies an aim or intention one is working toward for the future. Answers (A) and (B) refer to prizes for the winners of the race. In answer (D) the word "investment" refers to the act of giving money to a company or business with the expectations of making a profit or receiving an income, or receiving some satisfaction. By giving money to a cause you support, you are investing money for your own satisfaction, but the investment is not the cause; the investment goes to the cause.

17. Which of the following is NOT implied by the author?
   (A) Footraces appeal to a variety of people.
   (B) Walkers can compete for prizes.
   (C) Entering a race is a way to give support to an organization.
   (D) Running is a good way to strengthen the heart.

(D) Though answer (D) may be true, it is not stated or implied in the passage. Answer (A) is implied by the examples of runners that range from fast serious runners to babies to people in costume. Answer (B) is not stated, but it is implied that anyone can win, and winning something implies receiving a prize. Some races might have prizes for walkers as well as fast runners. Answer (C) is implied in the words "donate money to a good cause."

18. The word "beat" as used in line 4 could best be replaced by which of the following?
   (A) incline
   (B) overturn
   (C) outdo
   (D) undermine

(C) If you "beat" your time in a race, it means that you have run in a shorter amount of time. You have "out done" yourself, which means "exceed" or "do better." The verb "incline" means "lean" or "slope." The verb "overturn" means to turn over or turn upside down. The verb "undermine" means to subvert or weaken something.

19. As used in line 5, the word "strollers" refers to
   (A) cribs
   (B) wheelchairs
   (C) wagons
   (D) carriages

(D) A stroller is a carriage in which a baby sits or lies, and is pushed by someone else. A crib is a special bed where a baby sleeps. A wheelchair is a chair with wheels that is used by people who have difficulty walking. A wagon is a four-wheeled vehicle used for transporting something. A small wagon may be a toy for a child, while a large wagon may be used by a farmer.

20. In what lines does the author give reasons for why people enter footraces?
   (A) lines 1–5
   (B) lines 6–9
   (C) lines 10–12
   (D) lines 13–15

(A) In the first sentences the author states that people enter races to compete, to have fun, and to donate money.

21. The word "costumes" as used in line 13 most likely refers to
   (A) outfits
   (B) uniforms
   (C) cloaks
   (D) suits

(A) The words "costumes" and "outfits" refer to clothes that people wear, often for a special occasion, and sometimes as a joke. Uniforms are similar clothes that people wear for work. "Cloaks" are capes or robes. A "suit" is a set of clothes to be worn together such as a jacket and trousers or a skirt. A suit can also be called an "outfit," but an outfit or a costume is not always a suit.

22. Which of the following is NOT mentioned in this passage?
(A) Some runners looked like Elvis Presley.
(B) Some runners were ready to put out a fire.
(C) Some runners were participating in a wedding.
(D) Some runners were serious about winning.

(B) The author states that there were some firefighters who were carrying a firehose, but it does not say that the firehose is attached to water. We cannot assume that they were ready to put out a fire.

23. A "bystander" as used in line 17 refers to which of the following?
(A) a walker
(B) a participant
(C) a spectator
(D) a judge

(C) The words "bystander" and "spectator" both refer to someone who is watching an event or an activity rather than participating in it.

24. Which of the following best describes the organization of this passage?
(A) chronological order
(B) specific to general
(C) cause and result
(D) statement and example

(D) The first paragraph is a description of footraces in general. The second paragraph gives an example of one race, the Bay to Breakers race in San Francisco.

25. With what topic is the passage primarily concerned?
(A) the life and music of Tchaikovsky
(B) development of Tchaikovsky's music for ballets
(C) Tchaikovsky's relationship with Madame Von Meck
(D) the cause of Tchaikovsky's death

(A) This is a main topic question. The passage describes Tchaikovsky from his birth to his death. Several aspects of his life are covered and so answers (B), (C), and (D) are too specific. Answer (A) includes all topics of the paragraph.

26. Tchaikovsky's father was most probably
(A) a musician
(B) a supervisor
(C) a composer
(D) a soldier

(B) This is an inference/vocabulary question. Since the passage says that Tchaikovsky's father was a mining inspector, we can best assume that he was a supervisor of the miners.

27. Which of the the following is closest in meaning to the word "productivity" in line 3?
(A) fertility
(B) affinity
(C) creativity
(D) maturity

(C) Though the words "productive" and "creative" are not always synonymous, it is the best choice of the above answers. "Being productive" in this sentence means "creating much work." Answer (A) can also mean "productive," commonly when referring to land. When referring to people, "fertility" means the ability to have many children. Answer (B) means "a liking" or "a fondness" for something. Answer (D) means "full development" or "composure."

28. In line 4, the phrase "enjoyed the patronage of" probably means
(A) liked the company of
(B) was mentally attached to
(C) solicited the advice of
(D) was financially dependent upon

(D) This is a vocabulary/inference question. A clue for the answer can be found in the next line which states the amount of money Madame von Meck gave Tchaikovsky. The line after that mentions a "living allowance." These clues refer to finances. Answer (D) is the only answer that mentions finances.

29. Which of the following could best replace the word "terminated" in line 5?
(A) discontinued
(B) resolved
(C) exploited
(D) hated

(A) The verbs "to terminate" and "to discontinue" both mean "to end." Answer (B) means to "determine" or "decide." Answer (C) means "to utilize" or "take advantage of." Answer (D) means "to dislike" or "to despise."

30. According to the passage, all of the following describe Madame von Meck EXCEPT?
    (A) She had economic troubles.
    (B) She was generous.
    (C) She was never introduced to Tchaikovsky.
    (D) She enjoyed Tchaikovsky's music.

(D) This is a negative question. Though we might assume that she enjoyed Tchaikovsky's music since she was supporting him, we are not told that in the passage. It is possible that she admired him as a person, but did not particularly enjoy his music. Choice A is mentioned in lines 6–7; choice C is mentioned in line 5. The fact that Madame von Meck gave Tchaikovsky $1000 a year proves that she was generous.

31. Where in the passage does the author mention Tchaikovsky's influence on dance?
    (A) lines 1–3
    (B) lines 5–7
    (C) lines 7–9
    (D) lines 9–12

(D) This is an organization question that asks you to identify specific lines in the passage. Lines 9–11 discuss how Tchaikovsky's ballets were among the first to use serious dramatic music.

32. According to the passage, for what is Tchaikovsky's music most well known?
    (A) its repetitive monotonous tones
    (B) the ballet-like quality of the music
    (C) the richness and melodic drama of the music
    (D) its lively capricious melodies

(C) This is a restatement question. Neither answer (A) nor answer (B) is used to describe Tchaikovsky's music. Line 9 reads, "Tchaikovsky's music, well known for rich melodic and sometimes melancholy passages. . . ." Therefore (C) is the best answer.

33. According to the passage, *Swan Lake* and *The Sleeping Beauty* are
    (A) dances
    (B) songs
    (C) operas
    (D) plays

(A) The passage refers to *Swan Lake* and *The Sleeping Beauty* as ballets, which are dances.

34. Which of the following is NOT mentioned in the passage?
    (A) Tchaikovsky's influence on ballet music
    (B) Tchaikovsky's unhappiness leading to suicide
    (C) the patronage of Madame von Meck
    (D) Tchaikovsky's productivity in composing

(B) This is a negative question. The possibility that Tchaikovsky committed suicide is mentioned in the last line of the paragraph, but no reason is given. The other three answer choices are mentioned in the paragraph.

35. Which of the following is closest in meaning to the word "behind" as used in line 11?
    (A) supporting
    (B) in back of
    (C) going beyond
    (D) concealing

(A) In this sentence, the words "supporting" and "behind" both refer to the assistance that the music gives to the dance. At the ballet, most people are probably concentrating more on the dance than the music, but the two are complementary.

36. In line 11, the word "ostensibly" could best be replaced by
    (A) regretfully
    (B) assuredly
    (C) tragically
    (D) apparently

(D) This is a vocabulary question. One clue to the answer is the word "though" after the word "cholera," which implies that a different reason for Tchaikovsky's death is going to be given. "Ostensibly" and "apparently" both mean "seemingly." These words are used to refer to a comment that may be true but is not a fact.

37. What is the main topic of the passage?
    (A) the Bengal tiger
    (B) international boycotts
    (C) endangered species
    (D) problems with industrialization

(C) This is a main topic question. The passage gives an example of one endangered species and then ways that some countries are dealing with the problem.

38. Which of the following is closest in meaning to the word "alarming" in line 4?
    (A) dangerous
    (B) serious
    (C) gripping
    (D) distressing

(D) The words "distressing" and "alarming" both mean "disturbing" or "troubling." Answer (A) refers to something that is not safe. Answer (B) refers to something that is thoughtful and sincere. Answer (C) refers to something that is so interestng that it "holds" your attention.

39. Which of the following could best replace the word "case" as used in line 4?
    (A) act
    (B) situation
    (C) contrast
    (D) trade

(B) In this sentence "case" and "situation" both refer to "instance" or "example."

40. The word "poachers" as used in line 5 could best be replaced by which of the following?
    (A) illegal hunters
    (B) enterprising researchers
    (C) concerned scientists
    (D) trained hunters

(A) This is a vocabulary question. A poacher is someone who hunts illegally.

41. The word "callousness" in line 6 could best be replaced by which of the following?
    (A) indirectness
    (B) independence
    (C) incompetence
    (D) insensitivity

(D) "Callousness" or "insensitivity" means having no feelings for others or being indifferent to the feelings or thoughts of others.

42. The above passage is divided into two paragraphs in order to contrast
    (A) a problem and a solution
    (B) a statement and an illustration
    (C) a comparison and a contrast
    (D) specific and general information

(A) This is an organization question. The first paragraph presents the problem of endangered species, using the example of the tiger. The second paragraph describes some solutions to the problem.

43. What does the word "this" refer to in line 6?
    (A) endangered species that are increasing
    (B) Bengal tigers that are decreasing
    (C) poachers who seek personal gratification
    (D) sources that may not be accurate

(C) This is a referent question. The sentence just before the word "this" mentions poachers who want personal gratification, not just money.

44. Where in the passage does the author discuss a cause of extinction?
    (A) lines 1–3
    (B) lines 4–6
    (C) lines 10–12
    (D) lines 13–15

(B) This is an organization question. In lines 4–6 the author discusses poachers as one of the causes of the decreasing numbers of tigers.

45. Which of the following could best replace the word "allocated" in line 11?
    (A) set aside
    (B) combined
    (C) organized
    (D) taken off

(A) The verbs "to allocate" and "to set aside" mean to designate a certain amount for something else, or to put some money or land or some other object away for another time or purpose.

46. The word "defray" in line 12 is closest in meaning to which of the following?
    (A) lower
    (B) raise
    (C) make a payment on
    (D) make an investment toward

(C) When one "defrays" the cost of something, he or she uses other money or other assets to pay for it. Answer (A) is close in meaning, since by defraying part of the cost, the amount that is left is lowered. The overall cost, however, is the same. What is lowered is the amount left after the defrayment.

47. The author uses the phrase "stem the tide" in line 14 to mean
    (A) touch
    (B) stop
    (C) tax
    (D) save

(B) The verb "to stem" means "to stop" or "to restrain" or "to hold back." The whole expression infers that it will be difficult to stop something just as it is difficult to stop the tide of the ocean. The "tide" is the rising and falling of the surface level of the ocean.

48. Which of the following most likely reflects the author's attitude?
    (A) forgiving
    (B) concerned
    (C) vindictive
    (D) surprised

(B) This is an author's attitude question. The author seems worried or concerned about the future of endangered species and the planet. This attitude is apparent by the choice of words such as "alarming," "callousness," and "valuable," and by the final sentence of the passage.

49. With what topic is this passage primarily concerned?
    (A) the twenty types of amino acids
    (B) high- and low-quality proteins
    (C) the process of complementation
    (D) healthy diets for vegetarians

(D) This is a main topic question. The discussion in the entire passage leads to the concluding comments about vegetarians. Answers (A), (B), and (C) all refer to topics that relate to knowledge that a vegetarian should have in order to eat a healthy diet.

50. The word "lean" in line 2 could best be replaced by
    (A) thin
    (B) fat
    (C) tall
    (D) short

(A) The word "lean" means "thin." This word is also used to refer to meat, often beef, that is lacking in fat.

51. The word "ingest" in line 5 is closest in meaning to which of the following?
    (A) chew
    (B) swallow
    (C) suck
    (D) drink

(B) The verb "to ingest" means "to take something into the body by swallowing or absorbing." To "chew" means to crush (food) with the teeth to help swallow something. To "suck" is to draw (liquid) into the mouth. "Drink" refers to liquids only.

52. The word "ample" in line 8 is closest in meaning to which of the following?
    (A) meager
    (B) frequent
    (C) substantial
    (D) harmful

(C) The words "ample" and "substantial" mean "a lot," "more than enough," or "plenty." Answer (A) is the opposite. Answer (B) refers to time intervals, such as "often."

53. Which of the following would NOT be an example of a low-quality protein?
    (A) legumes
    (B) apples
    (C) grains
    (D) tuna

(D) This is a negative question. In lines 8–9 low-quality proteins are described as those that come from plant sources. Since tuna is a type of fish, it would contain high-quality protein. Legumes, apples, and grains are all plants.

54. As used in line 10, which of the following words is closest in meaning to "strict"?
    (A) responsible
    (B) casual
    (C) harmonious
    (D) rigid

(D) The words "strict" and "rigid" both refer to something that is "severe," "uncompromising," or "austere."

55. According to the passage, a vegetarian could die from a lack of protein if he or she
    (A) did not follow a varied and properly protein-complemented diet.
    (B) ate too many animal proteins and could not digest them properly.
    (C) did not follow a diet in which non-essential proteins were ingested.
    (D) ate too many low-quality proteins.

(A) This is an inference question. The answer is in lines 10–11, which stress that vegetarians should make sure to have a varied diet. A diet that is not varied may not include all of the essential amino acids needed for good health.

56. Which of the following is closest in meaning to the word "crippling" as used in line 13?
    (A) discouraging
    (B) betraying
    (C) incapacitating
    (D) amazing

(C) The words "crippling" and "incapacitating" both refer to the action of stopping or impairing normal activity.

57. Which of the following words could best replace the word "prolonged" in line 13?
    (A) narrow
    (B) hollow
    (C) hard-hearted
    (D) extended

(D) The words "prolonged" and "extended" both refer to lengthening or continuing something.

58. In line 14, the word "imperative" can best be replaced by
    (A) crucial
    (B) impossible
    (C) wonderful
    (D) satisfying

(A) This is a vocabulary question. "Imperative" and "crucial" both mean "absolutely necessary."

59. Which of the following best describes the author's tone in this passage?
    (A) forceful
    (B) light
    (C) casual
    (D) argumentative

(A) This is an author's tone question. Though the passage begins in a scientific and informative way, it ends with a strong warning to (or about) vegetarians. The passage ends with a mention of death and the words "it is imperative that. . . ." These are clues that the author is being forceful in the tone of this passage. These words are the opposite of "light" and "casual." The word "argumentative" describes a quarrel, which is not apparent in this passage.

60. Which statement best describes the organization of this passage?
    (A) Contrasting views concerning proteins are compared.
    (B) The author moves from a general comment to a specific argument.
    (C) A statement is given and its cause is then discussed.
    (D) Items are discussed in their order of importance.

(B) This is an organization question. The author presents a general comment and then follows it with specific discussion of the importance of high-quality proteins in the diet of a vegetarian.

Test 2 • Answers

ANSWER SHEET FOR PRACTICE TEST 3

Section 1: Listening Comprehension

1 2 3 4 5 6 7 8 9 10 11 12 13 14 15 16 17 18 19 20 21 22 23 24 25 26 27 28 29 30 31 32 33 34 35 36 37 38 39 40 41 42 43 44 45 46 47 48 49 50
Ⓐ Ⓐ
Ⓑ Ⓑ
Ⓒ Ⓒ
Ⓓ Ⓓ

Section 2: Structure and Written Expression

1 2 3 4 5 6 7 8 9 10 11 12 13 14 15 16 17 18 19 20 21 22 23 24 25 26 27 28 29 30 31 32 33 34 35 36 37 38 39 40
Ⓐ Ⓐ
Ⓑ Ⓑ
Ⓒ Ⓒ
Ⓓ Ⓓ

Section 3: Reading Comprehension

1 2 3 4 5 6 7 8 9 10 11 12 13 14 15 16 17 18 19 20 21 22 23 24 25 26 27 28 29 30 31 32 33 34 35 36 37 38 39 40 41 42 43 44 45 46 47 48 49 50 51 52 53 54 55 56 57 58 59 60
Ⓐ Ⓐ
Ⓑ Ⓑ
Ⓒ Ⓒ
Ⓓ Ⓓ

Date Taken _____

Number Correct

Section 1 _____
Section 2 _____
Section 3 _____

Practice Test 3

SECTION 1

Listening Comprehension

Time—approximately 30 minutes

NOTE: You can simulate actual TOEFL conditions by using the Listening Comprehension Cassettes that accompany this book. If you do not have the tape, ask a friend to read the tapescript for Listening Comprehension Test 3, which is in Part Four, pages 395–403 of this book.

Part A

Directions: In Part A you will hear short conversations between two people. After each conversation a third person will ask a question about what was said. You will hear the conversation only one time, so you must listen carefully to what each speaker says. After you hear the conversation and the question, read the four possible answers in your test booklet and pick the one which best answers the question. Then look on the answer sheet for the number of the question and fill in the oval that corresponds to the letter of your answer choice.

Listen to an example:

You will hear:

You will read:

Sample Answer

(A) He will call Pete before he goes home.
(B) He will call Pete after he gets home.
(C) He called Pete at home.
(D) He will call Pete tomorrow.

You learn from the conversation that the man will call Pete as soon as he gets home. The best answer to the question "What does the man mean?" is (B), "He will call Pete after he gets home." Therefore, the correct answer is (B).

Now listen to the tape: Test 3, Section 1, Listening Comprehension Part A

183

GO ON TO THE NEXT PAGE

1. (A) He is not interested in the news.
   (B) He is surprised that the woman knows.
   (C) He was also going to look for a job.
   (D) He thinks that the woman made a mistake.

2. (A) Victor is a good student.
   (B) Victor is shy.
   (C) Victor is intelligent.
   (D) Victor is a good friend.

3. (A) He'd rather live on a farm.
   (B) He's going on a trip to the country.
   (C) He'll go to the farmers market.
   (D) He'll try to eat more vegetables.

4. (A) They cannot go to the beach today.
   (B) They are expecting a plumber soon.
   (C) They have some guests coming to visit.
   (D) They should stay only a short time at the beach.

5. (A) He expected the movie would be good.
   (B) He liked the movie.
   (C) He missed the movie.
   (D) He wanted to go too.

6. (A) She doesn't like the man's idea.
   (B) She wants to keep warm.
   (C) She agrees with the man.
   (D) She will open the window.

7. (A) The afternoon will be less crowded.
   (B) The doctors are not well trained.
   (C) It's a busy year for the clinic.
   (D) A lot of people are sick during this season.

8. (A) He was sick, but he is getting better.
   (B) Only two classes were available to him.
   (C) He doesn't have enough time to study.
   (D) He has just returned from vacation.

9. (A) She has one more thing to do.
   (B) She is not scheduled to talk today.
   (C) She is busy working on the talk.
   (D) She's wondering how to prepare for it.

10. (A) Who is Sylvia?
    (B) What did Sylvia learn?
    (C) How did Sylvia find out?
    (D) What are some things Sylvia likes?

11. (A) Ask the woman to teach him to drive.
    (B) Learn to drive.
    (C) Leave the woman alone.
    (D) Teach the woman how to drive.

12. (A) He didn't stay up late last night.
    (B) He didn't sleep at all last night.
    (C) He was apologizing for disturbing her last night.
    (D) He slept comfortably all night.

13. (A) Dr. Byron has a new position.
    (B) The course has been cut this semester.
    (C) There are not enough students signed up for the class.
    (D) The department is hiring a new art history professor.

14. (A) He did poorly on the first exam.
    (B) He got more than eighty percent right.
    (C) Eighty percent of the students did well.
    (D) He did much better than he thought.

15. (A) that the woman hasn't learned anything yet
    (B) that the woman learned not to waste time
    (C) that the woman will become a manager after graduation
    (D) that the woman has done the right thing

16. (A) The coupon can be used only today.
    (B) The coupon will expire next week.
    (C) The coupon is not good.
    (D) He doesn't need this coupon.

17. (A) He cannot park here today.
    (B) Today is a normal day.
    (C) The street is very clean.
    (D) He needs to get a parking permit.

18. (A) He is going to stay home.
    (B) The meeting is mandatory.
    (C) He is interested in attending the meeting.
    (D) He'd like to invite more people to the meeting.

19. (A) The interviews are all written.
    (B) The interviews were difficult.
    (C) The man has more work to do.
    (D) The man is lazy.

20. (A) She wants the man to wait.
    (B) She is ready now.
    (C) She has decided not to go.
    (D) She thinks the man should change his clothes.

 GO ON TO THE NEXT PAGE

Part B

Directions: In Part B you will hear longer conversations between two people. After each conversation you will be asked some questions. You will hear the conversations and the questions only once, so listen carefully to what is said. After you hear a question, read the four possible answers in your test book and decide which one is the best answer to the question you heard. Then, on your answer sheet, find the number of the question and fill in the oval that corresponds to the letter of the answer you have chosen. Answer all questions based on what is stated or implied by the speakers.

Listen to the example on the tape.

You will hear:

Now listen to sample question number 1.   Sample Answer

You will read:

     (A) to the cafeteria
     (B) to the movie theater
     (C) to her dorm room
     (D) to the library

The best answer to the question "Where is the woman going?" is (D), "to the library." Therefore, the correct choice is (D).

Now listen to sample question number 2.   Sample Answer

You will hear:

You will read:

     (A) Term papers are easy for him.
     (B) He has a lot of essay exams.
     (C) He finds lab experiments easier than writing term papers.
     (D) He is busier this semester than last semester.

The best answer to the question "Which best describes the man's feelings about his classes?" is (C), "He finds lab experiments easier than writing term papers." Therefore, the correct answer is (C).

Now listen to the test. Remember, you are not allowed to take any notes or write in your test book.

21. (A) Saturday's game
    (B) Michigan's defense
    (C) pulled ligaments
    (D) getting into the coach's office

22. (A) soccer
    (B) baseball
    (C) football
    (D) basketball

23. (A) in the coach's office
    (B) on the playing field
    (C) at the doctor's office
    (D) in the auditorium

24. (A) to the hospital
    (B) to his home
    (C) to her office
    (D) to the library

25. (A) a lunch
    (B) an exam
    (C) a class
    (D) a trip

26. (A) rainforest tribes in Brazil
    (B) mountain tribes in Chile
    (C) Incas in Peru
    (D) cities of Colombia

27. (A) her paper due the next week
    (B) her most recent exam grade
    (C) the material on the exam
    (D) not being able to get lunch

28. (A) to take a nap
    (B) to study
    (C) to play football
    (D) to eat lunch

29. (A) a sandwich and a guest lecturer
    (B) a guest lecturer and ancient Egypt
    (C) anthropology and history
    (D) a sandwich and dessert

30. (A) anthropologist
    (B) doctor
    (C) teacher
    (D) student

31. (A) crafts of ancient Rome
    (B) ancient medicine
    (C) types of food in Egypt
    (D) job opportunities in anthropology

32. (A) in a classroom
    (B) in a doctor's office
    (C) in a cafeteria
    (D) in an apartment

33. (A) on a beach
    (B) on a dock
    (C) in a boat
    (D) in a swimming pool

34. (A) looking for his watch
    (B) listening to the radio
    (C) looking for his tanks
    (D) writing a letter

35. (A) summer break
    (B) Christmas break
    (C) fall break
    (D) Easter break

GO ON TO THE NEXT PAGE

Part C

Directions: In this part of the test, you will hear talks by a single person. After each talk, you will be asked some questions. You will hear the talks and the questions only once, so listen carefully to what is said. After you hear a question, read the four possible answers in your test book and decide which one is the best answer to the question you heard. Then find the number of the question on your answer sheet, and fill in the oval that corresponds to the letter of the answer you have chosen. Answer all questions based on what is stated or implied in the talk.

Listen to this sample talk.

You will hear:

Now listen to sample question number 1.   Sample Answer

You will read: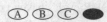

     (**A**) to demonstrate tutoring techniques
     (**B**) to explain school policies
     (**C**) to recruit childcare workers
     (**D**) to explain a service

The best answer to the question "What is the purpose of this announcement?" is (D), "to explain a service." Therefore, the correct choice is (D).

Now listen to sample question number 2.

You will hear: Sample Answer

You will read:

     (**A**) Give your child extra tutoring.
     (**B**) Take your child to the program today.
     (**C**) Apply as soon as you can.
     (**D**) Pay next month.

The best answer to the question "What does the speaker recommend? " is (C), "Apply as soon as you can." Therefore, the correct choice is (C).

Now begin. Remember, you are not allowed to write any notes in your test book.

GO ON TO THE NEXT PAGE

36. (A) types of bicycle frames
    (B) the diamond bicycle frame
    (C) an analysis of steel alloys
    (D) rigidity in bicycle frames

37. (A) lighter weight
    (B) more rigid structure
    (C) more visually appealing
    (D) easier to mount

38. (A) Mixte frames are better than diamond frames.
    (B) Bicycles haven't changed much in the last one hundred years.
    (C) Bicycles are difficult to build.
    (D) Diamond frames are better than mixte frames.

39. (A) new colors and paints
    (B) stronger plastic materials
    (C) lighter-weight metals
    (D) new popularity for cycling

40. (A) because the skin is good for boat-making
    (B) because the bones are used for traditional carvings
    (C) because the tusks are valuable
    (D) because the fur can be used in making coats

41. (A) Alaskans
    (B) coastal natives
    (C) park rangers
    (D) Fish and Wildlife workers

42. (A) money
    (B) weapons
    (C) drugs
    (D) food

43. (A) that the Fish and Wildlife Service will kill the animals
    (B) that they will not have enough walruses for food
    (C) that they will be blamed for illegal killings
    (D) that they will be attacked by walruses

44. (A) to discuss the university childcare programs
    (B) to advertise the merits of the kindergarten
    (C) to discuss eligibility requirements for the nursery
    (D) to argue for private schools as a better form of education

45. (A) two
    (B) three
    (C) four
    (D) five

46. (A) The parents must both be university students.
    (B) The parents must live in university housing.
    (C) The children must be at least six years old.
    (D) At least one parent must be studying for a doctorate degree.

47. (A) $100
    (B) $250
    (C) $500
    (D) $1,000

48. (A) He was the speaker's father.
    (B) He influenced the speaker's music.
    (C) He was the greatest jazz musician ever.
    (D) He helped the speaker produce his first record.

49. (A) the Ritz Carlton
    (B) the Poodle Dog Cafe
    (C) the Washingtonian
    (D) the Cotton Club

50. (A) piano
    (B) saxophone
    (C) guitar
    (D) trumpet

THIS IS THE END OF SECTION 1.
DO NOT READ OR WORK ON ANY OTHER SECTION OF THE TEST UNTIL TIME IS UP.

STOP   STOP   STOP   STOP   STOP

SECTION 2

Structure and Written Expression

Time—25 minutes

Part 1: Sentence Completion

Directions: Questions 1–15 are not complete sentences. One or more words are left out of each sentence. Under each sentence, you will see four words or phrases, marked (A), (B), (C), and (D). Choose the one word or phrase that completes the sentence correctly. Then, on your answer sheet, find the number of the question and fill in the oval that corresponds to the letter of your answer choice.

Example I▶

Birds make nests in trees _____ hide their young in the leaves and branches.

(A) can where they
(B) where they can
(C) where can they
(D) where can

Sample Answer

The sentence should read, "Birds make nests in trees where they can hide their young in the leaves and branches." Therefore, you should choose answer (B).

Example II▶

Sleeping, resting, and _____ are the best ways to care for a cold.

(A) to drink fluids
(B) drank fluids
(C) one drink fluids
(D) drinking fluids

Sample Answer

Ⓐ Ⓑ Ⓒ ●

The sentence should read, "Sleeping, resting, and drinking fluids are the best ways to care for a cold." Therefore, you should choose answer (D).

Now begin work on the questions.

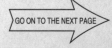
GO ON TO THE NEXT PAGE

1. Van Gogh's *Sunflowers* _____ $39.9 million, three times the previous record.
   (A) once sold for
   (B) for sale once
   (C) selling for once
   (D) for once sold

2. Some monkeys, _____, use their tails in a way similar to a hand.
   (A) like the spider monkey
   (B) spider monkey likes
   (C) to the spider monkey
   (D) the monkey likes the spider

3. Black, red, and even bright pink diamonds _____.
   (A) occasionally to find
   (B) occasionally found
   (C) have occasionally been found
   (D) have occasionally found

4. Between the California Coast Range and the Sierra Nevada _____.
   (A) great Central Valley
   (B) the great Central Valley
   (C) being the great Central Valley
   (D) lies the great Central Valley

5. It is gravity _____ objects toward the earth.
   (A) pulling
   (B) that pulls
   (C) to pull
   (D) what pulls

6. _____ their territories but rather than fight, they howl.
   (A) Wolves protectively jealous
   (B) Jealous of wolves
   (C) Protection of wolves
   (D) Wolves jealously protect

7. _____ strength of 70 horses, a forklift toils all day long in a warehouse lifting great weights.
   (A) Because the
   (B) With the
   (C) Some
   (D) The

8. The growth of two-income families in the United States _____ of people moving to a new social class.
   (A) has resulted in millions
   (B) results of millions
   (C) millions of results
   (D) resulting in millions

9. Using a globe can be _____ it is educational.
   (A) enjoyable
   (B) to enjoy as
   (C) as enjoyable
   (D) as enjoyable as

10. Each mediocre book we read means one less great book that we would otherwise have a chance _____.
    (A) to read them
    (B) read
    (C) reading
    (D) to read

11. Most accidents in the home can be prevented by _____ elimination of hazards.
    (A) that
    (B) that the
    (C) there is a
    (D) the

12. _____ problems in sailing in tropical seas is the coral reefs.
    (A) One of the biggest
    (B) The biggest one
    (C) Of the biggest one
    (D) There are the biggest

13. The strongest dump trucks work in rock quarries, _____ tons of rocks and soil at one time.
    (A) that they move
    (B) they move
    (C) where they move
    (D) which they move

14. Alice Freeman, _____ to head Wellesley College at age 27, is one of the youngest college presidents in history.
    (A) who was appointed
    (B) has been appointed
    (C) that is appointed
    (D) is appointed

GO ON TO THE NEXT PAGE

15. Helen Keller lost both her sight and hearing
after a severe illness _____ .
(A) of her age in 19 months
(B) she was 19 months old
(C) when she was 19 months old
(D) when 19 months old she was

Part 2: Error Identification

Directions: In questions 16–40 each sentence has four underlined words or phrases marked (A), (B), (C), and (D). Choose the one word or phrase that must be changed in order for the sentence to be correct. Then, on your answer sheet find the number of the question and fill in the oval that corresponds to the letter of your answer choice.

Example I▶

Aspirin is recommend to many people for its

      A   B   C

ability to thin the blood.

    D

Sample Answer

● Ⓑ Ⓒ Ⓓ

The sentence should read, "Aspirin is recommended to many people for its ability to thin the blood." Therefore, you should choose answer (A).

Example II▶

Some people believe that human beings will never use away all

         A   B

the natural resources on earth.

  C   D

Sample Answer

Ⓐ ● Ⓒ Ⓓ

The sentence should read, "Some people believe that human beings will never use up all the natural resources on earth." Therefore, you should choose answer (B).

Now begin work on the questions.

16. One of history's most spectacular executions were that of Damiens, the unsuccessful

    A   B   C   D

assassin of Louis XV of France.

17. Globes and maps have been important throughout history, but never many so than today.

                   A   B   C D

18. Since vitamins are contained in a wide variety of foods, people seldom lack of most of them.

        A   B   C   D

19. Psychological experiment indicate that people remember more math problems that

            A

they cannot solve than those they are able to solve.

      B   C   D

20. The sun is a huge fiery globe at a average distance of 93,000,000 miles from the Earth.

      A   B   C   D

21. Before becoming successful, Charles Kettering, former vice president of General

               A

Motors, was so poor that he has to use the hayloft of a barn as a laboratory.

      B   C   D

GO ON TO THE NEXT PAGE

22. Despite the metric system is used throughout the world, it is still not commonly used in the United States.
      A   B   C   D

23. Some gorillas beat their chests as an express of high spirits.
                 A   B C   D

24. Because Walter Reed's efforts and those of the people who worked with him, human beings
     A   B

   no longer fear the dreaded disease of yellow fever.
     C   D

25. Studying the science of logic is one way to cultivate one's reason skills.
     A   B   C   D

26. The continental shelves is the shallow area of the ocean floor that is closest to the continents.
              A   B   C   D

27. The average adult get two to five colds each year.
   A   B   C   D

28. Fishing have been found to contain a particular type of fat that may help lower blood cholesterol levels.
   A   B   C   D

29. Benjamin Franklin's ability to learn from observation and experience contributed greatly to
                A   B

   him success in public life.
    C   D

30. Industrial lasers are most often used for cutting, welding, drilling, and measure.
     A   B   C   D

31. In the last 10 years, Mexican government has reduced the number of its state-owned
                       A   B   C

   companies to about half.
     D

32. Psychologists at the University of Kansas has studied the effects of the color of a room
                              A   B   C

   on people's behavior.
    D

33. Montaigne, the illustrious French philosophy, was elected mayor of Bordeaux, which was his home town.
           A   B   C   D

34. Certain pollens are more likely to cause an allergic reaction than another.
     A   B   C   D

35. Computers have made access to information instantly available just by push a few buttons.
         A   B   C   D

36. Mined over 2,000 years ago, copper is one of the earliest know metals.
   A   B   C   D

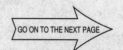 GO ON TO THE NEXT PAGE

37. Many of the early work of T.S. Eliot expresses the anguish and barrenness of modern
      A   B   C

life and the isolation of the individual.
      D

38. A sore throat interferes with daily life by making swallow difficult.
          A   B   C   D

39. A farmer's tractor is like a powerful horse, as it plows field, pulls trailers, and moves heavy loads.
              A   B   C   D

40. During wedding ceremonies in the United States guests are usually silence.
   A   B   C   D

THIS IS THE END OF SECTION 2.
DO NOT READ OR WORK ON ANY OTHER SECTION OF THE TEST UNTIL TIME IS UP.
STOP STOP STOP STOP STOP

SECTION 3

Reading Comprehension

Time — 55 minutes

Directions: In this this section you will read several passages. Each passage is followed by questions about it. Choose the one best answer, (A), (B), (C), or (D), for each question. Then, on your answer sheet, find the number of the question and fill in the oval that corresponds to the letter of your answer choice. Answer all questions based on what is stated or implied in the passage.

Read the following passage:

A new hearing device is now available for some hearing-impaired people. This device uses a magnet to hold the detachable sound-processing portion in place. Like other aids, it converts sound into vibrations. But it is unique in that it can transmit the vibrations directly to the magnet, and then to the inner ear. This produces a clearer sound. The new device will not help all hearing-impaired people, only those with a hearing loss caused by infection or some other problem in the middle ear. It will probably help no more than 20 percent of all people with hearing problems. Those people, however, who have persistent ear infections should find relief and restored hearing with the new device.

Example I▶

What is the author's main purpose?

Sample Answer

(A) to describe a new cure for ear infections
(B) to inform the reader of a new device
(C) to urge doctors to use a new device
(D) to explain the use of a magnet

Ⓐ ● Ⓒ Ⓓ

The author's main purpose is to inform the reader of a new device for hearing-impaired people. Therefore, you should choose answer (B).

Example II▶

The word "relief" in the last sentence means

Sample Answer

(A) less distress
(B) assistance
(C) distraction
(D) relaxation

● Ⓑ Ⓒ Ⓓ

The phrase "less distress" is similar in meaning to "relief" in this sentence. Therefore, you should choose answer (A).

Now begin with the questions.

Questions 1 to 13 are based on the following passage:

(1)   The peregrine falcon, a predatory bird indigenous to North America, was once in danger of extinction. In the 1960s, scientists discovered byproducts of the pesticide DDT in the birds' eggs, which caused them to be too soft to survive. The use of the pesticide had been banned in the United States, but the falcons were eating migratory birds from other places where DDT was still used. In order to increase the survival

(5)   rate, scientists were raising the birds in laboratories and then releasing them into mountainous areas. This practice achieved only moderate success, however, because many of the birds raised in captivity could not survive in the wild.

        There is now, however, a new alternative to releases in the wild. A falcon that has been given the name Scarlett chose to make her home on a ledge of the 33rd floor of a Baltimore, Maryland, office

(10)   building rather than in the wild, and, to the surprise of the scientists, she has managed to live quite well in the city. Following this example, programs have been initiated that release birds like Scarlett into cities rather than into their natural wild habitat. These urban releases are becoming a common way to strengthen the species. Urban homes have several benefits for the birds that wild spots do not. First, there is an abundance of pigeons and small birds as food sources. The peregrine in the city is also protected from its

(15)   main predator, the great horned owl. Urban release programs have been very successful in reestablishing the peregrine falcons along the East Coast. Though they are still an endangered species, their numbers increased from about 60 nesting pairs in 1975 to about 700 pairs in 1992. In another decade the species may flourish again, this time without human help.

1. What is the main topic of the passage?
(A) survival of peregrine falcons
(B) releases into the wild
(C) endangered species
(D) harmful effects of pesticides

2. In line 1, the phrase "indigenous to" could be best replaced by
(A) typical of
(B) protected by
(C) adapted to
(D) native to

3. The word "byproducts" in line 2 could best be replaced by which of the following?
(A) derivatives
(B) proceeds
(C) chemicals
(D) elements

4. In line 3, the word "banned" could be best replaced by
(A) authorized
(B) developed
(C) disseminated
(D) prohibited

5. Which of the following words is closest in meaning to the word "rate," as used in line 5?
(A) speed
(B) percentage
(C) continuation
(D) behavior

6. In line 5, the word "raising" most probably means
(A) breeding
(B) elevating
(C) collecting
(D) measuring

7. Why were the peregrine falcons in danger?
(A) because of pesticides used by American farmers
(B) because they migrated to countries where their eggs could not survive
(C) because they ate birds from other countries where DDT was still used
(D) because they were prized by hunters and hunted to near extinction

8. The word "releases" as used in line 8 most probably means
(A) internment
(B) regression
(C) distribution
(D) possessions

GO ON TO THE NEXT PAGE

9. The word "ledge" in line 9 is closest in meaning to
   (A) window
   (B) wall
   (C) terrace
   (D) shelf

10. According to the passage, which of the following is NOT a reason why a falcon might choose to live in a city?
    (A) There are high places to nest.
    (B) There are other falcons nearby.
    (C) There is a lack of predators.
    (D) There is abundant food.

11. According to the passage, which of the following are the falcon's main predators?
    (A) pigeons
    (B) rattlesnakes
    (C) owls
    (D) humans

12. As used in line 13, the word "spots" could best be replaced by
    (A) places
    (B) dilemmas
    (C) jungles
    (D) materials

13. According to the passage, where have the release programs been the most successful?
    (A) in office buildings
    (B) on the East Coast
    (C) in mountainous areas
    (D) in the wild

Questions 14 to 23 are based on the following passage:

(1)   Jan Dibbets may someday have his work revered as much as his Dutch predecessors: Vermeer, Van Gogh, and Rembrandt. At a time when the trends in art are toward abstraction and minimalism, Dibbets' work integrates these two disparate trends into one remarkable whole. In one series of composite works, he arranged sections of architectural photographs into rounded patterns. Then, with pen and ink and

(5)   watercolors, he connected the segments together into 360-degree circular forms blending the abstract with the real and the imagined. The imaginary images resemble the views of ceilings in gothic, baroque, and neo-classical buildings as they might be seen from the ground floor.

14. What does this passage mainly discuss?
(A) the life of Jan Dibbets
(B) new forms of art created by Jan Dibbets
(C) an exhibit of abstract art
(D) art that follows the style of Vermeer, Van Gogh, and Rembrandt

15. Which of the following words could best replace the word "revered" in line 1?
(A) honored
(B) possessed
(C) modeled
(D) handled

16. As used in line 2, what is the meaning of the word "time"?
(A) season
(B) period
(C) century
(D) interval

17. The word "disparate" in line 3 is closest in meaning to
(A) similar
(B) unspoken
(C) different
(D) unknown

18. The author implies that
(A) Dibbets is more well known to some people than Vermeer
(B) views of ceilings in gothic buildings are most beautiful when seen from the ground floor
(C) art is now becoming more abstract
(D) Dibbets preferred watercolor to photography

19. The word "remarkable" as used in line 3 could be best replaced by
(A) inseparable
(B) unified
(C) clever
(D) extraordinary

20. As used in line 3, the word "works" could be best replaced by which of the following?
(A) deeds
(B) mechanisms
(C) operations
(D) creations

21. As described in this passage, Dibbets used all of the following elements EXCEPT
(A) pen and ink
(B) watercolors
(C) architectural photographs
(D) still-life drawings

22. The word "segments" as used in line 5 refers to
(A) parts
(B) dots
(C) supports
(D) webs

23. The word "neo-classical" in line 7 refers to
(A) artistic patterns
(B) trends in art
(C) architectural styles
(D) museum decorations

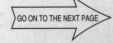
GO ON TO THE NEXT PAGE

Questions 24 to 36 are based on the following passage:

(1)   Carnegie Hall, the famous concert hall in New York City, has again undergone a restoration. While this is not the first, it is certainly the most extensive in the building's history. As a result of this new restoration, Carnegie Hall once again has the quality of sound that it had when it was first built.

        Carnegie Hall owes its existence to Andrew Carnegie, the wealthy owner of a steel company in the
(5)   late 1800s. The hall was finished in 1891 and quickly gained a reputation as an excellent performing arts hall where accomplished musicians gained fame. Despite its reputation, however, the concert hall suffered from several detrimental renovations over the years. During the Great Depression, when fewer people could afford to attend performances, the directors sold part of the building to commercial businesses. As a result, a coffee shop was opened in one corner of the building, for which the builders
(10)   replaced the brick and terra cotta walls with windowpanes. A renovation in 1946 seriously damaged the acoustical quality of the hall when the makers of the film *Carnegie Hall* cut a gaping hole in the dome of the ceiling to allow for lights and air vents. The hole was later covered with short curtains and a fake ceiling, but the hall never sounded the same afterwards.

        In 1960, the violinist Isaac Stern became involved in restoring the hall after a group of real estate
(15)   developers unveiled plans to demolish Carnegie Hall and build a high-rise office building on the site. This threat spurred Stern to rally public support for Carnegie Hall and encourage the City of New York to buy the property. The movement was successful, and the concert hall is now owned by the city. In the current restoration, builders tested each new material for its sound qualities, and they replaced the hole in the ceiling with a dome. The builders also restored the outer walls to their original appearance and closed the
(20)   coffee shop. Carnegie has never sounded better, and its prospects for the future have never looked more promising.

24. This passage is mainly about
  (A) changes to Carnegie Hall
  (B) the appearance of Carnegie Hall
  (C) Carnegie Hall's history during the Great Depression
  (D) damage to the ceiling in Carnegie Hall

25. The word "extensive" in line 2 could be best replaced by which of the following?
  (A) fabulous
  (B) thorough
  (C) devoted
  (D) continuous

26. In line 7, what is the meaning of the word "detrimental"?
  (A) dangerous
  (B) significant
  (C) extreme
  (D) harmful

27. What major change happened to the hall in 1946?
  (A) The acoustic dome was damaged.
  (B) Space in the building was sold to commercial businesses.
  (C) The walls were damaged in an earthquake.
  (D) The stage was renovated.

28. Who was Andrew Carnegie?
  (A) a violinist
  (B) an architect
  (C) a steel mill owner
  (D) mayor of New York City

29. Which of the following words could best replace the word "gaping" in line 11?
  (A) small
  (B) round
  (C) vital
  (D) wide

30. The word "fake" in line 12 is most similar to which of the following?
  (A) low
  (B) false
  (C) thin
  (D) handsome

 GO ON TO THE NEXT PAGE

31. What was Isaac Stern's relationship to
    Carnegie Hall?
    (A) He made the movie *Carnegie Hall* in 1946.
    (B) He performed on opening night in 1891.
    (C) He tried to save the hall, beginning in
        1960.
    (D) He opened a coffeeshop in Carnegie Hall
        during the Depression.

32. What was probably the most important aspect
    of the recent renovation?
    (A) restoring the outer wall
    (B) expanding the lobby
    (C) restoring the plaster trim
    (D) repairing the ceiling

33. Which of the following is closest in meaning to
    the word "unveiled" in line 15?
    (A) announced
    (B) restricted
    (C) overshadowed
    (D) located

34. The author uses the word "spurred" in line
    16 to show that Stern
    (A) predicted the result
    (B) probed the plans
    (C) was told in advance
    (D) was stimulated to act

35. How does the author seem to feel about the
    future of Carnegie Hall?
    (A) ambiguous
    (B) guarded
    (C) optimistic
    (D) negative

36. Which of the following would most likely be
    the topic of the next paragraph?
    (A) a scientific explanation of acoustics and
        the nature of sound
    (B) a description of people's reactions to the
        newly renovated hall
    (C) a discussion of the coffee shop that once
        was located in the building
    (D) further discussion about the activities of
        Isaac Stern in 1960

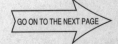

Questions 37 to 48 are based on the following passage:

(1) Situated in the central mountains of Alaska, a peak named Denali rises 20,320 feet above sea level. It is the highest peak in North America and the center of Denali National Park. One of America's greatest wilderness areas, the park has had limited access to visitors, but in spite of this tourism rose from under 6,000 visitors in 1950 to over 546,000 visitors in 1990. The increasing popularity of this park is prompting

(5) serious discussions about the future use of Denali as well as how to preserve wilderness areas in general.

One important issue of land use arises when parts of National Parks are owned by individuals. In Denali, though most of the land in this vast tract of more than a million acres is owned by the National Park Service, several thousand acres are still privately owned as mining tracts. These mining tracts in Denali were once abundant sources of gold, but they were sources of heavy metals such as arsenic and

(10) lead that polluted rivers and streams. Environmentalists were successful in getting the government to require mining companies to submit statements showing the potential impact of a mining project before they are allowed to begin mining. Because of this requirement, many individuals closed their mines and some sold their land to the National Park Service. Some land owners, however, are wondering if it is better to sell their land to the government or keep it for possible future use. Tourism in this previously remote

(15) area is bound to rise, as more roads are built to provide easier access to the park. This increase in the number of visitors creates a demand for hotels and other real estate development. The economic implications of this are of interest to the land owners, but are dismaying to those interested in preserving the wilderness.

37. What is the primary focus of this passage?
(A) controversies over land use in Denali
(B) miners selling their property in Denali
(C) Alaska building more roads to Denali
(D) limiting tourist access to Denali

38. The word "wilderness" in line 3 could be best replaced by the word
(A) dangerous
(B) natural
(C) rural
(D) pastoral

39. The word "prompting" in line 4 could best be replaced by which of the following?
(A) promising
(B) sanctioning
(C) initiating
(D) trapping

40. As used in line 5, which of the following is most similar to the word "preserve"?
(A) protect
(B) enclose
(C) investigate
(D) foster

41. The word "arises" in line 6 could be best replaced by
(A) surrenders
(B) occurs
(C) volunteers
(D) prospers

42. The word "tract" as used in line 7 refers to which of the following?
(A) trail
(B) resort
(C) frontier
(D) expanse

43. Which of the following is most similar to the word "abundant" in line 9?
(A) plentiful
(B) sparse
(C) hopeful
(D) absolute

44. According to the passage, which of the following are pollutants in the Denali area?
(A) gold
(B) pesticides
(C) human waste
(D) arsenic

45. Which of the following is closest in meaning to the phrase "potential impact" in line 11?
    (A) approximate cost
    (B) expected value
    (C) proposed size
    (D) possible effects

46. The author infers that some mine owners might hesitate to sell their land to the Park Service for which of the following reasons?
    (A) There may be increasing demand for the ore in the mines.
    (B) They might want to move to the towns.
    (C) They might receive more money selling their land to developers.
    (D) They might want to build a house on their property.

47. What is the author's purpose in writing this passage?
    (A) to demonstrate the changes in Denali National Park
    (B) to use Denali as an example of common park issues
    (C) to introduce the wonders of the wilderness area of Denali
    (D) to explain the problems occurring in Denali Park

48. Which of the following would most likely be the topic of the next paragraph in this passage?
    (A) conflict between land owners and environmentalists
    (B) the role of the National Park Service in development
    (C) tourist needs in Denali Park
    (D) wildlife in the park

GO ON TO THE NEXT PAGE

Questions 49 to 60 are based on the following passage:

(1) Sharks have gained an unfair reputation for being fierce predators of large sea animals. Humanity's unfounded fear and hatred of these ancient creatures is leading to a worldwide slaughter that may result in the extinction of many coastal shark species. The shark is the victim of a warped attitude of wildlife protection; we strive only to protect the beautiful, nonthreatening parts of our environment. And,

(5) in our efforts to restore only nonthreatening parts of our earth, we ignore other important parts.

A perfect illustration of this attitude is the contrasting attitude toward another large sea animal, the dolphin. During the 1980s, environmentalists in the United States protested the use of driftnets for tuna fishing in the Pacific Ocean since these nets also caught dolphins. The environmentalists generated enough political and economic pressure to prevent tuna companies from buying tuna that had been caught

(10) in driftnets. In contrast to this effort on behalf of the dolphins, these same environmentalists have done very little to help save the Pacific Ocean sharks whose population has decreased nearly to the point of extinction. Sharks are among the oldest creatures on earth, having survived in the seas for more than 350 million years. They are extremely efficient animals, feeding on wounded or dying animals, thus performing an important role in nature of weeding out the weaker animals in a species. Just the fact

(15) that species such as the Great White Shark have managed to live in the oceans for so many millions of years is enough proof of their efficiency and adaptability to changing environments. It is time for us humans, who may not survive another 1,000 years at the rate we are damaging the planet, to cast away our fears and begin considering the protection of sharks as an important part of a program for protection of all our natural environment.

49. With which of the following topics is this passage primarily concerned?
(A) Sharks are efficient creatures with bad reputations.
(B) Sharks are some of the oldest creatures on earth.
(C) Sharks illustrate a problem in wildlife protection.
(D) The campaign to save dolphins was not extended to save sharks.

50. Which of the following is most similar to the meaning of the word "warped" in line 3?
(A) distorted
(B) wasteful
(C) extravagant
(D) wanton

51. In line 7, the word "protested" is closest in meaning to which of the following?
(A) prescribed
(B) objected to
(C) protected
(D) reflected on

52. In line 8, the word "generated" could be best replaced by
(A) consumed
(B) absorbed
(C) designated
(D) produced

53. How did environmentalists manage to protect dolphins?
(A) They prevented fishermen from selling them for meat.
(B) They pressured fishermen into protecting dolphins by law.
(C) They brought political pressure against tuna companies.
(D) They created sanctuaries where dolphin fishing was not allowed.

54. About how long have sharks lived on the planet?
(A) 25 million years
(B) 150 million years
(C) 350 million years
(D) 500 million years

GO ON TO THE NEXT PAGE

55. The author uses the phrase "weeding out" in line 14 to mean
    (A) strengthening something that is weak
    (B) feeding something that is hungry
    (C) encouraging something that is efficient
    (D) getting rid of something that is unwanted

56. In line 15, the phrase "managed to live" is used to infer that
    (A) surviving was difficult
    (B) migration was common
    (C) procreation was expanding
    (D) roaming was necessary

57. The word "proof" in line 16 could be best replaced by which of the following?
    (A) characteristic
    (B) evidence
    (C) praise
    (D) customary

58. In line 17, the phrase "to cast away" means most nearly
    (A) to throw off
    (B) to bring in
    (C) to see through
    (D) to set apart

59. What is the author's tone in this passage?
    (A) explanatory
    (B) accusatory
    (C) gentle
    (D) proud

60. Which of the following best describes the organization of this passage?
    (A) order of importance
    (B) cause and effect
    (C) statement and example
    (D) chronological order

THIS IS THE END OF TEST 3

Practice Test 3

Answer Key

Section 1: Listening Comprehension

Part A

1. B	5. B	9. C	13. A	17. A
2. D	6. C	10. B	14. D	18. C
3. C	7. D	11. D	15. B	19. C
4. B	8. A	12. B	16. B	20. A

Part B

21. A	24. C	27. B	30. B	33. C
22. C	25. B	28. D	31. B	34. C
23. B	26. A	29. A	32. C	35. B

Part C

36. A	39. C	42. C	45. B	48. B
37. D	40. C	43. C	46. B	49. D
38. D	41. B	44. A	47. A	50. B

Section 2: Structure and Written Expression

Part 1: Sentence Completion

1. A	4. D	7. B	10. D	13. C
2. A	5. B	8. A	11. D	14. A
3. C	6. D	9. D	12. A	15. C

Part 2: Error Identification

16. C	21. C	26. A	31. A	36. D
17. C	22. A	27. B	32. A	37. A
18. D	23. C	28. A	33. B	38. C
19. A	24. A	29. C	34. D	39. C
20. C	25. D	30. D	35. D	40. D

Section 3: Reading Comprehension

1. A	13. B	25. B	37. A	49. C
2. D	14. B	26. D	38. B	50. A
3. A	15. A	27. A	39. C	51. B
4. D	16. B	28. C	40. A	52. D
5. B	17. C	29. D	41. B	53. C
6. A	18. C	30. B	42. D	54. C
7. C	19. D	31. C	43. A	55. D
8. C	20. D	32. D	44. D	56. A
9. D	21. D	33. A	45. D	57. B
10. B	22. A	34. D	46. C	58. A
11. C	23. C	35. C	47. B	59. B
12. A	24. A	36. B	48. A	60. C

Practice Test 3
Explanatory Answers

SECTION 1
Listening Comprehension

Part A

1. Woman: Barbara sure found a nice job!
    Man: So you know about it too?

    What can we assume about the man?
    (A) He is not interested in the news.
    (B) He is surprised that the woman knows.
    (C) He was also going to look for a job.
    (D) He thinks that the woman made a mistake.

(B) If the man thought the woman had known about Barbara's job, he would probably have agreed with her that it was a good job. Instead, his comment shows that he was surprised that the woman also knew about the job.

2. Man: Victor's always willing to help me.
    Woman: What a good buddy!

    What does the woman mean?
    (A) Victor is a good student.
    (B) Victor is shy.
    (C) Victor is intelligent.
    (D) Victor is a good friend.

(D) The word "buddy" is used to refer to someone who is a friend.

3. Woman: Simon, the vegetables at the farmers' market are fresher and cheaper than these.
    Man: Really, I guess I'd better try going there.

    What does the man mean?
    (A) He'd rather live on a farm.
    (B) He's going on a trip to the country.
    (C) He'll go to the farmers' market.
    (D) He'll try to eat more vegetables.

(C) The man says, "I'd better try going there." The word "there" refers to the farmers market, which is the topic of the conversation.

4. Man: I feel great today; shall we go to the beach?
    Woman: After the plumber finishes his work; he's coming shortly.

    What does the woman mean?
    (A) They cannot go to the beach today.
    (B) They are expecting a plumber soon.
    (C) They have some guests coming to visit.
    (D) They should stay only a short time at the beach.

(B) The word "shortly" means "very soon."

5. Woman: None of us enjoyed the movie very much.
    Man: I did.

    What does the man mean?
    (A) He expected the movie would be good.
    (B) He liked the movie.
    (C) He missed the movie.
    (D) He wanted to go too.

(B) The man's tone of voice shows that he is emphasizing his opinion, which is different from what the woman thinks.

6. Man: Do you mind if I open the window?
    Woman: Not a bad idea; we need some fresh air.

    What does the woman mean?
    (A) She doesn't like the man's idea.
    (B) She wants to keep warm.
    (C) She agrees with the man.
    (D) She will open the window.

(C) When the woman says, "Not a bad idea," she means that it is a good idea to open the window. Answer (D) is incorrect because it seems to be the man who will open the window, not the woman.

7.   Woman: The health clinic was so swamped
             with people that it took me three
             hours to get in.
      Man: Yeah, the clinic is always busy this
             time of year.

What does the man imply?
(A) The afternoon will be less crowded.
(B) The doctors are not well trained.
(C) It's a busy year for the clinic.
(D) A lot of people are sick during this season.

(D) Since the clinic is busy, we can infer that many
people are sick. The word "swamped" means "very
busy."

8.   Woman: Hi, Roger, good to see you again. So
             you're back at school now?
      Man: I'm still recovering, so I'm taking
             only two classes for the time being.

What does the man mean?
(A) He was sick, but he is getting better.
(B) Only two classes were available to him.
(C) He doesn't have enough time to study.
(D) He has just returned from vacation.

(A) Because the man says he is recovering, we can
assume that he was sick before. "Recovering"
means "getting better." The phrase "for the time being"
means "now."

9.   Man: Sarah, you're one of the speakers for
             today's presentation, aren't you?
      Woman: That's what I'm preparing for.

What does the woman mean?
(A) She has one more thing to do.
(B) She is not scheduled to talk today.
(C) She is busy working on the talk.
(D) She's wondering how to prepare for it.

(C) Since the woman says she is preparing for the talk,
we can assume that she is busy with her preparation.

10.   Woman: I just learned something really
             exciting!
      Man: What, Sylvia?

What does the man want to know?
(A) Who is Sylvia?
(B) What did Sylvia learn?
(C) How did Sylvia find out?
(D) What are some things Sylvia likes?

(B) The word "what" is a shortened form of "What did
you just learn?"

11.   Woman: Can you give me a driving lesson this
             afternoon, Will?
      Man: Yes, I guess I can, but I'm afraid I
             don't have much time.

What will the man probably do?
(A) Ask the woman to teach him to drive.
(B) Learn to drive.
(C) Leave the woman alone.
(D) Teach the woman how to drive.

(D) Even though he says he doesn't have much time, he
says, "Yes, I guess I can," so we can assume that he will
spend some time teaching the woman how to drive.

12.   Woman: You didn't stay up late last night, did
             you?
      Man: Not late, just all night.

What does the man imply?
(A) He didn't stay up late last night.
(B) He didn't sleep at all last night.
(C) He was apologizing for disturbing her last
    night.
(D) He slept comfortably all night.

(B) When he says, "Not late," the man is saying the
opposite of what he means. His tone of voice is a clue to
the meaning. The words "just all night" give the real
meaning.

13.   Man: Why isn't Dr. Byron teaching art
             history again this semester?
      Woman: No time. He just became department
             chair.

What does the woman mean?
(A) Dr. Byron has a new position.
(B) The course has been cut this semester.
(C) There are not enough students signed up for
    the class.
(D) The department is hiring a new art history
    professor.

(A) Since the man didn't know that Dr. Byron is
now chair of the department, we can assume that this is
a new job.

Test 3 • Answers

14. Woman: How did your first exam go?
     Man: I thought I did poorly, but I ended up with eighty percent, the highest grade in the class.

What does the man mean?
(A) He did poorly on the first exam.
(B) He got more than eighty percent right.
(C) Eighty percent of the students did well.
(D) He did much better than he thought.

(D) The man got 80% correct on this exam, which was evidently a high score for this test. He says he thought he did poorly, so we can assume that he was surprised that he did so well.

15. Woman: At least I've learned one thing at this university.
     Man: To manage your time, right?

What does the man mean?
(A) That the woman hasn't learned anything yet.
(B) That the woman learned not to waste time.
(C) That the woman will become a manager after graduation.
(D) That the woman has done the right thing.

(B) The man is guessing that the woman has learned to manage her time, which implies that she is now using her time wisely, not wasting it.

16. Man: Is this coupon still good?
     Woman: Till the end of this week.

What does the woman mean?
(A) The coupon can be used only today.
(B) The coupon will expire next week.
(C) The coupon is not good.
(D) He doesn't need this coupon.

(B) Since the coupon is valid until the end of the week, it must still be good all this week, but not after that.

17. Man: May I park here?
     Woman: You can normally, but today is street-cleaning day.

What does the woman mean?
(A) He cannot park here today.
(B) Today is a normal day.
(C) The street is very clean.
(D) He needs to get a parking permit.

(A) Since today is the day that the machines will clean the streets, the man cannot park there. On other days, he can.

18. Woman: Do you have to go to the meeting tonight?
     Man: I don't have to, but I'd like to know more about the university.

What does the man imply?
(A) He is going to stay home.
(B) The meeting is mandatory.
(C) He is interested in attending the meeting.
(D) He'd like to invite more people to the meeting.

(C) The man says he does not have to go to the meeting, but we can assume that he will go because he is interested in the information.

19. Man: I finally finished all my interviews.
     Woman: And now you need to write them up.

What does the woman mean?
(A) The interviews are all written.
(B) The interviews were difficult.
(C) The man has more work to do.
(D) The man is lazy.

(C) The woman comments that the man still needs to write up his interviews, so he has more work to do.

20. Man: Aren't you ready yet?
     Woman: Almost. Hang on a bit.

What does the woman mean?
(A) She wants the man to wait.
(B) She is ready now.
(C) She has decided not to go.
(D) She thinks the man should change his clothes.

(A) The phrase "hang on," in this context, means "wait."

Part B

21. What is the main topic of this conversation?
(A) Saturday's game
(B) Michigan's defense
(C) pulled ligaments
(D) getting into the coach's office

(A) This is a main idea question. The coach and player are talking about being ready for Saturday's game.

22. What sport are the coach and player talking about?
(A) soccer
(B) baseball
(C) football
(D) basketball

(C) This is a restatement question. The coach mentions the Michigan football team as the opposing team on Saturday.

23. Where does this conversation most likely take place?
(A) in the coach's office
(B) on the playing field
(C) at the doctor's office
(D) in the auditorium

(B) This is a location question. Since the speakers are at a football practice, a playing field would be the most likely location. They are not in the coach's office since the coach tells the player he can go to her office.

24. Where does the woman tell the man to go?
(A) to the hospital
(B) to his home
(C) to her office
(D) to the library

(C) This is a restatement question. The coach tells the player he can go to her office to watch the game films.

25. What is the main topic of this conversation?
(A) a lunch
(B) an exam
(C) a class
(D) a trip

(B) This is a main idea question. The two students are discussing their results on an exam.

26. What topic did the essay question cover?
(A) rainforest tribes in Brazil
(B) mountain tribes in Chile
(C) Incas in Peru
(D) cities of Colombia

(A) This is a restatement question. The essay was on the rainforest tribes in Brazil.

27. What is the woman upset about?
(A) her paper due the next week
(B) her most recent exam grade
(C) the material on the exam
(D) not being able to get lunch

(B) This is a restatement question. The woman says she didn't do well on her exam.

28. Where is the man going after they finish talking?
(A) to take a nap
(B) to study
(C) to play football
(D) to eat lunch

(D) This is a restatement question. The man asks the woman if she would like to eat lunch with him.

29. What two topics does this conversation focus on?
(A) a sandwich and a guest lecturer
(B) a guest lecturer and ancient Egypt
(C) anthropology and history
(D) a sandwich and dessert

(A) This is a main idea question. The two are talking about her sandwich and then begin talking about their last class together with a guest lecturer.

30. What was the occupation of the guest lecturer?
(A) anthropologist
(B) doctor
(C) teacher
(D) student

(B) This is a restatement question. The woman mentions that he is a doctor.

31. What did the guest lecturer speak about?
(A) crafts of ancient Rome
(B) ancient medicine
(C) types of food in Egypt
(D) job opportunities in anthropology

(B) This is a restatement question. The doctor discussed ancient medicine in China and Egypt.

32. Where would this conversation most likely take place?
    (A) in a classroom
    (B) in a doctor's office
    (C) in a cafeteria
    (D) in an apartment

(C) This is a location question. Because the woman mentions the long line of people waiting to get food, the cafeteria is the most likely location for the conversation.

33. Where are the woman and man talking?
    (A) on a beach
    (B) on a dock
    (C) in a boat
    (D) in a swimming pool

(C) This is a location question. The woman mentions that she may have placed the tanks in the back of the boat.

Part C

36. What is the main topic of this discussion?
    (A) types of bicycle frames
    (B) the diamond bicycle frame
    (C) an analysis of steel alloys
    (D) rigidity in bicycle frames

(A) This is a main idea question. The discussion includes advantages and disadvantages of the mixte and diamond frames.

37. What is one advantage of the mixte frame?
    (A) lighter weight
    (B) more rigid structure
    (C) more visually appealing
    (D) easier to mount

(D) This is a restatement question. The speaker says it is easier to mount.

34. What is the man doing?
    (A) looking for his watch
    (B) listening to the radio
    (C) looking for his tanks
    (D) writing a letter

(C) This is a restatement question. The man replies to the woman that he can't dive yet because he can't find his air tanks.

35. During what vacation is this conversation taking place?
    (A) summer break
    (B) Christmas break
    (C) fall break
    (D) Easter break

(B) This is a restatement question. The woman and man are vacationing during their Christmas break. They talk about their friends who are probably in colder climates, which generally typifies the Christmas break in December-January.

38. Which of the following statements most likely characterizes the speaker's opinion?
    (A) Mixte frames are better than diamond frames.
    (B) Bicycles haven't changed much in the last one hundred years.
    (C) Bicycles are difficult to build.
    (D) Diamond frames are better than mixte frames.

(D) This is an inference question. The woman is discussing how diamond frames are a good choice since they are stronger and lighter than the mixte frames.

39. What recent development has increased the demand for diamond frames?
    (A) new colors and paints
    (B) stronger plastic materials
    (C) lighter-weight metals
    (D) new popularity for cycling

(C) This is a restatement question. The use of lighter materials has made the diamond frame more popular.

40. Why do some people want to hunt walruses illegally?
    (A) because the skin is good for boat-making
    (B) because the bones are used for traditional carvings
    (C) because the tusks are valuable
    (D) because the fur can be used in making coats

(C) This is an inference question. The speaker says that the tusks are a source of ivory, which is illegal to sell in the United States.

41. What group of people are allowed to hunt the walrus for food and basic needs?
    (A) Alaskans
    (B) coastal natives
    (C) park rangers
    (D) Fish and Wildlife workers

(B) This is a restatement question. Only coastal natives are allowed to hunt the walruses, not all Alaskans.

42. According to the speaker, what are the tusks being traded for?
    (A) money
    (B) weapons
    (C) drugs
    (D) food

(C) This is a restatement question. Some people were found to have been trading tusks for illegal drugs.

43. What are some coastal residents afraid of?
    (A) that the Fish and Wildlife Service will kill the animals
    (B) that they will not have enough walruses for food
    (C) that they will be blamed for illegal killings
    (D) that they will be attacked by walruses

(C) This is a restatement question. The speaker ends by saying that some coastal natives fear they will be blamed for unlawful killings.

44. What is the purpose of this announcement?
    (A) to discuss the university childcare programs
    (B) to advertise the merits of the kindergarten
    (C) to discuss eligibility requirements for the nursery
    (D) to argue for private schools as a better form of education

(A) This is a main idea question. The discussion outlines the various programs and details requirements for participating in them.

45. How many programs does the childcare center offer?
    (A) two
    (B) three
    (C) four
    (D) five

(B) This is a restatement question. The speaker states that the childcare center offers three programs.

46. Which of the following is a requirement for having children qualify for the programs?
    (A) The parents must both be university students.
    (B) The parents must live in university housing.
    (C) The children must be at least six years old.
    (D) At least one parent must be studying for a doctorate degree.

(B) This is a restatement question. One of the several requirements mentioned is that the parents must live in university housing.

47. How much does the after-school daycare program cost per school term?
    (A) $100
    (B) $250
    (C) $500
    (D) $1,000

(A) This is a restatement question. The program costs $100 per school term.

48. What is the significance of Duke Ellington to this speaker?
    (A) He was the speaker's father.
    (B) He influenced the speaker's music.
    (C) He was the greatest jazz musician ever.
    (D) He helped the speaker produce his first record.

(B) This is an inference question. The speaker begins by stating that students ask him who the greatest influence on his musical style was, and he continues by discussing Duke Ellington.

49. What place was considered to be the center for all great jazz musicians in New York City?
    (A) the Ritz Carlton
    (B) the Poodle Dog Cafe
    (C) the Washingtonian
    (D) the Cotton Club

(D) This is a restatement question. The speaker says that the Cotton Club was considered to be the most popular club in New York for jazz musicians.

50. What instrument does the speaker play?
    (A) piano
    (B) saxophone
    (C) guitar
    (D) trumpet

(B) This is a restatement question. The speaker says that he plays saxophone.

SECTION 2

Structure and Written Expression

Part 1: Sentence Completion

1. Van Gogh's *Sunflowers* _____ $39.9 million, three times the previous record.
   - **(A)** once sold for
   - **(B)** for sale once
   - **(C)** selling for once
   - **(D)** for once sold

(A) Word order. The main verb of the sentence is in the past tense: "sold" because the word "once" means a past tense action, "at one time in the past." The preposition must be put just before the price, "for $39.9 million."

2. Some monkeys, _____, use their tails in a way similar to a hand.
   - **(A)** like the spider monkey
   - **(B)** spider monkey likes
   - **(C)** to the spider monkey
   - **(D)** the monkey likes the spider

(A) Word order. The word "like + noun" is used when giving an example of something. It is often set off by commas, as in this sentence.

3. Black, red, and even bright pink diamonds _____.
   - **(A)** occasionally to find
   - **(B)** occasionally found
   - **(C)** have occasionally been found
   - **(D)** have occasionally found

(C) Verb. The present perfect tense "have been found" is in the passive voice. It must be plural to agree with the plural noun "diamonds." In the active voice, this sentence would be "Some people have occasionally found black, red, and pink diamonds."

4. Between the California Coast Range and the Sierra Nevada _____.
   - **(A)** great Central Valley
   - **(B)** the great Central Valley
   - **(C)** being the great Central Valley
   - **(D)** lies the great Central Valley

(D) Word order/verb. This sentence is written in reversed subject/verb order. A standard subject/verb pattern would be, "The great Central Valley lies between the California Coast Range and the Sierra Nevada. Answers (A), (B), and (C) do not have a main verb, which this sentence needs.

5. It is gravity _____ objects toward the earth.
   - **(A)** pulling
   - **(B)** that pulls
   - **(C)** to pull
   - **(D)** what pulls

(B) Adjective clause. The word "that" introduces the clause that describes the noun "gravity."

6. _____ their territories but rather than fight, they howl.
   - **(A)** Wolves protectively jealous
   - **(B)** Jealous of wolves
   - **(C)** Protection of wolves
   - **(D)** Wolves jealously protect

(D) Word order/ Subject + verb. The correct answer must have a main subject and verb. None of the other answers includes a verb.

7. _____ strength of 70 horses, a forklift toils all day long in a warehouse lifting great weights.
   - **(A)** Because the
   - **(B)** With the
   - **(C)** Some
   - **(D)** The

(B) Preposition. The correct answer "with the" begins a prepositional phrase, which describes the forklift.

8. The growth of two-income families in the United States _____ of people moving to a new social class.
   - (A) has resulted in millions
   - (B) results of millions
   - (C) millions of results
   - (D) resulting in millions

(A) Word order/Verb. The sentence needs a present perfect verb, "has resulted," and in this sentence this verb must be followed by the preposition "in."

9. Using a globe can be _____ it is educational.
   - (A) enjoyable
   - (B) to enjoy as
   - (C) as enjoyable
   - (D) as enjoyable as

(D) Comparison. This type of comparison ("as . . . as") is used to compare two things of equal value. Answer (A) would be correct only if this were two sentences.

10. Each mediocre book we read means one less great book that we would otherwise have a chance _____.
    - (A) to read them
    - (B) read
    - (C) reading
    - (D) to read

(D) Infinitive. The infinitive "to read" follows the noun "chance."

11. Most accidents in the home can be prevented by _____ elimination of hazards.
    - (A) that
    - (B) that the
    - (C) there is a
    - (D) the

(D) Article. The article "the" must precede the noun "elimination."

12. _____ problems in sailing in tropical seas is the coral reefs.
    - (A) One of the biggest
    - (B) The biggest one
    - (C) Of the biggest one
    - (D) There are the biggest

(A) Superlative/Word order. The subject of this sentence is the word "one," and the main verb is "is." Answers (B) and (C) are incorrect because of the word "problems," which is plural, so it cannot follow "one." Answer (D) is incorrect because it has another verb, "are."

13. The strongest dump trucks work in rock quarries, _____ tons of rocks and soil at one time.
    - (A) that they move
    - (B) they move
    - (C) where they move
    - (D) which they move

(C) Word order/Adverb clause. The word "where" begins a clause that describes what happens in the rock quarries. The word "where" has the same meaning as "at which place."

14. Alice Freeman, _____ to head Wellesley College at age 27, is one of the youngest college presidents in history.
    - (A) who was appointed
    - (B) has been appointed
    - (C) that is appointed
    - (D) is appointed

(A) Relative clause/noun clause. The clause "who was appointed" describes the woman, Alice Freeman.

15. Helen Keller lost both her sight and hearing after a severe illness _____.
    - (A) of her age in nineteen months
    - (B) she was nineteen months old
    - (C) when she was nineteen months old
    - (D) when nineteen months old she was

(C) Adverb clause. The clause describes the time of the illness.

Part 2: Error Identification

16. One of history's most spectacular executions
    $\underline{\hspace{1.5cm}}$ $\underline{\hspace{1.5cm}}$
    A   **B**
    were that of Damiens, the unsuccessful
    $\underline{\hspace{1cm}}$ $\underline{\hspace{1.5cm}}$
    C   **D**
    assassin of Louis XV of France.

(C) Verb. The correct word is "was," a singular verb that goes with the subject of the sentence, "one." The "executions" is a part of the phrase, "history's most spectacular executions"; it is not the subject of the sentence.

17. Globes and maps have been important throughout
               $\underline{\hspace{3cm}}$
                   A
    history, but never many so than today.
        $\underline{\hspace{1cm}}$ $\underline{\hspace{1cm}}$ $\underline{\hspace{1cm}}$
        B   **C**   **D**

(C) Comparative. The correct word is "more" in the phrase, "never more so than today." This phrase compares "throughout history" with "today."

18. Since vitamins are contained in a wide variety of
            $\underline{\hspace{1cm}}$ $\underline{\hspace{1.5cm}}$ $\underline{\hspace{1cm}}$
            A   **B**   **C**
    foods, people seldom lack of most of them.
                $\underline{\hspace{1.5cm}}$
                  D

(D) Preposition/unnecessary word. The word "of" is not needed in this sentence. The preposition "of" can follow the word "lack" when "lack" is a verb, as in the above example. If "lack" is a noun, it is followed by "of," i.e., "I have a lack of paper."

19. Psychological experiment indicate that people
               $\underline{\hspace{2.5cm}}$
                 A
    remember more math problems that they cannot
    solve than those they are able to solve.
    $\underline{\hspace{1cm}}$ $\underline{\hspace{1cm}}$ $\underline{\hspace{1.5cm}}$
    B   **C**   **D**

(A) Singular/plural noun. Since the verb "indicate" is plural, the subject should be "experiments," a plural noun.

20. The sun is a huge fiery globe at a average distance
      $\underline{\hspace{0.5cm}}$ $\underline{\hspace{1.5cm}}$ $\underline{\hspace{0.5cm}}$
      A   **B**   **C**
    of 93,000,000 miles from the Earth.
             $\underline{\hspace{1.5cm}}$
              D

(C) Article. Since the word "average" begins with the letter "a," the article should be "an."

21. Before becoming successful, Charles Kettering,
              $\underline{\hspace{2cm}}$
                 A
    former vice-president of General Motors, was
    so poor that he has to use the hayloft of a barn as
    $\underline{\hspace{1cm}}$ $\underline{\hspace{1cm}}$ $\underline{\hspace{0.5cm}}$
    B   **C**   **D**
    a laboratory.

(C) Verb. Since this sentence describes a past-tense event, the verb should be "had to."

22. Despite the metric system is used throughout the
    $\underline{\hspace{1cm}}$ $\underline{\hspace{1cm}}$
    A   **B**
    world, it is still not commonly used in the United
             $\underline{\hspace{1cm}}$ $\underline{\hspace{1cm}}$
             C   **D**
    States.

(A) Connecting word. Because the first part of this sentence is a clause (. . . metric system is used . . .), the correct answer is either "despite the fact that . . . " or "even though." The word "despite" would be part of a phrase, with no verb, such as "despite it" or "despite this" or "despite the system. . . . "

23. Some gorillas beat their chests as an express of
           $\underline{\hspace{1cm}}$ $\underline{\hspace{0.5cm}}$ $\underline{\hspace{1cm}}$
           A   **B**   **C**
    high spirits.
    $\underline{\hspace{1cm}}$
    D

(C) Word form. The correct word is "expression," a noun. The word "express" can be an adjective or verb.

24. Because Walter Reed's efforts and those of the
    $\underline{\hspace{1cm}}$ $\underline{\hspace{1.5cm}}$
    A   **B**
    people who worked with him, human beings
    no longer fear the dreaded disease of yellow
         $\underline{\hspace{0.5cm}}$ $\underline{\hspace{1.5cm}}$
         C   **D**
    fever.

(A) Preposition. After the word, "because," there must be the preposition "of" in this sentence since "because" in this sentence begins a prepositional phrase. In other sentences, the word "because" begins a clause, i.e. "Because Walter Reed's efforts were very good, human beings. . . . "

25. Studying the science of logic is one way to
    $\underline{\hspace{1.5cm}}$ $\underline{\hspace{2cm}}$ $\underline{\hspace{0.5cm}}$
    A   **B**   **C**
    cultivate one's reason skills.
            $\underline{\hspace{1cm}}$
            D

(D) Word form. The correct word is "reasoning," an adjective that describes the type of skills. The word "reason" can be a noun or a verb.

26. The continental shelves is the shallow area of the
                          A   B
ocean floor that is closest to the continents.
      C   D

(A) Singular/plural noun. Since the main verb is singular, the subject must be "shelf."

27. The average adult get two to five colds each year.
        A   B   C   D

(B) Verb. Since the subject "adult," is singular, the verb must be "gets."

28. Fishing have been found to contain a particular
        A   B
type of fat that may help lower blood cholesterol
                              C
levels.
  D

(A) Word form. To make sense, the subject must be changed to "fish."

29. Benjamin Franklin's ability to learn from
                          A
observation and experience contributed greatly
                                  B
to him success in public life.
      C   D

(C) Pronoun. The correct word is "his," a subject pronoun that refers to the subject, "Benjamin Franklin."

30. Industrial lasers are most often used for cutting,
        A   B   C
welding, drilling, and measure.
                      D

(D) Parallel structure. The correct word is "measuring," which is a gerund, like "cutting," "welding," and "drilling."

31. In the last ten years, Mexican government
                              A
has reduced the number of its state-owned
    B   C
companies to about half.
              D

(A) Omitted word. Before the word "Mexican" must be the article "the."

32. Psychologists at the University of Kansas
has studied the effects of the color of a room
    A   B   C
on people's behavior.
      D

(A) Verb. Since the subject, "psychologists," is plural, the verb must be "have studied."

33. Montaigne, the illustrious French philosophy,
                                  A   B
was elected mayor of Bordeaux, which was his
      C   D
home town.

(B) Word form. Since Montaigne is a person, the correct word must be "philosopher," a word that describes a person. The word "philosophy" describes a field of study.

34. Certain pollens are more likely to cause
        A   B
an allergic reaction than another.
      C   D

(D) Pronoun. The word "another" refers to one more or one different, but since the word "pollens" is plural, the correct answer for this sentence is "others."

35. Computers have made access to information
                      A   B
instantly available just by push a few buttons.
              C   D

(D) Word form. The correct word is "pushing" since a noun or gerund must follow the word "by" in this type of sentence.

36. Mined over 2,000 years ago, copper is one of
        A   B
the earliest know metals.
      C   D

(D) Word form. The correct word is "known," an adjective that describes the metals. The word "know" is a verb.

37. Many of the early work of T.S. Eliot expresses
    $\underline{\text{A}}$ $\underline{\text{B}}$

    the anguish and barrenness of modern life and
                     $\underline{\text{C}}$

    the isolation of the individual.
              $\underline{\text{D}}$

(A) Adjective. The correct word is "much," since the word "work" is a mass (noncount) noun.

38. A sore throat interferes with daily life by making
                   $\underline{\text{A}}$ $\underline{\text{B}}$ $\underline{\text{C}}$

    swallow difficult.
        $\underline{\text{D}}$

(C) Word form. After the phrase, "by making," there must be a noun or gerund. The word "swallow" is a verb, but "swallowing" is a gerund (a verb +*ing* used as a noun).

39. A farmer's tractor is like a powerful horse, as it
                                  $\underline{\text{A}}$ $\underline{\text{B}}$

    plows field, pulls trailers, and moves heavy
          $\underline{\text{C}}$ $\underline{\text{D}}$

    loads.

(C) Singular/plural noun/parallel structure. The correct word is "fields," a plural noun that is parallel with "trailers" and "loads."

40. During wedding ceremonies in the United States,
           $\underline{\text{A}}$ $\underline{\text{B}}$

    guests are usually silence.
    $\underline{\text{C}}$ $\underline{\text{D}}$

(D) Word form. The correct word is "silent," an adjective. "Silence" is a noun.

SECTION 3
Reading Comprehension

1. What is the main topic of the passage?
   (A) survival of peregrine falcons
   (B) releases into the wild
   (C) endangered species
   (D) the pesticide DDT

(A) This is a main idea question. This passage first describes the falcons as endangered and then expands on how new urban nesting sites are providing for their survival.

2. In line 1, the phrase "indigenous to" could be best replaced by
   (A) typical of
   (B) protected by
   (C) adapted to
   (D) native to

(D) This is a vocabulary question. The word "indigenous" means "native" or "living or occurring naturally in an area."

3. The word "byproducts" in line 2 is most similar to which of the following?
   (A) derivatives
   (B) discoveries
   (C) chemicals
   (D) elements

(A) This is a vocabulary question. "Byproducts," which means something produced secondarily, is most similar to "derivatives," which means anything obtained or deduced from another material.

4. In line 3, the word "banned" could be best replaced by
   (A) authorized
   (B) developed
   (C) disseminated
   (D) prohibited

(D) The verbs "to ban" and "to prohibit" both mean "to forbid."

5. Which of the following words is closest in meaning to the word "rate," as used in line 5?
   (A) speed
   (B) percentage
   (C) continuation
   (D) behavior

(B) In this sentence, the word "rate" refers to the number of birds that survive, which is similar to the percentage of birds that survive.

6. In line 5, the word "raising" most probably means
   (A) breeding
   (B) elevating
   (C) collecting
   (D) measuring

(A) In this sentence, "raising" refers to the process of taking care of the birds as they grow. It may also include protecting the birds so that they can lay eggs that are hatched in the laboratories. The verb "breeding" also means "raising," "producing," or "growing."

7. Why were the peregrine falcons in danger?
   (A) because of the pesticides used by American farmers
   (B) because they migrated to countries where their eggs could not survive
   (C) because they ate birds from other countries where DDT was still used.
   (D) because they were prized by hunters and hunted to near extinction

(C) This is a restatement question. The passage states in lines 3–4 that the falcon ate birds from countries that were still using the pesticide DDT.

8. The word "release" as used in line 8 most probably means
  (A) internment
  (B) regression
  (C) distributions
  (D) possessions

(C) The word "releases" refers to the process of setting the birds free or letting them go, and the word "distributions" refers to the process of scattering something out or giving it out. Answer (A) is the opposite; it refers to keeping something in. Answer (B) refers to the process of moving backward or going into the past. Answer (D) refers to one's belongings.

9. The word "ledge" in line 9 is closest in meaning to
  (A) window
  (B) wall
  (C) terrace
  (D) shelf

(D) A "ledge" refers to something that protrudes horizontally. It may be a narrow walkway, something to stand on, or a decoration on a building. The closest in meaning is "shelf," since a shelf is also something that protrudes outward.

10. According to the passage, which of the following is NOT a reason why a falcon might choose to live in a city?
  (A) There are high places to nest.
  (B) There are other falcons nearby.
  (C) There is a lack of predators.
  (D) There is abundant food.

(B) This is a negative question. The author states all of the above reasons except (B). Answer (C) is not correct since the question is asking why the birds CHOOSE the city; it is not asking about the results of the release program. Even though there may be more falcons living in the city because of the new release programs, the passage states that the bird is still in danger of extinction, so the possibility of other falcons living nearby is small.

11. According to the passage, which of the following are the falcon's main predators?
  (A) pigeons
  (B) rattlesnakes
  (C) owls
  (D) humans

(C) This is a restatement question. Line 15 states that the falcon's main predator is the great horned owl.

12. As used in line 13, the word "spots" could be best replaced by
  (A) places
  (B) dilemmas
  (C) jungles
  (D) materials

(A) The words "spots" and "places" both refer to "locations."

13. According to the passage, where have the release programs been the most successful?
  (A) in office buildings
  (B) on the East Coast
  (C) in mountainous areas
  (D) in the wild

(B) This is a restatement question. Lines 15–16 state that the urban releases have been most successful on the East Coast of the United States.

14. What does this passage mainly discuss?
  (A) the life of Jan Dibbets
  (B) new forms of art created by Jan Dibbets
  (C) an exhibit of abstract art
  (D) art that follows the style of Vermeer, Van Gogh, and Rembrandt

(B) This is a main idea question. The passage is primarily concerned with the art created by Dibbets. There is not enough about Dibbets' career or life history to suggest (A) as the answer, nor does the passage mention an exhibit or give much information about Dibbets' predecessors.

15. Which of the following words could best replace the word "revered" in line 1?
    (A) honored
    (B) possessed
    (C) modeled
    (D) handled

(A) The verbs "to revere" and "to honor" both mean "to look up to" and "to respect."

16. As used in line 2, what is the meaning of the word "time"?
    (A) season
    (B) period
    (C) century
    (D) interval

(B) All of the above choices can mean "time" in some contexts. As used in line 2, however, answer (B) is the best. Answers (A) and (C) are too specific. Answer (D) refers to a period of time that is between two moments or events.

17. The word "disparate" in line 3 is closest in meaning to
    (A) similar
    (B) unspoken
    (C) different
    (D) unknown

(C) The word "disparate" means "different" or "dissimilar." It often implies that the two different things are so unlike as to be "at odds," "at variance," or "discordant" with each other.

18. The author implies that
    (A) Dibbets is more well known to some people than Vermeer
    (B) views of ceilings in Gothic buildings are most beautiful when seen from the ground floor
    (C) art is now becoming more abstract
    (D) Dibbets preferred watercolor to photography

(C) This is a restatement question. In the second line, the passage states that the trends in art are toward abstraction. The word "trend" refers to a movement in a general direction or a movement of events.

19. The word "remarkable" as used in line 3 could be best replaced by
    (A) inseparable
    (B) unified
    (C) clever
    (D) extraordinary

(D) The words "remarkable" and "extraordinary" both mean "beyond the usual."

20. As used in line 3, the word "works" could be best replaced by which of the following?
    (A) deeds
    (B) mechanisms
    (C) operations
    (D) creations

(D) The word "works" in this sentence refers to "works of art," which might also be referred to as "creations," "achievements," or "pieces."

21. As described in this passage, Dibbets used all of the following elements EXCEPT
    (A) pen and ink
    (B) watercolors
    (C) architectural photographs
    (D) still-life drawings

(D) This is a negative question. All the elements except still-life drawings are mentioned in the text.

22. The word "segments" as used in line 5 refers to
    (A) parts
    (B) dots
    (C) supports
    (D) webs

(A) "Segments" are the pieces or parts into which something is divided.

23. The word "neo-classical" in line 7 refers to
    (A) artistic patterns
    (B) trends in art
    (C) architectural styles
    (D) museum decoration

(C) This is a vocabulary question. Since the word "neo-classical" describes "buildings," we can infer that "neo-classical" is an architectural term.

24. This passage is mainly about
    (A) changes to Carnegie Hall
    (B) the appearance of Carnegie Hall
    (C) Carnegie Hall's history during the Great Depression
    (D) damage to the ceiling in Carnegie Hall

(A) This is a main idea question. Answers (B), (C), and (D) are too specific. (A) is the best answer because it addresses the overall discussion of renovations in the passage.

25. The word "extensive" in line 2 could best be replaced by which of the following?
    (A) fabulous
    (B) thorough
    (C) devoted
    (D) continuous

(B) The word "extensive" means that the renovation was broad; it included the rebuilding of a large part of the structure. The word "thorough" means that something is complete and careful. While these words do not have exactly the same meaning, they are the closest in meaning. Answer (A) means "wonderful." Answer (C) means "absorbed completely in some activity." And answer (D) means "non-stop."

26. In line 7, what is the meaning of the word "detrimental"?
    (A) dangerous
    (B) significant
    (C) extreme
    (D) harmful

(D) The words "detrimental" and "harmful" both refer to an activity that causes damage. The activity may or may not be dangerous, significant, or extreme.

27. What major change happened to the hall in 1946?
    (A) The acoustic dome was damaged.
    (B) Space in the building was sold to commercial businesses.
    (C) The walls were damaged in an earthquake.
    (D) The stage was renovated.

(A) This is a restatement question. The answer is in lines 11–12, which state that filmmarkers cut a hole in the ceiling because they needed more space for the lights and air vents.

28. Who was Andrew Carnegie?
    (A) a violinist
    (B) an architect
    (C) a steel mill owner
    (D) the mayor of New York City

(C) This is a restatement question. Line 4 states that Carnegie was the owner of a steel company.

29. Which of the following words could best replace the word "gaping" in line 11?
    (A) small
    (B) round
    (C) vital
    (D) wide

(D) The word "gaping" refers to the width of an opening, such as an open mouth. The word "wide" is the best synonym.

30. The word "fake" in line 12 is most similar to which of the following?
    (A) low
    (B) false
    (C) thin
    (D) handsome

(B) The word "fake" refers to something that is not genuine or is misleading. The closest in meaning is "false."

31. What was Isaac Stern's relationship to Carnegie Hall?
    (A) He made the movie *Carnegie Hall* in 1946.
    (B) He performed on opening night in 1891.
    (C) He tried to save the hall beginning in 1960.
    (D) He opened a coffeeshop in Carnegie Hall during the Depression.

(C) This is a restatement question. In lines 14–16, the passage states that Isaac Stern helped save Carnegie Hall from demolition.

32. What was probably the most important aspect of the recent renovation?
    (A) restoring the outer wall
    (B) expanding the lobby
    (C) restoring the plaster trim
    (D) repairing the ceiling

(D) This is an inference question. In several places in the passage, the acoustical quality is mentioned as being very important to the hall, and the damage to the ceiling greatly affected the quality of the acoustics.

33. Which of the following is closest in meaning to the word "unveiled" in line 15?
    (A) announced
    (B) restricted
    (C) overshadowed
    (D) located

(A) The verb " to unveil" means "to uncover" or "to reveal." When something is announced, it is revealed.

34. The author uses the word "spurred" in line 16 to show that Stern
    (A) predicted the result
    (B) probed the plans
    (C) was told in advance
    (D) was stimulated

(D) The verb "to spur" means "to stimulate," "to hasten," or "to encourage." The sentence means that Stern was stimulated to act quickly because of the plans to demolish the building.

35. How does the author seem to feel about the future of Carnegie Hall?
    (A) ambiguous
    (B) guarded
    (C) optimistic
    (D) negative

(C) This is an inference question. The final sentence of the passage states that the prospects for the future have never looked more promising. This is a very optimistic statement.

36. Which of the following would most likely be the topic of the next paragraph?
    (A) a scientific explanation of acoustics and the nature of sound
    (B) a description of people's reactions to the newly renovated hall
    (C) a discussion of the coffeeshop that once was located in the building
    (D) further discussion about the activities of Isaac Stern in 1960

(B) Since the passage ends with an optimistic comment about the renovations, the most likely next paragraph would continue with the topic of new renovations. The other answer choices are topics that were mentioned earlier in the passage.

37. What is the primary focus of this passage?
    (A) controversies over land use in Denali
    (B) miners selling their property in Denali
    (C) the building of new roads in the Denali area
    (D) limiting tourist access to Denali

(A) This is a main idea question. The first paragraph ends with the mention of the discussions about the future use of the area. The second paragraph alludes to a controversy between land owners and environmentalists.

38. The word "wilderness" in line 3 could be best replaced by the word
    (A) dangerous
    (B) natural
    (C) rural
    (D) pastoral

(B) A wilderness area is one that is left in its natural state. It may be dangerous, rural, or pastoral, but not necessarily any of these. "Rural" refers to the "country," not the city. "Pastoral" also refers to rural, country life.

39. The word "prompting" in line 4 could be best replaced by which of the following?
    (A) promising
    (B) sanctioning
    (C) initiating
    (D) trapping

(C) This is a vocabulary question. The verb "to prompt" means "to inspire discussion" or "to be the cause of beginning a discussion."

40. As used in line 5, which of the following is most similar to the word "preserve"?
    (A) protect
    (B) enclose
    (C) investigate
    (D) foster

(A) The verbs "to preserve" and "to protect" both refer to keeping something from danger, harm, or destruction.

41. The word "arises" in line 6 could be best replaced
    by
    (A) surrenders
    (B) occurs
    (C) volunteers
    (D) prospers

(B) The verb "to arise" means "to come into being" or
"to spring up." The verb "to occur" has a similar
meaning.

42. The word "tract" as used in line 7 refers to which of
    the following?
    (A) trail
    (B) resort
    (C) frontier
    (D) expanse

(D) A "tract" in this sentence refers to a large expanse
of land. In the following sentence, however, "a mining
tract" would more closely be replaced by a word such as
"area" or "zone."

43. Which of the following words is most similar to the
    word "abundant" in line 9?
    (A) plentiful
    (B) sparse
    (C) hopeful
    (D) absolute

(A) The words "abundant" and "plentiful" both refer to
a large or sufficient amount of something.

44. According to the passage, which of the following
    are pollutants in the Denali area?
    (A) gold
    (B) pesticides
    (C) human waste
    (D) arsenic

(D) This is a restatement question. Lines 9–10 state that
heavy metals such as arsenic and lead polluted rivers
and streams.

45. Which of the following is closest in meaning to the
    phrase "potential impact" in line 11?
    (A) approximate cost
    (B) expected value
    (C) proposed size
    (D) possible effects

(D) The word "potential" means "possible, but not yet
actual," and "impact" means "effect," often the initial
effect of something.

46. The author infers that mine owners might hesitate
    to sell their land to the Park Service for which of the
    following reasons?
    (A) There may be increasing demand for the ore in
        the mine.
    (B) They might want to move to the towns.
    (C) They might receive more money selling their
        land to developers.
    (D) They might want to build a house on their
        property.

(C) This is an inference question. The end of the passage
discusses the prospect of increased tourism as new
roads are built and the resulting demand for hotel and
tourist facilities. We can infer from this that the land
could become very valuable as future building sites and
that mine owners might make more money selling their
land to developers than to the National Park Service.

47. What is the author's purpose in writing this pas-
    sage?
    (A) to demonstrate the changes in Denali National
        Park
    (B) to use Denali as an example of common park
        issues
    (C) to introduce the wonders of the wilderness
        area of Denali
    (D) to explain the problems occurring in Denali
        Park

(B) This is an author's purpose question. At the end of
the first paragraph, the author states that there are
discussions "about how to preserve wilderness areas in
general." In addition, the first sentence of the second
paragraph talks about land use issues in general, and the
last sentence infers a general issue. The other answer
choices are all mentioned but are not the main purpose.
The "changes," the "wonders," and the "problems" all
relate to examples of common National Park issues.

48. Which of the following would most likely be the topic of the next paragraph in this passage?
- **(A)** conflict between land owners and environmentalists
- **(B)** the role of the National Park Service in development
- **(C)** tourist needs in Denali Park
- **(D)** wildlife in the park

(A) This is a question of the following topic. Since the passage ends with a mention of both land owners and those interested in preserving the wilderness (presumably environmentalists who are not land owners), we can infer that the next topic will be about both of these groups.

49. With which of the following topics is this passage primarily concerned?
- **(A)** Sharks are efficient creatures with bad reputations.
- **(B)** Sharks are some of the oldest creatures on earth.
- **(C)** Sharks illustrate a problem in wildlife protection.
- **(D)** The campaign to save dolphins was not extended to save sharks.

(C) This is a main idea question. The first paragraph argues that humans are interested in saving only certain of the earth's creatures, and that this is a problem because we are ignoring other important parts of our environment. The second paragraph begins with "A perfect illustration of this is. . . ." The shark as an endangered species is the example that supports the author's argument.

50. Which of the following is most similar to the meaning of the word "warped" in line 3?
- **(A)** distorted
- **(B)** wasteful
- **(C)** extravagant
- **(D)** wanton

(A) The words "warped" and "distorted" both refer to an idea that is "misrepresented" or "one-sided." Answer (B) means "misused" or "misspent." Answer (C) means "expensive" or "costly." It can also mean "wasteful." Answer (D) refers to a "deliberate" or "willful" act, usually of destruction.

51. In line 7, the word "protested" is closest in meaning to which of the following?
- **(A)** prescribed
- **(B)** objected to
- **(C)** protected
- **(D)** reflected on

(B) The verbs "to object to" and " to protest" both mean "to oppose something" or "to disapprove of" something.

52. In line 8, the word "generated" could be best replaced by
- **(A)** consumes
- **(B)** absorbed
- **(C)** designated
- **(D)** produced

(D) The words "generated" and "produced" both mean "to cause to exist" or "to make."

53. How did environmentalists manage to protect dolphins?
- **(A)** They prevented fishermen from selling them for meat.
- **(B)** They pressured fishermen to protect dolphins by law.
- **(C)** They brought political pressure against tuna companies.
- **(D)** They created sanctuaries where dolphin fishing was not allowed.

(C) This is a restatement question. In lines 8–9, the passage states that environmentalists helped protect the dolphin by putting political and economic pressure on tuna companies.

54. About how long have sharks lived on the planet?
- **(A)** 25 million years
- **(B)** 150 million years
- **(C)** 350 million years
- **(D)** 500 million years

(C) This is a restatement question. Lines 12–13 state that sharks have been around for about 350 million years.

55. The author uses the phrase "weeding out" in line 14 to mean
    (A) strengthening something that is weak
    (B) feeding something that is hungry
    (C) encouraging something that is efficient
    (D) getting rid of something that is unwanted

(D) A "weed" is a plant that is undesirable or unwanted. The phrase "weeding out" means to get rid of something that one doesn't want or to discourage something that is weak in order for another stronger thing to exist.

56. In line 15, the phrase "managed to live" is used to infer that
    (A) surviving was difficult
    (B) migration was common
    (C) procreation was expanding
    (D) roaming was necessary

(A) The phrase "managed to live" means that someone or something, although faced with difficulties, was able to survive.

57. The word "proof" in line 16 could be best replaced by which of the following?
    (A) characteristic
    (B) evidence
    (C) praise
    (D) customary

(B) The words "proof" and "evidence" both mean "documentation," "substantiation," or "verification" that something is true.

58. In line 17, the phrase "to cast away" means most nearly
    (A) to throw off
    (B) to bring in
    (C) to see through
    (D) to set apart

(A) The phrases "to cast away" and "to throw off" both refer to "flinging," "hurling," or "tossing" something away from oneself.

59. What is the author's tone in this passage?
    (A) explanatory
    (B) accusatory
    (C) gentle
    (D) proud

(B) In the first paragraph, the author accuses all people ("humanity" and "we") of a warped attitude toward wildlife protection. In the last sentence, the author accuses all people ("us," "humans," "we") of damaging the planet.

60. Which of the following best describes the organization of this passage?
    (A) order of importance
    (B) cause and effect
    (C) statement and example
    (D) chronological order

(C) The first paragraph is a general discussion about sharks having a bad reputation and how this reputation is based on an unfair attitude toward the preservation of wildlife. The second paragraph gives an example of how we have preserved the dolphin while ignoring sharks.

ANSWER SHEET FOR PRACTICE TEST 4

Section 1: Listening Comprehension

1 2 3 4 5 6 7 8 9 10 11 12 13 14 15 16 17 18 19 20 21 22 23 24 25 26 27 28 29 30 31 32 33 34 35 36 37 38 39 40 41 42 43 44 45 46 47 48 49 50 51 52 53 54 55 56 57 58 59 60

Ⓐ Ⓑ Ⓒ Ⓓ

61 62 63 64 65 66 67 68 69 70 71 72 73 74 75 76 77 78 79 80

Ⓐ Ⓑ Ⓒ Ⓓ

Section 2: Structure and Written Expression

1 2 3 4 5 6 7 8 9 10 11 12 13 14 15 16 17 18 19 20 21 22 23 24 25 26 27 28 29 30 31 32 33 34 35 36 37 38 39 40 41 42 43 44 45 46 47 48 49 50 51 52 53 54 55 56 57 58 59 60

Ⓐ Ⓑ Ⓒ Ⓓ

Section 3: Reading Comprehension

1 2 3 4 5 6 7 8 9 10 11 12 13 14 15 16 17 18 19 20 21 22 23 24 25 26 27 28 29 30 31 32 33 34 35 36 37 38 39 40 41 42 43 44 45 46 47 48 49 50 51 52 53 54 55 56 57 58 59 60

Ⓐ Ⓑ Ⓒ Ⓓ

61 62 63 64 65 66 67 68 69 70 71 72 73 74 75 76 77 78 79 80 81 82 83 84 85 86 87 88 89 90

Ⓐ Ⓑ Ⓒ Ⓓ

Date Taken ____________________

Number Correct

Section 1 __________

Section 2 __________

Section 3 __________

Practice Test 4: Long Form

This test is longer than the other practice tests in this book. It represents the longer form that is sometimes given during TOEFL examinations. See pages 4–5 for more information about the two forms of the TOEFL.

SECTION 1

Listening Comprehension

Time—approximately 50 minutes

NOTE: You can simulate actual TOEFL conditions by using the Listening Comprehension Cassettes that accompany this book. If you do not have the tape, ask a friend to read the tapescript for Listening Comprehension Test 4, which is in Part Four, pages 404–17 of this book.

Part A

Directions: In Part A you will hear short conversations between two people. After each conversation a third person will ask a question about what was said. You will hear the conversation only one time, so you must listen carefully to what each speaker says. After you hear the conversation and the question, read the four possible answers in your test booklet and pick the one which best answers the question. Then look on the answer sheet for the number of the question and fill in the oval that corresponds to the letter of your answer choice.

Listen to an example:

You will hear:

You will read:

Sample Answer

(A) He will call Pete before he goes home.
(B) He will call Pete after he gets home.
(C) He called Pete at home.
(D) He will call Pete tomorrow.

You learn from the conversation that the man will call Pete as soon as he gets home. The best answer to the question "What does the man mean?" is (B), "He will call Pete after he gets home." Therefore, the correct answer is (B).

Now listen to the tape: Test 4, Section 1, Listening Comprehension Part A.

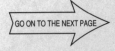

1. (A) Lisa is having a hard time in school.
   (B) Lisa is expecting a baby.
   (C) Lisa is very busy this term.
   (D) Lisa is often very tired.

2. (A) Her major was not chemistry.
   (B) She is an excellent student in chemistry.
   (C) She wanted to change her major.
   (D) She likes chemistry classes more than computer science classes.

3. (A) Mark has quit smoking.
   (B) Mark doesn't like to share a room with someone smoking.
   (C) Mark shouldn't smoke in the classroom.
   (D) Mark helped his roommate quit smoking.

4. (A) Not many people attended the workshop.
   (B) There were not many workshops available last night.
   (C) The workshop is more interesting than the show.
   (D) Last night's show was one of the few good ones.

5. (A) He didn't do very well in school.
   (B) He won't graduate this semester.
   (C) Steve needs some hands-on classes.
   (D) Steve is able to apply his knowlege.

6. (A) rent a videotape
   (B) fix the brakes on the car
   (C) begin packing for their move
   (D) see a film

7. (A) She will return the man's favor.
   (B) She will return the book on her way to work.
   (C) She can't return the book for the man.
   (D) She works at the school library.

8. (A) He is going to leave the room.
   (B) He is going to sit down.
   (C) He is going to buy a new chair.
   (D) He is going to bring the chair back.

9. (A) The man was excited by the lecture.
   (B) The man was very interested in the speech.
   (C) The man gave a long speech.
   (D) The man is tired.

10. (A) She wants to continue her studies right away.
    (B) She wants a break from studying.
    (C) She hasn't decided yet.
    (D) She'll find a job right after graduation.

11. (A) choose one class or the other
    (B) ask his advisor
    (C) let the professors make the decision
    (D) take both classes

12. (A) He doesn't have the book.
    (B) He had the book, but lost it.
    (C) He wants to read it again.
    (D) He has not read the book.

13. (A) He'll take his car and give the woman a ride.
    (B) He'll take his bicycle to school too.
    (C) He'll join her at her exercise class.
    (D) He'll teach the woman how to ride a bicycle.

14. (A) She didn't expect the books would have to be returned so soon.
    (B) She doesn't want to keep these books.
    (C) She doesn't think her library card is valid.
    (D) She has finished reading these books already.

15. (A) It will probably take five minutes to fix it.
    (B) She fixed it a few minutes ago.
    (C) Her machine is connected to the man's.
    (D) The electrical connection might be the problem.

16. (A) Thank you for dropping by.
    (B) Thank you for picking it up.
    (C) No thanks, I don't want any.
    (D) No thanks, I'm not going.

17. (A) show her how to make it work right
    (B) invite her as a guest
    (C) tell the woman the directions
    (D) take her there if necessary

18. (A) He already has a job.
    (B) He will probably work at the library.
    (C) He needs to study full time.
    (D) He plans to work at the library in the summer.

19. (A) He enjoys working on weekends.
    (B) He is different from the other workers.
    (C) He works at a different time on Saturdays and Sundays.
    (D) He's going out of town this weekend.

20. (A) Whether she'll have enough time to do it
    (B) Whether the professor will approve it
    (C) Whether she'll change her mind
    (D) Whether she has enough knowledge to do it

 GO ON TO THE NEXT PAGE

21. (A) She hopes that Laura will come back alone.
    (B) She wants Laura to return.
    (C) She doesn't want Laura to come back.
    (D) She knows Laura is thinking about coming back.

22. (A) Barbara mailed the letter too early.
    (B) Barbara is late in mailing the check.
    (C) Barbara took a week to send it.
    (D) Barbara mailed the check a week ago.

23. (A) He is going to keep the present.
    (B) He is going to resign his position.
    (C) He's going to continue working for now.
    (D) He is going to exercise as long as he can.

24. (A) Peter sleeps too much.
    (B) Peter should have rested for a longer time.
    (C) Peter was forced to stay away from his work.
    (D) Peter went on vacation.

25. (A) He doesn't know when it's open.
    (B) He doesn't want to go.
    (C) He thinks it is open in the evening.
    (D) He agrees with the woman.

26. (A) She's here permanently.
    (B) She hopes the change will be good.
    (C) It's a good place to work.
    (D) She can stay as long as the work is satisfactory.

27. (A) They don't have enough time to get there.
    (B) This way should take less time.
    (C) They are lost.
    (D) The road is winding through this area.

28. (A) It wasn't as easy as he thought it would be.
    (B) It was farther away than he thought.
    (C) He doesn't think he gave the appropriate compliments.
    (D) He thought it would be a lot harder.

29. (A) They were able to telephone the police.
    (B) They almost hit a boy.
    (C) Somebody tried to rob them.
    (D) Something frightened them.

30. (A) She found the right price.
    (B) She has decided what to buy.
    (C) She hasn't bought it yet.
    (D) She's beginning to think about it.

GO ON TO THE NEXT PAGE

Part B

Directions: In Part B you will hear longer conversations between two people. After each conversation you will be asked some questions. You will hear the conversations and the questions only once, so listen carefully to what is said. After you hear a question, read the four possible answers in your test book and decide which one is the best answer to the question you heard. Then, on your answer sheet, find the number of the question and fill in the oval that corresponds to the letter of the answer you have chosen. Answer all questions based on what is stated or implied by the speakers.

Listen to the example on the tape.

> *You will hear:*

Now listen to sample question number 1.

> *You will read:*

Sample Answer

Ⓐ Ⓑ Ⓒ ⬤

> **(A)** to the cafeteria
> **(B)** to the movie theater
> **(C)** to her dorm room
> **(D)** to the library

The best answer to the question "Where is the woman going?" is (D), "to the library." Therefore, the correct choice is (D).

Now listen to sample question number 2.

> *You will hear:*

Sample Answer

Ⓐ Ⓑ ⬤ Ⓓ

> *You will read:*

> **(A)** Term papers are easy for him.
> **(B)** He has a lot of essay exams.
> **(C)** He finds lab experiments easier than writing term papers.
> **(D)** He is busier this semester than last semester.

The best answer to the question "Which best describes the man's feelings about his classes?" is (C), "He finds lab experiments easier than writing term papers." Therefore, the correct answer is (C).

Now listen to the test. Remember, you are not allowed to take any notes or write in your test book.

31. (A) playing the guitar
    (B) working at a restaurant
    (C) singing in a rock concert
    (D) dancing in a ballet recital

32. (A) San Francisco
    (B) Washington
    (C) Chicago
    (D) New York

33. (A) in a restaurant
    (B) in a book shop
    (C) in a record store
    (D) in a theater

34. (A) New York
    (B) Chicago
    (C) Washington
    (D) San Francisco

35. (A) Nantucket
    (B) Woods Hole
    (C) her father's restaurant
    (D) on the coast

36. (A) Woods Hole
    (B) New York
    (C) his uncle's restaurant
    (D) his father's restaurant

37. (A) sea birds
    (B) sharks
    (C) whales
    (D) crabs

38. (A) because he will be visiting his grandparents
    (B) because he will be working for his uncle
    (C) because she will be working on a boat
    (D) because she will be working in a laboratory

39. (A) American history
    (B) American literature
    (C) English literature
    (D) chemistry

40. (A) to visit relatives
    (B) to give a lecture
    (C) to meet her publisher
    (D) to see museum exhibits

41. (A) to speak to his class
    (B) to deliver a message for him
    (C) to review an article for him
    (D) to lend him five dollars

42. (A) tomorrow's trip
    (B) tomorrow's practice
    (C) yesterday's exam
    (D) today's class

43. (A) basketball
    (B) marine biology
    (C) organic chemistry
    (D) geochemistry

44. (A) a ride to the beach
    (B) his notes from the last class
    (C) directions to the beach
    (D) help in moving from her apartment

45. (A) 3:30 A.M.
    (B) 4 A.M.
    (C) 5:30 P.M.
    (D) 6 P.M.

46. (A) nervous
    (B) scared
    (C) excited
    (D) hopeful

47. (A) 1
    (B) 4
    (C) 8
    (D) 16

48. (A) She wants to continue her study.
    (B) She hopes to find a job near Ed.
    (C) She hopes Ed is offered the job.
    (D) She hopes Ed finds a job near her.

49. (A) relieved
    (B) angry
    (C) frustrated
    (D) excited

50. (A) She thought it was a good idea.
    (B) She wanted to read about art first.
    (C) She didn't want to go.
    (D) She said she was too tired.

51. (A) Los Angeles
    (B) Chicago
    (C) San Francisco
    (D) New York

52. (A) study again
    (B) visit another museum
    (C) walk in a park
    (D) go to a restaurant

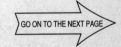
GO ON TO THE NEXT PAGE

53. (A) enroll in classes
    (B) get a new phone
    (C) convince her friend to register
    (D) contact her counselor

54. (A) that she should wait until later
    (B) that she should change her schedule
    (C) that she should enroll in classes
    (D) that she should see a counselor

55. (A) relaxed
    (B) worried
    (C) scared
    (D) excited

Part C

Directions: In this part of the test, you will hear talks by a single person. After each talk, you will be asked some questions. You will hear the talks and the questions only once, so listen carefully to what is said. After you hear a question, read the four possible answers in your test book and decide which one is the best answer to the question you heard. Then find the number of the question on your answer sheet, and fill in the oval that corresponds to the letter of the answer you have chosen. Answer all questions based on what is stated or implied in the talk.

Listen to this sample talk.

You will hear:

Now listen to sample question number 1.   Sample Answer

You will read: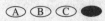

      (A) to demonstrate tutoring techniques
      (B) to explain school policies
      (C) to recruit childcare workers
      (D) to explain a service

The best answer to the question "What is the purpose of this announcement?" is (D), "to explain a service." Therefore, the correct choice is (D).

Now listen to sample question number 2.   Sample Answer

You will hear:

You will read:

      (A) Give your child extra tutoring.
      (B) Take your child to the program today.
      (C) Apply as soon as you can.
      (D) Pay next month.

The best answer to the question "What does the speaker recommend?" is (C), "Apply as soon as you can." Therefore the correct choice is (C).

Now begin. Remember, you are not allowed to write any notes in your test book.

GO ON TO THE NEXT PAGE

56. (A) the life of James Joyce
    (B) a book called *Dubliners*
    (C) writers in Paris
    (D) Irish novelists

57. (A) scientist
    (B) painter
    (C) writer
    (D) doctor

58. (A) Paris
    (B) Dublin
    (C) New York
    (D) Zurich

59. (A) Dublin
    (B) Paris
    (C) London
    (D) New York

60. (A) to explain recent fossil discoveries
    (B) to argue theories of the "straight crab"
    (C) to tell the history of the Institute
    (D) to contrast the fossil discoveries in America and Australia

61. (A) scientists
    (B) tourists
    (C) English teachers
    (D) administrators

62. (A) reptiles
    (B) mammals
    (C) crabs
    (D) insects

63. (A) Dr. Sawyer's discoveries
    (B) the Australian team's recent findings
    (C) theories about the "straight crab"
    (D) the descendants of the "straight crab"

64. (A) University of Washington
    (B) University of Iowa
    (C) Harvard University
    (D) University of North Carolina

65. (A) It is the oldest public university.
    (B) It is the largest public university.
    (C) It is the least expensive public university.
    (D) It is the most beautiful university.

66. (A) war
    (B) plagues
    (C) lack of funding
    (D) fire

67. (A) music
    (B) science
    (C) baseball
    (D) arts

68. (A) in a cafeteria
    (B) in an auditorium
    (C) in a classroom
    (D) in a gymnasium

69. (A) to be camp counselors
    (B) to maintain the equipment
    (C) to drive the campers
    (D) to work as teachers

70. (A) to California
    (B) to high school
    (C) to Washington
    (D) to college

71. (A) that they leave the water
    (B) that they dig a hole in the sand
    (C) that they rip open their nests
    (D) that they eat their babies

72. (A) in a hole
    (B) in the water
    (C) under the mother's tail
    (D) in the mother's mouth

73. (A) to keep them warm
    (B) to protect them from harm
    (C) to transport them to the water
    (D) to clean them

74. (A) 5 weeks
    (B) 10 weeks
    (C) 12 weeks
    (D) 15 weeks

75. (A) to improve low-yielding varieties of wheat
    (B) to receive the Nobel Peace prize
    (C) to take over his father's farm
    (D) to be the "father of the green revolution"

76. (A) the Nobel Prize
    (B) the Rockefeller Foundation
    (C) his family farm
    (D) the Green Revolution

77. (A) introduced new technology
    (B) became a plant pathologist
    (C) worked for peace
    (D) got a doctorate degree

GO ON TO THE NEXT PAGE

78. (A) The coal has polluted the river.
    (B) It's a beautiful place to visit.
    (C) The water is too cold for swimming.
    (D) It is an unusual border between two countries.

79. (A) Detroit and Duluth were established.
    (B) The Great Lakes were linked with the Atlantic Ocean.
    (C) Cargo boats began carrying grain on the river.
    (D) Canals and locks were built on the river.

80. (A) an area of tree-covered islands
    (B) a series of castles near the river
    (C) a place where cargo ships carry coal
    (D) a destination of ocean-going vessels

THIS IS THE END OF SECTION 1.
DO NOT READ OR WORK ON ANY OTHER SECTION OF THE TEST UNTIL TIME IS UP.

STOP   STOP   STOP   STOP   STOP

SECTION 2

Structure and Written Expression

Time—35 minutes

Part 1: Sentence Completion

Directions: Questions 1–23 are not complete sentences. One or more words are left out of each sentence. Under each sentence, you will see four words or phrases, marked (A), (B), (C), and (D). Choose the one word or phrase that completes the sentence correctly. Then, on your answer sheet, find the number of the question and fill in the oval that corresponds to the letter of your answer choice.

Example I▷

Birds make nests in trees _____ hide their young in the leaves and branches.

Sample Answer

Ⓐ ● Ⓒ Ⓓ

    (A) can where they
    (B) where they can
    (C) where can they
    (D) where can

The sentence should read, "Birds make nests in trees where they can hide their young in the leaves and branches." Therefore, you should choose answer (B).

Example II▷

Sleeping, resting, and _____ are the best ways to care for a cold.

Sample Answer

Ⓐ Ⓑ Ⓒ ●

    (A) to drink fluids
    (B) drank fluids
    (C) one drink fluids
    (D) drinking fluids

The sentence should read, "Sleeping, resting, and drinking fluids are the best ways to care for a cold." Therefore, you should choose answer (D).

Now begin work on the questions.

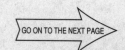
GO ON TO THE NEXT PAGE ▷

1. Because aluminum is lighter and cheaper
   _____, it is frequently used for high-
   tension power transmission.
   (A) as copper
   (B) than copper
   (C) for copper
   (D) more copper

2. It is only recently that ballets have been based on
   themes _____ American life.
   (A) reflecting
   (B) reflects
   (C) is reflecting
   (D) reflected

3. Poison oak generates irritating poisons _____
   even if people merely brush against the plants.
   (A) they can affect people
   (B) that can affect people
   (C) what can effect people
   (D) which do they affect

4. _____ ants live in colonies, keep farms, go
   to war, carry off slaves, and have a society
   somewhat like human beings.
   (A) Studies of ant life show that
   (B) Studies of ant life that
   (C) That is studied
   (D) That the studies of ant life

5. Generic medications are just as _____, and
   much less expensive.
   (A) effectively brand-name products
   (B) brand-name products effective
   (C) brand-name products as effective
   (D) effective as brand-name products

6. _____ is no way to tell the exact number of
   heroin addicts in the United States.
   (A) It
   (B) There
   (C) What
   (D) Each

7. Ernest Hemingway is _____ of modern
   fiction.
   (A) one of the molders
   (B) the molders one
   (C) who is one of the molders
   (D) the molders who is the one

8. _____ occasions for congratulations.
   (A) Birthdays that usually considered
   (B) Usually considering birthdays
   (C) Birthdays are usually considered
   (D) That considered birthdays usually

9. "Forty-niners" _____ to California for gold
   in 1848.
   (A) rushed
   (B) are rushed
   (C) have rushed
   (D) rushing

10. In order for people to work together effectively,
    they need _____ each other's needs.
    (A) to be sensitive to
    (B) is sensitive for
    (C) sensitivity
    (D) sensitive

11. It is good form to use the name of the person
    _____.
    (A) who are greeting
    (B) you are greeting
    (C) which you are greeting
    (D) greeting for you

12. _____ the promotion of health and to
    helping people avoid injury and disease.
    (A) To commit the Red Cross
    (B) The Red Cross to commit
    (C) Committed to the Red Cross is
    (D) The Red Cross is committed to

13. People usually can get a sufficient amount of the
    calcium their bodies _____ from the food
    they consume.
    (A) need
    (B) needs
    (C) needing
    (D) to need

14. It is possible _____ may assist some trees in
    saving water in the winter.
    (A) the leaves are lost
    (B) when leaves have lost
    (C) that the loss of leaves
    (D) to lose leaves

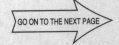 GO ON TO THE NEXT PAGE

15. Hollywood, the heart of America's motion picture industry, _____ of Los Angeles a century ago.
    (A) was only a quiet suburb
    (B) only quiet suburb was
    (C) quiet suburb only was
    (D) suburb was quiet only

16. Kitchen appliances called blenders became _____ in the 1930s, when Stephen J. Poplawski developed a machine that excelled at making his favorite drink.
    (A) establish
    (B) establishing
    (C) established
    (D) which establish

17. Built at the beginning of the century, the Library of Congress houses one of the largest _____ collections of books in the world.
    (A) and fine
    (B) and finest
    (C) or finest
    (D) yet fine

18. In the preparation of fibrous material for production uses, stiff woody fibers from plants _____ fibers from animal sources.
    (A) the most heat the
    (B) need more heat than
    (C) than more heat needed
    (D) need the more heat than

19. A partnership is an association of two or more individuals who _____ together to develop a business.
    (A) worked
    (B) they work
    (C) work
    (D) working

20. Chosen as the nation's capital at the end of the American Civil War, _____ a city of over a million people.
    (A) Washington, D.C., is now
    (B) for Washington, D.C.,
    (C) to Washington, D.C.,
    (D) now in Washington, D.C.,

21. Within an area of only 100 miles, Death Valley sinks to 282 feet below sea level while Mount Whitney _____ to a height of 14,494 feet.
    (A) soaring
    (B) soar
    (C) soared
    (D) soars

22. The cosmopolitan flavor of San Francisco is enhanced by _____ shops and restaurants.
    (A) an ethnic
    (B) its many ethnic
    (C) its ethnicity
    (D) ethnicity

23. _____ that increasing numbers of compact-disc players will be bought by consumers in the years to come.
    (A) They are anticipated
    (B) In anticipation
    (C) Anticipating
    (D) It is anticipated

GO ON TO THE NEXT PAGE

Part 2: Error Identification

Directions: In questions 24–60 each sentence has four underlined words or phrases, marked (A), (B), (C), and (D). Choose the one word or phrase that must be changed in order for the sentence to be correct. Then, on your answer sheet find the number of the question and fill in the oval that corresponds to the letter of your answer choice.

Example I►

Aspirin is recommend to many people for its
    A   B   C

ability to thin the blood.
    D

Sample Answer

● Ⓑ Ⓒ Ⓓ

The sentence should read, "Aspirin is recommended to many people for its ability to thin the blood." Therefore, you should choose answer (A).

Example II►

Some people believe that human beings will never
              A

use away all the natural resources on earth.
  B   C   D

Sample Answer

Ⓐ ● Ⓒ Ⓓ

The sentence should read, "Some people believe that human beings will never use up all the natural resources on earth." Therefore, you should choose answer (B).

Now begin work on the questions.

24. How the Earth is in the shadow of the moon, we see an eclipse of the sun.
  A   B   C   D

25. The children's television program called *Sesame Street* was seeing in 84 countries in 1989.
      A   B   C   D

26. Some research suggests what there is a link between the body's calcium balance and tooth decay.
        A   B   C   D

27. Luther Burbank earned the funds to go west by sale his new ideas about growing potatoes.
                A   B   C   D

28. Louisa May Alcott infused her own life into the character of Jo in book *Little Women*.
            A   B   C D

29. Rock music was original a mixture of country music and rhythm and blues.
  A   B   C   D

30. An increasing number of office works use computer programs as daily routine.
    A   B   C   D

31. Traveling ballet companies were uncommon before her Augusta Maywood formed the first traveling troupe.
  A   B   C   D

32. The virtues of ordinary life is the focus of many poems.
  A   B   C   D

33. Economic goods often consist to material items, but they can also be services to people.
      A   B   C   D

34. *Moby-Dick* is a novel that telling the story of a ship captain's single-minded hatred of a huge white whale.
            A   B   C   D

35. Earwax lubricates and protects the ear from foreign matter such water and insects.
    A   B   C   D

GO ON TO THE NEXT PAGE

36. Before creating the telegraph, Samuel Morse made their living as a painter.
   _____A_____   __B__ __C__ __D__

37. Some jellyfish make daily journeys from deep water to the surface and back, while others migrate horizontal.
              __A__   __B__   __C__   __D__

38. Putting a large amount of information on a map, a variety of symbols are used.
   __A__   __B__   __C__   __D__

39. Before the nineteenth century it was rarely to find organized systems of adult education.
   __A__   __B__ __C__   __D__

40. Smoking is the number one prevent cause of death in the United States.
   __A__ __B__   __C__   __D__

41. Not single alphabet has ever perfectly represented the sounds of any of Earth's natural languages.
   __A__   __B__   __C__ __D__

42. When the Second World War, almost a third of a million people were killed.
   __A__   __B__ __C__   __D__

43. The ozone layer must be protected because it shields the Earth from excessive ultraviolet radiations.
                __A__   __B__   __C__   __D__

44. Carbohydrates and fats are two essential sources of energy for animal grow.
                __A__   __B__   __C__   __D__

45. By passing sunlight through a prism, the light is separate into a spectrum of colors.
   __A__   __B__   __C__   __D__

46. In spite modern medical technology, many diseases caused by viruses are still not curable.
   __A__   __B__   __C__   __D__

47. Though Pablo Picasso was primarily a painting, he also became a fine sculptor, engraver, and ceramist.
   __A__   __B__ __C__   __D__

48. People who live in small towns often seem more warm and friendly than people who live in populated densely
                          __A__   __B__   __C__   __D__

   areas.

49. It took eight years to complete the Erie Canal, the 365-mile waterway which it connects Albany and Buffalo
   __A__   __B__   __C__   __D__

   in New York State.

50. Every candidate under considering for a federal job must undergo a thorough medical examination.
                      __A__ __B__   __C__   __D__

51. The masterpiece A Christmas Carol wrote by Charles Dickens in 1843.
   __A__   __B__ __C__   __D__

52. Species like snakes, lizards, coyotes, squirrels, and jack rabbits seems to exist quite happily in the desert.
                __A__   __B__   __C__ __D__

53. The disposable camera, a single-use camera preloaded with print film, has appeared in the late 1980s, and
                              __A__   __B__   __C__

   has become very popular.
   __D__

GO ON TO THE NEXT PAGE

54. Until recently, photocopy machines were regarded strict as business and professional office equipment
 ‾‾A‾‾   ‾‾B‾‾ ‾‾C‾‾

 that required a lot of expensive servicing.
 ‾‾‾‾D‾‾‾‾

55. Before bridges were built, all transport across major rivers in the United States were by ferryboat.
        ‾‾A‾‾ ‾‾B‾‾   ‾‾C‾‾ ‾D‾

56. Public health experts say that the money one spends avoiding illness is less than the cost to be sick.
                              ‾‾A‾‾   ‾‾B‾‾   ‾‾C‾‾   ‾‾D‾‾

57. People in the world differ in his beliefs about the cause of sickness and health.
                      ‾‾A‾‾   ‾‾B‾‾ ‾‾C‾‾   ‾‾D‾‾

58. In the 1840s, hundreds of families pioneer moved west in their covered wagons.
 ‾‾A‾‾   ‾‾B‾‾   ‾‾C‾‾   ‾‾D‾‾

59. When children get their first pair of glasses, they are often surprise to see that trees and flowers
 ‾‾A‾‾   ‾‾B‾‾   ‾‾C‾‾

 have sharp clear outlines.
 ‾‾D‾‾

60. The indiscriminate and continual use of any drug without medical supervision can be danger.
                              ‾‾A‾‾   ‾‾B‾‾ ‾‾C‾‾   ‾‾D‾‾

THIS IS THE END OF SECTION 2.
DO NOT READ OR WORK ON ANY OTHER SECTION OF THE TEST UNTIL TIME IS UP.
STOP   STOP   STOP   STOP   STOP

SECTION 3
Reading Comprehension

Time—75 minutes

Directions: In this section you will read several passages. Each passage is followed by questions about it. Choose the one best answer, (A), (B), (C), or (D), for each question. Then, on your answer sheet, find the number of the question and fill in the oval that corresponds to the letter of your answer choice. Answer all questions based on what is stated or implied in the passage.

Read the following passage:

> A new hearing device is now available for some hearing-impaired people. This device uses a magnet to hold the detachable sound-processing portion in place. Like other aids, it converts sound into vibrations. But it is unique in that it can transmit the vibrations directly to the magnet, and then to the inner ear. This produces a clearer sound. The new device will not help all hearing-impaired people, only those with a hearing loss caused by infection or some other problem in the middle ear. It will probably help no more than 20 percent of all people with hearing problems. Those people, however, who have persistent ear infections should find relief and restored hearing with the new device.

Example I▷ What is the author's main purpose?

(A) to describe a new cure for ear infections
(B) to inform the reader of a new device
(C) to urge doctors to use a new device
(D) to explain the use of a magnet

Sample Answer

 (A) ● (C) (D)

The author's main purpose is to inform the reader of a new device for hearing-impaired people. Therefore, you should choose answer (B).

Example II▷ The word "relief" in the last sentence means

(A) less distress
(B) assistance
(C) distraction
(D) relaxation

Sample Answer

● (B) (C) (D)

The phrase "less distress" is similar in meaning to "relief" in this sentence. Therefore, you should choose answer (A).

Now begin with the questions.

 GO ON TO THE NEXT PAGE

Questions 1 to 12 are based on the following passage:

(1)   It is very difficult to succeed in the music business; nine out of ten bands that release a first record fail to produce a second. Surviving in the music industry requires luck and patience, but most of all it requires an intricate knowledge of how a record company functions. The process begins when a representative of a company's Artists and Repertoire (A & R) department visits bars and night clubs, scouting for young,

(5)   talented bands. After the representative identifies a promising band, he or she will work to negotiate a contract with that band. The signing of this recording contract is a slow process. A company will spend a long time investigating the band itself as well as current trends in popular music. During this period, it is important that a band reciprocate with an investigation of its own, learning as much as possible about the record company and making personal connections within the different departments that will handle

(10)   their recordings.

Once a band has signed the contract and has finished recording an album, the Publicity and Promotions department takes over. This department decides whether or not to mass produce and market the band's album. Most bands fail to make personal contacts in this second department, thus losing their voice in the important final process of producing and marketing their album. This loss of voice often

(15)   contributes to the band's failure as a recording group.

1. Which of the following statements best expresses the main idea of the passage?
    (A) Nine out of ten bands fail to produce a second record.
    (B) It is important for a band to have an intricate knowledge of how a recording company works.
    (C) Making personal connections will help the band in the final decisions about the promotion of their album.
    (D) The main factors in a band's success are luck and patience.

2. As used in line 1, what is the meaning of the word "release"?
    (A) distribute
    (B) pay for
    (C) overturn
    (D) itemize

3. The phrase "an intricate" in line 3 could be best replaced by which of the following?
    (A) a fleeting
    (B) a straightforward
    (C) an extraneous
    (D) a detailed

4. According to the passage, the initial contact between a band and a recording company is made by
    (A) the band's manager
    (B) a band member
    (C) an A&R representative
    (D) the Publicity and Promotions department

5. The word "reciprocate" as used in line 8 could be best replaced by which of the following?
    (A) commence
    (B) respond
    (C) practice
    (D) confirm

6. The word "investigation" in line 8 is closest in meaning to which of the following?
    (A) production
    (B) betrothal
    (C) credential
    (D) examination

7. Which of the following words is most similar to the word "handle" as used in line 9?
    (A) touch
    (B) control
    (C) manipulate
    (D) protect

8. As used in line 12, what is the meaning of "takes over"?
    (A) takes charge
    (B) takes pleasure
    (C) takes advice
    (D) takes blame

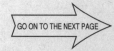
GO ON TO THE NEXT PAGE

9. The author mentions that a band's success is dependent on all of the following factors EXCEPT
   (A) having patience
   (B) making personal contacts with people in the company
   (C) understanding how a record company functions
   (D) playing music that sounds like music of famous bands

10. According to the passage, the Publicity and Promotions department
    (A) has the final decision in producing an album
    (B) handles the recording arrangements for the band
    (C) sends representatives to look for new talent
    (D) visits bars and night clubs

11. The author uses the phrase "losing their voice" in lines 13–14 to illustrate that they
    (A) are forbidden to speak
    (B) are unable to visit
    (C) have no representation
    (D) are too shy to express their desires

12. It can be inferred from the passage that
    (A) the music industry is full of opportunities for young bands
    (B) the A&R department has a very large staff
    (C) most bands do not fully understand how record companies operate
    (D) the cost of recording an album is very expensive

GO ON TO THE NEXT PAGE

Questions 13 to 24 are based on the following passage:

(1) About 200 million years ago, as the Triassic Period came to a close, many species of animals disappeared from the face of the Earth. Scientists previously believed that the series of extinctions happened over a period of 15 to 20 million years. Recent discoveries in Nova Scotia suggest, however, that the extinctions may have happened over a much shorter period of time, perhaps less than 850,000 years.

(5) Evidence for a rapid extinction of species at the end of the Triassic Period is found in the McCoy Brook Formation along the Bay of Fundy in Nova Scotia. Fossils found in this formation indicate a rapid disappearance of species rather than a slow and gradual change over time. One explanation for a relatively sudden extinction at the end of the Triassic may be that a large meteorite struck the earth at the time and is responsible for a 70-kilometer hole nearby. If geologists and other researchers can find evidence, such

(10) as shocked quartz in the rock formations, that a meteorite did strike the earth, it would give more credence to the theory of rapid Triassic extinctions. It is possible, however, that even if a rapid extinction happened in and around Nova Scotia, it did not necessarily occur in the rest of the world.

13. What is the main topic of this passage?
   (A) the disappearance of animal species at the end of the Triassic Period
   (B) evidence of a relatively sudden extinction of species
   (C) the possibility of an extinction happening simultaneously throughout the world
   (D) a meteorite hole in the Bay of Fundy in Nova Scotia

14. Which of the following could best replace the word "close" as used in line 1?
   (A) connection
   (B) dispersion
   (C) separation
   (D) end

15. The author uses the phrase "the face of the Earth" in line 2 in order to
   (A) emphasize the disappearance
   (B) focus on one part of the Earth
   (C) focus on one period of time
   (D) point out the reference to land, not water

16. All of the following were mentioned in the passage EXCEPT
   (A) the extinction of late Triassic animals
   (B) the duration of time for the extinction
   (C) a large meteorite hitting the Earth 10 million years ago
   (D) the use of types of rock in scientific research

17. Which of the following is closest in meaning to the word "relatively" in line 7?
   (A) comparatively
   (B) independently
   (C) phenomenally
   (D) visibly

18. Where in the passage does the author give evidence for the argument?
   (A) Lines 1–3
   (B) Lines 5–7
   (C) Lines 8–9
   (D) Lines 10–12

19. According to the passage, what would give evidence that a meteorite struck the earth?
   (A) a gradual change in species over time
   (B) a change in the quartz
   (C) gold deposits in the veins of rocks
   (D) a change in the waters of the Bay of Fundy

20. Which of the following could best replace the word "struck" as used in line 8?
   (A) affected
   (B) discovered
   (C) devastated
   (D) hit

21. Which of the following is most probably the meaning of "shocked quartz" in line 10?
   (A) narrow chasms
   (B) tiny lines
   (C) hardened ores
   (D) cracked minerals

GO ON TO THE NEXT PAGE

22. In line 10, "it" refers to
  (A) evidence
  (B) an extinction
  (C) the Earth
  (D) a meteorite

23. Which of the following could best replace the word "credence" in line 10?
  (A) demonstration
  (B) elevation
  (C) suitability
  (D) credibility

24. Which of the following best describes the author's tone?
  (A) aggressive
  (B) explanatory
  (C) apologetic
  (D) cynical

Questions 25 to 36 are based on the following passage:

(1)   Alzheimer's disease impairs a person's ability to recall memories, both distant and as recent as a few hours before. Although there is not yet a cure for the illness, there may be hope for a cure with a protein called nerve growth factor. The protein is produced by nerve cells in the same region of the brain where Alzheimer's occurs. Based on this relationship, scientists from the University of Lund in Sweden and the

(5)   University of California at San Diego designed an experiment to test whether doses of nerve growth factor could reverse the effects of memory loss caused by Alzheimer's. Using a group of rats with impaired memory, the scientists gave half of the rats doses of nerve growth factor while giving the other half a blood protein as a placebo, thus creating a control group. At the end of the four-week test, the rats given the nerve growth factor performed equally to rats with normal memory abilities. While the experiments do not show

(10)   that nerve growth factor can stop the general process of deterioration caused by Alzheimer's, they do show potential as a means to slowing the process significantly.

25. With what topic is this passage mainly concerned?
    (A) impaired memory of patients
    (B) cures for Alzheimer's disease
    (C) the use of rats as experimental subjects
    (D) nerve growth factor as a cure for Alzheimer's

26. The word "impairs" in line 1 is most similar to which of the following?
    (A) affects
    (B) destroys
    (C) enhances
    (D) diminishes

27. According to the passage, where is nerve growth factor produced in the body?
    (A) in nerve cells in the spinal column
    (B) in red blood cells in the circulatory system
    (C) in nerve cells in the brain
    (D) in the pituitary gland

28. Which of the following is closest in meaning to the word "region" as used in line 3?
    (A) vicinity
    (B) plain
    (C) expanse
    (D) orbit

29. Which of the following is closest in meaning to the word "doses" in line 5?
    (A) measures
    (B) pieces
    (C) injections
    (D) stipends

30. Which of the following could best replace the word "reverse" as used in line 6?
    (A) foster
    (B) prompt
    (C) override
    (D) match

31. Which of the following can be inferred from the passage?
    (A) Alzheimer's disease is deadly.
    (B) Though unsuccessful, the experiments did show some benefits derived from nerve growth factor.
    (C) The experiments did not show any significant benefits from nerve growth factor.
    (D) More work needs to be done to understand the effects of nerve growth factor.

32. The passage most closely resembles which of the following patterns of organization?
    (A) chronological order
    (B) statement and illustration
    (C) cause/effect
    (D) alphabetical order

33. Which of the following is closest in meaning to the word "deterioration" in line 10?
    (A) depression
    (B) deduction
    (C) decline
    (D) disconnection

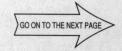GO ON TO THE NEXT PAGE

34. Which of the following could best replace the word "potential" in line 11?

(A) possibility

(B) capability

(C) dependability

(D) creativity

35. Which of the following could best replace the word "significantly" in line 11?

(A) considerably

(B) knowingly

(C) suggestively

(D) tirelessly

36. The relationship between nerve growth factor and a protein is similar to the relationship between Alzheimer's and

(A) forgetfulness

(B) a disease

(C) a cure

(D) a cancer

GO ON TO THE NEXT PAGE

Questions 37 to 48 are based on the following passage:

(1)   Until recently, hunting for treasure from shipwrecks was mostly fantasy; with recent technological advances, however, the search for sunken treasure has become more popular as a legitimate endeavor. This has caused a debate between those wanting to salvage the wrecks and those wanting to preserve them.

Treasure hunters are spurred on by the thought of finding caches of gold coins or other valuable objects (5)   on a sunken ship. One team of salvagers, for instance, searched the wreck of the RMS *Republic,* which sank outside the Boston harbor in 1909. The search party, using side-scan sonar, a device that projects sound waves across the ocean bottom and produces a profile of the sea floor, located the wreck in just two and a half days. Before the use of this new technology, such searches could take months or years. The team of 45 divers searched the wreck for two months, finding silver tea services, crystal dinnerware, and (10)   thousands of bottles of wine, but they did not find the five and a half tons of American Gold Eagle coins they were searching for.

Preservationists focus on the historic value of a ship. They say that even if a shipwreck's treasure does not have a high monetary value, it can be an invaluable source of historic artifacts that are preserved in nearly mint condition. But once a salvage team has scoured a site, much of the archaeological value (15)   is lost. Maritime archaeologists who are preservationists worry that the success of salvagers will attract more treasure-hunting expeditions and thus threaten remaining undiscovered wrecks. Preservationists are lobbying their state lawmakers to legally restrict underwater searches and unregulated salvages. To counter their efforts, treasure hunters argue that without the lure of gold and million-dollar treasures, the wrecks and their historical artifacts would never be recovered at all.

37. What is the main idea of this passage?
  (A) Searching for wrecks is much easier with new technologies like side-scan sonar.
  (B) Maritime archaeologists are concerned about the unregulated searching of wrecks.
  (C) The search of the RMS *Republic* failed to produce the hoped-for coins.
  (D) The popularity of treasure seeking has spurred a debate between preservationists and salvagers.

38. The word "sunken" in line 2 is closest in meaning to which of the following words?
  (A) broken
  (B) underwater
  (C) ancient
  (D) hollow

39. Which of the following is closest in meaning to the word "legitimate" in line 2?
  (A) justified
  (B) innocent
  (C) prudent
  (D) fundamental

40. Which of the following could best replace the phrase "a profile" as used in line 7?
  (A) a projection
  (B) an execution
  (C) a highlight
  (D) an outline

41. Which of the following statements is best supported by the author?
  (A) The value of a shipwreck depends on the quantity of its artifacts.
  (B) Preservationists are fighting the use of technological advances such as side-scan sonar.
  (C) Side-scan sonar has helped to legitimize salvaging.
  (D) The use of sound waves is crucial to locating shipwrecks.

42. The author uses the word "services" in line 9 to refer to which of the following?
  (A) cups
  (B) sets
  (C) containers
  (D) decorations

GO ON TO THE NEXT PAGE

43. The author uses the phrase "mint condition" in line 14 to describe
   (A) somcething perfect
   (B) something significant
   (C) something tolerant
   (D) something magical

44. All of the following were found on the RMS *Republic* EXCEPT
   (A) wine bottles
   (B) silver tea services
   (C) American Gold Eagle coins
   (D) crystal dinnerware

45. From the passage, you can infer that a preservationist would be most likely to
   (A) shun treasure-seeking salvagers
   (B) be a diver
   (C) put treasures in a museum
   (D) do archaeological research

46. The word "scoured" in line 14 is most similar to which of the following?
   (A) scraped away
   (B) scratched over
   (C) scrambled around
   (D) searched through

47. In line 18, what is the closest meaning to the word "lure"?
   (A) knowledge
   (B) attraction
   (C) luxury
   (D) glare

48. The second and third paragraphs are an example of
   (A) chronological order
   (B) explanation
   (C) specific to general
   (D) definition

GO ON TO THE NEXT PAGE

Questions 49 to 60 are based on the following passage:

(1)　Are you interested in seeing the beautiful fall foliage of New England but tired of traffic jams and overbooked hotels? Then this year forget the crowds in New England and see the beautiful colors of autumn in the Catskills.

　　These rugged mountains in New York State, just 90 miles northwest of New York City, are famous
(5)　for the legendary tales of Rip Van Winkle, and more recently for the summer hotels that sprang up in the region during the 1940s, 1950s, and 1960s. Families trying to escape the heat of New York City found the Catskills to be the perfect place to stay for a month or so each summer. By the late 1950s there were over 500 resorts and hotels offering nighttime entertainment as well as all kinds of outdoor activities. Famous comedians like Jackie Gleason, Joan Rivers, and Sid Caesar all got their start touring the hotel
(10)　clubs here. Since the introduction of air-conditioning and cheaper air travel, however, families have stopped coming to the Catskills in such large numbers, choosing instead more distant locations at different times of the year. Many of the Catskill hotels closed in the 1970s, but some remain and have expanded and changed their facilities to meet the needs of today's visitors.

　　Currently, there are many activities available to the traveler besides witnessing the changing colors
(15)　of the leaves. There is an all-organic sheep farm where visitors can see how a traditional sheep farm operates. There are also hundreds of miles of scenic drives in the area. Route 42, for instance, is an excellent site for spotting bald eagles. For more information on vacations in the Catskills, call the Office of Public Information.

49. What is the author's main purpose in this passage?
- **(A)** to promote the Catskills as a vacation destination
- **(B)** to introduce visitors to famous Catskills entertainers
- **(C)** to describe the history of the Catskills region
- **(D)** to compare the Catskills to New England

50. The word "rugged" in line 4 could be best replaced by which of the following?
- **(A)** barren
- **(B)** rough
- **(C)** tall
- **(D)** lush

51. According to the passage, which of the following caused the decline in the number of resorts in the 1970s?
- **(A)** television
- **(B)** shorter vacations
- **(C)** affordable air travel
- **(D)** more traffic

52. Which of the following is closest in meaning to the word "legendary" in line 5?
- **(A)** foolish
- **(B)** perplexing
- **(C)** mythical
- **(D)** humorous

53. The phrase "sprang up" in line 5 most probably refers to something that has
- **(A)** burst forth
- **(B)** spread out
- **(C)** operated vigorously
- **(D)** joined together

54. In what season would a tourist most likely have visited the Catskills in the 1950s?
- **(A)** fall
- **(B)** winter
- **(C)** spring
- **(D)** summer

55. Which of the following most reflects the author's tone in this passage?
- **(A)** light and encouraging
- **(B)** informative and scientific
- **(C)** humorous and sceptical
- **(D)** regretful and reminiscent

56. What does the passage imply that a visitor might be lucky enough to do?
- **(A)** see fall leaves in color
- **(B)** see a kind of bird
- **(C)** work on a sheep farm
- **(D)** drive on scenic roads

 GO ON TO THE NEXT PAGE

57. As used in line 14, the word "witnessing" could best be replaced by
    (A) attending
    (B) certifying
    (C) viewing
    (D) validating

58. As used in line 16, the word "drives" refers to
    (A) excursions
    (B) tracks
    (C) paths
    (D) canyons

59. As used in line 17, which of the following could best replace the word "spotting"?
    (A) photographing
    (B) seeing
    (C) painting
    (D) shooting

60. The author implies that in the Catskills there are few
    (A) leaves
    (B) eagles
    (C) people
    (D) sheep

GO ON TO THE NEXT PAGE

Questions 61 to 70 are based on the following passage:

(1)   It's hard to find artifacts that are genuinely American, but the present day banjo may be one of them. Even though its ancestry is African, the modern banjo is nothing like the early instruments first brought by Africans to the southern plantations. In the nineteenth century the banjo was a standard instrument in minstrel shows, and, as it continued to be used, it was changed in various ways. Machined pegs were added

(5)   for precise tuning, frets were added for better intonation, and vellum heads were added to improve the tension. The number of strings also continued to change. Early banjos had four strings, while later models had as many as nine. In the late 1800s, the five-string banjo was developed, a model that had a small unfretted drone string that was played with the thumb. This was the instrument that country singer Earl Scruggs played, and was the type used to produce that great style of music known as American bluegrass.

(10)   In the 1920s, the four-string tenor banjo made a remarkable comeback, as banjo bands became popular in schools and clubs from coast to coast. Again in the 1960s there was a renewed interest in folk and country music that brought the banjo back into the forefront of American music. It's an American instrument that continues to live on.

61. What does this passage mainly discuss?
    (A) the lasting effects of bluegrass music
    (B) the development of an American instrument
    (C) the life of a banjo
    (D) changes in music in the nineteenth and twentieth centuries

62. The banjo originally came from
    (A) southern plantations
    (B) folk and country music
    (C) minstrel shows
    (D) Africa

63. The word "plantations" in line 3 most probably refers to
    (A) types of farms in the South
    (B) southern states
    (C) southern musical theaters
    (D) bands common in the South

64. Which of the following words is most similar to the word "pegs" in line 4?
    (A) holes
    (B) bars
    (C) pins
    (D) strings

65. The word "precise" in line 5 could best be replaced by which of the following?
    (A) accurate
    (B) confirmed
    (C) processed
    (D) forthcoming

66. According to the passage, all of the following are true of the five-string banjo EXCEPT:
    (A) It was used by Earl Scruggs.
    (B) It was famous in the production of bluegrass music.
    (C) It had an unfretted string.
    (D) It was a tenor banjo.

67. Which of the following is most similar to the meaning of "comeback" in line 10?
    (A) performance
    (B) reappearance
    (C) gain
    (D) achievement

68. The word "renewed" in line 11 could be best replaced by which of the following?
    (A) rescued
    (B) remarkable
    (C) revived
    (D) renowned

69. Which of the following means most nearly the same as the word "forefront" as used in line 12?
    (A) forcast
    (B) spotlight
    (C) footnote
    (D) record

70. Which of the following best indicates the author's attitude toward the banjo?
    (A) It is a unique instrument.
    (B) It should be in a museum.
    (C) It should be used more.
    (D) It must be kept alive.

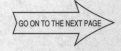 GO ON TO THE NEXT PAGE

Questions 71 to 80 are based on the following passage:

(1)   Franklin D. Roosevelt, the 32nd president of the United States, was from a wealthy, well-known family. As a child, he attended private school, had private tutors, and traveled with his parents to Europe. He attended Harvard University, and afterward studied law. At age 39 Roosevelt suddenly developed polio, a disease that left him without the full use of his legs for the rest of his life. Even through the worst of

(5)   his illness, however, he continued his life in politics. In 1924 he appeared at the Democratic National Convention to nominate Al Smith for president, and eight years after that he himself was nominated for the same office. Roosevelt was elected to the presidency during the Great Depression of the 1930s, at a time when more than 5,000 banks had failed and thousands of people were out of work. Roosevelt took action. First he declared a bank holiday that closed all the banks so no more could fail; then he reopened

(10)   the banks little by little with government support. Roosevelt believed in using the full power of government to help what he called the "forgotten people." And it was these workers, the wage earners, who felt the strongest affection toward Roosevelt. There were others, however, who felt that Roosevelt's policies were destroying the American system of government, and they opposed him in the same intense way that others admired him.

(15)   In 1940 the Democrats nominated Roosevelt for an unprecedented third term. No president in American history had ever served three terms, but Roosevelt felt an obligation not to quit while the United States' entry into World War II was looming in the future. He accepted the nomination and went on to an easy victory.

71. What does the passage mainly discuss?
(A) political aspects of Roosevelt's life
(B) problems during the Great Depression
(C) Roosevelt's upbringing
(D) criticisms of Roosevelt's actions

72. Which one of the following statements is NOT mentioned in the passage?
(A) Roosevelt was elected during the Great Depression.
(B) Roosevelt voted for Al Smith.
(C) Roosevelt had difficulty walking during his presidency.
(D) Roosevelt supported strong government powers.

73. The phrase "took action" in lines 8–9 is used to illustrate the idea that Roosevelt
(A) performed admirably
(B) exerted himself physically
(C) responded immediately
(D) got assistance

74. As used in line 10, the phrase "little by little" means that Roosevelt
(A) opened the smaller banks first
(B) opened the banks for minimal services
(C) opened the banks a few at a time
(D) opened the bank for a short time

75. The word "full" in line 10 could best be replaced by which of the following?
(A) packed
(B) loaded
(C) overflowing
(D) complete

76. Where in the passage does the author discuss Roosevelt's response to the Great Depression?
(A) lines 1–4
(B) lines 5–8
(C) lines 9–11
(D) lines 12–14

77. The word "affection" as used in line 12 could best be replaced by which of the following?
(A) fascination
(B) fondness
(C) lure
(D) appeal

78. The word "unprecedented" in line 15 could best be replaced by
(A) unimportant
(B) unheard of
(C) unjustified
(D) unhampered

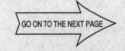

79. It can be inferred from the passage that the people who liked Roosevelt best were

(A) poor people
(B) bankers
(C) rich people
(D) average workers

80. In line 17, the author uses the word "looming" to indicate a feeling of

(A) reservation
(B) determination
(C) regret
(D) threat

GO ON TO THE NEXT PAGE

Questions 81 to 90 are based on the following passage:

(1)   Our eyes and ears might be called transformers since they sense the light and sound around us and turn them into electrical impulses that the brain can interpret. These electrical impulses that have been transformed by the eye and ear reach the brain and are turned into messages that we can interpret. For the eye, the process begins as the eye admits light waves, bends them at the cornea and lens, and then

(5)   focuses them on the retina. At the back of each eye, nerve fibers bundle together to form optic nerves, which join and then split into two optic tracts. Some of the fibers cross, so that part of the input from the right visual field goes into the left side of the brain, and vice versa. The process in the ear is carried out through sensory cells that are carried in fluid-filled canals and that are extremely sensitive to vibration. Sound that is transformed into electricity travels along nerve fibers in the auditory nerve. These fibers

(10)   form a synapse with neurons that carry the messages to the auditory cortex on each side of the brain.

81. According to the author, we might call our eyes and ears "transformers" because
(A) they sense light and sound
(B) they create electrical impulses
(C) the brain can interpret the input
(D) the messages travel in the brain

82. Which of the following is closest in meaning to the word "admits" in line 4?
(A) selects
(B) interprets
(C) lets in
(D) focuses on

83. In line 4, what does the word "them" refer to?
(A) light waves
(B) processes
(C) eyes
(D) messages

84. The word "bundle" in line 5 could best be replaced by which of the following?
(A) group
(B) grow
(C) branch
(D) settle

85. The word "split" as used in line 6 is closest in meaning to which of the following?
(A) tear
(B) fracture
(C) separate
(D) crack

86. Which of the following is closest in meaning to the word "cross" as used in line 6?
(A) intersect
(B) cancel
(C) assemble
(D) match

87. According to the passage, when input from the right visual field goes into the left side of the brain, what happens?
(A) The nerve fibers bundle together.
(B) The optic nerves split.
(C) The retina receives light waves.
(D) Input from the left field goes to the right side.

88. The phrase "carried out" in line 7 could best be replaced by which of the following?
(A) brought over
(B) taken away
(C) accomplished
(D) maintained

89. Which of the following is most similar to the word "vibration" as used in line 8?
(A) sound
(B) movement
(C) light
(D) heat

90. According to the passage, optic nerves eventually
(A) bend
(B) split
(C) admit light waves
(D) become messages

THIS IS THE END OF TEST 4

Practice Test 4
Answer Key

Section 1: Listening Comprehension

Part A

1. C	7. C	13. B	19. C	25. A
2. A	8. B	14. A	20. A	26. A
3. A	9. D	15. D	21. B	27. B
4. A	10. A	16. B	22. B	28. A
5. D	11. A	17. C	23. C	29. D
6. D	12. D	18. A	24. B	30. C

Part B

31. C	36. C	41. A	46. D	51. A
32. B	37. C	42. A	47. B	52. B
33. C	38. C	43. B	48. D	53. A
34. D	39. B	44. A	49. A	54. D
35. B	40. C	45. B	50. C	55. A

Part C

56. A	61. A	66. A	71. D	76. B
57. C	62. D	67. B	72. A	77. A
58. B	63. A	68. C	73. C	78. B
59. B	64. D	69. A	74. C	79. D
60. A	65. A	70. C	75. A	80. A

Section 2: Structure and Written Expression

Part 1: Sentence Completion

1. B	6. B	11. B	16. C	21. D
2. A	7. A	12. D	17. B	22. B
3. B	8. C	13. A	18. B	23. D
4. A	9. A	14. C	19. C	
5. D	10. A	15. A	20. A	

Part 2: Error Identification

24. A	32. C	40. C	48. D	56. D
25. C	33. B	41. A	49. D	57. B
26. B	34. B	42. A	50. B	58. C
27. C	35. C	43. D	51. B	59. C
28. D	36. C	44. D	52. B	60. D
29. B	37. D	45. C	53. C	
30. C	38. A	46. A	54. C	
31. C	39. C	47. C	55. C	

Section 3: Reading Comprehension

1. B	13. B	25. D	37. D	49. A
2. A	14. D	26. D	38. B	50. B
3. D	15. A	27. C	39. A	51. C
4. C	16. C	28. A	40. D	52. C
5. B	17. A	29. A	41. C	53. A
6. D	18. B	30. C	42. B	54. D
7. B	19. B	31. D	43. A	55. A
8. A	20. D	32. B	44. C	56. B
9. D	21. D	33. C	45. A	57. C
10. A	22. A	34. A	46. D	58. A
11. C	23. D	35. A	47. B	59. B
12. C	24. B	36. B	48. B	60. C

61. B	67. B	73. C	79. D	85. C
62. D	68. C	74. C	80. D	86. A
63. A	69. B	75. D	81. B	87. D
64. C	70. A	76. C	82. C	88. C
65. A	71. A	77. B	83. A	89. B
66. D	72. B	78. B	84. A	90. B

Practice Test 4
Explanatory Answers

SECTION 1

Listening Comprehension

Part A

1.   Man: I didn't expect Lisa to spend so much of her time helping me.

    Woman: She really has a tight schedule this semester, doesn't she?

What are the speakers saying about Lisa?
(A) Lisa is having a hard time in school.
(B) Lisa is expecting a baby.
(C) Lisa is very busy this term.
(D) Lisa is often very tired.

(C) A "tight schedule" refers to a very busy schedule. The two speakers agree that Lisa is busy.

2.   Woman: Guess what? I'll be a teaching assistant for Chemistry 1B.

    Man: I thought your major was computer science.

What had the man assumed about the woman?
(A) Her major was not chemistry.
(B) She is an excellent student in chemistry.
(C) She wanted to change her major.
(D) She likes chemistry classes more than computer science classes.

(A) Since the man says he thinks her major is computer science, he must think that it is not chemistry.

3.   Woman: Mark sure smokes a lot when he studies hard.

    Man: Not any more he doesn't.

What does the man mean?
(A) Mark has quit smoking.
(B) Mark doesn't like to share a room with someone smoking.
(C) Mark shouldn't smoke in the classroom.
(D) Mark helped his roommate quit smoking.

(A) When the man says, "not any more," he means, "Mark doesn't smoke a lot anymore." The man's comment could mean that Mark has quit smoking. It could also mean that now Mark smokes less than he did before, but this is not an answer choice. So (A) is the best answer.

4.   Woman: Dozens of people signed up for the workshop.

    Man: But only a few showed up, didn't they?

What does the man imply?
(A) Not many people attended the workshop.
(B) There were not many workshops available last night.
(C) The workshop is more interesting than the show.
(D) Last night's show was one of the few good ones.

(A) If "only a few showed up," it means that not many people were there.

5. Man: Steve won't graduate until this summer, but did you know that he has already started his own computer consulting company?

    Woman: Boy, he's really using what he's learned.

    What does the woman say about Steve?
    (A) He didn't do very well in school.
    (B) He won't graduate this semester.
    (C) Steve needs some hands-on classes.
    (D) Steve is able to apply his knowlege.

(D) The words "using what he's learned" means the same as "applying one's knowledge."

6. Man: I need to take a break.
    Woman: Let's go to the movies tonight.

    What are the speakers going to do?
    (A) Rent a videotape.
    (B) Fix the brakes on the car.
    (C) Begin packing for their move.
    (D) See a film.

(D) The words "movies" and "film" are often used interchangeably in the United States. If the speakers were going to rent a videotape, they would say, "Let's go *get* a movie," rather than "Let's go *to* a movie."

7. Man: Would you please drop this book at the library for me when you go to school?

    Woman: I would if I were going, but I have to work today.

    What does the woman imply?
    (A) She will return the man's favor.
    (B) She will return the book on her way to work.
    (C) She can't return the book for the man.
    (D) She works at the school library.

(C) The woman is using the conditional tense. She means, "I would (return your book) if I were going to the library, but I am not going to the library."

8. Man: Excuse me, but is this seat taken?
    Woman: No, somebody just left.

    What is the man probably going to do?
    (A) He is going to leave the room.
    (B) He is going to sit down.
    (C) He is going to buy a new chair.
    (D) He is going to bring the chair back.

(B) When a person asks, "Is this seat taken?", it usually means that the person wants to sit there. This is a polite question to ask before sitting down next to someone in a public place.

9. Woman: The professor seems exhausted after that long lecture he gave.
    Man: So am I.

    What does the man mean?
    (A) The man was excited by the lecture.
    (B) The man was very interested in the speech.
    (C) The man gave a long speech.
    (D) The man is tired.

(D) When the man says, "so am I," he means that he is feeling the same thing. The word "exhausted" means "very tired."

10. Man: You don't want to start graduate school right after graduation, do you?
    Woman: Well, actually I do.

    What does the woman mean?
    (A) She wants to continue her studies right away.
    (B) She wants a break from studying.
    (C) She hasn't decided yet.
    (D) She'll find a job right after graduation.

(A) The woman's response "actually I do" means that she feels the opposite of what the man says. The man asked a negative question, "you don't want to . . . ," and the woman's response is positive.

11. Man: Two of the classes I want to take have conflicting schedules.
    Woman: Then you need to make a decision.

    What does the woman suggest the man do?
    (A) Choose one class or the other.
    (B) Ask his advisor.
    (C) Let the professors make the decision.
    (D) Take both classes.

(A) The woman means that the man needs to make a decision about which class to take since two of them are at the same time.

12. Woman: You've already read this book, haven't you?
    Man: I wish I had.

    What does the man mean?
    (A) He doesn't have the book.
    (B) He had the book, but lost it.
    (C) He wants to read it again.
    (D) He has not read the book.

(D) The man's statement is a conditional. If he wishes he had done something, it means that he has not done it.

13. Woman: Bill, I think I'll ride my bike to school today; do you want to go with me?

Man: Sure, the exercise will do me good.

What does the man mean?

(A) He'll take his car and give the woman a ride.

(B) He'll take his bicycle to school too.

(C) He'll join her at her exercise class.

(D) He'll teach the woman how to ride a bicycle.

(B) The man's response is positive, as shown by his word "sure."

14. Man: Uh-oh, these two books are due tomorrow.

Woman: Already?

What does the woman mean?

(A) She didn't expect the books would have to be returned so soon.

(B) She doesn't want to keep these books.

(C) She doesn't think her library card is valid.

(D) She has finished reading these books already.

(A) The woman's tone of voice is important in this conversation. Her word "already?" could be expanded to "Are these books already due at the library?"

15. Man: This is the second time my machine has broken since I started working five minutes ago.

Woman: Let me try to fix it for you, it's probably a bad connection.

What does the woman mean?

(A) It will probably take five minutes to fix it.

(B) She fixed it a few minutes ago.

(C) Her machine is connected to the man's.

(D) The electrical connection might be the problem.

(D) The words "a bad connection" refer to a connection between electric wires.

16. Man: Excuse me. Did you drop this?

Woman: Oh, thanks.

What does the woman mean?

(A) Thank you for dropping by.

(B) Thank you for picking it up.

(C) No thanks, I don't want any.

(D) No thanks, I'm not going.

(B) We can assume that the man has just picked up something the woman dropped, and she is thanking him for picking it up.

17. Man: Do you know how to get there?

Woman: I think so, but give me the directions, just in case.

What is the man probably going to do?

(A) Show her how to make it work right.

(B) Invite her as a guest.

(C) Tell the woman the directions.

(D) Take her there if necessary.

(C) The woman is asking for directions, so we can assume that the man will give her the directions.

18. Woman: Mark, the university library is hiring now; are you still looking for a job?

Man: I've found one, but thank you anyway.

What does the man mean?

(A) He already has a job.

(B) He will probably work at the library.

(C) He needs to study full time.

(D) He plans to work at the library in the summer.

(A) When the word "thank you" is said as "but thank you anyway," it means that the speaker is being polite in saying no.

19. Woman: Jack, do you work on weekends too?

Man: Yes, but the hours are different.

What does the man mean?

(A) He enjoys working on weekends.

(B) He is different from the other workers.

(C) He works at a different time on Saturdays and Sundays.

(D) He's going out of town this weekend.

(C) The weekend is Saturday and Sunday. The man says that his working hours are different on these days. He works either more or fewer hours.

20. Woman: Jill is very excited about her new project.

Man: But is it feasible for her to complete it within a year?

What is the man's concern about Jill's project?

(A) Whether she'll have enough time to do it.

(B) Whether the professor will approve it.

(C) Whether she'll change her mind.

(D) Whether she has enough knowledge to do it.

(A) The word "feasible" means "possible." The man is questioning whether one year will be enough time to finish the project.

21.　　Man:　If only Laura would come back!
　　Woman:　I know; I feel the same.

What does the woman mean?
(A) She hopes that Laura will come back alone.
(B) She wants Laura to return.
(C) She doesn't want Laura to come back.
(D) She knows Laura is thinking about coming back.

(B) The expression "come back" means the same as "return." Answer (A) is incorrect because the speaker does not say that she wants Laura to be alone when she comes back.

22.　　Man:　Barbara should have mailed the check a week ago.
　　Woman:　I wonder what happened?

What are the man and woman talking about?
(A) Barbara mailed the letter too early.
(B) Barbara is late in mailing the check.
(C) Barbara took a week to send it.
(D) Barbara mailed the check a week ago.

(B) The modal "should have" implies that an action was not done. In this case it implies that Barbara did not mail the check. The speakers may be assuming that she will mail the check but that it is already late, since it was not mailed last week.

23.　　Woman:　You'd better hang on to your present job.
　　Man:　At least for a while.

What does the man mean?
(A) He is going to keep the present.
(B) He is going to resign his position.
(C) He's going to continue working for now.
(D) He is going to exercise as long as he can.

(C) The idiom "hang on to" means "to keep." In this sentence, the man says he will keep his job, but he implies that he may not keep it for very long. The expression "for now" implies that something is happening at this moment, but may not continue into the future.

24.　　Woman:　Peter would be better now if he hadn't gone back to work so soon.
　　Man:　Yes, but we couldn't force him to stay home.

What do the man and woman think?
(A) Peter sleeps too much.
(B) Peter should have rested for a longer time.
(C) Peter was forced to stay away from his work.
(D) Peter went on vacation.

(B) The woman's statement is in the past conditional. She implies that Peter was sick and that he stayed home for a while, but that he went back to work sooner than she wanted him to. Her sentence also implies that he got sick again after he went back to work. The man also implies that he thinks Peter should have stayed home longer.

25.　　Woman:　The recreation room is open four nights a week, isn't it?
　　Man:　Let's find out.

What does the man mean?
(A) He doesn't know when it's open.
(B) He doesn't want to go.
(C) He thinks it is open in the evening.
(D) He agrees with the woman.

(A) Since the man says, "let's find out," we can assume that he does not know the answer to the woman's question.

26.　　Man:　Hey, Linda, how long are you staying this time?
　　Woman:　Oh, I'm here for good now.

What does the woman mean?
(A) She's here permanently.
(B) She hopes the change will be good.
(C) It's a good place to work.
(D) She can stay as long as the work is satisfactory.

(A) The expression "for good" means that something is permanent or that it will last a long time or that there are no plans to change it.

27.   Man: Sue, are you sure this is the right way to get there?

   Woman: Sure. This is a shortcut; we'll be there in no time.

What does the woman mean?
(A) They don't have enough time to get there.
(B) This way should take less time.
(C) They are lost.
(D) The road is winding through this area.

(B) The expression "in no time" means "very little time" or "a short time." The woman says that this is a shortcut, which means a quicker way or a shorter distance.

28.   Woman: What took you so long?

   Man: I didn't think it would be so complicated.

What does the man mean?
(A) It wasn't as easy as he thought it would be.
(B) It was farther away than he thought.
(C) He doesn't think he gave the appropriate compliments.
(D) He thought it would be a lot harder.

(A) This answer gives the man's statement in the opposite form. The man didn't think it would be complicated, which means that it was complicated, and therefore was not easy.

29.   Man: Boy, that was a close call.

   Woman: Yeah, I was really scared.

What do the man and woman mean?
(A) They were able to telephone the police.
(B) They almost hit a boy.
(C) Somebody tried to rob them.
(D) Something frightened them.

(D) Answers (A), (B), and (C) are too specific. We don't know why the speakers were scared or what they did. We only know from their words that they were scared about something. Whatever it was did not actually happen. The phrase "close call" means that something almost happened, but didn't.

30.   Man: Have you gone shopping for Jimmy's present yet?

   Woman: I'm waiting for the sale to begin.

What does the woman mean?
(A) She found the right price.
(B) She has decided what to buy.
(C) She hasn't bought it yet.
(D) She's beginning to think about it.

(C) Since the woman says she is waiting, we can assume that she hasn't done it yet. We don't know from her words whether she knows the price or has decided what to buy. We also don't know whether she is just now thinking about it, or whether she has been thinking about it for a long time.

Part B

31. What was the man doing the previous night?
   (A) playing the guitar
   (B) working at a restaurant
   (C) singing in a rock concert
   (D) dancing in a ballet recital

(C) This is a restatement question. The woman says, "Your singing was great."

32. Where will the man play next week?
   (A) San Francisco
   (B) Washington
   (C) Chicago
   (D) New York

(B) This is a restatement question. The man says, "maybe you can see us next week when we play in Washington."

33. Where is the woman working?
   (A) in a restaurant
   (B) in a book shop
   (C) in a record store
   (D) in a theater

(C) This is an inference question. The woman tries to help the man find a record in the store and then directs him to try another record store to find the album. It is implied from this conversation that she works in a store selling records.

Test 4 • Answers

34. Where is the woman going for her vacation?
    (A) New York
    (B) Chicago
    (C) Washington
    (D) San Francisco

(D) This is a restatement question. The woman says that she will be going to San Francisco for vacation.

35. Where is the woman going to work for the summer?
    (A) Nantucket
    (B) Woods Hole
    (C) her father's restaurant
    (D) on the coast

(B) This is a restatement question. The woman says she is going to Woods Hole, Massachusetts, to study whales.

36. Where will the man be working during the summer?
    (A) Woods Hole
    (B) New York
    (C) his uncle's restaurant
    (D) his father's restaurant

(C) This is a restatement question. Tom states he will be working in his uncle's restaurant.

37. What is the woman going to study?
    (A) sea birds
    (B) sharks
    (C) whales
    (D) crabs

(C) This is a restatement question. The woman states that she will be studying whales.

38. Why can't the woman visit the man in the month of July?
    (A) because he will be visiting his grandparents
    (B) because he will be working for his uncle
    (C) because she will be working on a boat
    (D) because she will be working in a laboratory

(C) This is a restatement question. The woman says she will be away on a boat for the month of July.

39. What field of study are these two speakers most likely teaching?
    (A) American history
    (B) American literature
    (C) English literature
    (D) chemistry

(B) This is an inference question. The woman is writing a book about an American poet and the man is teaching a class in American literature. Based on this information it can be inferred that the teachers are most likely teaching American literature.

40. Why is the woman going to Washington next week?
    (A) to visit relatives
    (B) to give a lecture
    (C) to meet her publisher
    (D) to see museum exhibits

(C) This is a restatement question. She is traveling to meet a publisher and discuss the last chapter of the book she is writing.

41. What favor does the man ask of the woman?
    (A) to speak to his class
    (B) to deliver a message for him
    (C) to review an article for him
    (D) to lend him five dollars

(A) This is a restatement question. He asks her to speak to his American literature class.

42. What is the main topic of this conversation?
    (A) tomorrow's trip
    (B) tomorrow's practice
    (C) yesterday's exam
    (D) today's class

(A) This is a main idea question. The two students are talking about traveling to the place for the next day's class.

43. What is the most likely subject of the class the students are taking?
    (A) basketball
    (B) marine biology
    (C) organic chemistry
    (D) geochemistry

(B) This is an inference question. Since the students are talking about diving and studying sharks, the most likely subject is marine biology.

44. What is the woman asking for from the man?
    (A) a ride to the beach
    (B) his notes from the last class
    (C) directions to the beach
    (D) help in moving from her apartment

(A) This is an inference question. She doesn't exactly ask him for a ride. Instead she asks first if he is driving and second what time he is leaving. At the beginning of the conversation we can assume that she wants a ride. Later on it is clear that she will ride with him.

45. What time is the man planning to leave the next day?
    (A) 3:30 A.M.
    (B) 4 A.M.
    (C) 5:30 P.M.
    (D) 6 P.M.

(B) This is a restatement question. He says that he will leave at 4 A.M.

46. How does the man seem to feel after this interview?
    (A) nervous
    (B) scared
    (C) excited
    (D) hopeful

(D) This is a restatement question. At the beginning of the conversation the man says that he is "pretty hopeful this time."

47. How many people have been asked back for a second interview?
    (A) 1
    (B) 4
    (C) 8
    (D) 16

(B) This is a restatement question. The man says that they interviewed 16 the first time, but that only 4 of them were asked to return this time.

48. What does the man's girlfriend want?
    (A) She wants to continue her study.
    (B) She hopes to find a job near Ed.
    (C) She hopes Ed is offered the job.
    (D) She hopes Ed finds a job near her.

(D) This is a restatement question. The man says that his girlfriend doesn't want to leave her family, and that she hopes he finds a job close to home.

49. How does the woman feel at the beginning of the conversation?
    (A) relieved
    (B) angry
    (C) frustrated
    (D) excited

(A) This is a restatement question. The woman says that she finished her two term papers, and can now "see the light." The idiomatic expression "see the light" refers to finally being able to understand something, or being free from a load of work or problems.

50. What was the woman's first response to the man's suggestion?
    (A) She thought it was a good idea.
    (B) She wanted to read about art first.
    (C) She didn't want to go.
    (D) She said she was too tired.

(C) This is an inference question. When the man asks her to go to the art exhibit, her first response is "Oh, I don't know." This implies that she doesn't want to go or can't go.

51. Which city will the art exhibit go to next?
    (A) Los Angeles
    (B) Chicago
    (C) San Francisco
    (D) New York

(A) This is a restatement question. The man says, "Next week it will go to Los Angeles."

52. What does the man suggest they do after going to the art museum?
    (A) study again
    (B) visit another museum
    (C) walk in a park
    (D) go to a restaurant

(B) This is a restatement question. The man says, "we could hit both of them." The idiomatic expression "hit" in this case means "go to."

53. What is the woman trying to do?
    (A) enroll in classes
    (B) get a new phone
    (C) convince her friend to register
    (D) contact her counselor

(A) This is a restatement. In the beginning the woman says she just finished trying the new telephone system to enroll in classes.

54. What does the man suggest?
(A) that she should wait until later
(B) that she should change her schedule
(C) that she should enroll in classes
(D) that she should see a counselor

(D) This is a restatement question. The man says, "Maybe you should see a counselor."

55. How does the man seem to feel?
(A) relaxed
(B) worried
(C) scared
(D) excited

(A) This is a restatement question. The man says, "I don't think I'll have any trouble . . . last semester it was easy."

Part C

56. What is the main topic of this lecture?
(A) the life of James Joyce
(B) a book called *Dubliners*
(C) writers in Paris
(D) Irish novelists

(A) This is a main idea question. The discussion outlines the major events of James Joyce's life.

57. What was James Joyce's occupation?
(A) scientist
(B) painter
(C) writer
(D) doctor

(C) This is an inference question. In the passage, the speaker mentions that several works were published. Publishing is an activity associated with books and printed material, so we can infer that Joyce is a writer.

58. Where did James Joyce attend college?
(A) Paris
(B) Dublin
(C) New York
(D) Zurich

(B) This is a restatement question. The speaker says that Joyce attended two colleges in Dublin.

59. Where did Joyce live in his later years?
(A) Dublin
(B) Paris
(C) London
(D) New York

(B) This is a restatement question. Joyce spent his later years living in Paris.

60. What is the main purpose of the discussion?
(A) to explain recent fossil discoveries
(B) to argue theories of the "straight crab"
(C) to tell the history of the Institute
(D) to contrast the fossil discoveries in America and Australia

(A) This is a main topic question. The main topic of the discussion is to introduce Dr. Sawyer and to explain the significance of the discovery of the fossils of the "straight crab."

61. What kinds of people are most likely to be listening to this conversation?
(A) scientists
(B) tourists
(C) English teachers
(D) administrators

(A) This is an inference question. Since the discussion takes place at the Institute of Natural History, it is most likely to involve scientists. The subject is very specific and would not be of general interest to tourists who might visit a museum or institute. The subject area is paleontology and the study of insect fossils. Both English teachers and administrators work in very different fields and are not likely to be attending this talk.

62. Which does the speaker say might be descendents of the "straight crab"?
(A) reptiles
(B) mammals
(C) crabs
(D) insects

(D) This is a restatement question. The speaker describes the "straight crab" as possibly the "parent of all insects."

63. What will probably be discussed next?
    (A) Dr. Sawyer's discoveries
    (B) the Australian team's recent findings
    (C) theories about the "straight crab"
    (D) the descendants of the "straight crab"

(A) This is a question about a following topic. The speaker ends by introducing Dr. Sawyer, the chief researcher for the American team, and states that Dr. Sawyer will now explain his findings.

64. What is the name of the university where the speech is taking place?
    (A) University of Washington
    (B) University of Iowa
    (C) Harvard University
    (D) University of North Carolina

(D) This is a restatement question. The chancellor is talking about the history of the University of North Carolina.

65. According to the speaker, which of the following facts is true of the university?
    (A) It is the oldest public university.
    (B) It is the largest public university.
    (C) It is the least expensive public university.
    (D) It is the most beautiful university.

(A) This is a restatement question. The speaker says that the school is the oldest public university in the United States.

66. What once caused the university to close?
    (A) war
    (B) plagues
    (C) lack of funding
    (D) fire

(A) This is a restatement question. The speaker says that the university once closed because of the Civil War.

67. What type of summer camp is announced?
    (A) music
    (B) science
    (C) baseball
    (D) arts

(B) This is a main idea question. The teacher is announcing that a summer science camp is looking for students to serve as camp counselors.

68. Where is this discussion most likely taking place?
    (A) in a cafeteria
    (B) in an auditorium
    (C) in a classroom
    (D) in a gymnasium

(C) This is a location question. The most likely location would be a classroom, since the teacher says he is about to begin today's lecture.

69. Why does the camp need college students?
    (A) to be camp counselors
    (B) to maintain the equipment
    (C) to drive the campers
    (D) to work as teachers

(A) This is a restatement question. The announcement is calling for students to apply for jobs as counselors.

70. Where will all campers travel in July?
    (A) to California
    (B) to high school
    (C) to Washington
    (D) to college

(C) This is a restatement question. The speaker says that the campers are scheduled to travel to Washington.

71. What does the speaker say is the common misconception about crocodile mothers?
    (A) that they leave the water
    (B) that they dig a hole in the sand
    (C) that they rip open their nests
    (D) that they eat their babies

(D) This is a restatement question. The speaker says, "Many people have heard that crocodiles eat their babies . . . in fact they don't."

72. Where do the young hatch?
    (A) in a hole
    (B) in the water
    (C) under the mother's tail
    (D) in the mother's mouth

(A) This is a restatement question. The speaker says that the crocodile digs a hole and then lays her eggs in it.

73. Why does the crocodile put her babies in her mouth?

(A) to keep them warm

(B) to protect them from harm

(C) to transport them to the water

(D) to clean them

(C) This is a restatement question. The speaker says that the mother "takes the young into a pouch of skin in her lower jaw and carries them to the safety of the water." Answer (B) is close, since of course she is also protecting the young, but the main reason to put them into her mouth is to transport them.

74. How long does the mother wait for the young to hatch?

(A) 5 weeks

(B) 10 weeks

(C) 12 weeks

(D) 15 weeks

(C) This is a restatement question. The speaker says she guards her nest for 12 weeks.

75. Which of the following was Borlaug's goal?

(A) to improve low-yielding varieties of wheat

(B) to receive the Nobel Peace Prize

(C) to take over his father's farm

(D) to be the "father of the green revolution"

(A) This is a restatement question. The speaker says Borlaug's goal was to improve low-yielding wheat.

76. What helped finance Borlaug's trip abroad?

(A) the Nobel Prize

(B) the Rockefeller Foundation

(C) his family farm

(D) the Green Revolution

(B) This is an inference question. The speaker says that Borlaug was chosen by the Rockefeller Foundation to go abroad. This happened before the Nobel Peace Prize was given to him.

77. What did Borlaug do when he left the United States?

(A) introduced new technology

(B) became a plant pathologist

(C) worked for peace

(D) got a doctorate degree

(A) This is a restatement question. The speaker says that Borlaug went abroad to introduce new agricultural technology to farmers.

78. What can you best infer about the speaker's attitude toward the St. Lawrence River?

(A) The coal has polluted the river.

(B) It's a beautiful place to visit.

(C) The water is too cold for swimming.

(D) It is an unusual border between two countries.

(B) This is an inference question. The speaker refers to the beauty of the homes and castles on the islands in the river. The other choices are not mentioned at all.

79. What happened in 1959?

(A) Detroit and Duluth were established.

(B) The Great Lakes were linked with the Atlantic Ocean.

(C) Cargo boats began carrying grain on the river.

(D) Canals and locks were built on the river.

(D) This is a restatement question. The speaker says that "it's only been since 1959 that a series of canals, locks, and dams have made the river navigable."

80. Which of the following best describes the Thousand Islands?

(A) an area of tree-covered islands

(B) a series of castles near the river

(C) a place where cargo ships carry coal

(D) a destination of ocean-going vessels

(A) This is a restatement question. The speaker says that the Thousand Islands is an area dotted with tree-covered islands.

SECTION 2
Structure and Written Expression

Part 1: Sentence Completion

1. Because aluminum is lighter and cheaper _____, it is frequently used for high-tension power transmission.
   - (A) as copper
   - (B) than copper
   - (C) for copper
   - (D) more copper

(B) Comparison. After the comparative ending -er, the word "than" is necessary.

2. It is only recently that ballets have been based on themes _____ American life.
   - (A) reflecting
   - (B) reflects
   - (C) is reflecting
   - (D) reflected

(A) Adjective phrase. The phrase "reflecting American life" describes the noun "themes."

3. Poison oak has irritating poisons _____ even if people merely brush against the plants.
   - (A) they can affect people
   - (B) that can affect people
   - (C) what can effect people
   - (D) which do they affect

(B) Connecting word/adjective clause. The clause "that can affect people" describes the noun "poisons."

4. _____ ants live in colonies, keep farms, go to war, carry off slaves, and have a society somewhat like human beings.
   - (A) Studies of ant life show that
   - (B) Studies of ant life that
   - (C) That is studied
   - (D) That the studies of ant life

(A) Subject + verb. The main subject and verb of the sentence are "Studies . . . show...." The rest of the sentence is a clause that begins with the word "that" and describes what the studies show.

5. Generic medications are just as _____, and much less expensive.
   - (A) effectively brand-name products
   - (B) brand-name products effective
   - (C) brand-name products as effective
   - (D) effective as brand-name products

(D) Comparison. This is an "as...as" comparison. Two things are compared: the generic medications and brand-name medications. A "generic" medication is one that is not produced and sold by a specific company, but is the general medicine that is used by all the companies.

6. _____ is no way to tell the exact number of heroin addicts in the United States.
   - (A) It
   - (B) There
   - (C) What
   - (D) Each

(B) Subject. The expletive "there" is the subject of this sentence. The main verb is "is." Answer (C) is incorrect because the word "what" before "is" would begin a question, and this is not a question. Answer (D) is incorrect because it does not make sense to say, "each is no way." The expletive "it" would refer to something in this sentence, but there is nothing for it to refer to.

7. Ernest Hemingway is _____ of modern fiction.
   - (A) one of the molders
   - (B) the molders one
   - (C) who is one of the molders
   - (D) the molders who is the one

(A) The word "one" refers to Ernest Hemingway. The sentence means that Hemingway is one of the many writers who shaped modern writing.

8. _____ occasions for congratulations.
   - (A) Birthdays that usually considered
   - (B) Usually considering birthdays
   - (C) Birthdays are usually considered
   - (D) That considered birthdays usually

(C) Subject + verb. The main verb of the sentence is "considered." Answers (A) and (D) incorrectly add the word "that" which is a connecting word for a clause. They are incorrect because there is no other verb for a clause. Answer (B) is incorrect because it does not bring a main verb to the sentence.

9. "Forty-niners" _____ to California for gold in 1848.
   - (A) rushed
   - (B) are rushed
   - (C) have rushed
   - (D) rushing

(A) Verb. This is a past tense sentence that can only have a past tense verb.

10. In order for people to work together effectively, they need _____ each other's needs.
   - (A) to be sensitive to
   - (B) is sensitive for
   - (C) sensitivity
   - (D) sensitive

(A) The verb "need" must be followed by the preposition "to."

11. It is good form to use the name of the person _____.
   - (A) who are greeting
   - (B) you are greeting
   - (C) which you are greeting
   - (D) greeting for you

(B) The word "you" in answer (B) is a general word that refers to all people. The sentence could also be "...the person that you are greeting." Answer (C) is incorrect because "which" does not refer to people.

12. _____ the promotion of health and to helping people avoid injury and disease.
   - (A) To commit the Red Cross
   - (B) The Red Cross to commit
   - (C) Committed to the Red Cross is
   - (D) The Red Cross is committed to

(D) Subject + verb. This sentence is a parallel construction: "...commited to the promotion of health and [committed] to helping people...."

13. People usually can get a sufficient amount of the calcium their bodies _____ from the food they consume.
   - (A) need
   - (B) needs
   - (C) needing
   - (D) to need

(A) The verb "need" is a present tense verb that goes with "bodies."

14. It is possible _____ may assist some trees in saving water in the winter.
   - (A) the leaves are lost
   - (B) when leaves have lost
   - (C) that the loss of leaves
   - (D) to lose leaves

(C) The clause "that the loss of leaves may assist . . ." follows "possible that...." The other answers add another verb.

15. Hollywood, the heart of America's motion picture industry, _____ of Los Angeles a century ago.
   - (A) was only a quiet suburb
   - (B) only quiet suburb was
   - (C) quiet suburb only was
   - (D) suburb was quiet only

(A) Verb. The main noun of this sentence is "Hollywood," and the main verb is "was." The other answers have an incorrect order of adjectives.

16. Kitchen appliances called blenders became _____ in the 1930s, when Stephen J. Poplawski developed a machine that excelled at making his favorite drink.
   - (A) establish
   - (B) establishing
   - (C) established
   - (D) which establish

(C) Verb. This is a passive form of the verb.

17. Built at the beginning of the century, the Library of Congress houses one of the largest _____ collections of books in the world.
   - (A) and fine
   - (B) and finest
   - (C) or finest
   - (D) yet fine

(B) Conjunction. The two words that are connected are "largest" and "finest."

18. In the preparation of fibrous material for production uses, stiff woody fibers from plants _____ fibers from animal sources.
- **(A)** the most heat the
- **(B)** need more heat than
- **(C)** than more heat needed
- **(D)** need the more heat than

(B) Comparison. The correct phrase includes the main verb "need" plus the comparison "more heat than fibers from animal sources."

19. A partnership is an association of two or more individuals who _____ together to develop a business.
- **(A)** worked
- **(B)** they work
- **(C)** work
- **(D)** working

(C) Verb. The sentence is all in the present tense, as shown by the first verb, "is."

20. Chosen as the nation's capital at the end of the American Civil War, _____ a city of over a million people.
- **(A)** Washington, D.C., is now
- **(B)** for Washington, D.C.,
- **(C)** to Washington, D.C.,
- **(D)** now in Washington, D.C.,

(A) Subject + verb. Answer (A) is the only answer that includes a verb.

21. Within an area of only 100 miles, Death Valley sinks to 282 feet below sea level while Mount Whitney _____ to a height of 14,494 feet.
- **(A)** soaring
- **(B)** soar
- **(C)** soared
- **(D)** soars

(D) Verb/parallel construction. The two verbs that must be parallel are "sinks" and "soars." "Sinks" means to go down, while "soars" means to rise up.

22. The cosmopolitan flavor of San Francisco is enhanced by _____ shops and restaurants.
- **(A)** an ethnic
- **(B)** its many ethnic
- **(C)** its ethnicity
- **(D)** ethnicity

(B) Adjective. The answer is part of the noun phrase, "its many ethnic shops and restaurants." The word "ethnicity" is a noun, and would not fit here. Answer (A) is incorrect since the word "shops" is plural.

23. _____ that increasing numbers of compact-disc players will be bought by consumers in the years to come.
- **(A)** They are anticipated
- **(B)** In anticipation
- **(C)** Anticipating
- **(D)** It is anticipated

(D) Explicit *it*. This is also called "empty *it*." The word "it" has no meaning and is put in the sentence to fill the subject position.

Part 2: Error Identification

24. How the Earth is in the shadow of the moon,
<u>A</u>   <u>B</u>   <u>C</u>

we see an eclipse of the sun.
<u>D</u>

(A) Adverb. The wrong word has been put in this sentence. The correct word is "when," which tells the time at which we can see an eclipse of the sun.

25. The children's television program called
<u>A</u>   <u>B</u>

Sesame Street was seeing in 84 countries in
<u>C</u>   <u>D</u>

1989.

(C) Verb. The correct verb tense is "was seen," which is written in the passive voice. The active voice could be "Many people saw the television program called *Sesame Street* in 1989."

26. Some research suggests what there is a
<u>A</u>   <u>B</u>

link between the body's calcium balance and
<u>C</u>   <u>D</u>

tooth decay.

(B) Connecting word/noun clause. The correct word is "that," which answers the question, "what"; i.e., "What does some research suggest? Some research suggests that. . . ."

27. Luther Burbank earned the funds to go west by
<u>A</u>   <u>B</u>

sale his new ideas about growing potatoes.
<u>C</u>   <u>D</u>

(C) Word form. After the word "by" must be the *ing* form: "selling." This is an adverb phrase that answers the question, "how"; i.e., "How did Luther Burbank earn the funds to go west? By selling his new ideas. . . ."

28. Louisa May Alcott infused her own life into the
<u>A</u>   <u>B</u>

character of Jo in book *Little Women*.
<u>C</u> <u>D</u>

(D) Omitted word/article. The correct phrase is "in the book." There must be an article before the singular noun "book."

29. Rock music was original a mixture of
<u>A</u>   <u>B</u>

country music and rhythm and blues.
<u>C</u>   <u>D</u>

(B) Word form. An adverb is needed to refer to the time that rock music was a combination of country music and blues. The correct answer is "originally."

30. An increasing number of office works use
<u>A</u>   <u>B</u>   <u>C</u>

computer programs as daily routine.
<u>D</u>

(C) Word form. The sentence is referring to people, so the correct word is "workers."

31. Traveling ballet companies were uncommon
<u>A</u>   <u>B</u>

before her Augusta Maywood formed the first
<u>C</u>

traveling troupe.
<u>D</u>

(C) Unnecessary word. The word "her" is not needed in this sentence, since both the pronoun "her" and the name refer to the same person. The correct phrase is "before Augusta Maywood formed. . . ."

32. The virtues of ordinary life is the focus of many
<u>A</u>   <u>B</u>   <u>C</u>   <u>D</u>

poems.

(C) Verb. Since the subject is "virtues," a plural noun, the verb must be "are."

33. Economic goods often consist to material
<u>A</u>   <u>B</u>

items, but they can also be services to people.
<u>C</u>   <u>D</u>

(B) Preposition. After the verb "consist," comes the preposition "of."

34. *Moby-Dick* is a novel that telling the story of a
<u>A</u>   <u>B</u>

ship captain's single-minded hatred of a huge
<u>C</u>   <u>D</u>

white whale.

(B) Word form. The correct phrase is "that tells the story. . . ." This begins an adjective clause that answers the question "what kind of," i.e., "What kind of novel is *Moby-Dick?* It is a novel that tells the story of a ship captain. . . ." The verb "tells" is the simple present tense.

35. Earwax lubricates and protects the ear from
    _____ _____
            A

    foreign matter such water and insects.
    _____   _____   _____
        B   C   D

(C) Omitted word. The correct answer is "such as," as a connecting phrase that introduces an example.

36. Before creating the telegraph, Samuel Morse
    _____
            A

    made their living as a painter.
    _____ _____   _____
      B   C   D

(C) Pronoun. Since Samuel Morse is one person, the pronoun must be singular. The correct answer is "made his living."

37. Some jellyfish make daily journeys from deep
    _____   _____
            A   B

    water to the surface and back, while others
    _____   _____
                                      C

    migrate horizontal.
    _____ _____
            D

(D) Word form. The correct word is "horizontally," an adverb that describes how the jellyfish migrate.

38. Putting a large amount of information on a
    _____   _____
      A   B

    map, a variety of symbols are used.
        _____   _____
            C   D

(A) Infinitive/gerund. The correct answer is "To put. . . ." This sentence could also be written, "In order to put a large amount of information on a map. . . ." The infinitive gives the idea of a future action, and is used as an adverb. It answers the question, "why," i.e., "Why are a variety of symbols used? To put a large amount of information on a map." The gerund, in contrast, is part of the noun-subject. It answers the question, "what," i.e., "What is difficult? Putting a large amount of information on a map is difficult."

39. Before the nineteenth century it was rarely to
    _____   _____ _____
      A   B   C

    find organized systems of adult education
         _____
             D

(C) Word form. This sentence needs the adjective, "rare," not the adverb. The phrase "it was rare" is grammatically similar to a sentence such as, "it was beautiful" or "it was funny."

40. Smoking is the number one prevent cause
    _____   _____ _____
      A   B   C

    of death in the United States.
    _____
        D

(C) Word form. The correct word is "preventable," an adjective that describes the noun "cause."

41. Not single alphabet has ever perfectly repre-
    _____   _____
      A   B

    sented the sounds of any of Earth's natural
           _____ _____
               C   D

    languages.

(A) Negative adverb. The correct answer is "no single alphabet." It would also be correct to say, "not a single alphabet." The word "not" cannot come directly before a noun.

42. When the Second World War, almost a third of
    _____   _____   _____
      A   B   C

    a million people were killed.
               _____
                   D

(A) Adverb. The correct word to make sense in the sentence is "during," which begins an adverb phrase that answers the question "when," i.e., "When were . . . people killed? During the Second World War." It would also be correct to begin this sentence with a clause, such as, "When the Second World War ended, almost a third of a million people had been killed."

43. The ozone layer must be protected because it
    _____   _____
              A   B

    shields the Earth from excessive ultraviolet
           _____
               C

    radiations.
    _____
        D

(D) Singular/plural noun. The word "radiation" is a mass noun that does not have a plural form.

44. Carbohydrates and fats are two essential
    _____
              A

    sources of energy for animal grow.
    _____   _____   _____
        B   C   D

(D) Word form. This sentence should end in a noun, "growth." The phrase "for animal growth" describes the reason that energy is essential. The word "animal" in this sentence is used as an adjective that describes the type of growth.

Test 4 • Answers

45. By passing sunlight through a prism, the light
<u>A</u>   <u>B</u>

is separate into a spectrum of colors.
<u>C</u>   <u>D</u>

(C) Verb. The correct answer is "is separated," a passive form of the verb. The active voice could be, "something separates the light into . . . colors."

46. In spite modern medical technology, many
<u>A</u>   <u>B</u>

diseases caused by viruses are still not curable.
<u>C</u>   <u>D</u>

(A) Connecting phrase/omitted word. The correct phrase is "in spite of. . . ." It would also be correct to say, "Despite modern medical technology. . . ."

47. Though Pablo Picasso was primarily a painting,
<u>A</u>   <u>B</u>   <u>C</u>

he also became a fine sculptor, engraver, and
<u>D</u>

ceramist.

(C) Word form. Since Picasso is a person, the word to describe him must be "painter."

48. People who live in small towns often seem
<u>A</u>   <u>B</u>

more warm and friendly than people who live
<u>C</u>

in populated densely areas.
<u>D</u>

(D) Reversed words. The correct phrase is "densely populated areas." The adverb "densely" describes the word "populated."

49. It took eight years to complete the Erie Canal,
<u>A</u>   <u>B</u>

the 365-mile waterway which it connects
<u>C</u>   <u>D</u>

Albany and Buffalo in New York State.

(D) Unnecessary word. The word "it" is not necessary in this phrase. It is correct to say that the waterway connects Albany and Buffalo.

50. Every candidate under considering for a federal
<u>A</u>   <u>B</u>

job must undergo a thorough medical
<u>C</u>   <u>D</u>

examination.

(B) Word form. The correct phrase is "under consideration."

51. The masterpiece *A Christmas Carol* wrote by
<u>A</u>   <u>B</u> <u>C</u>

Charles Dickens in 1843.
<u>D</u>

(B) Verb. The verb should be the passive form, "was written."

52. Species like snakes, lizards, coyotes, squirrels,
<u>A</u>

and jack rabbits seems to exist quite happily in
<u>B</u>   <u>C</u>

the desert.
<u>D</u>

(B) Verb. The correct verb is the plural form, "seem to," to go with the plural noun "species."

53. The disposable camera, a single-use camera
<u>A</u>

preloaded with print film, has appeared in the
<u>B</u>   <u>C</u>

late 1980s, and has become very popular.
<u>D</u>

(C) Verb. The correct verb is in the simple past tense, "appeared," since a specific date is given from a past time.

54. Until recently, photocopy machines
<u>A</u>

were regarded strict as business and
<u>B</u>   <u>C</u>

professional office equipment that required a
<u>D</u>

lot of expensive servicing.

(C) Adverb. The correct word is "strictly." This means the same as "only" or "inflexibly."

55. Before bridges were built, all transport across
                    A   B

major rivers in the United States were by
                                   C D

ferryboat.

(C) Verb. The verb should be singular, "was," in order to go with the main noun "transport."

56. Public health experts say that the money one
                                      A

spends avoiding illness is less than the cost
               B   C

to be sick.
 D

(D) Infinitive/gerund. The correct phrase is "the cost of being sick."

57. People in the world differ in his beliefs about
                         A   B   C

the cause of sickness and health.
               D

(B) Pronoun. The word "his" cannot be the pronoun that carries the meaning of "people," since "people" is plural and "his" is singular. The correct pronoun is "their."

58. In the 1840s, hundreds of families pioneer
        A   B   C

moved west in their covered wagons.
             D

(C) Reversed words. The correct phrase is "pioneer families." The word "pioneer" describes the type of families.

59. When children get their first pair of glasses,
        A   B

they are often surprise to see that trees and
               C

flowers have sharp clear outlines.
           D

(C) Verb/word form. The correct answer is "surprised." It is the passive form of the verb.

60. The indiscriminate and continual use of any
                                 A

drug without medical supervison can be danger.
          B   C   D

(D) Word form. The correct word is "dangerous," an adjective that describes that rest of the sentence: "the indiscriminate and continual use of any drug without medical supervision."

Test 4 • Answers

SECTION 3
Reading Comprehension

1. Which of the following statements best expresses the main idea of the passage?
   (A) Nine out of ten bands fail to produce a second record.
   (B) It is important for a band to have an intricate knowledge of how a recording company works.
   (C) Making personal connections will give the band a voice in the final decisions about the promotion of their album.
   (D) The main factors in a band's success are luck and patience.

(B) This is a main idea question. Answer (B) is the best choice because the entire passage discusses how a recording company works. (A) is only a fact that supports the claim that the industry is very competitive. Answer (C) is a strategy that is a part of the main idea. Answer (D) is mentioned in the beginning, but the sentence says that luck and patience are not as important as knowledge.

2. As used in line 1, what is the meaning of the word "release"?
   (A) distribute
   (B) pay for
   (C) overturn
   (D) itemize

(A) To "release" a record is to let it out to the public so people can buy it. The word "distribute" means "give out."

3. The phrase "an intricate" in line 3 could be best replaced by which of the following?
   (A) a fleeting
   (B) a straightforward
   (C) an extraneous
   (D) a detailed

(D) To have an "intricate" and "detailed" knowledge means to know much about all the many complex parts of the company.

4. According to the passage, the initial contact between a band and a recording company is made by
   (A) the band's manager
   (B) a band member
   (C) an A&R representative
   (D) the Publicity and Promotions department

(C) This is a restatement question. In lines 3–5, the passage states that a representative from the A&R department visits night clubs and bars to look for new talent.

5. The word "reciprocate" as used in line 8 could be replaced by which of the following?
   (A) commence
   (B) respond
   (C) practice
   (D) confirm

(B) The verb "to reciprocate" means to do the same thing in return that someone has done to you. "Respond" is the closest in meaning. "To reciprocate" is to respond in a similar manner.

6. The word "investigation" in line 8 is closest in meaning to which of the following?
   (A) production
   (B) betrothal
   (C) credential
   (D) examination

(D) An investigation and an examination both refer to a systematic inquiry into something.

7. Which of the following words is most similar to the word "handle" as used in line 9?
   (A) touch
   (B) control
   (C) manipulate
   (D) protect

(B) All of the above words could mean "handle" in some situations, but in this situation "to handle" means "to take charge" or "to do the work."

8. As used in line 12, what is the meaning of "takes over"?
    (A) takes charge
    (B) takes pleasure
    (C) takes advice
    (D) takes blame

(A) "To take over" means to do all the work, to take the power, or "to take charge."

9. The author mentions that a band's success is dependent on all of the following factors EXCEPT
    (A) having patience
    (B) making personal contacts with people in the company
    (C) understanding how a record company functions
    (D) playing music that sounds like music of famous bands

(D) This is a restatement question. Answer (D) is not mentioned anywhere in the passage.

10. According to the passage, the Publicity and Promotions department
    (A) has the final decision in producing an album
    (B) handles the recording arrangements for the band
    (C) sends representatives to look for new talent
    (D) visits bars and night clubs

(A) This is an inference question. From the statement that this department "decides whether or not to mass produce and market the band's album," we can infer that the department has the final say.

11. The author uses the phrase "losing their voice" in lines 13–14 to illustrate that they
    (A) are forbidden to speak
    (B) are unable to visit
    (C) have no representation
    (D) are too shy to express their desires

(C) The phrase "to have a voice" means "to be able to give one's viewpoint or ideas." If one "loses one's voice" then one cannot share one's ideas. This does not necessarily mean that one cannot speak or visit but that there is no one who will listen. The phrase "have no representation" is the closest in meaning.

12. It can be inferred from the passage that
    (A) the music industry is full of opportunities for young bands
    (B) the A&R department has a very large staff
    (C) most bands do not fully understand how record companies operate
    (D) the cost of recording an album is very high

(C) This is an inference question. Answer (A) is the opposite assumption to that stated in the first sentence. Answers (B) and (D) are incorrect since neither the size of the staff nor the costs of production are mentioned in the paragraph. We can infer answer (C) since the author is explaining why some bands fail to produce records.

13. What is the main topic of this passage?
    (A) the disappearance of animal species at the end of the Triassic Period
    (B) evidence of a relatively sudden extinction of species
    (C) the possibility of an extinction happening simultaneously throughout the world
    (D) a meteorite hole in the Bay of Fundy in Nova Scotia

(B) The author begins the passage by explaining that recent discoveries suggest that extinctions may have happened over a much shorter period of time than had previously been thought.

14. Which of the following could best replace the word "close" as used in line 1?
    (A) connection
    (B) dispersion
    (C) separation
    (D) end

(D) The word "close" can be a noun, an adjective, or a verb. In this sentence, it is a noun and it means the same as "the end."

15. The author uses the phrase "the face of the Earth" in line 2 in order to
    (A) emphasize the disappearance
    (B) focus on one part of the Earth
    (C) focus on one period of time
    (D) point out the reference to land, not water

(A) The phrase "the face of the Earth" does not mean anything different from the phrase "the Earth." It is used only to emphasize that many species of animals completely disappeared from the Earth.

16. All of the following were mentioned in the passage EXCEPT
    (A) the extinction of late Triassic animals
    (B) the duration of time for the extinction
    (C) a large meteorite hitting the Earth 10 million years ago
    (D) the use of types of rock in scientific research

(C) The passage states that a large meteorite *may* have struck the earth at the end of the Triassic Period; the beginning of the passage states that the Triassic Period was 200 million years ago, not 10 million years ago.

17. Which of the following is closest in meaning to the word "relatively" in line 7?
    (A) comparatively
    (B) independently
    (C) phenomenally
    (D) visibly

(A) The words "relatively" and "comparatively" both mean considering something in comparison with another thing.

18. Where in the passage does the author give evidence for the argument?
    (A) lines 1–3
    (B) lines 5–7
    (C) lines 8–9
    (D) lines 10–12

(B) The author states in lines 5–7 that the evidence is in the McCoy Brook Formation along the Bay of Fundy in Nova Scotia.

19. According to the passage, what would give evidence that a meteorite struck the earth?
    (A) a gradual change in species over time
    (B) a change in the quartz
    (C) gold deposits in the veins of rocks
    (D) a change in the waters of the Bay of Fundy

(B) The final paragragh mentions shocked quartz as an example of evidence that a meteorite struck the earth.

20. Which of the following could best replace the word "struck" as used in line 8?
    (A) affected
    (B) discovered
    (C) devastated
    (D) hit

(D) The word "struck" is to the past tense of "strike," which means "to hit." Both words in this sentence mean "to collide with."

21. Which of the following is most probably the meaning of "shocked quartz" in line 10?
    (A) narrow chasms
    (B) tiny lines
    (C) hardened ores
    (D) cracked minerals

(D) "Quartz" is a type of mineral that is transparent and crystallized. If it has been shocked, it probably has cracks in it.

22. In line 10, the word "it" refers to
    (A) evidence
    (B) an extinction
    (C) the Earth
    (D) a meteorite

(A) This is a referent question. The head noun before the word "it" is "evidence." The word "meteorite" explains the "evidence," and the word "Earth" is connected in meaning to "meteorite." The word "extinction" follows the word "it" and does not explain it.

23. Which of the following could best replace the word "credence" in line 10?
    (A) demonstration
    (B) elevation
    (C) suitability
    (D) credibility

(D) The words "credence" and "credibility" are similar in meaning to "belief," "confidence," and "trust."

24. Which of the following best describes the author's tone?
    (A) aggressive
    (B) explanatory
    (C) apologetic
    (D) cynical

(B) This question asks for the author's tone. The author is primarily concerned with a description of the evidence for a new theory. There are no words to suggest any of the other answers.

25. With what topic is this passage mainly concerned?
    (A) impaired memory of patients
    (B) cures for Alzheimer's disease
    (C) the use of rats as experimental subjects
    (D) nerve growth factor as a cure for Alzheimer's

(D) This is a main idea question. Both (A) and (B) are more general than the scope of the passage. (C) is not relative to the main idea.

26. The word "impairs" in line 1 is most similar to which of the following?
    (A) affects
    (B) destroys
    (C) enhances
    (D) diminishes

(D) In the context of this passage, the word "impair" means to cause a deterioration in memory. Answer (A) is not specific enough, and answer (B) is too extreme. Answer (C) is the opposite of deterioration.

27. According to the passage, where is nerve growth factor produced in the body?
    (A) in nerve cells in the spinal column
    (B) in red blood cells in the circulatory system
    (C) in nerve cells in the brain
    (D) in the pituitary gland

(C) This is a restatement question. Lines 3–4 of the passage state that the nerve growth factor is produced in the same part of the brain where Alzheimer's occurs.

28. Which of the following is closest in meaning to the word "region" as used in line 3?
    (A) vicinity
    (B) plain
    (C) expanse
    (D) orbit

(A) The words "region" and "vicinity" both refer to a locality around something. Answer (B) refers to a flat level area, answer (C) refers to a large area, and answer (D) refers to the revolving or circular path of an object.

29. Which of the following is closest in meaning to the word "doses" in line 5?
    (A) measures
    (B) pieces
    (C) injections
    (D) stipends

(A) The words "measures" and "doses" both refer to "quantities" or "amounts" of something, often medicines. Answer (B) refers to bits of solid material. Answer (C) refers to a syringe or needle that forces a drug into the body. Answer (D) generally refers to a regular or fixed payment such as a salary.

30. Which of the following could best replace the word "reverse" as used in line 6?
    (A) foster
    (B) prompt
    (C) override
    (D) match

(C) The verb "to reverse" means "to do the opposite." The word "override" means "to disregard something" or "to take precedence over something." In this case, the nerve growth factor would take precedence over effects of the memory loss, thereby reversing the effect. Answer (A) means the opposite. Answer (B) means "punctual" or "immediate." Answer (D) means "identical" or something that "goes together."

31. Which of the following can be inferred from the passage?
    (A) Alzheimer's disease is deadly.
    (B) Though unsuccessful, the experiments did show some benefits derived from nerve growth factor.
    (C) The experiments did not show any significant benefits from nerve growth factor.
    (D) More work needs to be done to understand the effects of nerve growth factor.

(D) This is an inference question. Answer (A) is not true; the passage describes the disease as only in terms of a gradual deterioration of memory. Answers (B) and (C) each contain some information that is false according to the passage. Answer (D) can be inferred since the final sentence of the passage states that there is potential in this experiment. This implies that we do not yet know enough about it.

32. The passage most resembles which of the following patterns of organization?
    (A) chronological order
    (B) statement and illustration
    (C) cause/effect
    (D) alphabetical order

(B) This is an organization question. Neither (A) nor (D) is correct since the passage is not ordering things chronologically or alphabetically. Answer (C) is not correct since the passage does not focus on the experiments and the results. Instead, there is a statement of the main idea, which is that there is a potential cure for Alzheimer's disease, followed by a discussion of nerve growth factor, which illustrates this potential cure.

33. Which of the following is closest in meaning to the
    word "deterioration" in line 10?
    (A) depression
    (B) deduction
    (C) decline
    (D) disconnection

(C) The words "deterioration" and "decline" both mean
that something is getting worse.

34. Which of the following could best replace the word
    "potential" in line 11?
    (A) possibility
    (B) capability
    (C) dependability
    (D) creativity

(A) The word "potential" refers to the possibility of
something developing in the future.

35. Which of the following could best replace the word
    "significantly" in line 11?
    (A) considerably
    (B) knowingly
    (C) suggestively
    (D) tirelessly

(A) The word "significantly" indicates that there is
enough of something to make it important. The word
"considerably" means "enough" or "importantly."

36. The relationship between nerve growth factor and
    a protein is similar to the relationship between
    Alzheimer's and
    (A) forgetfulness
    (B) a disease
    (C) a cure
    (D) a cancer

(B) This is an analogy question. For this type of question, the answer must form a parallel sentence with the
question. A nerve growth factor is an example of a
protein, just as Alzheimer's is an example of a disease.

37. What is the main idea of this passage?
    (A) Searching for wrecks is much easier with new
        technologies like side-scan sonar.
    (B) Maritime archaeologists are concerned about
        the unregulated searching of wrecks.
    (C) The search of the RMS *Republic* failed to
        produce the hoped-for coins.
    (D) The popularity of treasure seeking has
        spurred a debate between preservationists and
        salvagers.

(D) This is a main idea question. Each of the other
answers are ideas in the passage but are only part of the
main idea.

38. The word "sunken" in line 2 is closest in meaning
    to which of the following words?
    (A) broken
    (B) underwater
    (C) ancient
    (D) hollow

(B) This is a vocabulary question. The word "sunken"
comes from the verb "to sink," which implies that an
object has gone underwater.

39. Which of the following is closest in meaning to the
    word "legitimate" in line 2?
    (A) justified
    (B) innocent
    (C) prudent
    (D) fundamental

(A) The words "legitimate" and "justified" both refer to
something that has been shown to have value or has
been approved. In this case, the use of new technological devices has given credence and respectability to the
act of searching for sunken treasures since it now can be
done scientifically.

40. Which of the following could best replace the
    phrase "a profile" as used in line 7?
    (A) a projection
    (B) an execution
    (C) a highlight
    (D) an outline

(D) A "profile" and an "outline" are both sketches or
diagrams that show the contour of an object.

41. Which of the following statements is best supported by the author?
    (A) The value of a shipwreck depends on the quantity of its artifacts.
    (B) Preservationists are fighting the use of technological advances such as side-scan sonar.
    (C) Side-scan sonar has helped to legitimize shipwreck salvaging.
    (D) The use of sound waves is crucial to locating shipwrecks.

(C) This is an author's support question. The first sentence states that treasure seeking is now seen as legitimate because of new technology. The fifth sentence states that one of the new technological advances is side-scan sonar. Answer (A) is not correct since the passage infers that a sunken ship may have value as an historic object, even if it has no monetary value from treasures. Answer (B) is not correct; it may be inferred, but it is not "best supported" by the author. Answer (D) is not correct since the use of sound waves is not stated as being crucial, only as being a new advance that has improved and sped up the process of discovery.

42. The author uses the word "services" in line 9 to refer to which of the following?
    (A) cups
    (B) sets
    (C) containers
    (D) decorations

(B) A "tea service" refers to a group of items, such as a tray containing a teapot, a small bowl for sugar, a small jug for cream, and maybe a spoon.

43. The author uses the phrase "mint condition" in line 14 to describe
    (A) something perfect
    (B) something significant
    (C) something tolerant
    (D) something magical

(A) The phrase "mint condition" refers to something that is like new, in perfect condition. It comes from the noun and verb "mint," referring to the place and process of producing coins. At a mint, all coins are brand new and in perfect condition.

44. All of the following were found on the RMS *Republic* EXCEPT
    (A) wine bottles
    (B) silver tea services
    (C) American Gold Eagle coins
    (D) crystal dinnerware

(C) This is a negative question. The answer lies in lines 9–10, where the author lists the items found and states that the crew did not find any American Gold Eagle coins.

45. From the passage, you can infer that a preservationist would be most likely to
    (A) shun treasure-seeking salvagers
    (B) be a diver
    (C) put treasures in a museum
    (D) do archaeological research

(A) This is an inference question. Because preservationists are critical of the activities of treasure hunters, and because the passage says they are fighting each other in the courts, it would be most likely that preservationists would shun salvagers. The verb "to shun" means "to avoid deliberately."

46. The word "scoured" in line 14 is most similar to which of the following?
    (A) scraped away
    (B) scratched over
    (C) scrambled through
    (D) searched through

(D) In this sentence, the verbs "to scour" and "to search through" mean "to comb through" or "to rummage through." Scour infers that the search involves turning things over to look under them. In other instances the verb "to scour" means "to wash vigorously."

47. As used in line 18, what is the closest meaning to the word "lure"?
    (A) knowledge
    (B) attraction
    (C) luxury
    (D) glare

(B) The nouns "lure" and "attraction" both refer to something that is appealing, such as a reward or pleasure.

48. The second and third paragraphs are an example of
  (A) chronological order
  (B) explanation
  (C) specific to general
  (D) definition

(B) This is an organization question. The second and third paragraphs give an explanation of two opposing groups of people: preservationists and treasure seekers (also called "treasure hunters" and "salvagers"). Answer (D), "definition," is too narrow since the paragraphs give more information than just a definition of the types of people.

49. What is the author's main purpose in this passage?
  (A) to promote the Catskills as a vacation destination
  (B) to introduce visitors to famous Catskills entertainers
  (C) to describe the history of the Catskills region
  (D) to compare the Catskills to New England

(A) This is a question of the author's purpose. Answer (B) is incorrect because the entertainers are mentioned only as one reason to visit the Catskills. Answer (C) is also mentioned only as a way to promote the region. Answer (D) is incorrect because there is no similar discussion of New England's features as a vacation destination.

50. The word "rugged" in line 4 could best be replaced by which of the following?
  (A) barren
  (B) rough
  (C) tall
  (D) lush

(B) The words "rugged" and "rough" both refer to something that is uneven or jagged, such as the mountains. Answer (A) refers to a place that has little vegetation growing, while answer (D) is just the opposite in that it refers to a place that is very green and is filled with growing plants.

51. According to the passage, which of the following caused the decline in the number of Catskills resorts in the 1970s?
  (A) television
  (B) shorter vacations
  (C) affordable air travel
  (D) more traffic

(C) This is a restatement question. Lines 10–11 give cheaper air travel and air-conditioning as reasons why families stopped coming to the hotels and why the hotels later closed.

52. Which of the following is closest in meaning to the word "legendary" in line 5?
  (A) foolish
  (B) perplexing
  (C) mythical
  (D) humorous

(C) A "legendary" story is one that is probably not true but is well known in a particular culture. "Mythical" also refers to a story that is not true but is well known.

53. The phrase "sprang up" in line 5 most probably refers to something that has
  (A) burst forth
  (B) spread out
  (C) operated vigorously
  (D) joined together

(A) The phrases "to spring up" and "to burst forth" both refer to something that appears suddenly.

54. In what season would a tourist most likely have visited the Catskills in the 1950s?
  (A) fall
  (B) winter
  (C) spring
  (D) summer

(D) This is an inference question. Lines 5–6 describe the Catskills in the 1950s as a summer vacation spot.

55. Which of the following most reflects the author's tone in this passage?
    (A) light and encouraging
    (B) informative and scientific
    (C) humorous and sceptical
    (D) regretful and reminiscent

(A) This is an author's-tone question. Throughout the passage, the author is speaking directly to the reader in a light-hearted way to encourage the reader to visit the Catskills. Whereas much of the passage is "informative," it is not written in a scientific way. There are no words to suggest humor, scepticism, regret, or reminiscence.

56. What does the passage imply that a visitor might be lucky enough to do?
    (A) see fall leaves in color
    (B) see a kind of bird
    (C) work on a sheep farm
    (D) drive on scenic roads

(B) this is an inference question. The final paragraph mentions several things that a visitor might be able to do. The only answer that implies being "lucky" is answer (B), "spotting bald eagles." An eagle is a bird. The word "spot" implies a quick look at something, which could also be "discern," "detect," or "pick out." All these verbs imply that it is not always easy to see the object, and one may get only a glance at it. Seeing the fall colors, mentioned in answer (A), is written of as an expected activity, not a "lucky" one. Answers (C) and (D) are both mentioned as things visitors can do; there is no implication that the visitor must be "lucky" to do them.

57. As used in line 14, the word "witnessing" could best be replaced by
    (A) attending
    (B) certifying
    (C) viewing
    (D) validating

(C) All of the above words can mean "witnessing" in some contexts, but in this sentence "witnessing" simply means "observing," "seeing," or "viewing." It implies viewing with interest.

58. As used in line 16, the word "drives" refers to
    (A) excursions
    (B) tracks
    (C) paths
    (D) canyons

(A) In this sentence, the word "drives" refers to places that people can drive to in their cars for pleasure. The word "excursion" refers to the same activity. Answers (B) and (C) do not imply automobile tourism, as does "drives." One might walk on a track or path. On a scenic drive, a tourist might view a canyon, but the word "drive" refers to the road, not the canyon itself.

59. As used in line 17, which of the following could best replace the word "spotting"?
    (A) photographing
    (B) seeing
    (C) painting
    (D) shooting

(B) The verb "to spot" refers to seeing or viewing something briefly or with difficulty.

60. The author implies that in the Catskills there are few
    (A) leaves
    (B) eagles
    (C) people
    (D) sheep

(C) This is an inference question. The passage begins with the implication that few people go to the Catskills since there are no traffic jams or overbooked hotels.

61. What does this passage mainly discuss?
    (A) the lasting effects of bluegrass music
    (B) the development of an American instrument
    (C) the life of a banjo
    (D) changes in music in the nineteenth and twentieth centuries

(B) This is a main idea question. Answer (A) can be inferred but is not the main subject. Answers (C) is too specific and answer (D) is too broad.

62. The banjo originally came from
    (A) southern plantations
    (B) folk and country music
    (C) minstrel shows
    (D) Africa

(D) This is a restatement question. The passage states that the "ancestry [of the banjo] is African."

63. The word "plantation" in line 3 most probably refers to
(A) types of farms in the South
(B) southern states
(C) southern musical theater
(D) bands common in the South

(A) A "plantation" is an area that consists of fields for planting crops and homes for the landowners and fielf workers.

64. Which of the following words is most similar to the word "pegs" in line 4?
(A) holes
(B) bars
(C) pins
(D) strings

(C) A "peg" is a type of small pin, often made of wood.

65. The word "precise" in line 5 could best be replaced by which of the following?
(A) accurate
(B) confirmed
(C) processed
(D) essential

(A) This is a vocabulary question. The words "precise" and "accurate" both mean "exact."

66. According to the passage, all of the following are true of the five-string banjo EXCEPT
(A) It was used by Earl Scruggs.
(B) It was famous in the production of bluegrass music.
(C) It had an unfretted string.
(D) It was a tenor banjo.

(D) This is a negative question. Answers (A), (B), and (C) are all stated in the passage.

67. Which of the following is most similar to the meaning of "comeback" in line 10?
(A) performance
(B) reappearance
(C) gain
(D) achievement

(B) A "comeback" means a "reappearance." In this sense, it means to return and become famous or popular again.

68. The word "renewed" in line 11 could best be replaced by which of the following?
(A) rescued
(B) remarkable
(C) revived
(D) renowned

(C) The words "renewed" and "revived" both mean to become important again, "to be brought to life" again.

69. Which of the following means most nearly the same as the word "forefront" as used in line 12?
(A) forcast
(B) spotlight
(C) footnote
(D) record

(B) To be in the "forefront" means to be in the extreme front or "the position of most importance." To be in the "spotlight" means to be in a place of prominence.

70. Which of the following best indicates the author's attitude toward the banjo?
(A) It is a unique instrument.
(B) It should be in a museum.
(C) It should be used more.
(D) It must be kept alive.

(A) This is an author's attitude question. We can infer that the author thinks that the banjo is unique in part from the first sentence, which says that it is hard to find artifacts that are genuinely American.

71. What does the passage mainly discuss?
(A) political aspects of Roosevelt's life
(B) problems during the Great Depression
(C) Roosevelt's upbringing
(D) criticisms of Roosevelt's actions

(A) This is a main idea question. Though all of the above are mentioned, answer (A) is the most comprehensive.

72. Which one of the following statements is NOT mentioned in the passage?
(A) Roosevelt was elected during the Great Depression.
(B) Roosevelt voted for Al Smith.
(C) Roosevelt had difficulty walking during his presidency.
(D) Roosevelt supported strong government powers.

(B) This is a negative question. We know that Roosevelt nominated Al Smith, but the passage does not say that Roosevelt voted for him.

73. The phrase "took action" in lines 8–9 is used to illustrate the idea that Roosevelt
    (A) performed admirably
    (B) exerted himself physically
    (C) responded immediately
    (D) got assistance

(C) The phrase "to take action" means to take charge of something, usually a task that needs to be done. In this case, the action was that Roosevelt responded to the problem of bank failure. We can assume from the sentence that he acted quickly to solve the problem.

74. As used in line 10, the phrase "little by little" means that Roosevelt
    (A) opened the smaller banks first
    (B) opened the banks for minimal services
    (C) opened the banks a few at a time
    (D) opened the banks for a short time

(C) The phrase "little by little" means doing something in small doses.

75. The word "full" in line 10 could best be replaced by which of the following?
    (A) packed
    (B) loaded
    (C) overflowing
    (D) complete

(D) All of these choices might mean "full" in some situations, but only "complete" is appropriate in this sentence. The "full power" of the government means *all* the power of the government.

76. Where in the passage does the author discuss Roosevelt's response to the Great Depression?
    (A) lines 1–4
    (B) lines 5–8
    (C) lines 8–10
    (D) lines 12–14

(C) This is an organization question. Lines 8–9 say that Roosevelt "took action" by closing the banks.

77. The word "affection" as used in line 12 could best be replaced by which of the following?
    (A) fascination
    (B) fondness
    (C) lure
    (D) appeal

(B) The words "affection" and "fondness" indicate a warm emotional feeling or attachment toward someone or something.

78. The word "unprecedented" in line 15 could best be replaced by
    (A) unimportant
    (B) unheard of
    (C) unjustified
    (D) unhampered

(B) This is a vocabulary question. "Unprecedented" and "unheard of" both mean something that is unusual and may not have happened before.

79. It can be inferred from the passage that the people who liked Roosevelt best were
    (A) poor people
    (B) bankers
    (C) rich people
    (D) average people

(D) The passage refers to "forgotten people," "workers," and "wage earners" as those who like Roosevelt best. This would not be referring mainly to poor people since poor people may not be earning regular wages. It would probably not be referring to bankers or rich people since we might infer that these people would not be called "forgotten people." The term "wage earners" usually refers to people who are earning regular wages but are not rich.

80. In line 17, the author uses the word "looming" to indicate a feeling of
    (A) reservation
    (B) determination
    (C) regret
    (D) threat

(D) The word "looming" refers to something that appears or rises before us. This word often gives the idea that the thing appearing may be large and possibly threatening.

81. According to the author, we might call our eyes and ears "transformers" because
    (A) they sense light and sound
    (B) they create electrical impulses
    (C) the brain can interpret the input
    (D) the messages travel in the brain

(B) This is a restatement question. The first sentence says that light and sound are turned into electrical impulses. The "transformation," then, is the making of electrical impulses.

82. Which of the following is closest in meaning to the word "admits" in line 4?
    (A) selects
    (B) interprets
    (C) lets in
    (D) focuses on

(C) The verbs "to admit" and "to let in" both refer to allowing something to enter.

83. In line 4, what does the first use of the word "them" refer to?
    (A) light waves
    (B) processes
    (C) eyes
    (D) messages

(A) This is a referent question. The word "them" refers back to the previous noun, "light waves."

84. The word "bundle" in line 5 could best be replaced by which of the following?
    (A) group
    (B) grow
    (C) branch
    (D) settle

(A) This is a vocabulary question. The word "bundle" is a verb in this sentence, referring to an assortment of things that come together, possibly being wrapped or tied together. The word "group" is the closest of the above words.

85. The word "split" as used in line 6 is closest in meaning to which of the following?
    (A) tear
    (B) fracture
    (C) separate
    (D) crack

(C) All of the above words can mean "split" in some contexts. In this sentence, "split" means "to divide" or "to separate." The words "tear," "fracture," and "crack" all connote something negative. "Crack" and "fracture" refer to the breaking of something that is hard and brittle, while "tear" means to pull apart something by force.

86. Which of the following is closest in meaning to the word "cross" as used in line 6?
    (A) intersect
    (B) cancel
    (C) assemble
    (D) match

(A) The verbs "to cross" and "to intersect" both mean "to go across" or "to go over" something else.

87. According to the passage, when input from the right visual field goes into the left side of the brain, what happens?
    (A) The nerve fibers bundle together.
    (B) The optic nerves split.
    (C) The retina receives light waves.
    (D) Input from the left field goes to the right side.

(D) This is a restatement question. In line 7 the phrase "vice versa" means that the opposite happens.

88. The phrase "carried out" in line 7 could best be replaced by which of the following?
    (A) brought over
    (B) taken away
    (C) accomplished
    (D) maintained

(C) The verbs "to carry out" and "to accomplish" both refer to getting something done or achieving some purpose.

89. Which of the following is most similar to the word "vibration" as used in line 8?
    (A) sound
    (B) movement
    (C) light
    (D) heat

(B) A vibration is a movement like a tremble, a flutter, or a quiver.

90. According to the passage, optic nerves eventually
    (A) bend
    (B) split
    (C) admit light waves
    (D) become messages

(B) This is a restatement question. Lines 5–6 say that optic nerves join and split into two optic tracts.

ANSWER SHEET FOR PRACTICE TEST 5

Section 1: Listening Comprehension

1 2 3 4 5 6 7 8 9 10 11 12 13 14 15 16 17 18 19 20 21 22 23 24 25 26 27 28 29 30 31 32 33 34 35 36 37 38 39 40 41 42 43 44 45 46 47 48 49 50
Ⓐ Ⓑ Ⓒ Ⓓ

Section 2: Structure and Written Expression

1 2 3 4 5 6 7 8 9 10 11 12 13 14 15 16 17 18 19 20 21 22 23 24 25 26 27 28 29 30 31 32 33 34 35 36 37 38 39 40
Ⓐ Ⓑ Ⓒ Ⓓ

Section 3: Reading Comprehension

1 2 3 4 5 6 7 8 9 10 11 12 13 14 15 16 17 18 19 20 21 22 23 24 25 26 27 28 29 30 31 32 33 34 35 36 37 38 39 40 41 42 43 44 45 46 47 48 49 50 51 52 53 54 55 56 57 58 59 60
Ⓐ Ⓑ Ⓒ Ⓓ

Date Taken _____

Number Correct

Section 1 _____

Section 2 _____

Section 3 _____

Practice Test 5

SECTION 1

Listening Comprehension

Time—approximately 30 minutes

NOTE: You can simulate actual TOEFL conditions by using the Listening Comprehension Cassettes that accompany this book. If you do not have the tape, ask a friend to read the tapescript for Listening Comprehension Test 5, which is in Part Four, pages 418–25 of this book.

Part A

Directions: In Part A you will hear short conversations between two people. After each conversation a third person will ask a question about what was said. You will hear the conversation only one time, so you must listen carefully to what each speaker says. After you hear the conversation and the question, read the four possible answers in your test booklet and pick the one which best answers the question. Then look on the answer sheet for the number of the question and fill in the oval that corresponds to the letter of your answer choice.

Listen to an example:

You will hear:

You will read:

Sample Answer

(A) He will call Pete before he goes home.
(B) He will call Pete after he gets home.
(C) He called Pete at home.
(D) He will call Pete tomorrow.

You learn from the conversation that the man will call Pete as soon as he gets home. The best answer to the question "What does the man mean?" is (B), "He will call Pete after he gets home." Therefore, the correct answer is (B).

Now listen to the tape: Test 5, Section 1, Listening Comprehension Part A.

GO ON TO THE NEXT PAGE
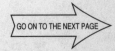

1. (A) The shirt is old-fashioned.
   (B) The shirt is the wrong color.
   (C) The shirt is too dirty.
   (D) The shirt doesn't fit.

2. (A) There are fewer people than usual.
   (B) There will be more people in the restaurant at dinner time.
   (C) They don't have any lunch specials today.
   (D) It's very busy.

3. (A) He wants to pay with cash.
   (B) He wants to get money.
   (C) He wants to charge something.
   (D) He wants to check something.

4. (A) She has finished eating dinner.
   (B) She is going to make some dessert.
   (C) She did the cooking.
   (D) She is happy dining with him.

5. (A) He thinks she will do a good job.
   (B) He will impress everybody with the presentation.
   (C) She has good reason to worry.
   (D) She will be fine if she practices more.

6. (A) bus driver
   (B) airline ticket agent
   (C) post office clerk
   (D) department store salesperson

7. (A) The school offers more classes now.
   (B) This is a small section.
   (C) It's difficult to get into this class.
   (D) Last fall the class was better.

8. (A) She has had enough chicken.
   (B) She doesn't eat vegetables.
   (C) She doesn't eat meat.
   (D) She is not hungry.

9. (A) He goes fishing sometimes.
   (B) He went fishing once.
   (C) He had to quit fishing.
   (D) He has other hobbies now.

10. (A) She is surprised.
    (B) She can't help him.
    (C) She doesn't understand him.
    (D) She is angry.

11. (A) sit down and rest
    (B) pay the money
    (C) take the boat tour
    (D) visit the exihibit

12. (A) He drinks a lot of water during the day.
    (B) He doesn't usually drink this much water.
    (C) He has never been so thirsty.
    (D) He likes soft drinks more than water.

13. (A) They will go eat with their friends.
    (B) The Johnsons are coming over.
    (C) She will take a dish to the Johnson's house.
    (D) She is tired of cooking.

14. (A) He is tired of standing up all day.
    (B) He is finishing his homework.
    (C) He has a lot of school work.
    (D) He has been working at home.

15. (A) The car didn't get washed.
    (B) Don and Mary washed the car together.
    (C) Mary washed the car.
    (D) Don washed the car for Mary.

16. (A) This grocery store doesn't accept checks.
    (B) Check your shopping list while you are shopping.
    (C) This store doesn't have what she wants.
    (D) Check to see if the grocery store is next to the gas station.

17. (A) He used the wrong bus schedule.
    (B) He's going to get a bus schedule.
    (C) He likes to ride the bus.
    (D) He missed the bus.

18. (A) John has his hair cut every month.
    (B) John has his hair cut twice as often as Peter does.
    (C) John had a haircut two weeks ago.
    (D) This month Peter didn't have his hair cut.

19. (A) She is financially independent now.
    (B) She needs a financial advisor.
    (C) She applied for a job this year.
    (D) She's happy with her financial plan.

20. (A) She should turn right on Second Street.
    (B) She is supposed to turn right at this stop sign.
    (C) She should turn left at the stop sign after this one.
    (D) She should turn left after she turns right.

GO ON TO THE NEXT PAGE

Part B

Directions: In Part B you will hear longer conversations between two people. After each conversation you will be asked some questions. You will hear the conversations and the questions only once, so listen carefully to what is said. After you hear a question, read the four possible answers in your test book and decide which one is the best answer to the question you heard. Then, on your answer sheet, find the number of the question and fill in the oval that corresponds to the letter of the answer you have chosen. Answer all questions based on what is stated or implied by the speakers.

Listen to the example on the tape.

> *You will hear:*

Now listen to sample question number 1.

You will read:

Sample Answer

    (A) to the cafeteria
    (B) to the movie theater
    (C) to her dorm room
    (D) to the library

The best answer to the question "Where is the woman going?" is (D), "to the library." Therefore, the correct choice is (D).

Now listen to sample question number 2.

Sample Answer

> *You will hear:*

> *You will read:*

    (A) Term papers are easy for him.
    (B) He has a lot of essay exams.
    (C) He finds lab experiments easier than writing term papers.
    (D) He is busier this semester than last semester.

The best answer to the question "Which best describes the man's feelings about his classes?" is (C), "He finds lab experiments easier than writing term papers." Therefore, the correct answer is (C).

Now listen to the test. Remember, you are not allowed to take any notes or write in your test book.

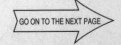
GO ON TO THE NEXT PAGE

21. (A) because she failed her last exam
    (B) in order to complete her homework
    (C) in order to prepare for her exams
    (D) because she has fallen behind in her work

22. (A) to her room
    (B) to the dining hall
    (C) to the pool
    (D) to the gymnasium

23. (A) eating dinner
    (B) swimming
    (C) studying for an exam
    (D) taking a nap

24. (A) The man will have an exam.
    (B) The man and the woman will have lunch together.
    (C) The man will be in a swim meet at 1 P.M.
    (D) The man and the woman will study together.

25. (A) advanced economics
    (B) biology 110
    (C) introductory economics
    (D) advanced biology

26. (A) walking on campus
    (B) waiting in a dormitory lounge
    (C) eating at a dining hall
    (D) sitting on a campus bench

27. (A) 40
    (B) 100
    (C) 200
    (D) 400

28. (A) She took the class last semester.
    (B) She read about it in the school newspaper.
    (C) She heard about it on the school radio station.
    (D) Her roommate took the course last semester.

29. (A) He wanted to ask her to do something for him.
    (B) They both live in the same dorm.
    (C) They both had the same exam the next day.
    (D) He wanted to borrow her car.

30. (A) 6:00 A.M.
    (B) 7:00 A.M.
    (C) 7:30 A.M.
    (D) 8:00 A.M.

31. (A) in Katrina's room
    (B) in front of the dormitory
    (C) next to the dean's office
    (D) inside the parking garage

32. (A) He has been expelled from school.
    (B) He has to go to a relative's funeral.
    (C) He is going to his sister's wedding.
    (D) He has finished his exams.

33. (A) watching a football game on television
    (B) going out to dinner tonight
    (C) arranging to meet at a championship game
    (D) getting ready to play a game.

34. (A) car trouble
    (B) studying for an exam
    (C) choir practice
    (D) a late dinner

35. (A) in Section C
    (B) in Section D
    (C) behind the benches
    (D) behind the goals

GO ON TO THE NEXT PAGE

Part C

Directions: In this part of the test, you will hear talks by a single person. After each talk, you will be asked some questions. You will hear the talks and the questions only once, so listen carefully to what is said. After you hear a question, read the four possible answers in your test book and decide which one is the best answer to the question you heard. Then find the number of the question on your answer sheet, and fill in the oval that corresponds to the letter of the answer you have chosen. Answer all questions based on what is stated or implied in the talk.

Listen to this sample talk.

> *You will hear:*

Now listen to sample question number 1.　　　　　　　　　　　　　　　　Sample Answer

> *You will read:*　　　　　　　　　　　　　　　　　　　　　　Ⓐ Ⓑ Ⓒ ⬤

> **(A)** to demonstrate tutoring techniques
> **(B)** to explain school policies
> **(C)** to recruit childcare workers
> **(D)** to explain a service

The best answer to the question "What is the purpose of this announcement?" is (D), "to explain a service." Therefore, the correct answer is (D).

Now listen to sample question number 2.　　　　　　　　　　　　　　　　Sample Answer

> *You will hear:*　　　　　　　　　　　　　　　　　　　　　Ⓐ Ⓑ ⬤ Ⓓ

> *You will read:*

> **(A)** Give your child extra tutoring.
> **(B)** Take your child to the program today.
> **(C)** Apply as soon as you can.
> **(D)** Pay next month.

The best answer to the question "What does the speaker recommend?" is (C), "Apply as soon as you can." Therefore the correct choice is (C).

Now begin. Remember, you are not allowed to write any notes in your test book.

GO ON TO THE NEXT PAGE

36. (A) one to two pages
    (B) 10 to 12 pages
    (C) 19 to 20 pages
    (D) no limit was mentioned

37. (A) during the first week of school
    (B) by the middle of the term
    (C) sometime before the last week of school
    (D) at anytime during the term

38. (A) because they are more likely to have problems writing the paper
    (B) because the teaching assistant prefers to work with first-year students
    (C) because it is the policy of the university
    (D) because the professor wants them to have more work

39. (A) April 6
    (B) April 13
    (C) April 20
    (D) April 27

40. (A) arriving passengers
    (B) departing passengers
    (C) people boarding a boat
    (D) people departing from a train

41. (A) Walk straight ahead.
    (B) Turn to the left to Terminal B.
    (C) Wait for transportation to bring their luggage.
    (D) Walk to their right to get their baggage.

42. (A) at Carousel B
    (B) at the blue area
    (C) near the green sign
    (D) next to the white buses

43. (A) at the departure gate
    (B) at Carousel B
    (C) under the green sign
    (D) in the yellow loading zone

44. (A) American natural history
    (B) English children's literature
    (C) zoos in the western world
    (D) bears of North America

45. (A) a child
    (B) a bear
    (C) an author
    (D) a pig

46. (A) in the woods
    (B) at a zoo
    (C) at a school
    (D) in a garden

47. (A) the invention of the elevator
    (B) modern elevators
    (C) the Crystal Palace Exhibition
    (D) inventions of the nineteenth century

48. (A) London
    (B) Chicago
    (C) San Francisco
    (D) New York

49. (A) steel cables
    (B) guide rails
    (C) strong ropes
    (D) an open carriage

50. (A) other inventions at the Crystal Palace Exhibition
    (B) the first tall buildings
    (C) further developments in elevators
    (D) the life of Elisha Otis

THIS IS THE END OF SECTION 1.
DO NOT READ OR WORK ON ANY OTHER SECTION OF THE TEST UNTIL TIME IS UP.

STOP   STOP   STOP   STOP   STOP

SECTION 2
Structure and Written Expression

Time—25 minutes

Part 1: Sentence Completion

Directions: Questions 1–15 are not complete sentences. One or more words are left out of each sentence. Under each sentence, you will see four words or phrases, marked (A), (B), (C), and (D). Choose the one word or phrase that completes the sentence correctly. Then, on your answer sheet, find the number of the question and fill in the oval that corresponds to the letter of your answer choice.

Example I ▷

Birds make nests in trees _____ hide their young in the leaves and branches.

Sample Answer

Ⓐ ● Ⓒ Ⓓ

    (A) can where they
    (B) where they can
    (C) where can they
    (D) where can

The sentence should read, "Birds make nests in trees where they can hide their young in the leaves and branches." Therefore, you should choose answer (B).

Example II ▷

Sleeping, resting, and _____ are the best ways to care for a cold.

Sample Answer

Ⓐ Ⓑ Ⓒ ●

    (A) to drink fluids
    (B) drank fluids
    (C) one drink fluids
    (D) drinking fluids

The sentence should read, "Sleeping, resting, and drinking fluids are the best ways to care for a cold." Therefore, you should choose answer (D).

Now begin work on the questions.

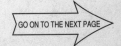
GO ON TO THE NEXT PAGE

1. Birds all over the world _____ in distances up to thousands of miles.
   (A) migrating
   (B) migrated
   (C) migrate
   (D) are migrated

2. Cellulose, which _____ for making paper, can be found in all plants.
   (A) is used
   (B) uses
   (C) are used
   (D) is using

3. _____ , human beings have relatively constant body temperature.
   (A) Alike all mammal
   (B) Alike all mammals
   (C) Like all mammals
   (D) Like all mammal

4. So far there is no vaccine _____ in sight for the common cold.
   (A) or curing
   (B) has cured
   (C) or cure
   (D) having cured

5. The Louisiana Territory, an area _____ the size of France, was bought by the United States from France for $15,000,000 in 1803.
   (A) than more four times
   (B) more than four times
   (C) four times than more
   (D) is four times more than

6. Despite claims that filters and low-tar tobacco make smoking somewhat safer, in fact they only marginally reduce, _____ eliminate, the hazards.
   (A) none
   (B) no
   (C) not
   (D) nor

7. _____ many of the designs for the new capital were considered lost forever, Benjamin Banneker helped reproduce the original plans.
   (A) When
   (B) During
   (C) If as
   (D) How

8. A few natural elements exist in _____ that they are rarely seen in their natural environments.
   (A) such small quantities
   (B) so small quantities
   (C) very small quantities
   (D) small quantity

9. Generally speaking, every person_____ the potential to be a teacher, to some extent.
   (A) has
   (B) to have
   (C) having
   (D) have

10. _____ business, a merger is a combination of two or more corporations under one management.
    (A) The
    (B) At
    (C) On
    (D) In

11. _____ of commodities by air began in the 1920s at the same time as airmail service.
    (A) The shipping
    (B) A ship
    (C) The shipped
    (D) To ship

12. Jan Malzeliger's invention, the "shoe-lasting" machine, _____ production but it also cut the cost of shoe production by half.
    (A) not only increased
    (B) not increased only
    (C) increased only
    (D) only have increased

13. It can sometimes _____ a home.
    (A) to take months to sell
    (B) take several months to sell
    (C) selling takes several months
    (D) to sell taking several months

14. Jellyfish are probably _____ on Earth.
    (A) most numerous predators
    (B) the most numerous predators
    (C) most numerous of predators
    (D) the most predators

15. In the United States _____ is the most concentrated is New Orleans.
    (A) French influence the city
    (B) the city where French influence
    (C) where the city influences French
    (D) where the French influence the city

GO ON TO THE NEXT PAGE

Part 2: Error Identification

Directions: In questions 16–40 each sentence has four underlined words or phrases marked (A), (B), (C), and (D). Choose the one word or phrase that must be changed in order for the sentence to be correct. Then, on your answer sheet, find the number of the question and fill in the oval that corresponds to the letter of your answer choice.

Example I▷

Aspirin is recommend to many people for its
        A   **B**   **C**

ability to thin the blood.
    D

Sample Answer

● Ⓑ Ⓒ Ⓓ

The sentence should read, "Aspirin is recommend to many people for its ability to thin the blood." Therefore, you should choose answer (A).

Example II▷

Some people believe that human beings will
            A

never use away all the natural resources on earth.
    B   **C**   **D**

Sample Answer

Ⓐ ● Ⓒ Ⓓ

The sentence should read, "Some people believe that human beings will never use up all the natural resources on earth." Therefore, you should choose answer (B).

Now begin work on the questions.

16. In 1931 Jane Addams was a Nobel Peace Prize recipient for she humanitarian achievements.
  A   **B**   **C**   **D**

17. Even on the most careful prepared trip, problems will sometimes develop.
    A   **B**   **C**   **D**

18. Many people say that California is a state of geographic remarkable diversity.
    A   **B**   **C**   **D**

19. An uncultivated tea plant might grow about 30 feet height.
      A   **B**   **C**   **D**

20. A galaxy, where may include billions of stars, is held together by gravitational attraction.
       A   **B** **C**   **D**

21. Rocks can be broken apart by water that seeps into the cracks and freeze in low temperatures.
          A   **B**   **C**   **D**

22. Alexander Graham Bell was once a teacher who run a school for the deaf in Massachusetts.
                A   **B**   **C**   **D**

23. Some fish use their sense of smell as a guide when return to a spawning site.
      A **B**   **C**   **D**

24. In Quebec, Canada, the flowing of the maple sap is one of the first sign of spring.
  A   **B**   **C**   **D**

25. Antique auctions are getting more and more popular in the United States because increasing public awareness
      A   **B**   **C**

of the value of investing in antiques.
    D

GO ON TO THE NEXT PAGE▷

26. Archaeological evidence reveals that Native Americans lived on the East Coast of the United States 13 centuries
              A   B   C

    before.
    D

27. Diamond itself is the only material hard enough to cut and polishes diamonds.
        A   B   C   D

28. The change from day to night results the rotation of the Earth.
        A   B C   D

29. As Ingrid Bergman lived a life of courage, she also approached die with courage.
    A   B   C   D

30. Residents in some cities can call an electrical inspector to have the wiring in their house is checked.
             A   B   C   D

31. The best way to eliminate a pest is to controlling the food accessible to it.
     A   B   C   D

32. The Earth depends the sun for its heating.
      A   B   C   D

33. The famous aviator Charles Lindbergh was a early supporter of rocket research.
       A   B   C   D

34. Cholesterol help the body by making hormones and building cell walls, but too much cholesterol can cause
        A   B   C   D

    heart problems.

35. Luther Burbank was a pioneer in the process of graft immature plants onto fully mature plants.
             A   B   C   D

36. With its compound eyes, dragonflies can see moving insects approximately 18 feet away.
      A   B   C   D

37. An X-ray microscope enables a person to see on solid materials such as metal and bone.
           A   B   C   D

38. The United States has a younger population as most other major industrial countries.
        A   B C   D

39. Before the invention of the printing press, books have been all printed by hand.
     A   B   C   D

40. As the Asian economic miracle spreads throughout the Pacific, wage increases everywhere is affecting
    A   B   C

    millions of consumers.
    D

THIS IS THE END OF SECTION 2.
DO NOT READ OR WORK ON ANY OTHER SECTION OF THE TEST UNTIL TIME IS UP.
STOP   STOP   STOP   STOP   STOP

SECTION 3

Reading Comprehension

Time—55 minutes

Directions: In this section you will read several passages. Each passage is followed by questions about it. Choose the one best answer, (A), (B), (C) or (D), for each question. Then, on your answer sheet, find the number of the question and fill in the oval that corresponds to the letter of your answer choice. Answer all questions based on what is stated or implied in the reading passage.

Read the following passage:

A new hearing device is now available for some hearing-impaired people. This device uses a magnet to hold the detachable sound-processing portion in place. Like other aids, it converts sound into vibrations. But it is unique in that it can transmit the vibrations directly to the magnet, and then to the inner ear. This produces a clearer sound. The new device will not help all hearing-impaired people, only those with a hearing loss caused by infection or some other problem in the middle ear. It will probably help no more than 20 percent of all people with hearing problems. Those people, however, who have persistent ear infections should find relief and restored hearing with the new device.

Example I▷

What is the author's main purpose?

(A) to describe a new cure for ear infections
(B) to inform the reader of a new device
(C) to urge doctors to use a new device
(D) to explain the use of a magnet

Sample Answer

The author's main purpose is to inform the reader of a new device for hearing-impaired people. Therefore, you should choose answer (B).

Example II▷

The word "relief" in the last sentence means

(A) less distress
(B) assistance
(C) distraction
(D) relaxation

Sample Answer

The phrase "less distress" is similar in meaning to "relief" in this sentence. Therefore, you should choose answer (A).

Now begin with the questions.

Questions 1 to 12 are based on the following passsage:

(1)   Lead poisoning in children is a major health concern. Both low and high doses of paint can have serious effects. Children exposed to high doses of lead often suffer permanent nerve damage, mental retardation, blindness, and even death. Low doses of lead can lead to mild mental retardation, short attention spans, distractibility, poor academic performance, and behavioral problems.

(5)   This is not a new concern. As early as 1904, lead poisoning in children was linked to lead-based paint. Microscopic lead particles from paint are absorbed into the bloodstream when children ingest flakes of chipped paint, plaster, or paint dust from sanding. Lead can also enter the body through household dust, nailbiting, thumb sucking, or chewing on toys and other objects painted with lead-based paint. Although American paint companies today must comply with strict regulations regarding the amount of lead used

(10)   in their paint, this source of lead poisoning is still the most common and most dangerous. Children living in older, dilapidated houses are particularly at risk.

1. What is the main topic of the passage?
   (A) problems with household paint
   (B) major health concerns for children
   (C) lead poisoning in children
   (D) lead paint in older homes

2. Which part of the passage discusses symptoms and consequences of lead poisoning?
   (A) lines 1–4
   (B) lines 5–8
   (C) lines 9–10
   (D) lines 10–11

3. The phrase "exposed to" in line 2 could best be replaced by which of the following?
   (A) familiar with
   (B) in contact with
   (C) displaying
   (D) conducting

4. As used in line 2, which of the following is closest in meaning to the word "suffer"?
   (A) experience
   (B) reveal
   (C) feel pain from
   (D) grieve with

5. Which of the following does the passage infer?
   (A) Paint companies can no longer use lead in their paint.
   (B) Paint companies aren't required to limit the amount of lead used in their paint.
   (C) Paint companies must limit the amount of lead used in their lead.
   (D) Paint companies have always followed restrictions regarding the amount of lead used in their paint.

6. Which of the following is closest in meaning to the phrase "linked to" in line 5?
   (A) endorsed by
   (B) threatened by
   (C) combined with
   (D) associated with

7. The word "absorbed" in line 6 could best be replaced by
   (A) fixed
   (B) assimilated
   (C) soaked
   (D) accepted

8. In line 6, the word "ingest" could best be replaced by which of the following?
   (A) inhale
   (B) digest
   (C) inject
   (D) eat

9. Which of the following is closest in meaning to the word "chipped" as used in line 7?
   (A) fragmented
   (B) canned
   (C) sprayed
   (D) unhealthy

10. In line 11, the word "dilapidated" is closest in meaning to which of the following?
    (A) poorly painted
    (B) unpainted
    (C) falled down
    (D) broken down

 GO ON TO THE NEXT PAGE

11. According to the passage, what is the most common source of lead poisoning in children?
    (A) household dust
    (B) lead-based paint
    (C) painted toys
    (D) dilapidated houses

12. What does the author imply in the final sentence of the passage?
    (A) Lead-based paint chips off more easily than newer paints.
    (B) Poor people did not comply with the regulations.
    (C) Old homes were painted with lead-based paint.
    (D) Old homes need to be rebuilt in order to be safe for children.

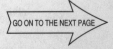

Questions 13 to 24 are based on the following passage:

(1) Although they are an inexpensive supplier of vitamins, minerals, and high-quality protein, eggs also contain a high level of blood cholesterol, one of the major causes of heart disease. One egg yolk, in fact, contains a little more than two-thirds of the suggested daily cholesterol limit. This knowledge has caused egg sales to plummet in recent years, which in turn has brought about the development of

(5) several alternatives to eating regular eggs. One alternative is to eat substitute eggs. These egg substitutes are not really eggs, but they look somewhat like eggs when they are cooked. They have the advantage of having lower cholesterol rates, and they can be scrambled or used in baking. One disadvantage, however, is that they are not good for frying, poaching, or boiling. A second alternative to regular eggs is a new type of egg, sometimes called "designer" eggs. These eggs are produced by hens that are fed low-fat diets

(10) consisting of ingredients such as canola oil, flax, and rice bran. In spite of their diets, however, these hens produce eggs that contain the same amount of cholesterol as regular eggs. Yet, the producers of these eggs claim that eating their eggs will not raise the blood cholesterol in humans.

Egg producers claim that their product has been portrayed unfairly. They cite scientific studies to back up their claim. And, in fact, studies on the relationship between eggs and human cholesterol levels

(15) have brought mixed results. It may be that it is not the type of egg that is the main determinant of cholesterol but the person who is eating the eggs. Some people may be more sensitive to cholesterol derived from food than other people. In fact, there is evidence that certain dietary fats stimulate the body's production of blood cholesterol. Consequently, while it still makes sense to limit one's intake of eggs, even designer eggs, it seems that doing this without regulating dietary fat will probably not help reduce

(20) the blood cholesterol level.

13. What is the main purpose of this passage?
(A) to inform people about the relationship between eggs and cholesterol
(B) to convince people to eat "designer" eggs and egg substitutes
(C) to persuade people that eggs are unhealthy and should not be eaten
(D) to introduce the idea that dietary fat increases the blood cholesterol level

14. As used in line 4, the word "plummet" refers to which of the following?
(A) drop abruptly
(B) rise gently
(C) hesitate unexpectantly
(D) bounce uncertainly

15. According to the passage, which of the following is a cause of heart disease?
(A) minerals
(B) cholesterol
(C) vitamins
(D) canola oil

16. As used in line 6, which of the following could best replace the word "somewhat"?
(A) indefinitely
(B) in fact
(C) a little
(D) a lot

17. According to the passage, what has been the cause for changes in the sale of eggs?
(A) dietary changes in hens
(B) decreased production
(C) increasing price
(D) a shrinking market

18. According to the passage, one egg yolk contains approximately what fraction of the suggested daily limit for human consumption of cholesterol?
(A) 1/3
(B) 1/2
(C) 2/3
(D) 3/4

19. As used in line 12, the word "claim" means
(A) guarantee
(B) assert
(C) deny
(D) confirm

20. The word "portrayed" in line 13 could best be replaced by which of the following?
(A) described
(B) studied
(C) destroyed
(D) tested

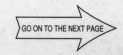GO ON TO THE NEXT PAGE

21. As used in line 14, what is the meaning of the phrase "back up"?
(A) reverse
(B) advance
(C) support
(D) block

22. What does the author mean by the phrase "mixed results" in line 15?
(A) The results are blended.
(B) The results are inconclusive.
(C) The results are a composite of things.
(D) The results are mingled together.

23. According to the passage, egg substitutes cannot be used to make any of the following types of eggs EXCEPT
(A) scrambled
(B) fried
(C) poached
(D) boiled

24. According to the author, which of the following may reduce blood cholesterol?
(A) reducing egg intake but not fat intake
(B) increasing egg intake and fat intake
(C) increasing egg intake but not fat intake
(D) decreasing egg intake and fat intake

GO ON TO THE NEXT PAGE

Questions 25 to 36 are based on the following passage:

(1)   A team of Russian scientists has challenged the theory that the woolly mammoths became extinct 10,000 years ago at the end of the Ice Age. The scientists have reported that the beasts may have survived until 2000 B.C. on an island off the coast of Siberia, where researchers uncovered 29 fossilized woolly mammoth teeth ranging in age from 4,000 to 7,000 years. The question to be asked now is, how did these

(5)   prehistoric pachyderms survive in their island environment? One possibility is that they adapted to their confined surroundings by decreasing their bulk. This theory is based on their smaller tooth size, which has led scientists to believe that they were only 6 feet tall at the shoulder compared with 10 feet of their full-sized counterpart. But would this be enough to enable them to survive thousands of years beyond that of other mammoths? Researchers are still working to uncover the reasons for this isolated group's belated

(10)   disappearance.

25. With which topic is this passage mainly concerned?
(A) Some scientists have challenged a theory.
(B) Some small teeth have been discovered.
(C) Some mammoths lived longer than others.
(D) Some pachyderms survived on an island.

26. According to the passage, some researchers suggest that mammoths became extinct
(A) about 2,000 years ago
(B) about 4,000 years ago
(C) about 7,000 years ago
(D) about 10,000 years ago

27. The word "woolly" as used in this passage refers to the animal's
(A) body size
(B) feet size
(C) hair
(D) teeth

28. The word "uncovered" as used in line 3 is closest in meaning to which of the following?
(A) unearthed
(B) unburdened
(C) undisturbed
(D) unfolded

29. The word "adapted" in line 5 could best be replaced with
(A) lept
(B) penetrated
(C) revealed
(D) accommodated

30. In line 6, the word "confined" could best be replaced by
(A) imprisoned
(B) swampy
(C) restricted
(D) fenced

31. The author uses the word "counterpart" in line 8 to refer to
(A) mammoths with more feet
(B) mammoths in an earlier time
(C) mammoths with smaller teeth
(D) larger mammoths on the island

32. The word "enable" in line 8 could best be replaced by which of the following?
(A) authorize
(B) enjoin
(C) undertake
(D) allow

33. The word "belated" in line 9 is closest in meaning to which of the following?
(A) delayed
(B) early
(C) sudden
(D) gradual

34. According to the scientists, the woolly mammoths may have managed to survive because they
(A) shed their hair
(B) grew smaller teeth
(C) became herbivores
(D) decreased in size

35. According to the passage, the reason for the disappearance of the mammoths on the island is
(A) that the temperature changed
(B) is not yet known
(C) that they were isolated
(D) that larger mammoths killed them

36. Which of the following terms from the passage is NOT used to refer to the mammoths?
(A) beasts
(B) pachyderms
(C) bulk
(D) group

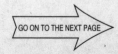 GO ON TO THE NEXT PAGE

Questions 37 to 48 are based on the following passage:

(1)   The rules of etiquette in American restaurants depend upon a number of factors: the physical location of the restaurant, e.g., rural or urban; the type of restaurant, e.g., informal or formal; and certain standards that are more universal. In other words, some standards of etiquette vary significantly while other standards apply almost anywhere. Learning the proper etiquette in a particular type of restaurant in a

(5)   particular area may sometimes require instruction, but more commonly it simply requires sensitivity and experience. For example, while it is acceptable to read a magazine in a coffee shop, it is inappropriate to do the same in a more luxurious setting. And, if you are eating in a very rustic setting it may be fine to tuck your napkin into your shirt, but if you are in a sophisticated urban restaurant this behavior would demonstrate a lack of manners. It is safe to say, however, that in virtually every restaurant it is unaccept-

(10)   able to indiscriminately throw your food on the floor. The conclusion we can most likely draw from the above is that while the types and locations of restaurants determine etiquette appropriate to them, some rules apply to all restaurants.

37. With what topic is this passage primarily concerned?
(A) rules of etiquette
(B) instruction in proper etiquette
(C) the importance of good manners
(D) variable and universal standards of etiquette

38. According to the passage, which of the following is a universal rule of etiquette?
(A) tucking a napkin in your shirt
(B) not throwing food on the floor
(C) reading a magazine at a coffee shop
(D) eating in rustic settings

39. What does the word "it" refer to in line 5?
(A) learning the proper etiquette
(B) clear instruction
(C) knowing the type of restaurant
(D) sensitivity

40. Which of the following could best replace the word "luxurious" in line 7?
(A) lurid
(B) austere
(C) elegant
(D) romantic

41. Which of the following words is most similar to the meaning of "rustic" in line 7?
(A) agricultural
(B) ancient
(C) unsophisticated
(D) urban

42. Which of the following is closest in meaning to the word "tuck" in line 8?
(A) put
(B) set
(C) hold
(D) fold

43. The word "sophisticated" in line 8 could best be replaced by
(A) expensive
(B) cultured
(C) famous
(D) exclusive

44. The word "manners" in line 9 could best be replaced by which of the following?
(A) experience
(B) character
(C) ceremony
(D) tact

45. The author uses the phrase "safe to say" in line 9 in order to demonstrate that the idea is
(A) somewhat innocent
(B) quite certain
(C) very clever
(D) commonly reported

46. The word "indiscriminately" in line 10 could best be replaced by which of the following?
(A) randomly
(B) angrily
(C) noisily
(D) destructively

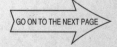
GO ON TO THE NEXT PAGE

47. The author uses the word "draw" in line 10 to mean
- **(A)** pick out
- **(B)** drag away
- **(C)** evoke
- **(D)** infer

48. What is the author's main purpose in this passage?
- **(A)** to assist people in learning sophisticated manners
- **(B)** to describe variations in restaurant manners
- **(C)** to simplify rules of restaurant etiquette
- **(D)** to compare sophisticated and rustic restaurants

GO ON TO THE NEXT PAGE

Questions 49 to 60 are based on the following passage:

(1)   Marian Anderson's brilliant singing career began at age six when she sang spirituals at the Union Baptist Church in her hometown of Philadelphia. She toured Europe in the 1920s, drawing vast acclaim; however, when she returned to the United States she was still barred from performing on the American operatic stage. After she was prevented from singing in Washington's segregated Constitution Hall in 1939,

(5)   Eleanor Roosevelt intervened and arranged for Miss Anderson to perform at the Lincoln Memorial. A crowd of 75,000 people came to watch her sing before the Memorial. Marian Anderson's beautiful contralto voice broke down racial barriers, showing white Americans that blacks had a profound contribution to make to America's cultural life. Eventually, in 1955, she became the first African-American singer to perform at New York's Metropolitan Opera. In her many years of touring she had to

(10) endure a racism that forced her to enter concert halls and hotels through service entrances. Her grace under this stress showed a moral perseverance that paralleled that of the famous Martin Luther King, Jr.

49. We can conclude from the passage that Marian Anderson first toured Europe instead of the United States because
(A) it was too expensive to tour in the United States
(B) she was paid more in Europe
(C) she was not allowed to perform in the United States
(D) there were better operatic facilities in Europe

50. The word "vast" in line 2 could best be replaced by which of the following?
(A) widespread
(B) positive
(C) enthusiastic
(D) respectable

51. The word "barred" in line 3 could best be replaced by which of the following?
(A) purged
(B) released
(C) prohibited
(D) overpowered

52. The significance of Anderson's Lincoln Memorial performance was that
(A) 75,000 people came
(B) she was a black performer
(C) Eleanor Roosevelt arranged it
(D) her contralto voice was beautiful

53. In line 5, the word "intervened" means that Eleanor Roosevelt
(A) got up
(B) took in
(C) set up
(D) stepped in

54. In line 7, the phrase "broke down . . . barriers" means
(A) disclosed opportunities
(B) shattered obstacles
(C) revealed inaccuracies
(D) analyzed destinations

55. In line 7, the word "profound" could best be replaced by
(A) broad
(B) deep
(C) full-sized
(D) spacious

56. The word "eventually" in line 8 could best be replaced by which of the following?
(A) later
(B) at last
(C) in the long run
(D) recently

57. The word "grace" in line 10 is similar in meaning to which of the following?
(A) awkwardness
(B) cruelty
(C) elegance
(D) saintliness

58. According to the passage, what did Marian Anderson have in common with Martin Luther King, Jr?
(A) moral perseverance
(B) a clear strong voice
(C) a performance at the Lincoln Memorial
(D) singing in church

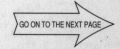GO ON TO THE NEXT PAGE

59. The author's tone in this passage is
    (A) instructive
    (B) critical
    (C) respectful
    (D) regretful

60. In line 11, what does the word "this" refer to?
    (A) touring for many years
    (B) racist attitudes toward her
    (C) performing before thousands of people
    (D) being like Martin Luther King, Jr.

THIS IS THE END OF TEST 5

Practice Test 5
Answer Key

Section 1: Listening Comprehension

Part A

1. D	5. A	9. A	13. A	17. D
2. A	6. C	10. A	14. C	18. B
3. B	7. C	11. D	15. D	19. A
4. A	8. C	12. B	16. C	20. C

Part B

21. C	24. B	27. D	30. B	33. C
22. D	25. C	28. D	31. B	34. D
23. B	26. A	29. A	32. D	35. A

Part C

36. B	39. B	42. A	45. C	48. D
37. B	40. A	43. C	46. B	49. B
38. A	41. D	44. B	47. A	50. C

Section 2: Structure and Written Expression

Part 1: Sentence Completion

1. C	4. C	7. A	10. D	13. B
2. A	5. B	8. A	11. A	14. B
3. C	6. C	9. A	12. A	15. B

Part 2: Error Identification

16. C	21. C	26. D	31. B	36. A
17. B	22. B	27. D	32. B	37. B
18. C	23. D	28. C	33. B	38. B
19. D	24. D	29. D	34. A	39. C
20. A	25. C	30. D	35. B	40. C

Section 3: Reading Comprehension

1. C	13. A	25. C	37. D	49. C
2. A	14. A	26. B	38. B	50. A
3. B	15. B	27. C	39. A	51. C
4. A	16. C	28. A	40. C	52. B
5. C	17. D	29. D	41. C	53. D
6. D	18. C	30. C	42. A	54. B
7. B	19. B	31. B	43. B	55. B
8. D	20. A	32. D	44. D	56. A
9. A	21. C	33. A	45. B	57. C
10. D	22. B	34. D	46. A	58. A
11. B	23. A	35. B	47. D	59. C
12. C	24. D	36. C	48. C	60. B

Practice Test 5
Explanatory Answers

SECTION 1

Listening Comprehension

Part A

1.   Man: I really like this shirt, but I'm afraid it's not my size.
   Woman: Don't worry, we can exchange it.

   What is the problem?
   (A) The shirt is old-fashioned.
   (B) The shirt is the wrong color.
   (C) The shirt is too dirty.
   (D) The shirt doesn't fit.

   (D) If the shirt is not his size, it doesn't fit him.

2.   Man: It's usually crowded here at lunch time.
   Woman: Usually. I know; I wonder why it's not today?

   What does the woman imply about the restaurant?
   (A) There are fewer people than usual.
   (B) There will be more people in the restaurant at dinner time.
   (C) They don't have any lunch specials today.
   (D) It's very busy.

   (A) When the woman says, "it's not today," she means "it's not crowded." Therefore, she implies that fewer people than usual are in the restaurant at this time

3.   Woman: Next customer please.
      Man: Hi, I would like to cash this check.

   What does the man mean?
   (A) He wants to pay with cash.
   (B) He wants to get money.
   (C) He wants to charge something.
   (D) He wants to check something.

   (B) To "cash a check" means to exchange the check for money (cash).

4.   Man: Have you finished? We're going to have some dessert.
   Woman: I'm done.

   What does the woman mean?
   (A) She has finished eating dinner.
   (B) She is going to make some dessert.
   (C) She did the cooking.
   (D) She is happy dining with him.

   (A) The comment "I'm done" answers the man's question, "Have you finished?"

5.   Woman: I'm worried about the speech I'm going to give tonight.
      Man: You'll be just fine. Everyone was really impressed with your last one.

   What does the man mean?
   (A) He thinks she will do a good job.
   (B) He will impress everybody with the presentation.
   (C) She has good reason to worry.
   (D) She will be fine if she practices more.

   (A) The man is being very supportive and positive to the woman when he says, "You'll be just fine."

6.   Woman: How long will it take this package to get to New York?
      Man: How do you want to send it?

   What most probably is the man's occupation?
   (A) bus driver
   (B) airline ticket agent
   (C) post office clerk
   (D) department store salesperson

   (C) Since the woman is sending a package, the most likely place for this conversation is in the post office.

7.   Man: I was hoping to take this class last fall.
      Woman: Me too, but we're lucky to get in now.

What does the woman mean?
(A) The school offers more classes now.
(B) This is a small section.
(C) It's difficult to get into this class.
(D) Last fall the class was better.

(C) Since the woman says, "we're lucky," we can infer that "it is difficult to get in."

8.   Man: Would you like some chicken?
      Woman: No, thanks, I'm a vegetarian.

What does the woman mean?
(A) She has had enough chicken.
(B) She doesn't eat vegetables.
(C) She doesn't eat meat.
(D) She is not hungry.

(C) A vegetarian is a person who does not eat meat.

9. Woman: Do you still have time for fishing?
      Man: Only once in a while now, but I still consider it my hobby.

What does the man mean?
(A) He goes fishing sometimes.
(B) He went fishing once.
(C) He had to quit fishing.
(D) He has other hobbies now.

(A) The phrase "once in a while" has a similar meaning to "sometimes."

10.   Man: I'd like to send a card to my mother for Mother's day.
      Woman: Oh, I didn't know you had that tradition in your country.

What does the woman imply?
(A) She is surprised.
(B) She can't help him.
(C) She doesn't understand him.
(D) She is angry.

(A) When the woman says, "I didn't know. . . , " she indicates surprise.

11. Woman: Bob, you'd better get down to the museum tomorrow if you want to see the exhibit.
      Man: Yeah, I don't want to miss it again!

What is the man probably going to do?
(A) Sit down and rest.
(B) Pay the money.
(C) Take the boat tour.
(D) Visit the exhibit.

(D) The verb "to miss" means that a person did not do something or was not able to do something, and he or she regrets it. Since the man doesn't want to miss the exhibit, it means that he will try to visit the museum.

12. Woman: Do you usually drink so much water?
      Man: Only after this much exercise.

What does the man mean?
(A) He drinks a lot of water during the day.
(B) He doesn't usually drink this much water.
(C) He has never been so thirsty.
(D) He likes soft drinks more than water.

(B) The man says that he only drinks a lot of water after he exercises a lot. Since he says "only" we can assume that he usually drinks less.

13.   Man: What are you going to cook tonight?
      Woman: Nothing. The Johnsons invited us over.

What does the woman mean?
(A) They will go eat with their friends.
(B) The Johnsons are coming over.
(C) She will take a dish to the Johnson's house.
(D) She is tired of cooking.

(A) The phrase "the Johnsons invited us over" means that they are planning to go to the Johnsons' house. We can assume that the Johnsons are their friends.

14. Woman: Hi, how's it going?
      Man: OK, but I can't stand all the homework.

What does the man mean?
(A) He is tired of standing up all day.
(B) He is finishing his homework.
(C) He has a lot of school work.
(D) He has been working at home.

(C) The word "all" in the phrase "all the homework" implies that there is a lot of homework. The idiom "I can't stand something" means "I don't like something."

15. Man: Mary, did you wash the car yourself?
     Woman: No, I got Don to do it.

What happened to the car?
(A) The car didn't get washed.
(B) Don and Mary washed the car together.
(C) Mary washed the car.
(D) Don washed the car for Mary.

(D) The construction "to get [someone] to do [something]" means that you ask someone to do it.

16. Woman: Do you carry containers for a microwave oven?
     Man: Umm . . . check the grocery store next to the gas station to see if they have any.

What does the man imply?
(A) This grocery store doesn't accept checks.
(B) Check your shopping list while you are shopping.
(C) This store doesn't have what she wants.
(D) Check to see if the grocery store is next to the gas station.

(C) Since the man says to check the other store, we can assume that the item is not for sale at this store.

17. Woman: Mr. Blake misread the bus schedule.
     Man: So he wasn't able to get there in time.

What do they imply about Mr. Blake?
(A) He used the wrong bus schedule.
(B) He's going to get a bus schedule.
(C) He likes to ride the bus.
(D) He missed the bus.

(D) The verb "to misread" means "read incorrectly." We can assume that he read the wrong time for the bus, and got to the bus stop too late.

18. Woman: John has his hair cut every two weeks.
     Man: But Peter has his cut every month.

What do they say about John and Peter?
(A) John has his hair cut every month.
(B) John has his hair cut twice as often as Peter does.
(C) John had a haircut two weeks ago.
(D) This month Peter didn't have his hair cut.

(B) This sentence requires you to compute the answer. One month is twice as long as two weeks.

19. Man: Pat, are your parents still supporting you?
     Woman: I'm on my own now.

What does the woman mean?
(A) She is financially independent now.
(B) She needs a financial advisor.
(C) She applied for a job this year.
(D) She's happy with her financial plan.

(A) The phrase "on my own" means that she can live on her own salary, without getting money from her parents.

20. Woman: I'm supposed to turn left at the second stop sign, right?
     Man: Right.

What does the man mean?
(A) She should turn right on Second Street.
(B) She is supposed to turn right at this stop sign.
(C) She should turn left at the stop sign after this one.
(D) She should turn left after she turns right.

(C) The "second stop sign" is the stop sign after this one.

Part B

21. Why has the woman been studying a lot recently?
  (A) because she failed her last exam
  (B) in order to complete her homework
  (C) in order to prepare for her exams
  (D) because she has fallen behind in her work

(C) Inference. In the beginning of the conversation the woman says that all of her exams are during the same week. We can infer that she is studying a lot, so that she will be prepared for her exams. We have no information about whether she has failed her last exam or has fallen behind in her studies. She says nothing about doing homework.

22. Where is the woman going?
  (A) to her room
  (B) to the dining hall
  (C) to the pool
  (D) to the gymnasium

(D) Restatement. The woman says she is headed to the gym to work out. The phrase "headed to" means "going to."

23. What has the man just finished doing?
  (A) eating dinner
  (B) swimming
  (C) studying for an exam
  (D) taking a nap

(B) Restatement. The man states that he has just had swim practice.

24. What will happen tomorrow?
  (A) The man will have an exam.
  (B) The man and the woman will have lunch together.
  (C) The man will be in a swim meet at 1 P.M.
  (D) The man and the woman will study together.

(B) Inference. We can infer that the man and woman will meet for lunch tomorrow since they both agree to meet, and she says, "I'll see you there."

25. What class is the man trying to find?
  (A) advanced economics
  (B) biology 110
  (C) introductory economics
  (D) advanced biology

(C) Restatement. The man says he is taking the introductory economics class.

26. Where does this conversation most probably take place?
  (A) walking on campus
  (B) waiting in a dormitory lounge
  (C) eating at a dining hall
  (D) sitting on a campus bench

(A) Inference. We can assume that the conversation is taking place while the two students are walking. The conversation ends with the man telling the woman that they are at her classroom. Therefore, they had been walking to the class during the conversation.

27. Approximately how many students were in the economics class last semester?
  (A) 40
  (B) 100
  (C) 200
  (D) 400

(D) Restatement. The woman states that there were over 400 students in her roommate's economics class last semester.

28. How does the woman know that the economics class has a lot of students?
  (A) She took the class last semester.
  (B) She read about it in the school newspaper.
  (C) She heard about it on the school radio station.
  (D) Her roommate took the course last semester.

(D) Restatement. The woman says her roommate took the course and told her about it.

29. Why did the man want to talk to the woman?
  (A) He wanted to ask her to do something for him.
  (B) They both live in the same dorm.
  (C) They both had the same exam the next day.
  (D) He wanted to borrow her car.

(A) Restatement. The man says he wants to ask a favor. Answer (D), "borrow her car," is not correct because the man says, "give me a ride," which means "drive me." Answer (B) is not correct because we cannot assume they live in the same dorm simply because they were in the room together.

30. At what time does the man's flight leave?
- (A) 6:00 A.M.
- (B) 7:00 A.M.
- (C) 7:30 A.M.
- (D) 8:00 A.M.

(B) Restatement. The man states that his flight leaves at 7:00 A.M.

31. Where will the two students meet tomorrow morning?
- (A) in Katrina's room
- (B) in front of the dormitory
- (C) next to the dean's office
- (D) inside the parking garage

(B) Restatement. The woman states that she will meet the man in front of the dormitory.

32. Why is the man leaving tomorrow morning?
- (A) He has been expelled from school.
- (B) He has to go to a relative's funeral.
- (C) He is going to his sister's wedding.
- (D) He has finished his exams.

(D) Restatement. The man states that he has finished his exams and needs to catch a flight. None of the other options is mentioned.

33. What are the students talking about?
- (A) watching a football game on television
- (B) going out to dinner tonight
- (C) arranging to meet at a championship game
- (D) getting ready to play a game

(C) Inference. The man begins the conversation by asking the woman if she is going to the game. The rest of the conversation is about arrangements for how she can get there in time and where her friends are sitting.

34. What would prevent the woman from seeing the game?
- (A) car trouble
- (B) studying for an exam
- (C) choir practice
- (D) a late dinner

(D) Restatement. The woman states that she will come to the game if dinner does not run too late.

35. Where will the man be sitting?
- (A) in Section C
- (B) in Section D
- (C) behind the benches
- (D) behind the goals

(A) Restatement. The man states that he will be sitting in Section C.

Part C

36. How long does the paper have to be?
- (A) One to two pages
- (B) 10 to 12 pages
- (C) 19 to 20 pages
- (D) No limit was mentioned

(B) This is a restatement question. In the first sentence the speaker states that the paper must be 10 to 12 pages.

37. By when must the students discuss a potential topic with their teaching assistants?
- (A) During the first week of school
- (B) By the middle of the term
- (C) Sometime before the last week of school
- (D) At anytime during the term

(B) This is a restatement question. The speaker says that the students must meet their teaching assistants before the middle of the term.

38. Why are first year students advised to write a rough draft?
- (A) Because they are more likely to have problems writing the paper
- (B) Because the teaching assistant prefers to work with first-year students
- (C) Because it is the policy of the university
- (D) Because the professor wants them to have more work

(A) This is an inference question. The reason that the professor wants first-year students to write a rough draft is that they are more likely to have difficulties writing the paper. The professor says that the teaching assistant will help them write the paper. Nowhere is it implied that this is "university policy." Rather it seems to be the professor's personal opinion.

39. When is the paper due for those not writing a rough draft?
- **(A)** April 6
- **(B)** April 13
- **(C)** April 20
- **(D)** April 27

(B) This is a restatement question. The professor states that the paper is due April 13th for everyone who does not hand in a first draft to the teaching assistant.

40. To whom is this announcement most likely directed?
- **(A)** arriving passengers
- **(B)** departing passengers
- **(C)** people boarding a boat
- **(D)** people departing from a train

(A) This is an inference question. The speaker talks about exiting the plane. From this we infer that the announcement is most likely directed to passengers who are arriving at an airport.

41. When the passengers exit, what should they do?
- **(A)** Walk straight ahead.
- **(B)** Turn to the left to Terminal B.
- **(C)** Wait for transportation to bring their luggage.
- **(D)** Walk to their right to get their baggage.

(D) This is a restatement question. The speaker tells the passengers to walk to their right when they exit the plane.

42. Where will the baggage arrive?
- **(A)** at Carousel B
- **(B)** at the blue area
- **(C)** near the green sign
- **(D)** next to the white buses

(A) This is a restatement question. The speaker tells the passengers that their baggage will arrive at Carousel B in about 10 minutes.

43. Where can the passengers find airport transportation?
- **(A)** at the departure gate
- **(B)** at Carousel B
- **(C)** under the green sign
- **(D)** in the yellow loading zone

(C) This is a restatement question. The speaker says that airport transportation is available under greens signs outside the baggage claim area.

44. What general subject is this lecture most likely a part of?
- **(A)** American natural history
- **(B)** English children's literature
- **(C)** zoos in the western world
- **(D)** bears of North America

(B) This is an inference question. Since the speaker is beginning the first day of class with some English literature, we can assume that the class is a literature class.

45. Who is Milne?
- **(A)** a child
- **(B)** a bear
- **(C)** an author
- **(D)** a pig

(C) This is a restatement question. The speaker says that the story was written by A. A. Milne.

46. Where did the author get the idea for the main character of his book?
- **(A)** in the woods
- **(B)** at a zoo
- **(C)** at a school
- **(D)** in a garden

(B) This is a restatement question. The speaker talks about how A. A. Milne and his son would go to the zoo and see a small bear.

47. What is the main topic of this lecture?
- **(A)** the invention of the elevator
- **(B)** modern elevators
- **(C)** the Crystal Palace Exhibition
- **(D)** inventions of the nineteenth century

(A) This is a main idea question. Throughout the talk there are references to the first safe elevator.

48. Where was the Crystal Palace Exhibition of 1853?
- **(A)** London
- **(B)** Chicago
- **(C)** San Francisco
- **(D)** New York

(D) This is a restatement question. The speaker states that the first Exhibition was in New York.

49. What was special about Otis's elevator?
  (A) steel cables
  (B) guide rails
  (C) strong ropes
  (D) an open carriage

(B) This is a restatement question. The speaker says that Otis's elevator was attached to two guide rails that held the elevator tightly.

50. Which of the following topics is the lecturer most likely to discuss next?
  (A) other inventions at the Crystal Palace Exhibition
  (B) the first tall buildings
  (C) further developments in elevators
  (D) the life of Elisha Otis

(C) This is an inference question. Since the speaker ends her talk by mentioning that people have been riding in elevators ever since Otis's demonstration, it seems likely that she will continue to talk about elevators. Answer (B) is incorrect because the tall buildings were only mentioned at the beginning as an introduction to the idea of elevators. Answers (A) and (D) were subtopics of the general topic of the development of elevators.

SECTION 2

Structure and Written Expression

Part 1: Sentence Completion

1. Birds all over the world _____ in distances up to thousands of miles.
   (A) migrating
   (B) migrated
   (C) migrate
   (D) are migrated

(C) Verb. This is the main verb of the sentence. It is a present tense verb indicating a statement of fact.

2. Cellulose, which _____ for making paper, can be found in all plants.
   (A) is used
   (B) uses
   (C) are used
   (D) is using

(A) Verb. The adjective phrase "which is used for making paper" has a passive form of the verb.

3. _____ , human beings have relatively constant body temperature.
   (A) Alike all mammal
   (B) Alike all mammals
   (C) Like all mammals
   (D) Like all mammal

(C) The phrase "like all mammals" needs a plural form of the noun because of the word "all." The word "alike" is incorrect since it must follow a verb, i.e., "They are alike."

4. So far there is no vaccine _____ in sight for the common cold.
   (A) or curing
   (B) has cured
   (C) or cure
   (D) having cured

(C) Parallel construction. The word "cure" is a noun that follows the other noun, "vaccine."

5. The Louisiana Territory, an area _____ the size of France, was bought by the United States from France for $15,000,000 in 1803.
   (A) than more four times
   (B) more than four times
   (C) four times than more
   (D) is four times more than

(B) Word order/Comparative. The correct comparative form is "more than." Answer (D) is incorrect because of the verb "is" which cannot be included in this adjective phrase.

6. Despite claims that filters and low-tar tobacco make smoking somewhat safer, in fact they only marginally reduce, _____ eliminate, the hazards.
   (A) none
   (B) no
   (C) not
   (D) nor

(C) Conjunction. This sentence contrasts two verbs "to reduce" and "to eliminate." The word "not" comes before the verb "eliminate." The word "do" would have to come before a noun.

7. _____ many of the designs for the new capital were considered lost forever, Benjamin Banneker helped reproduce the original plans.
   (A) When
   (B) During
   (C) If as
   (D) How

(A) Conjunction. The word "when" in this sentence means "at the time that."

8. A few natural elements exist in _____ that they are rarely seen in their natural environments.
   - (A) such small quantities
   - (B) so small quantities
   - (C) very small quantities
   - (D) small quantity

(A) Conjunction. The clue in this sentence is the word "that." The correct answer is the phrase "such [adjective/plural noun] that. . . ." The phrase "so . . . that" needs a singular noun or an adjective, i.e., "so small a quantity that. . . ."

9. Generally speaking, every person _____ the potential to be a teacher, to some extent.
   - (A) has
   - (B) to have
   - (C) having
   - (D) have

(A) Verb. The main subject "person" is singular and must be followed by a present tense verb in this sentence.

10. _____ business, a merger is a combination of two or more corporations under one management.
    - (A) The
    - (B) At
    - (C) On
    - (D) In

(D) Preposition. The word "in" refers to the concept of "in the field of business. . . ."

11. _____ of commodities by air began in the 1920s at the same time as airmail service.
    - (A) The shipping
    - (B) A ship
    - (C) The shipped
    - (D) To ship

(A) Noun phrase. The word "shipping" in this sentence is a verb used as a noun (a gerund). The whole phrase "The shipping of commodities by air" is the subject of the sentence.

12. Jan Malzeliger's invention, the "shoe-lasting" machine, _____ production but it also cut the cost of shoe production by half.
    - (A) not only increased
    - (B) not increased only
    - (C) increased only
    - (D) only have increased

(A) Word order. The clue in this sentence is the phrase "but also," which goes with "not only."

13. It can sometimes _____ a home.
    - (A) to take months to sell
    - (B) take several months to sell
    - (C) selling takes several months
    - (D) to sell taking several months

(B) Word order. The main verb in this sentence is "can . . . take," which is separated by the word "sometimes."

14. Jellyfish are probably _____ on Earth.
    - (A) most numerous predators
    - (B) the most numerous predators
    - (C) most numerous of predators
    - (D) the most predators

(B) Superlative. The word "most" is a superlative that must be preceded by "the." Answer (D) is incorrect because the word "predators" does not make any sense without the word "numerous," which refers to how many predators there are.

15. In the United States, _____ is the most concentrated is New Orleans.
    - (A) French influence the city
    - (B) the city where French influence
    - (C) where the city influences French
    - (D) where the French influence the city

(B) Word order. The word "influence" can be both a noun and a verb. In this sentence, the correct answer uses the word as a noun. Answers (A), (C), and (D) all use influence as a verb, and this conflicts with the next verb in the sentence, "is."

Part 2: Error Identification

16. In 1931 Jane Addams was a Nobel Peace Prize
    _A_   _B_
    recipient for she humanitarian achievements.
                    _C_   _D_

(C) Pronoun. The correct word is "her," a pronoun that
is the object of the preposition "for."

17. Even on the most careful prepared trip, problems
    _A_   _B_   _C_
    will sometimes develop.
    _D_

(B) Word form. The correct word is "carefully," an
adverb that describes the adjective "prepared."

18. Many people say that California is a state of
    _A_   _B_
    geographic remarkable diversity.
    _C_   _D_

(C) Reversed words. The correct phrase is "of remarkable geographic diversity." The adjective "remarkable"
comes before the adjective "geographic." Both of these
adjectives describe the noun "diversity."

19. An uncultivated tea plant might grow about 30
        _A_   _B_   _C_
    feet height.
    _D_

(D) Omitted word. The correct phrase could be "30 feet
in height" or "30 feet high." The word "height" is a
noun, and "high" is an adjective.

20. A galaxy, where may include billions of stars, is
            _A_   _B_   _C_
    held together by gravitational attraction.
    _D_

(A) Pronoun. The correct answer is "which." The main
subject and verb of this sentence are "galaxy . . . is held
together." The adjective clause "which may include
billions of stars" describes the subject.

21. Rocks can be broken apart by water that seeps into
            _A_   _B_
    the cracks and freeze in low temperatures.
                    _C_   _D_

(C) Verb/parallel construction. The correct answer is
"freezes," which is the present tense: ". . . water seeps
. . . and freezes."

22. Alexander Graham Bell was once a teacher who
                                        _A_
    run a school for the deaf in Massachusetts.
    _B_   _C_   _D_

(B) Verb. The correct answer is "ran," simple past tense.
Since the main verb is "was," the verb in the clause must
also be in the past tense.

23. Some fish use their sense of smell as a guide when
    _A_   _B_   _C_
    return to a spawning site.
    _D_

(D) Adverb phrase. The correct answer is "when returning. . . ." An -*ing* form follows the word "when," just as
it follows a preposition, such as "by returning."

24. In Quebec, Canada, the flowing of the maple sap
    _A_   _B_
    is one of the first sign of spring.
    _C_   _D_

(D) Singular/plural noun. The correct phrase is "one of
the first signs of spring. . . . " Any phrase that begins
"one of the" must refer to a plural noun since you are
referring to one of a number of things.

25. Antique auctions are getting more and more popu-
                        _A_   _B_
    lar in the United States because increasing public
                            _C_
    awareness of the value of investing in antiques.
    _D_

(C) Preposition/omitted word. The correct answer is
"because of increasing public awareness. . . . " The
phrase "because of " is a connector for a noun phrase.
Since "awareness" is a noun, it must be preceded by
"because of." The word "because" is not a preposition;
rather it begins an adjective clause.

26. Archaeological evidence reveals that Native
$$\underline{\hspace{1cm}}$$
                                           A
Americans lived on the East Coast of the United
         $$\underline{\hspace{1cm}}$$ $$\underline{\hspace{1cm}}$$
              B   C
States 13 centuries before.
                $$\underline{\hspace{1cm}}$$
                      D

(D) Adverb. The correct word in this sentence is "ago," an adjective that refers to some time in the past. The word "before" is an adverb conjunction that refers to time or sequence; i.e. , "13 centuries before they came to the West Coast."

27. Diamond itself is the only material hard enough to
          $$\underline{\hspace{1cm}}$$ $$\underline{\hspace{1cm}}$$ $$\underline{\hspace{1cm}}$$
              A   B   C
cut and polishes diamonds.
      $$\underline{\hspace{1cm}}$$
          D

(D) Verb/parallel construction. The correct answer is "polish." It is an infinitive that goes with "to cut." It would also be correct to say "hard enough to cut and to polish diamonds."

28. The change from day to night results the rotation
      $$\underline{\hspace{1cm}}$$ $$\underline{\hspace{1cm}}$$ $$\underline{\hspace{1cm}}$$
          A   B   C
of the Earth.
    $$\underline{\hspace{1cm}}$$
        D

(C) Preposition/omitted word. The correct answer is "results from." The verb "result" is a two-word verb followed by "from" or "in." The word "result" is also a noun that is followed by "of," as in "It is a result of. . . ."

29. As Ingrid Bergman lived a life of courage, she
    $$\underline{\hspace{1cm}}$$ $$\underline{\hspace{1cm}}$$ $$\underline{\hspace{1cm}}$$
        A   B   C
also approached die with courage.
                  $$\underline{\hspace{1cm}}$$
                      D

(D) Word form. The correct word is "death," a noun. The word "die" is a verb.

30. Residents in some cities can call an electrical
                      $$\underline{\hspace{1cm}}$$ $$\underline{\hspace{1cm}}$$
                          A   B
inspector to have the wiring in their house
          $$\underline{\hspace{1cm}}$$
              C
is checked.
$$\underline{\hspace{1cm}}$$
    D

(D) Verb/unnecessary word. The correct answer is "to have the wiring in their house checked." This is a causative construction that is followed by the base form of the verb (without "to"). The phrase "to have [something] checked" means to ask someone else to check something. Another verb used in this way is "make," e.g., "I made John do my work."

31. The best way to eliminate a pest is to controlling
      $$\underline{\hspace{1cm}}$$ $$\underline{\hspace{1cm}}$$
          A   B
the food accessible to it.
      $$\underline{\hspace{1cm}}$$ $$\underline{\hspace{1cm}}$$
          C   D

(B) Infinitive. The correct answer is "to control." The infinitive form of the verb cannot combine "to" and "-ing."

32. The Earth depends the sun for its heating.
      $$\underline{\hspace{1cm}}$$ $$\underline{\hspace{1cm}}$$ $$\underline{\hspace{1cm}}$$ $$\underline{\hspace{1cm}}$$
          A   B   C   D

(B) Preposition/omitted word. The correct answer is ". . . Earth depends on the sun. . . ." The verb "depend" is a two-word verb that is followed by "on" or "upon."

33. The famous aviator Charles Lindbergh was
          $$\underline{\hspace{1cm}}$$
              A
a early supporter of rocket research.
$$\underline{\hspace{1cm}}$$ $$\underline{\hspace{1cm}}$$ $$\underline{\hspace{1cm}}$$
  B   C   D

(B) Article. The correct answer is "an early supporter...." Since the word "early" begins with the sound of a vowel, it must be preceded by "an."

34. Cholesterol help the body by making hormones
      $$\underline{\hspace{1cm}}$$ $$\underline{\hspace{1cm}}$$
          A   B
and building cell walls, but too much cholesterol
                              $$\underline{\hspace{1cm}}$$
                                  C
can cause heart problems.
    $$\underline{\hspace{1cm}}$$
        D

(A) Verb. The correct word is "helps," the singular form of the verb that goes with the mass noun "cholesterol."

35. Luther Burbank was a pioneer in the process of
    _____A_____

    graft immature plants onto fully mature plants.
    __B__   __C__   __D__

(B) Word form. The correct answer is "of graft-ing . . . plants." The word "grafting" is a gerund, a noun form of the verb "to graft." The noun form is required as the object of the preposition.

36. With its compound eyes, dragonflies can see
    ___A___

    moving insects approximately 18 feet away.
    _____B_____ _____C_____   __D__

(A) Pronoun. The correct word is "their," a plural pronoun that refers to the plural noun, "dragonflies."

37. An X-ray microscope enables a person to see on
    _____A_____   __B__

    solid materials such as metal and bone.
    _____C_____   __D__

(B) Preposition. The correct answer is "to see through." There are many prepositions that can follow the verb "see." Understanding the meaning of the sentence is important here. An X-ray allows a person to see through (into, behind, on the other side of) metal. A doctor can look inside a person's body with X-rays; the doctor can see through the skin.

38. The United States has a younger population as
    ___A___   __B__

    most other major industrial countries.
    __C__   __D__

(B) Comparative. The correct answer is "younger . . . than most other. . . ." The comparative form *-er* is followed by the word "than."

39. Before the invention of the printing press, books
    _____A_____   _____B_____

    have been all printed by hand.
    _____C_____   __D__

(C) Verb. The correct answer is "books had been . . . printed. . . ." This is a sentence in the past perfect tense. It refers to two events in the past: (1) the invention of the printing press, and (2) books printed by hand. The order of events is important; the hand printing occurred before the invention of the printing press.

40. As the Asian economic miracle spreads through-
    __A__   _____B_____

    out the Pacific, wage increases everywhere is
                                                  __C__

    affecting millions of consumers.
    _____D_____

(C) Verb. The correct answer is "are affecting," a plural form of the present continuous tense that goes with the plural noun "increases."

SECTION 3

Reading Comprehension

1. What is the main topic of the passage?
 (A) problems with household paint
 (B) major health concerns for children
 (C) lead poisoning in children
 (D) lead paint in older homes

(C) This is a main topic question. Answers (A) and (B) are too general. Answer (D) is too specific, indicating one of the issues discussed but not the main topic.

2. Which part of the passage discusses symptoms and consequences of lead poisoning?
 (A) lines 1–4
 (B) lines 5–8
 (C) lines 9–10
 (D) lines 10–11

(A) This is an organization question. Lines 1–4 discuss the physical and behavioral symptoms and effects (or consequences) of high and low doses of lead poisoning.

3. The phrase "exposed to" in line 2 could best be replaced by which of the following?
 (A) familiar with
 (B) in contact with
 (C) displaying
 (D) conducting

(B) The phrases "exposed to" and "in contact with" both refer to someone being physically close to something. Answer (A) means "knowledge" of something. Answer (C) means "demonstrating" or "showing," which makes sense in this sentence but is a different meaning. Answer (D) means "leading."

4. As used in line 2, which of the following is closest in meaning to the word "suffer"?
 (A) experience
 (B) reveal
 (C) feel pain from
 (D) grieve with

(A) This is a vocabulary question. In this sentence, the verb "to suffer" means to undergo or experience something painful. A person may or may not feel pain or may or may not grieve with this disease or impairment. Answer (B) means "to tell something previously unknown by others."

5. Which of the following does the passage infer?
 (A) Paint companies can no longer use lead in their paint.
 (B) Paint companies are not required to limit the amount of lead used in their paint.
 (C) Paint companies must limit the amount of lead used in their paint.
 (D) Paint companies have always followed restrictions regarding the amount of lead used in their paint.

(C) This is an inference question. Lines 9–10 state that the amount of lead that paint companies can use in their paint is strictly regulated (limited or controlled) and that these regulations did not exist or were not as strict in the past.

6. Which of the following is closest in meaning to the phrase "linked to" in line 5?
 (A) endorsed by
 (B) threatened by
 (C) combined with
 (D) associated with

(D) This is a vocabulary question. The phrases "linked to" and "associated with" both mean that there is a connection between two things. Answer (A) means "support," "approve," or "recommend." Answer (B) means "being warned of an intent to do harm." Answer (C) means "to unite" or "to merge" two or more things.

7. The word "absorbed" in line 6 could best be replaced by
 (A) fixed
 (B) assimilated
 (C) soaked
 (D) accepted

(B) This is a vocabulary question. The verbs "to absorb" and "to assimilate" both refer to the process of one thing being taken in by another. Answer (A) means "to make something firm" or "to repair something." Answer (C) can also mean "absorbed," but it is used when something is "immersed," "wet," or "saturated" with liquid. Answer (D) means "received" or "acknowledged."

8. In line 6, the word "ingest" could best be replaced by which of the following?
   (A) inhale
   (B) digest
   (C) inject
   (D) eat

(D) This is a vocabulary question. The word "ingest" means to take food or other substances into the body through the mouth," or "to eat."

9. Which of the following is closest in meaning to the word "chipped" as used in line 7?
   (A) fragmented
   (B) canned
   (C) sprayed
   (D) unhealthy

(A) This is a vocabulary question. A "chip" is a small piece of something. "Chipped paint," then, refers to small pieces of paint that have come off the wall. The word "fragmented" also refers to pieces broken from a whole.

10. In line 11, the word "dilapidated" is closest in meaning to which of the following?
    (A) poorly painted
    (B) unpainted
    (C) fallen down
    (D) broken down

(D) This is a vocabulary question. Both "dilapidated" and "broken down" mean "in poor condition" and "badly needing repair." Such houses generally have a lot of old, chipped paint. The words "fallen down" mean that the house is not standing.

11. According to the passage, what is the most common source of lead poisoning in children?
    (A) household dust
    (B) lead-based paint
    (C) painted toys
    (D) dilapidated houses

(B) This is a restatement question. The last paragraph of the passage states that lead used in paint is still the most common source of lead poisoning. The other choices are all lesser sources of lead poisoning.

12. What does the author imply in the final sentence of the passage?
    (A) Lead-based paint chips off more easily than newer paints.
    (B) Poor people did not comply with the regulations.
    (C) Old homes were painted with lead-based paint.
    (D) Old homes need to be rebuilt in order to be safe for children.

(C) This is an inference question. The inference is that the older houses were painted before paint companies were forced to regulate the amount of lead they could use in their paints. Therefore, the paint used in older houses contains more lead than is allowed today, leaving children who live in these older houses more at risk.

13. What is the main purpose of this passage?
    (A) to inform people about the relationship between eggs and cholesterol
    (B) to convince people to eat "designer" eggs and egg substitutes
    (C) to persuade people that eggs are unhealthy and should not be eaten
    (D) to introduce the idea that dietary fat increases the blood cholesterol level

(A) This a question about the author's purpose. The author is primarily concerned with informing people about eggs and blood cholesterol. Each paragraph focuses on these topics. Answer choices (B) and (C) are the opposite of what the passage says. Answer choice (D) is mentioned, but only as part of the final paragraph.

14. As used in line 4, the word "plummet" refers to which of the following?
    (A) drop abruptly
    (B) rise gently
    (C) hesitate unexpectedly
    (D) bounce uncertainly

(A) The word "plummet" means "to fall straight down" or "drop suddenly."

15. According to the passage, which of the following is a cause of heart disease?
    (A) minerals
    (B) cholesterol
    (C) vitamins
    (D) canola oil

(B) This is a restatement question. In the first sentence, cholesterol is noted to be a major cause of heart disease.

16. As used in line 6, which of the following could best replace the word "somewhat"?
    (A) indefinitely
    (B) in fact
    (C) a little
    (D) a lot

(C) The words "somewhat" and "a little" both mean "some amount, but not very much."

17. According to the passage, what has been the cause for changes in the sale of eggs?
    (A) dietary changes in hens
    (B) decreased production
    (C) increasing price
    (D) a shrinking market

(D) This is an inference question. The author states that the knowledge of the high level of cholesterol in eggs and the health hazard this poses have caused egg sales to plummet (drop). We can infer, therefore, that people are not buying eggs. If people do not buy a product we say that there is no market for that product. The phrase "a shrinking market" means that fewer people are buying something because there is less desire for that item. The word "shrinking" means "getting smaller."

18. According to the passage, one egg yolk contains approximately what fraction of the suggested daily limit for human consumption of cholesterol?
    (A) 1/3
    (B) 1/2
    (C) 2/3
    (D) 3/4

(C) This is a restatement question. In the second sentence the author states that eggs contain a little more than two-thirds of the daily cholesterol level.

19. As used in line 12, the word "claim" means
    (A) guarantee
    (B) assert
    (C) deny
    (D) confirm

(B) The verbs "to claim" and "to assert" both mean "to state something strongly" or "to declare."

20. The word "portrayed" in line 13 could best be replaced by which of the following?
    (A) described
    (B) studied
    (C) destroyed
    (D) tested

(A) The verbs "to portray" and "to describe" both refer to the way something is represented to someone.

21. As used in line 14, what is the meaning of the phrase "back up"?
    (A) reverse
    (B) advance
    (C) support
    (D) block

(C) The phrase "to back up" someone or something means to give it support or to give evidence of its reliability.

22. What does the author mean by the phrase "mixed results" in line 15?
    (A) The results are blended.
    (B) The results are inconclusive.
    (C) The results are a composite of things.
    (D) The results are mingled together.

(B) The phrase "mixed results" means that there is no clear answer; some test results indicate one thing and other test results indicate another.

23. According to the passage, egg substitutes cannot be used to make any of the following types of eggs EXCEPT
    (A) scrambled
    (B) fried
    (C) poached
    (D) boiled

(A) This is a negative question. In line 8, the author states that substitute eggs cannot be used for frying, poaching, or boiling. The word "scrambled" is not mentioned.

24. According to the author, which of the following may reduce blood cholesterol?
    (A) reducing egg intake but not fat intake
    (B) increasing egg intake and fat intake
    (C) increasing egg intake but not fat intake
    (D) decreasing egg intake and fat intake

(D) This is an inference question. At the end of the last paragraph, the author says that some fats may stimulate the production of cholesterol. From this we can infer the opposite, that fewer fats may result in less cholesterol. We can also infer that eating fewer eggs may lower the cholesterol. The author states that there are mixed results on the relationship between eggs and cholesterol and that some people may be more sensitive to cholesterol from food than others. It is important to note the word "may" in these answer choices. The answers do not say that cholesterol will be lower, only that there is a chance that it may be.

25. With what topic is this passage mainly concerned?
    (A) Some scientists have challenged a theory.
    (B) Some small teeth have been discovered.
    (C) Some mammoths lived longer than others.
    (D) Some pachyderms survived on an island.

(C) Answers (A), (B), and (D) are all aspects of (C). The main idea is that these woolly mammoths did not become extinct when the others did. The evidence is (B), and answer (D) is a question to be answered to give a clue to why they survived longer.

26. According to the passage, some researchers suggest that mammoths became extinct
    (A) about 2,000 years ago
    (B) about 4,000 years ago
    (C) about 7,000 years ago
    (D) about 10,000 years ago

(B) This is a restatement question. The previous theory is that woolly mammoths became extinct 10,000 years ago, but this has been challenged. Researchers now suggest that the mammoths lived until 2,000 B.C., which was about 4,000 years ago.

27. The word "woolly," as often used in this passage, refers to the animal's
    (A) body size
    (B) feet size
    (C) hair
    (D) teeth

(C) The word "woolly" refers to the hair of the animal. "Woolly" hair is thick and matted, like the wool of a sheep.

28. The word "uncovered" as used in line 3 is closest in meaning to which of the following?
    (A) unearthed
    (B) unburdened
    (C) undisturbed
    (D) unfolded

(A) The verbs "to uncover" and "to unearth" both mean "to dig up" or "to excavate."

29. The word "adapt" in line 5 could best be replaced with
    (A) lept
    (B) penetrated
    (C) revealed
    (D) accommodated

(D) This is a vocabulary question. The verbs "to adapt" and "to accommodate" both mean "to change," "to conform," or "to adjust" to something.

30. In line 6, the word "confined" could best be replaced by
    (A) imprisoned
    (B) swampy
    (C) restricted
    (D) fenced

(C) This is a vocabulary question. In this context the word "confined" implies that the animals had a restricted or limited area in which to live compared to their previous living conditions. Both "confined" and "restricted" imply that there was very little room to move around. Answers (A) and (D) imply the work of human beings who are not mentioned in this passage.

31. The author uses the word "counterpart" in line 8 to refer to
    (A) mammoths with more feet
    (B) mammoths in an earlier time
    (C) mammoths with smaller teeth
    (D) larger mammoths on the island

(B) The "full-sized counterpart" refers to the larger mammoths who became extinct 10,000 years ago, not the ones on the island.

32. The word "enable" in line 8 could best be replaced by which of the following?
    (A) authorize
    (B) enjoin
    (C) undertake
    (D) allow

(D) The verbs "to enable" and "to allow" both mean "to make something possible" or "to assist." Answer (A) means "to give permission." Answer (B) means "to advise," "to warn," or "to beg." Answer (C) means "to attempt" or "to begin" doing something.

33. The word "belated" in line 9 is closest in meaning to which of the following?
    (A) delayed
    (B) early
    (C) sudden
    (D) gradual

(A) The words "belated" and "delayed" both mean "late."

34. According to the scientists, the woolly mammoths may have managed to survive because they
    (A) shed their hair
    (B) grew smaller teeth
    (C) became herbivores
    (D) decreased in size

(D) This is a restatement question. Line 6 states that the animals decreased in bulk, which means they "got smaller." The theory is based on the smaller tooth size, but that does not mean that they survived because they had smaller teeth.

35. According to the passage, the reason for the disappearance of the mammoths on the island
    (A) is that the temperature changed
    (B) is not yet known
    (C) is that they were isolated
    (D) is that larger mammoths killed them

(B) The final sentence says that researchers are still working to uncover the reasons. This means that they do not yet know, or that they are not sure of, the reasons.

36. Which of the following terms from the passage is NOT used to refer to the mammoths?
    (A) beasts
    (B) pachyderms
    (C) bulk
    (D) group

(C) The word "bulk" refers to the size of the mammoth, not the animal itself.

37. With what topic is this passage primarily concerned?
    (A) rules of etiquette in different restaurants
    (B) instruction in proper etiquette
    (C) the importance of good manners
    (D) variable and universal standards of etiquette

(D) This is a main-idea question. The main idea is that rules for good manners may vary depending on the setting but that there are general rules as well.

38. According to the passage, which of the following is a universal rule of etiquette?
    (A) tucking a napkin in your shirt
    (B) not throwing food on the floor
    (C) reading a magazine at a coffee shop
    (D) eating in rustic settings

(B) This is an inference question. A universal rule is one that applies to any setting. According to the passage, answer (B) is a rule that can probably apply to any restaurant. Answers (A) and (C) are appropriate only in specific settings. Answer (D) is not a rule of etiquette.

39. What does the word "it" refer to in line 5?
    (A) learning the proper etiquette
    (B) clear instruction
    (C) knowing the type of restaurant
    (D) sensitivity

(A) This is a referent question. In the phrase "it simply requires sensitivity and experience," the word "it" refers to "learning the proper etiquette," the main subject of the sentence.

40. Which of the following could best replace the word "luxurious" in line 7?
    (A) lurid
    (B) austere
    (C) elegant
    (D) romantic

(C) In this sentence, the word "luxurious" refers to a place that is "elegant" and "expensive." Answer (A) means "vivid" or "shocking." Answer (B) is the opposite of "luxurious." Answer (D) refers to romance, love, or devotion.

41. Which of the following words is most similar to the meaning of "rustic" in line 7?
    (A) agricultural
    (B) ancient
    (C) unsophisticated
    (D) urban

(C) This is a vocabulary question. While the word "rustic" can mean rural and may be associated with agricultural areas, its meaning in the context of this passage is "unsophisticated."

42. Which of the following is closest in meaning to the word "tuck" in line 8?
    (A) put
    (B) set
    (C) hold
    (D) fold

(A) The verb "to tuck" means "to insert." In this case, the word "put" has the same meaning.

43. The word "sophisticated" in line 8 could best be replaced by
    (A) expensive
    (B) cultured
    (C) famous
    (D) exclusive

(B) The words "sophisticated" and "cultured" both refer to something that is "refined" or "polished."

44. The word "manners" in line 9 could best be replaced by which of the following?
    (A) experience
    (B) character
    (C) ceremony
    (D) tact

(D) The words "manners" and "tact" both refer to having politeness and/or using discretion.

45. The author uses the phrase "safe to say" in line 9 in order to demonstrate that the idea is
    (A) somewhat innocent
    (B) quite certain
    (C) very clever
    (D) commonly reported

(B) The phrase "it is safe to say" means that probably no one will disagree; therefore, one is quite certain of what one is saying.

46. The word "indiscriminately" in line 10 could best be replaced by which of the following?
    (A) randomly
    (B) angrily
    (C) noisily
    (D) destructively

(A) The words "indiscriminately" and "randomly" both refer to being "haphazard" or "unsystematic."

47. The author uses the word "draw" in line 10 to mean
    (A) pick out
    (B) drag away
    (C) evoke
    (D) infer

(D) The word "draw" is often used in the phrase "to draw a conclusion." In this sense, it means "to infer" a conclusion or an idea.

48. What is the author's main purpose in this passage?
    (A) to assist people in learning sophisticated manners
    (B) to describe variations in restaurant manners
    (C) to simplify rules of restaurant etiquette
    (D) to compare sophisticated and rustic restaurants

(C) This is an author's-purpose question. It requires inference. The author states that learning the proper etiquette does not usually require instruction; it usually simply requires sensitivity and experience. The author also states that there are many rules that apply to all settings. From this we can infer that the author is simplifying the reader's understanding of rules of etiquette.

49. We can infer from the passage that Marian Anderson toured Europe instead of the United States because
    (A) it was too expensive to tour in the United States
    (B) she was paid more in Europe
    (C) she was not allowed to perform in the United States
    (D) there were better operatic facilities in Europe

(C) This is an inference question. Lines 3–4 say that she was "still barred from performing on the American operatic stage." This means she was not allowed to perform.

50. The word "vast" in line 2 could best be replaced by which of the following?
    (A) widespread
    (B) positive
    (C) enthusiastic
    (D) respectable

(A) This is a vocabulary question. The words "vast" and "widespread" in this context both mean "very large" or "enormous."

51. The word "barred" in line 3 could best be replaced by which of the following?
    (A) purged
    (B) released
    (C) prohibited
    (D) overpowered

(C) This is a vocabulary question. The words "barred" and "prohibited" both mean "prevented" or "banned."

52. The significance of Anderson's Lincoln Memorial performance was that
    (A) 75,000 people came
    (B) she was a black performer
    (C) Eleanor Roosevelt arranged it
    (D) her contralto voice was beautiful

(B) This is an inference question. The passage states that her singing was "breaking down racial barriers." From this we can infer that the significant part of the performance was that she was black and had previously been barred from performing on stage.

53. In line 5, the word "intervened" means that Eleanor Roosevelt
    (A) got up
    (B) took in
    (C) set up
    (D) stepped in

(D) The words "intervened" and "stepped in" both mean "to take a decisive role" in changing some event. In this case Roosevelt played an active role in getting Anderson to be allowed to sing at the Lincoln Memorial.

54. In line 7, the phrase "breaking down . . . barriers" means
    (A) disclosing opportunites
    (B) shattering obstacles
    (C) revealing inaccuracies
    (D) analyzing destinations

(B) The verb "to break down" means "to destroy" or "to begin to get rid of." The verb "to shatter" means "to break into pieces." The words "barriers" and "obstacles" refer to something that prevents someone from doing something. The meaning of this sentence is that the people who heard Anderson's beautiful voice may have begun to think of black people in a more positive way.

55. In line 7, the word "profound" could best be replaced by
    (A) broad
    (B) deep
    (C) full-sized
    (D) spacious

(B) This is a vocabulary question. In this sentence, the words "profound" and "deep" both mean "thoughtful," "intellectual," or "reflective."

56. The word "eventually" in line 8 could best be replaced by which of the following?
    (A) later
    (B) at last
    (C) in the long run
    (D) recently

(A) The word "eventually" refers to something happening at a future date, or "later." The words "at last" mean "finally" or "at an end." The phrase "in the long run" means "over a long period of time." The word "recently" means "a short time ago."

57. The word "grace" in line 10 is similar in meaning
to which of the following?
- **(A)** awkwardness
- **(B)** cruelty
- **(C)** elegance
- **(D)** saintliness

(C) The words "grace" and "elegance" both refer to an
"ease of movement" and "effortless beauty" or "refined
appearance."

58. According to the passage, what did Marian Ander-
son have in common with Dr. Martin Luther King,
Jr.?
- **(A)** moral perseverance
- **(B)** a clear strong voice
- **(C)** a performance at the Lincoln Memorial
- **(D)** singing in church

(A) This is a restatement question. While King had a
clear strong voice, gave a speech at the Lincoln Memorial, and sang in church, it is only answer (A) that is
clearly stated (in the last sentence) as a similarity
between Anderson and King.

59. The author's tone in this passage is
- **(A)** instructive
- **(B)** critical
- **(C)** respectful
- **(D)** regretful

(C) This is a question about the author's tone. The final
sentence gives a good clue about the author's respect for
Anderson, as do such words as "endure racism," "profound contribution," and "brilliant career."

60. In line 11, what does the word "this" refer to?
- **(A)** touring for many years
- **(B)** racist attitudes toward her
- **(C)** performing before thousands of people
- **(D)** being like Martin Luther King, Jr.

(B) This is a referent question. The word "this" refers
back to "racism that had forced her to enter concert halls
and hotels through service entrances," which is similar
to "racist attitudes toward her."

ANSWER SHEET FOR PRACTICE TEST 6

Section 1: Listening Comprehension

1	2	3	4	5	6	7	8	9	10	11	12	13	14	15	16	17	18	19	20	21	22	23	24	25	26	27	28	29	30	31	32	33	34	35	36	37	38	39	40	41	42	43	44	45	46	47	48	49	50
A	A	A	A	A	A	A	A	A	A	A	A	A	A	A	A	A	A	A	A	A	A	A	A	A	A	A	A	A	A	A	A	A	A	A	A	A	A	A	A	A	A	A	A	A	A	A	A	A	A
B	B	B	B	B	B	B	B	B	B	B	B	B	B	B	B	B	B	B	B	B	B	B	B	B	B	B	B	B	B	B	B	B	B	B	B	B	B	B	B	B	B	B	B	B	B	B	B	B	B
C	C	C	C	C	C	C	C	C	C	C	C	C	C	C	C	C	C	C	C	C	C	C	C	C	C	C	C	C	C	C	C	C	C	C	C	C	C	C	C	C	C	C	C	C	C	C	C	C	C
D	D	D	D	D	D	D	D	D	D	D	D	D	D	D	D	D	D	D	D	D	D	D	D	D	D	D	D	D	D	D	D	D	D	D	D	D	D	D	D	D	D	D	D	D	D	D	D	D	D

Section 2: Structure and Written Expression

1	2	3	4	5	6	7	8	9	10	11	12	13	14	15	16	17	18	19	20	21	22	23	24	25	26	27	28	29	30	31	32	33	34	35	36	37	38	39	40
A	A	A	A	A	A	A	A	A	A	A	A	A	A	A	A	A	A	A	A	A	A	A	A	A	A	A	A	A	A	A	A	A	A	A	A	A	A	A	A
B	B	B	B	B	B	B	B	B	B	B	B	B	B	B	B	B	B	B	B	B	B	B	B	B	B	B	B	B	B	B	B	B	B	B	B	B	B	B	B
C	C	C	C	C	C	C	C	C	C	C	C	C	C	C	C	C	C	C	C	C	C	C	C	C	C	C	C	C	C	C	C	C	C	C	C	C	C	C	C
D	D	D	D	D	D	D	D	D	D	D	D	D	D	D	D	D	D	D	D	D	D	D	D	D	D	D	D	D	D	D	D	D	D	D	D	D	D	D	D

Section 3: Reading Comprehension

1	2	3	4	5	6	7	8	9	10	11	12	13	14	15	16	17	18	19	20	21	22	23	24	25	26	27	28	29	30	31	32	33	34	35	36	37	38	39	40	41	42	43	44	45	46	47	48	49	50	51	52	53	54	55	56	57	58	59	60
A	A	A	A	A	A	A	A	A	A	A	A	A	A	A	A	A	A	A	A	A	A	A	A	A	A	A	A	A	A	A	A	A	A	A	A	A	A	A	A	A	A	A	A	A	A	A	A	A	A	A	A	A	A	A	A	A	A	A	A
B	B	B	B	B	B	B	B	B	B	B	B	B	B	B	B	B	B	B	B	B	B	B	B	B	B	B	B	B	B	B	B	B	B	B	B	B	B	B	B	B	B	B	B	B	B	B	B	B	B	B	B	B	B	B	B	B	B	B	B
C	C	C	C	C	C	C	C	C	C	C	C	C	C	C	C	C	C	C	C	C	C	C	C	C	C	C	C	C	C	C	C	C	C	C	C	C	C	C	C	C	C	C	C	C	C	C	C	C	C	C	C	C	C	C	C	C	C	C	C
D	D	D	D	D	D	D	D	D	D	D	D	D	D	D	D	D	D	D	D	D	D	D	D	D	D	D	D	D	D	D	D	D	D	D	D	D	D	D	D	D	D	D	D	D	D	D	D	D	D	D	D	D	D	D	D	D	D	D	D

Date Taken ____________________

Number Correct

Section 1 __________

Section 2 __________

Section 3 __________

Practice Test 6

SECTION 1

Listening Comprehension

Time—approximately 30 minutes

NOTE: You can simulate actual TOEFL conditions by using the Listening Comprehension Cassettes that accompany this book. If you do not have the tape, ask a friend to read the tapescript for Listening Comprehension Test 6, which is in Part Four, pages 426–33 of this book.

Part A

Directions: In Part A you will hear short conversations between two people. After each conversation a third person will ask a question about what was said. You will hear the conversation only one time, so you must listen carefully to what each speaker says. After you hear the conversation and the question, read the four possible answers in your test booklet and pick the one which best answers the question. Then look on the answer sheet for the number of the question and fill in the oval that corresponds to the letter of your answer choice.

Listen to an example:

You will hear:

You will read:

Sample Answer

(A) He will call Pete before he goes home.
(B) He will call Pete after he gets home.
(C) He called Pete at home.
(D) He will call Pete tomorrow.

You learn from the conversation that the man will call Pete as soon as he gets home. The best answer to the question "What does the man mean?" is (B), "He will call Pete after he gets home." Therefore, the correct answer is (B).

Now listen to the tape: Test 6, Section 1, Listening Comprehension, Part A.

335

1. (A) Adam will repair the car.
   (B) Adam helped to pull the car to the repair shop.
   (C) Fred and Adam both fixed the car.
   (D) The car cannot be fixed any more.

2. (A) Jeff agreed to take the oral exam again.
   (B) Jeff passed the oral exam and went on a vacation.
   (C) It took Jeff a long time to pass his exam.
   (D) Jeff didn't take the oral exam.

3. (A) He has been waiting for Ron for a long time.
   (B) Ron is not a new librarian.
   (C) Ron did a lot of work for the man.
   (D) He needs to collect some information from Ron.

4. (A) He would like to help the woman typing.
   (B) He wonders how much he should pay her.
   (C) He wants the woman to help him.
   (D) He prefers to type the paper by himself.

5. (A) Why the man needs to return.
   (B) What makes the man happy.
   (C) Which classroom the man is going to.
   (D) What book the man needs to get.

6. (A) Mary is going to the airport.
   (B) Mary is not going to the party.
   (C) Mary is not very kind.
   (D) Mary should not be driving.

7. (A) She doesn't need an escort.
   (B) She will call the night escort by herself.
   (C) She would like the man to get a night escort for her.
   (D) She's afraid the man won't help her.

8. (A) The fee for charging is more than $15.
   (B) He cannot use a credit card if he spends less than $15.
   (C) The store does not accept credit cards.
   (D) She cannot accept cash.

9. (A) The woman has to wait in line to register.
   (B) It may be too late for the woman to get into the speech class.
   (C) The woman needs to take another class before registering for this class.
   (D) The woman should go by herself to sign up for the class.

10. (A) Students can bring their books to the exam.
    (B) Dr. Jones will be the next department chair.
    (C) Dr. Jones will probably not give an open-book exam.
    (D) It's up to the students.

11. (A) He doesn't know how to take care of the phone.
    (B) He's going to leave too.
    (C) He will answer the telephone for the woman.
    (D) He is coming back soon.

12. (A) She can manage much more.
    (B) She will take one.
    (C) She doesn't care how many she gets.
    (D) She will not take any.

13. (A) He needs a roommate to share the expenses.
    (B) He lives alone without anybody to bother him.
    (C) Things are all right at this point.
    (D) His apartment is far away from school.

14. (A) The university policy has not changed enough.
    (B) He agrees with the woman's opinion.
    (C) He doesn't know what the old policy was.
    (D) The university needs to change their policy more.

15. (A) She was very frightened.
    (B) She had a heart problem.
    (C) She lost the race.
    (D) Overall, she was happy.

16. (A) It's not a good time or place to talk.
    (B) I'm thinking about making this place better.
    (C) This is a good place for a conversation.
    (D) You'd better leave this place now.

17. (A) It's expensive to get a 10-speed bicycle.
    (B) He commutes to school by bike.
    (C) He would really like a fast bicycle.
    (D) He can borrow his friend's bicycle whenever he wants.

18. (A) She doesn't like cheap things.
    (B) It was two dollars cheaper than usual.
    (C) It was too expensive.
    (D) She bought something cheaper.

GO ON TO THE NEXT PAGE

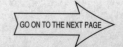

19. **(A)** She was expecting someone to visit.
    (B) She didn't like to get up early.
    (C) She got up early and went out.
    (D) Someone called her early in the morning.

20. **(A)** Jim washed his friend's car.
    (B) Jim's car was not very well cleaned.
    (C) Jim didn't wash his car this time.
    (D) Jim once had a job washing cars.

Part B

Directions: In Part B you will hear longer conversations between two people. After each conversation you will be asked some questions. You will hear the conversations and the questions only once, so listen carefully to what is said. After you hear a question, read the four possible answers in your test book and decide which one is the best answer to the question you heard. Then, on your answer sheet, find the number of the question and fill in the oval that corresponds to the letter of the answer you have chosen. Answer all questions based on what is stated or implied by the speakers.

Listen to the example on the tape.

> *You will hear:*

Now listen to sample question number 1.   Sample Answer

> *You will read:*   Ⓐ Ⓑ Ⓒ ●

> **(A)** to the cafeteria
> **(B)** to the movie theater
> **(C)** to her dorm room
> **(D)** to the library

The best answer to the question "Where is the woman going?" is (D), "to the library." Therefore, the correct choice is (D).

Now listen to sample question number 2.   Sample Answer

> *You will hear:*   Ⓐ Ⓑ ● Ⓓ

> *You will read:*

> **(A)** Term papers are easy for him.
> **(B)** He has a lot of essay exams.
> **(C)** He finds lab experiments easier than writing term papers.
> **(D)** He is busier this semester than last semester.

The best answer to the question "Which best describes the man's feelings about his classes?" is (C), "He finds lab experiments easier than writing term papers." Therefore, the correct answer is (C).

Now listen to the test. Remember, you are not allowed to take any notes or write in your test book.

GO ON TO THE NEXT PAGE

21. **(A)** to a park downtown
    (B) to the Ocean Palace
    (C) to the cinema
    (D) to a bookstore

22. **(A)** two free dinners
    (B) $50 worth of books
    (C) a $30 gift certificate
    (D) four movie passes

23. **(A)** by going to the bookstore
    (B) by sending a letter in the mail
    (C) by calling on the phone
    (D) by going to the ticket office

24. **(A)** go with the man
    (B) make a phone call
    (C) buy a ticket
    (D) go to the library

25. **(A)** a fight
    (B) cooking
    (C) manners
    (D) a problem

26. **(A)** student
    (B) bartender
    (C) waiter
    (D) cook

27. **(A)** because something was wrong
    (B) because she wanted to pay her bill
    (C) because she needed to order her meal
    (D) because she needed to be seated

28. **(A)** angry
    (B) concerned
    (C) pleased
    (D) disappointed

29. **(A)** in a restaurant
    (B) in a classroom
    (C) in a library
    (D) at a park

30. **(A)** study
    (B) eat dinner
    (C) see a movie
    (D) work

31. **(A)** working
    (B) studying
    (C) dancing
    (D) eating

32. **(A)** to set a time to meet again
    (B) to complain about school
    (C) to explain working hours
    (D) to request help in finding books

33. **(A)** Canada
    (B) Alaska
    (C) Alabama
    (D) Washington

34. **(A)** that he was a president
    (B) that he was a scientist
    (C) that he liked peanuts
    (D) that he was a Native American

35. **(A)** dedicated
    (B) angry
    (C) excited
    (D) uninformed

GO ON TO THE NEXT PAGE

Part C

Directions: In this part of the test, you will hear talks by a single person. After each talk, you will be asked some questions. You will hear the talks and the questions only once, so listen carefully to what is said. After you hear a question, read the four possible answers in your test book and decide which one is the best answer to the question you heard. Then find the number of the question on your answer sheet, and fill in the oval that corresponds to the letter of the answer you have chosen. Answer all questions based on what is stated or implied in the talk.

Listen to this sample talk.

You will hear:

Now listen to sample question number 1.

You will read:

Sample Answer

Ⓐ Ⓑ Ⓒ ⬤

(A) to demonstrate tutoring techniques
(B) to explain school policies
(C) to recruit childcare workers
(D) to explain a service

The best answer to the question "What is the purpose of this announcement?" is (D), "to explain a service." Therefore, the correct choice is (D).

Now listen to sample question number 2.

Sample Answer

Ⓐ Ⓑ ⬤ Ⓓ

You will hear:

You will read:

(A) Give your child extra tutoring.
(B) Take your child to the program today.
(C) Apply as soon as you can.
(D) Pay next month.

The best answer to the question "What does the speaker recommend?" is (C), "Apply as soon as you can." Therefore the correct choice is (C).

Now begin. Remember, you are not allowed to write any notes in your test book.

GO ON TO THE NEXT PAGE

36. (A) history of the Smithsonian
    (B) introduction to archeology
    (C) Native Americans in the Western States
    (D) hiking and backpacking techniques

37. (A) to the university
    (B) to a lecture
    (C) to Wyoming
    (D) to the Smithsonian Institute

38. (A) searching for plant and animal fossils
    (B) building homes for the poor
    (C) rock climbing
    (D) white water rafting

39. (A) $1,250
    (B) $1,500
    (C) $2,000
    (D) $2,500

40. (A) an animation festival
    (B) a drama festival
    (C) an exhibit featuring the *Mona Lisa*
    (D) *Mona Lisa Descending a Staircase*

41. (A) Italian history
    (B) art history
    (C) sociology
    (D) architecture

42. (A) *The Prince and the Princess*
    (B) Francis Bacon
    (C) the Louvre
    (D) KKED radio

43. (A) at the KKED radio station
    (B) at the Art Exhibition Hall
    (C) at the Palace of Fine Arts
    (D) at the Historical Museum

44. (A) European expeditions in the 1700s
    (B) the growth of Los Angeles
    (C) famous sites in Los Angeles
    (D) the entertainment industry

45. (A) the oceans and the gold rush
    (B) tourism and the entertainment industry
    (C) the railroads and the discovery of oil
    (D) sea trade and the airplane industry

46. (A) 50 years
    (B) 100 years
    (C) 200 years
    (D) 300 years

47. (A) Washington, D.C.
    (B) New York City
    (C) Chicago
    (D) Denver

48. (A) to prevent diseases among military personnel
    (B) to investigate serious crimes in the military
    (C) to find ways of identifying bodies of soldiers
    (D) to store old military journals and diaries

49. (A) working with DNA
    (B) wearing a necklace
    (C) taking blood samples
    (D) making identification tags

50. (A) biology
    (B) geology
    (C) history
    (D) political science

THIS IS THE END OF SECTION 1.
DO NOT READ OR WORK ON ANY OTHER SECTION OF THE TEST UNTIL TIME IS UP.
STOP   STOP   STOP   STOP   STOP

SECTION 2

Structure and Written Expression

Time—25 minutes

Part 1: Sentence Completion

Directions: Questions 1–15 are not complete sentences. One or more words are left out of each sentence. Under each sentence, you will see four words or phrases, marked (A), (B), (C), and (D). Choose the one word or phrase that completes the sentence correctly. Then, on your answer sheet, find the number of the question and fill in the oval that corresponds to the letter of your answer choice.

Example I▷

Birds make nests in trees _____ hide their young in the leaves and branches.

(A) can where they
(B) where they can
(C) where can they
(D) where can

Sample Answer

Ⓐ ● Ⓒ Ⓓ

The sentence should read, "Birds make nests in trees where they can hide their young in the leaves and branches." Therefore, you should choose answer (B).

Example II▷

Sleeping, resting, and _____ are the best ways to care for a cold.

(A) to drink fluids
(B) drank fluids
(C) one drink fluids
(D) drinking fluids

Sample Answer

Ⓐ Ⓑ Ⓒ ●

The sentence should read, "Sleeping, resting, and drinking fluids are the best ways to care for a cold." Therefore, you should choose answer (D).

Now begin with the questions.

GO ON TO THE NEXT PAGE

1. A log grabber has a long arm _____, which stretches out to pick up logs.
   (A) calls a jib
   (B) calling a jib
   (C) a jib called
   (D) called a jib

2. A home computer _____ an opportunity for convenient and efficient work at home.
   (A) provides
   (B) to be providing
   (C) which provides
   (D) providing it

3. Eli Whitney's milling machine remained unchanged for a century and a half because _____ was so efficient.
   (A) it
   (B) he
   (C) of
   (D) its

4. Some of the rainwater from clouds evaporates before _____.
   (A) reaching the ground
   (B) to reach the ground
   (C) reach the ground
   (D) the ground reaches

5. Once an offending allergen has been identified _____ tests, it is possible for the doctor to give specific desensitizing injections.
   (A) means of
   (B) by means of
   (C) of the means by
   (D) by means

6. Sometimes _____ wears people out and is worse than the lack of sleep itself.
   (A) to sleep the desire
   (B) the desire to sleep
   (C) to desire sleep is
   (D) the desire to sleep who

7. Although dissimilar in almost every other respect, birds and insects have both evolved efficient _____ capabilities.
   (A) fly
   (B) flying
   (C) to fly
   (D) is flying

8. The wheel, _____ has remained important for 4,000 years, is one of mankind's first inventions.
   (A) how
   (B) when
   (C) which
   (D) about

9. _____ children master the basics, advanced development becomes easier.
   (A) The
   (B) Once
   (C) That
   (D) Even

10. _____ there is a close correlation between stress and illness.
    (A) Some psychologists believe
    (B) Believed some psychologists
    (C) Some psychologists to believe
    (D) Some psychologists believing

11. _____ is often used in soups and sauces.
    (A) Parsley, an inexpensive herb,
    (B) Parsley is an inexpensive herb
    (C) Inexpensive parsley, herb
    (D) An herb is inexpensive parsley,

12. Perspiration increases _____ vigorous exercise or hot weather.
    (A) during
    (B) when
    (C) at the time
    (D) for

13. Goddard developed the first rocket to fly faster _____.
    (A) than sound is
    (B) does sound
    (C) sound
    (D) than sound

14. Even if the unemployment rate _____ sharply, the drop may still be temporary.
    (A) to drop
    (B) dropping
    (C) have dropped
    (D) drops

GO ON TO THE NEXT PAGE

15. Studies indicate _____ collecting art today
    than ever before.
    - (A) there are that more people
    - (B) more people that are
    - (C) that there are more people
    - (D) people there are more

Part 2: Error Identification

Directions: In questions 16–40 each sentence has four underlined words or phrases, marked (A), (B), (C), and (D). Choose the one word or phrase that must be changed in order for the sentence to be correct. Then, on your answer sheet find the number of the question and fill in the oval that corresponds to the letter of your answer choice.

Example I▷

Aspirin is recommend to many people for its
          A   B   C
ability to thin the blood.
          D

Sample Answer

● Ⓑ Ⓒ Ⓓ

The sentence should read, "Aspirin is recommended to many people for its ability to thin the blood." Therefore, you should choose answer (A).

Example II▷

Some people believe that human beings will never use away all
                    A   B
the natural resources on earth.
          C   D

Sample Answer

Ⓐ ● Ⓒ Ⓓ

The sentence should read, "Some people believe that human beings will never use up all the natural resources on earth." Therefore, you should choose answer (B).

Now begin work on the questions.

16. The surface of the tongue covered with tiny taste buds.
                        A   B   C   D

17. Cosmic distance is measured on light-years.
       A   B   C   D

18. A million of tourists from all over the world visit New York every year.
    A   B   C   D

19. Whereas Earth has one moon, the planet call Mars has two small ones.
        A   B   C   D

20. An ardent feminist, Margaret Fuller, through her literature, asked that women be given a fairly chance.
                              A   B   C   D

21. No longer is scientific discovery a matter of one person alone working.
    A   B   C   D

22. The scientific method consists of forming hypotheses, collect data, and testing results.
              A   B   C   D

23. All data in computer are changed into electronic pulses by an input unit.
              A   B   C   D

GO ON TO THE NEXT PAGE

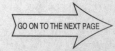

24. The basic <u>law</u> of addition, subtraction, multiplication and division <u>are</u> <u>taught</u> to all elementary school students.
    <u> A </u>   B   C   D

25. A <u>largely</u> <u>percentage</u> of Canadian export business <u>is</u> <u>with</u> the United States.
       A   B   C D

26. The <u>famous</u> Jim Thorpe won <u>both</u> the pentathlon <u>or</u> <u>decathlon</u> in the 1912 Olympic Games.
         A   B   C   D

27. Acute pharyngitis <u>pain</u> is <u>most often</u> caused by a viral infection, for <u>who</u> antibiotics <u>are ineffective</u>.
                 A   B   C   D

28. <u>Knowledges</u> about cultures <u>provides</u> <u>insights</u> into the <u>learned</u> behaviors of groups.
          A   B   C   D

29. A <u>fiber-optic</u> cable across the Pacific <u>went</u> into service in <u>April</u> 1989, <u>link</u> the United States and Japan.
           A   B   C   D

30. <u>Dislike</u> the gorilla, the <u>male</u> adult chimpanzee <u>weighs</u> <u>under</u> 200 pounds.
      A   B   C   D

31. Before lumberjacks had <u>mechanical equipments</u>, they used horses and ropes to <u>drag</u> logs.
      A   B   C   D

32. George Gershwin <u>not only</u> composed popular songs for musicals, <u>also</u> wrote <u>more</u> serious <u>concerts</u>.
                       A   B   C   D

33. <u>Among</u> the world's 44 <u>richest</u> countries, <u>there has been</u> not war <u>since</u> 1945.
      A   B   C   D

34. Caricature, a <u>type</u> of comic <u>exaggeration</u>, is <u>common</u> <u>used</u> in political cartoons.
              A   B   C   D

35. <u>One</u> and more sentences <u>related</u> to the <u>same</u> topic <u>form</u> a paragraph.
      A   B   C   D

36. Mirrors <u>done</u> of shiny metal <u>were used</u> by the Egyptians <u>in</u> ancient <u>times</u>.
       A   B   C   D

37. Mark Twain's *Adventures of Huckleberry Finn* <u>are</u> <u>one</u> of America's <u>national</u> <u>treasures</u>.
                                   A B   C   D

38. In his early days as a <u>direct</u>, Charlie Chaplin <u>produced</u> 62 <u>short</u>, silent comedy films <u>in</u> four years.
      A   B   C   D

39. Some studies show that <u>young</u> babies prefer <u>the smell</u> of milk <u>to those</u> of <u>other</u> liquids.
                 A   B   C   D

40. Plants <u>absorb</u> water and nutrients and <u>anchoring</u> themselves in the <u>soil</u> with their <u>roots</u>.
           A   B   C   D

THIS IS THE END OF SECTION 2.
DO NOT READ OR WORK ON ANY OTHER SECTION OF THE TEST UNTIL TIME IS UP.

STOP STOP STOP STOP STOP

SECTION 3

Reading Comprehension

Time—55 minutes

Directions: In this section you will read several passages. Each passage is followed by questions about it. Choose the one best answer, (A), (B), (C), or (D), for each question. Then, on your answer sheet, find the number of the question and fill in the space that corresponds to the letter of your answer choice. Answer all questions based on what is stated or implied in the passage.

Read the following passage:

A new hearing device is now available for some hearing-impaired people. This device uses a magnet to hold the detachable sound-processing portion in place. Like other aids, it converts sound into vibrations. But it is unique in that it can transmit the vibrations directly to the magnet, and then to the inner ear. This produces a clearer sound. The new device will not help all hearing-impaired people, only those with a hearing loss caused by infection or some other problem in the middle ear. It will probably help no more than 20 percent of all people with hearing problems. Those people, however, who often have persistent ear infections should find relief and restored hearing with the new device.

Example I▷   What is the author's main purpose in this passage?

Sample Answer

(A) to describe a new cure for ear infections
(B) to inform the reader of a new device
(C) to urge doctors to use a new device
(D) to explain the use of a magnet

The author's main purpose is to inform the reader of a new device for hearing-impaired people. Therefore, you should choose answer (B).

Example II▷   The word "relief" in the last sentence means

Sample Answer

(A) less distress
(B) assistance
(C) distraction
(D) relaxation

The phrase "less distress" is similar in meaning to "relief" in this sentence. Therefore, you should choose answer (A).

Now begin with the questions.

Questions 1 to 12 are based on the following passage:

(1)   Another common blues instrument that flourished in the rural South during the 1920s and 1930s was the blues harp or harmonica. It was played mainly in bands called jug bands that commonly performed on street corners, in saloons, and at country stores. Jug bands used a variety of instruments including the banjo, guitar, washboard, kazoo, fiddle, jugs, and blues harp. In these bands, the blues harp was used

(5)   primarily for melodic and rhythmic support. The earliest evidence of the harp used as a solo or lead instrument in the jug bands was in the late 1920s, as heard in the recordings of George "Bullet" Williams. Other good harpmen, such as Sonny Terry, Little Walter, and Sonny Boy Williamson, followed Williams, revolutionizing the harp's role as a lead instrument.

1. What does the passage mainly discuss?
(A) twentieth-century music of the South
(B) a change in the role of the blues harp
(C) good harpmen of the traditional blues harp
(D) the variety of instruments in jug bands

2. The blues harp is another name for the
(A) harpsichord
(B) guitar
(C) harmonica
(D) banjo

3. The word "flourished" as used in line 1 could best be replaced by which of the following?
(A) began to burgeon
(B) was profound
(C) appeared
(D) entertained

4. The author uses the phrase "rural South" in line 1 to refer to the Southern
(A) landscape
(B) metropolis
(C) countryside
(D) nation

5. It can be inferred that George "Bullet" Williams
(A) was the best blues harp player
(B) became friends with later harpmen
(C) played lead guitar in his band
(D) influenced some of the later harpmen

6. As used in line 5, the word "primarily" could best be replaced by
(A) chiefly
(B) peculiarly
(C) favorably
(D) advantageously

7. According to the author, when was the harp first used as a lead instrument?
(A) 1920–1925
(B) 1925–1930
(C) 1930–1935
(D) 1935–1940

8. The word "lead" as used in line 6 is closest in meaning to which of the following?
(A) model
(B) only
(C) control
(D) principal

9. In line 6, the word "recordings" most likely refers to
(A) readings
(B) tapes
(C) records
(D) movies

10. The word "revolutionizing" in line 8 could best be replaced by which of the following?
(A) reforming
(B) fighting
(C) resisting
(D) turning

11. Which of the following would most likely be the topic of the previous paragraph?
(A) the use of instruments for rythmic support in rural southern music in the 1920s
(B) lead instruments in rural southern music of the 1920s
(C) music in the American rural South before 1920
(D) jug bands and their role in 1920s southern music

12. According to the passage, jug bands were likely to perform in all of the following places EXCEPT
(A) on street corners
(B) at country suppers
(C) in concert halls
(D) in saloons

GO ON TO THE NEXT PAGE

Questions 13 to 24 are based on the following passage:

(1)   Over the past 600 years, English has grown from a language of few speakers to become the dominant language of international communication. English as we know it today emerged around 1350, after having incorporated many elements of French that were introduced following the Norman invasion of 1066. Until the 1600s, English was, for the most part, spoken only in England and had not extended even as

(5)   far as Wales, Scotland, or Ireland. However, during the course of the next two centuries, English began to spread around the globe as a result of exploration, trade (including slave trade), colonization, and missionary work. Thus, small enclaves of English speakers became established and grew in various parts of the world. As these communities proliferated, English gradually became the primary language of international business, banking, and diplomacy.

(10)   Currently, about 80 percent of the information stored on computer systems worldwide is in English. Two-thirds of the world's science writing is in English, and English is the main language of technology, advertising, media, international airports, and air traffic controllers. Today there are more than 700 million English users in the world, and over half of these are nonnative speakers, constituting the largest number of nonnative users than any other language in the world.

13. What is the main topic of this passage?
    (A) the number of nonnative users of English
    (B) the French influence on the English language
    (C) the expansion of English as an international language
    (D) the use of English for science and technology

14. The word "emerged" in line 2 could best be replaced by which of the following?
    (A) appeared
    (B) hailed
    (C) frequented
    (D) engaged

15. As used in line 3, the word "elements" is most similar to which of the following?
    (A) declaration
    (B) features
    (C) curiosities
    (D) customs

16. The word "extended" as used in line 4 is more similar to which of the following?
    (A) experienced
    (B) conferred
    (C) spread
    (D) stretched

17. Approximately when did English begin to be used beyond England?
    (A) in 1066
    (B) around 1350
    (C) before 1600
    (D) after 1600

18. According to the passage, all of the following contributed to the spread of English around the world EXCEPT
    (A) the slave trade
    (B) the Norman invasion
    (C) missionaries
    (D) colonization

19. As used in line 5, which of the following is closest in meaning to the word "course"?
    (A) subject
    (B) policy
    (C) time
    (D) track

20. The word "enclaves" in line 7 could best be replaced by which of the following?
    (A) communities
    (B) organizations
    (C) regions
    (D) countries

21. The word "proliferated" in line 8 is closest in meaning to which of the following?
    (A) prospered
    (B) organized
    (C) disbanded
    (D) expanded

GO ON TO THE NEXT PAGE

22. Which of the following is closest in meaning to the word "stored" as used in line 10?

    (A) bought
    (B) saved
    (C) spent
    (D) valued

23. Which of the following is closest in meaning to the word "constituting" in line 13?

    (A) looking over
    (B) setting down
    (C) doing in
    (D) making up

24. According to the passage, approximately how many nonnative users of English are there in the world today?

    (A) a quarter million
    (B) half a million
    (C) 350 million
    (D) 700 million

Questions 25 to 36 are based on the following passage:

(1)   As heart disease continues to be the number-one killer in the United States, researchers have become increasingly interested in identifying the potential risk factors that trigger heart attacks. High-fat diets and "life in the fast lane" have long been known to contribute to the high incidence of heart failure. But according to new studies, the list of risk factors may be significantly longer and quite surprising.

(5)   Heart failure, for example, appears to have seasonal and temporal patterns. A higher percentage of heart attacks occur in cold weather, and more people experience heart failure on Monday than on any other day of the week. In addition, people are more susceptible to heart attacks in the first few hours after waking. Cardiologists first observed this morning phenomenon in the mid-1980, and have since discovered a number of possible causes. An early-morning rise in blood pressure, heart rate, and

(10)   concentration of heart stimulating hormones, plus a reduction of blood flow to the heart, may all contribute to the higher incidence of heart attacks between the hours of 8:00 A.M. and 10:00 A.M.

In other studies, both birthdays and bachelorhood have been implicated as risk factors. Statistics reveal that heart attack rates increase significantly for both females and males in the few days immediately preceding and following their birthdays. And unmarried men are more at risk for heart attacks than their

(15)   married counterparts. Though stress is thought to be linked in some way to all of the aforementioned risk factors, intense research continues in the hope of further comprehending why and how heart failure is triggered.

25. What does the passage mainly discuss?
(A) risk factors in heart attacks
(B) seasonal and temporal patterns of heart attacks
(C) cardiology in the 1980s
(D) diet and stress as factors in heart attacks

26. In line 2, the word "potential" could best be replaced by which of the following?
(A) harmful
(B) primary
(C) unknown
(D) possible

27. The word "trigger" as used in line 2 is closest in meaning to which of the following?
(A) involve
(B) affect
(C) cause
(D) encounter

28. Which of the following could best replace the word "incidence" as used in line 3?
(A) increase
(B) rate
(C) chance
(D) factor

29. The author uses the word "temporal" in line 5 to mean
(A) affected by
(B) of a certain date
(C) expected
(D) regularly

30. The phrase "susceptible to " in line 7 could best be replaced by
(A) aware of
(B) affected by
(C) accustomed
(D) prone to

31. According to the passage, which of the following is NOT a possible cause of many heart attacks?
(A) decreased blood flow to the heart
(B) increased blood pressure
(C) lower heart rate
(D) increase in hormones

32. The word "phenomenon" in line 8 refers to which of the following?
(A) habit
(B) illness
(C) occurrence
(D) activity

GO ON TO THE NEXT PAGE

33. The word "implicated" in line 12 could best be replaced by which of the following?
    - (A) indicated
    - (B) disregarded
    - (C) investigated
    - (D) discovered

34. Which of the following is NOT cited as a possible risk factor?
    - (A) having a birthday
    - (B) getting married
    - (C) eating fatty foods
    - (D) being under stress

35. Which of the following does the passage infer?
    - (A) We now fully understand how risk factors trigger heart attacks.
    - (B) We recently began to study how risk factors trigger heart attacks.
    - (C) We have not identified many risk factors associated with heart attacks.
    - (D) We do not fully understand how risk factors trigger heart attacks.

36. As used in line 13, which of the following could best replace the word "reveal"?
    - (A) show
    - (B) observe
    - (C) mean
    - (D) explain

GO ON TO THE NEXT PAGE

Questions 37 to 48 are based on the following passage:

(1) Baseball has been dubbed "America's favorite sport," and many fans contend that there is no greater thrill than watching a good pitcher throw the ball skillfully in a series of expertly delivered "fast" and "curve" balls. Two such pitches, the "rising fastball" and the "breaking curveball" are particularly exasperating to batters because these balls tend to veer in one direction or the other just as they reach home plate.

(5) The "rising fastball" zooms forward only to jump up and over the bat as the batter swings. The "breaking curveball" curves toward home plate, but plunges downward unexpectedly at the last moment. Batters attempt to anticipate these pitches, and respond accordingly, while pitchers work at perfecting their "fast" and "curve" ball deliveries.

But, according to studies conducted by a team of engineers and psychologists, the "rising fastball"

(10) and the "breaking curveball" do not actually exist; they are merely optical illusions. The studies revealed that batters perceive the ball as approaching more slowly or falling more quickly than it actually is, and it is this misperception that produces the visual illusion. Batters tend to have difficulty tracking a ball continuously as it approaches and will briefly divert their eyes to the spot where they think the ball will cross the plate. When a batter has misjudged the speed or angle of a pitch, and shifts his or her gaze in

(15) this way, the ball will appear to suddenly rise or dip, and the batter will often miss.

How will this finding affect "America's favorite pastime"? No doubt some will vehemently reject the notion that the "rising fastball" and the "breaking curveball" are mere illusions. But for others, the findings may imbue the game with a new level of intrigue as batters attempt to respond to pitches that don't exist.

37. What does this passage mainly discuss?
   (A) the difference between fastballs and curveballs
   (B) America's favorite pastime
   (C) illusions about the movements of pitched balls
   (D) perceptional problems among baseball players

38. As used in line 1, the word "contend" could best be replaced by which of the following?
   (A) maintain
   (B) operate
   (C) propose
   (D) suppose

39. Which of the following words could best replace the word "thrill" in line 1?
   (A) activity
   (B) excitement
   (C) remedy
   (D) issue

40. In line 3, the word "exasperating" could best be replaced by which of the following?
   (A) challenging
   (B) exhausting
   (C) exciting
   (D) frustrating

41. As used in line 5, the word "zooms" is closest in meaning to which of the following?
   (A) falls
   (B) rolls
   (C) speeds
   (D) bounces

42. Which of the following words could best replace the word "plunges" as used in line 6?
   (A) drops
   (B) withdraws
   (C) emerges
   (D) tips

43. According to the author, why is it difficult for the batter to hit the "rising fastball" and the "breaking curveball"?
   (A) because the ball approaches too quickly
   (B) because the ball veers just before reaching home plate
   (C) because the batter misjudges the pitcher's intention
   (D) because the batter misjudges the speed and angle of the ball

GO ON TO THE NEXT PAGE

44. In line 10, what does the word "they" refer to?
    (A) the "rising fastball" and the "breaking curveball"
    (B) the engineers and psychologists
    (C) the research studies
    (D) the optical illusions

45. Which of the following is closest in meaning to the word "gaze" as used in line 14?
    (A) to glance rapidly
    (B) to blink rapidly
    (C) to look steadily
    (D) to peek briefly

46. According to the passage, how is the illusion of the "rising fastball" and the "breaking curveball" produced?
    (A) by the pitcher's delivery
    (B) by the batter's failing to track the ball accurately
    (C) by the speed and angle of the ball
    (D) by the studies of engineers and psychologists

47. Which of the following could best replace the word "vehemently" in line 16?
    (A) certainly
    (B) impassively
    (C) socially
    (D) furiously

48. The word "imbue" in line 18 is closest in meaning to which of the following?
    (A) fill
    (B) spoil
    (C) affect
    (D) change

GO ON TO THE NEXT PAGE

Questions 49 to 60 are based on the following passage:

(1)   The Timber rattlesnake, once widespread throughout the eastern United States, is now on the endangered species list and is extinct in two eastern states in which it once thrived. Compared to its western cousins, the Timber rattlesnake may be especially vulnerable because of certain behaviors adapted for coping with the cold climate in which it lives.

(5)   Rattlesnakes are generally found in warm climates because, like all reptiles, they cannot generate or regulate their own body temperature internally and must rely on the sun's warmth for heat. But Timber rattlesnakes migrated into colder northern areas about 8,000 years ago when glaciers retreated. In these northern regions, the snakes developed a number of adaptive strategies to survive, but ultimately these behaviors make them more vulnerable to human predation, their main threat.

(10)   One survival strategy the snakes have developed is hibernation. For approximately eight months of the year, the rattlers remain motionless in deep frost-free crevices, with their body temperature dropping as low as 40 degrees. In the spring when they emerge, they must warm their chilled bodies by sunning for three or four days on rocks in the open. This behavior, coupled with the fact that Timber rattlesnakes tend to concentrate in large numbers at their wintering sites, makes them easy prey. Gestating

(15)   females are particularly vulnerable because they spend much of their time basking in the sun in order to produce live young from eggs. In addition, females have very long interbirth intervals, producing live young only every three to five years. If a frost or cold spell comes late in the year, the entire litter of six to twelve young may die.

         Efforts are underway to protect the Timber rattlesnake and its habitat from further human

(20)   depredation, but in many states it is already too late.

49. What is the main topic of the passage?
(A) why Timber rattlesnakes hibernate
(B) how Timber rattlesnakes are surviving
(C) how Timber rattlesnakes adapted to northern climates
(D) why Timber rattlesnakes are endangered

50. Which of the following is closest in meaning to the word "vulnerable" in line 3?
(A) unprotected
(B) impervious
(C) insensitive
(D) deprived

51. Which of the following is true about Timber rattlesnakes?
(A) They migrated to eastern states.
(B) They migrated northward during a warming period.
(C) They migrated to escape a cold climate.
(D) They migrated to the South to seek a warmer climate.

52. In line 11, the word "crevices" could be replaced by which of the following?
(A) tombs
(B) rocks
(C) cracks
(D) tunnels

53. Which of the following could best replace the word "emerge" in line 12?
(A) come out
(B) set off
(C) get up
(D) see through

54. In which of the following places might a person be most likely to find Timber rattlesnakes in the spring?
(A) in the woods
(B) in meadows
(C) in bushy areas
(D) in canyons

55. Which of the following could best replace the phrase "coupled with" in line 13?
(A) compared with
(B) combined with
(C) controlled with
(D) supported with

GO ON TO THE NEXT PAGE

56. The phrase "easy prey" in line 14 could best be replaced by which of the following?
    (A) relaxed
    (B) protective
    (C) victims
    (D) sociable

57. Which of the following words can best replace the word "basking" in line 15?
    (A) washing
    (B) eating
    (C) sleeping
    (D) lying

58. According to the passage, which of the following does NOT contribute to the rattlesnake being an endangered animal?
    (A) hibernating for eight months
    (B) basking in the sun
    (C) congregating together
    (D) having long intervals between births

59. Which of the following could best replace the word "depredation" in line 20?
    (A) fear
    (B) habitation
    (C) destruction
    (D) depression

60. What is the author's tone attitude toward the topic?
    (A) accusative
    (B) nostalgic
    (C) regretful
    (D) humorous

THIS IS THE END OF TEST 6

Practice Test 6
Answer Key

Section 1: Listening Comprehension

Part A

1. A	5. A	9. B	13. C	17. C
2. C	6. D	10. C	14. B	18. C
3. B	7. C	11. C	15. A	19. A
4. C	8. B	12. B	16. C	20. C

Part B

21. A	24. A	27. A	30. A	33. C
22. B	25. D	28. C	31. A	34. B
23. C	26. C	29. C	32. A	35. D

Part C

36. B	39. B	42. A	45. C	48. C
37. C	40. A	43. C	46. B	49. A
38. A	41. B	44. B	47. A	50. A

Section 2: Structure and Written Expression

Part 1: Sentence Completion

1. D	4. A	7. B	10. A	13. D
2. A	5. B	8. C	11. A	14. D
3. A	6. B	9. B	12. A	15. C

Part 2: Error Identification

16. B	21. D	26. C	31. B	36. A
17. C	22. C	27. C	32. C	37. A
18. B	23. A	28. A	33. D	38. B
19. C	24. A	29. D	34. C	39. C
20. D	25. A	30. A	35. A	40. B

Section 3: Reading Comprehension

1. B	13. C	25. A	37. C	49. D
2. C	14. A	26. D	38. A	50. A
3. A	15. B	27. C	39. B	51. B
4. C	16. C	28. B	40. D	52. C
5. D	17. D	29. A	41. C	53. A
6. A	18. B	30. D	42. A	54. B
7. B	19. C	31. C	43. D	55. B
8. D	20. A	32. C	44. A	56. C
9. C	21. D	33. A	45. C	57. D
10. A	22. B	34. B	46. B	58. A
11. B	23. D	35. D	47. D	59. C
12. C	24. C	36. A	48. A	60. C

Practice Test 6
Explanatory Answers

SECTION 1
Listening Comprehension

Part A

1. Woman: Fred, have you done anything about that strange noise in the car?
   Man: Oh, I'll have Adam fix it.

   What does the man mean?
   (A) Adam will repair the car.
   (B) Adam helped to pull the car to the repair shop.
   (C) Fred and Adam both fixed the car.
   (D) The car cannot be fixed any more.

   (A) The construction "to have someone do something" means to ask someone to do something.

2. Woman: Did you hear that Jeff has passed his oral exam?
   Man: Finally.

   What does the man imply?
   (A) Jeff agreed to take the oral exam again.
   (B) Jeff passed the oral exam and went on a vacation.
   (C) It took Jeff a long time to pass his exam.
   (D) Jeff didn't take the oral exam.

   (C) The meaning of this sentence is in the tone of voice of the man. His answer of "finally" indicates that it took a long time, but he finally passed it.

3. Woman: How do you like the new librarian at the information desk?
   Man: You mean Ron? He's been here as long as I have!

   What does the man imply?
   (A) He has been waiting for Ron for a long time.
   (B) Ron is not a new librarian.
   (C) Ron did a lot of work for the man.
   (D) He needs to collect some information from Ron.

   (B) The man's comment "he's been here as long as I have" indicates that Ron is not a new employee.

4. Woman: Would you like me to type your paper this time?
   Man: Would I? Please do.

   What does the man mean?
   (A) He would like to help the woman typing.
   (B) He wonders how much he should pay her.
   (C) He wants the woman to help him.
   (D) He prefers to type the paper by himself.

   (C) This is another answer in which the meaning is in the speaker's voice. The question "Would I?" actually means "I really would."

5. Man: I have to go back to the classroom again.
   Woman: What's up?

   What does the woman want to know?
   (A) Why the man needs to return.
   (B) What makes the man happy.
   (C) Which classroom the man is going to.
   (D) What book the man needs to get.

   (A) The question "What's up?" means "What is going on?" or "What is the matter?" or "Why?" She means "Why do you need to go back to the classroom?"

6. Woman: Mary is going to give me a ride to the party.
   Man: How could she? She doesn't have her license yet.

   What does the man mean?
   (A) Mary is going to the airport.
   (B) Mary is not going to the party.
   (C) Mary is not very kind.
   (D) Mary should not be driving.

   (D) Since the man says that Mary does not have a driving license, we can assume that Mary should not be driving.

7.   Man: Would you like me to call a night escort?
      Woman: If possible.

What does the woman mean?
(A) She doesn't need an escort.
(B) She will call the night escort by herself.
(C) She would like the man to get a night escort for her.
(D) She's afraid the man won't help her.

(C) When the woman says, "If possible," she means, "Yes, I would like you to call a night escort if it is possible for you to do so." In this sentence, a night escort is a service provided by a school or workplace in which a person will walk with another person to that person's car or home or bus at night. This service is provided as a safety precaution.

8.   Man: Do you accept credit cards?
      Woman: Only if the charge is more than $15.

What does the woman mean?
(A) The fee for charging is more than $15.
(B) He cannot use a credit card if he spends less than $15.
(C) The store does not accept credit cards.
(D) She cannot accept cash.

(B) The woman says that she will only accept a credit card if the man spends more than $15.

9.   Woman: I hope I still can register for the speech class.
      Man: I heard there was a waiting list.

What does the man mean?
(A) The woman has to wait in line to register.
(B) It may be too late for the woman to get into the speech class.
(C) The woman needs to take another class before registering for this class.
(D) The woman should go by herself to sign up for the class.

(B) When the man says there is a waiting list, he means that there are no more spaces left for students in the speech class, but a list has been written for those who would like to take the class. We can assume that if some of the people who are in the class decide not to take the class, then some of the people on the waiting list may be able to.

10.   Man: Dr. Jones, is it possible for the exam to be an open-book exam?
      Woman: Well it would be OK with me, but we have to follow the department regulations.

What does the woman mean?
(A) Students can bring their books to the exam.
(B) Dr. Jones will be the next department chair.
(C) Dr. Jones will probably not give an open-book exam.
(D) It's up to the students.

(C) Since Dr. Jones says, "but we must follow the department regulations," we can assume that the department does not allow open-book exams. An open-book exam is an exam in which the students can look for information in their books during the test.

11. Woman: Could you take my phone calls for me while I am away?
      Man: Sure, when will you be back?

What does the man mean?
(A) He doesn't know how to take care of the phone.
(B) He's going to leave too.
(C) He will answer the telephone for the woman.
(D) He is coming back soon.

(C) The man answers, "Sure," so he is agreeing to help the woman. The woman's request to "take my phone calls" means "please answer my phone and take the messages."

12.   Man: You really shouldn't take any more.
      Woman: Well, one more, and then no more.

What does the woman mean?
(A) She can manage much more.
(B) She will take one.
(C) She doesn't care how many she gets.
(D) She will not take any.

(B) The woman seems to want more, but is not allowing herself to take more. We might imagine that it is candy that she is taking. She would like to take more, but has decided to take only one piece.

13. Woman: How are you and your roommates getting along?
Man: So far, so good.

What does the man mean?
(A) He needs a roommate to share the expenses.
(B) He lives alone without anybody to bother him.
(C) Things are all right at this point.
(D) His apartment is far away from school.

(C) The expression "so far, so good" means "At this point in time, things are fine."

14. Woman: The university policy has changed a lot
since I've been here.
Man: Hasn't it.

What does the man mean?
(A) The university policy has not changed enough.
(B) He agrees with the woman's opinion.
(C) He doesn't know what the old policy was.
(D) The university needs to change their policy more.

(B) This is a question for which the speaker's tone of voice is important. Since his voice has a falling tone, it means that he agrees. He is repeating the verb of the woman's comment "hasn't it changed," but the comment is a statement, not a question: "hasn't it changed a lot!"

15. Man: You weren't scared, were you?
Woman: Not much, I wasn't! My heart was beat-
ing fast and tears were running down my
face, that's all.

What does the woman mean?
(A) She was very frightened.
(B) She had a heart problem.
(C) She lost the race.
(D) Overall, she was happy.

(A) This is a question for which the speaker's tone of voice is important. In fact, the speaker says the opposite of what she means. Her comment "Not much" actually means "a lot."

16. Woman: Shall we sit here and talk?
Man: There is no better place than here.

What does the man mean?
(A) It's not a good time or place to talk.
(B) I'm thinking about making this place better.
(C) This is a good place for a conversation.
(D) You'd better leave this place now.

(C) If there is no better place, then this place must be good, or at least the best place there is in this area.

17. Woman: What would you like for your present?
Man: A racing bike; that's what I've always
wanted.

What does the man mean?
(A) It's expensive to get a 10-speed bicycle.
(B) He commutes to school by bike.
(C) He would really like a fast bicycle.
(D) He can borrow his friend's bicycle whenever he wants.

(C) A racing bike is a bike that can go very fast. The man says that he has always wanted a racing bike. He does not say that it is expensive (though it probably is), or that he commutes to school by bike (though he might).

18. Man: Why didn't you buy it?
Woman: If it had been only two dollars cheaper, I
would have.

What does the woman mean?
(A) She doesn't like cheap things.
(B) It was two dollars cheaper than usual.
(C) It was too expensive.
(D) She bought something cheaper.

(C) The woman says that she would have bought the item if it had been two dollars less. We can infer that it is too expensive for her to buy it.

19. Man: Marie, why did you get up so early
today?
Woman: I thought someone was coming over.

What does the woman mean?
(A) She was expecting someone to visit.
(B) She didn't like to get up early.
(C) She got up early and went out.
(D) Someone called her early in the morning.

(A) The phrase "to come over" means "to visit someone at home."

20. Woman: Usually Jim washes his car himself.
Man: Yeah, but this time he took it to the
carwash.

What do they say about Jim?
(A) Jim washed his friend's car.
(B) Jim's car was not very well cleaned.
(C) Jim didn't wash his car this time.
(D) Jim once had a job washing cars.

(C) The word "but" is an indication that the sentence expresses an opposite idea. Usually Jim washes his car, but this time he didn't.

Part B

21. Where is the man going?
 (A) to a park downtown
 (B) to the Ocean Palace
 (C) to the cinema
 (D) to a bookstore

(A) This is a restatement question. At the beginning of the conversation the man says he is going downtown to the auction. Later he adds that he is going to the park, where the auction will be held. We can assume that the park is downtown.

22. What did the man previously get at an auction?
 (A) two free dinners
 (B) $50 worth of books
 (C) a $30 gift certificate
 (D) four movie passes

(B) This is a restatement question. The man states that he once got a gift certificate for $50, but he paid only $30 for it. So he was able to get $50 worth of books for only $30.

23. How can a person get an item at the auction?
 (A) by going to the bookstore
 (B) by sending a letter in the mail
 (C) by calling on the phone
 (D) by going to the ticket office

(C) This is a restatement question. The man tells the woman that there are two ways to get things at the auction. One way is by listening to the radio and calling to say the amount you want to pay for an item. The other way is by going to the auction in the park. This second way is not one of the choices above. The man says nothing about any of the other choices.

24. What is the woman going to do?
 (A) go with the man
 (B) make a phone call
 (C) buy a ticket
 (D) go to the library

(A) This is a restatement question. At the end of the conversation, the woman says, "You talked me into it. Let's go." She means that the man convinced her to join him.

25. What is this conversation mainly about?
 (A) a fight
 (B) cooking
 (C) manners
 (D) a problem

(D) This is an inference question. When the woman says, "There is something in my soup," she means that there is something wrong with her soup. She is making a complaint because of a problem.

26. What is the man's occupation?
 (A) student
 (B) bartender
 (C) waiter
 (D) cook

(C) This is an inference question. The woman calls the man "waiter," and he is serving her food at a restaurant.

27. Why did the woman get the attention of the man?
 (A) because something was wrong
 (B) because she wanted to pay her bill
 (C) because she needed to order her meal
 (D) because she needed to be seated

(A) This is an inference question. The woman says that there is "an insect or something" in her soup.

28. At the end of the conversation, how does the woman feel?
 (A) angry
 (B) concerned
 (C) pleased
 (D) disappointed

(C) This is an inference question. The woman seems pleased as is shown by her comment "That's great. I can use a free lunch."

29. Where does this conversation take place?
 (A) in a restaurant
 (B) in a classroom
 (C) in a library
 (D) at a park

(C) This is a restatement question. The woman says that she has to stay late at the library.

30. What is the woman going to do until eleven o'clock?
  (A) study
  (B) eat dinner
  (C) see a movie
  (D) work

(A) This is a restatement question. The woman says that she is going to study until eleven o'clock.

31. What is the man doing?
  (A) working
  (B) studying
  (C) dancing
  (D) eating

(A) This is a restatement question. The man states that he has to work at the library until eleven o'clock.

32. What seems to be the main purpose of this conversation?
  (A) to set a time to meet again
  (B) to complain about school
  (C) to explain working hours
  (D) to request help in finding books

(A) This is an inference question. Though the woman may be interpreted as making a complaint about school, and the man does talk about the hours he is working, the best answer is that the two people are making a date and time to meet again. The man first asks her if she wants to meet at eleven o'clock, and then the woman asks the man if he wants to get together on another day.

33. Where is Tuskegee located?
  (A) Canada
  (B) Alaska
  (C) Alabama
  (D) Washington

(C) This is a restatement question. The woman states that Tuskegee is in the state of Alabama.

34. What does the woman say about George Washington Carver?
  (A) that he was a president
  (B) that he was a scientist
  (C) that he liked peanuts
  (D) that he was a Native American

(B) This is a restatement question. The woman says that George Washington Carver was a great scientist.

35. What quality most clearly describes the man?
  (A) dedicated
  (B) angry
  (C) excited
  (D) uninformed

(D) This is an inference question. The man indicates that he does not know where Tuskegee is, why it is famous, or who Carver is. He is uninformed about all of these.

Part C

36. What class are the students most likely taking?
    (A) history of the Smithsonian
    (B) introduction to archeology
    (C) Native Americans in the Western States
    (D) hiking and backpacking techniques

(B) This is an inference question. The announcer talks about archeological digging and paleontology. She also says that this trip would be a good way to learn about archeology, and that students will get class credit from their department.

37. Where will the volunteers go?
    (A) to the university
    (B) to a lecture
    (C) to Wyoming
    (D) to the Smithsonian Institute

(C) This is a restatement question. The announcer says that the volunteers will explore some current archeological digs in Wyoming.

38. What will the field workers be doing?
    (A) searching for plant and animal fossils
    (B) building homes for the poor
    (C) rock climbing
    (D) white water rafting

(A) This is a restatement question. The announcer says that the volunteer field workers will search for remains of plants and vertebrates.

39. How much does the trip cost?
    (A) $1,250
    (B) $1,500
    (C) $2,000
    (D) $2,500

(B) This is a restatement question. The woman says the trip will cost $1,500.

40. What is the main topic of this announcement?
    (A) an animation festival
    (B) a drama festival
    (C) an exhibit featuring the *Mona Lisa*
    (D) *Mona Lisa Descending a Staircase*

(A) This is a main idea question. The speaker begins by saying that he is announcing the opening of the annual festival of animation. It includes the movie *Mona Lisa Descending a Staircase*, but that is only part of the topic.

41. What academic subject is expressed in the film *Mona Lisa Descending a Staircase*?
    (A) Italian history
    (B) art history
    (C) sociology
    (D) architecture

(B) This is a restatement question. The speaker says that this movie is a journey through several hundred years of art history.

42. What is featured at the festival?
    (A) *The Prince and the Princess*
    (B) Francis Bacon
    (C) the Louvre
    (D) KKED radio

(A) This is a restatement question. The speaker says that one highlight of the festival is the French movie *The Prince and the Princess*.

43. Where is the festival being held?
    (A) at the KKED radio station
    (B) at the Art Exhibition Hall
    (C) at the Palace of Fine Arts
    (D) at the Historical Museum

(C) This is a restatement question. The speaker says that the festival begins April 16 at the Palace of Fine Arts.

44. What is this talk about?
    (A) European expeditions in the 1700s
    (B) the growth of Los Angeles
    (C) famous sites in Los Angeles
    (D) the entertainment industry

(B) This is a main idea question. The lecture begins and ends with information about the size of Los Angeles.

45. What two factors caused the town to begin to grow?
    (A) the oceans and the gold rush
    (B) tourism and the entertainment industry
    (C) the railroads and the discovery of oil
    (D) sea trade and the airplane industry

(C) This is a restatement question. The tour guide describes these two factors as the cause of the beginning of the city's growth in the late 1800s. Later on, the entertainment industry was the cause of more growth.

46. Approximately how many years ago did Los Angeles begin growing into a large city?
- **(A)** 50 years
- **(B)** 100 years
- **(C)** 200 years
- **(D)** 300 years

(B) This is a restatement question. The speaker ends by saying that Los Angeles has grown into a sprawling metropolis in the past one hundred years. The word "sprawling" means "spread out without a regular pattern." A metropolis is a large city.

47. Where did the woman work the previous summer?
- **(A)** Washington, D.C.
- **(B)** New York City
- **(C)** Chicago
- **(D)** Denver

(A) This is a restatement question. She begins her talk by saying that she worked in Washington, D.C.

48. What is the purpose of the program the woman is discussing?
- **(A)** to prevent diseases among military personnel
- **(B)** to investigate serious crimes in the military
- **(C)** to find ways of identifying bodies of soldiers
- **(D)** to store old military journals and diaries

(C) This is a restatement question. The woman begins by saying that the job was awful because the purpose was to identify the remains of soliders in wars.

49. What did the speaker say was exciting about her work?
- **(A)** working with DNA
- **(B)** wearing a necklace
- **(C)** taking blood samples
- **(D)** making identification tags

(A) This is a restatement question. The woman says that she was excited because she was working with a scientist on DNA structures.

50. In what class would the student most likely be making this presentation?
- **(A)** biology
- **(B)** geology
- **(C)** history
- **(D)** political science

(A) This is an inference question. Since the woman was talking about DNA, a genetic material, the subject is most likely biology.

SECTION 2

Structure and Written Expression

Part 1: Sentence Completion

1. A log grabber has a long arm _____, which stretches out to pick up logs.
   - (A) calls a jib
   - (B) calling a jib
   - (C) a jib called
   - (D) called a jib

(D) Adjective phrase. The phrase "called a jib" could also be "which is called a jib." It describes the arm of the log grabber.

2. A home computer _____ an opportunity for convenient and efficient work at home.
   - (A) provides
   - (B) to be providing
   - (C) which provides
   - (D) providing it

(A) Verb. The subject of the sentence is "computer" and the verb "provides" is present tense.

3. Eli Whitney's milling machine remained unchanged for a century and a half because _____ was so efficient.
   - (A) it
   - (B) he
   - (C) of
   - (D) its

(A) Pronoun. The word "it" refers to the main noun, "machine."

4. Some of the rainwater from clouds evaporates before _____.
   - (A) reaching the ground
   - (B) to reach the ground
   - (C) reach the ground
   - (D) the ground reaches

(A) Gerund. After the preposition "before" the -ing form of the verb is used.

5. Once an offending allergen has been identified _____ tests, it is possible for the doctor to give specific desensitizing injections.
   - (A) means of
   - (B) by means of
   - (C) of the means by
   - (D) by means

(B) The phrase "by means of" refers to how something is done.

6. Sometimes _____ wears people out and is worse than the lack of sleep itself.
   - (A) to sleep the desire
   - (B) the desire to sleep
   - (C) to desire sleep is
   - (D) the desire to sleep who

(B) Noun phrase. The complete phrase "the desire to sleep" is the subject of this sentence. The main verb is a two-word verb "to wear out," meaning "to become very tired or exhausted."

7. Although dissimilar in almost every other respect, birds and insects have both evolved efficient _____ capabilities.
   - (A) fly
   - (B) flying
   - (C) to fly
   - (D) is flying

(B) Adjective. The word "flying," though usually a verb, in this sentence is a word that describes the type of capabilities.

8. The wheel, _____ has remained important for 4,000 years, is one of mankind's first inventions.
   - (A) how
   - (B) when
   - (C) which
   - (D) about

(C) Adjective. The word "which" begins the adjective clause that describes the wheel: "which has remained important for 4,000 years."

9. _____ children master the basics, advanced development becomes easier.
   - (A) The
   - (B) Once
   - (C) That
   - (D) Even

(B) Adverb. The word "once" means "as soon as" or "whenever."

10. _____ there is a close correlation between stress and illness.
    (A) Some psychologists believe
    (B) Believed some psychologists
    (C) Some psychologists to believe
    (D) Some psychologists believing

(A) Subject and verb. This is the main subject and verb of the sentence.

11. _____ is often used in soups and sauces.
    (A) Parsley, an inexpensive herb,
    (B) Parsley is an inexpensive herb,
    (C) Inexpensive parsley, herb,
    (D) An herb is inexpensive parsley,

(A) Noun phrase. The main noun of the sentence is "parsley" and the phrase after "parsley" describes what it is.

12. Perspiration increases _____ vigorous exercise or hot weather.
    (A) during
    (B) when
    (C) at the time
    (D) for

(A) Conjunction. The word "during" is correct since it precedes two nouns ("exercise" and "weather"). Answer (C) would be correct if it said "at the time of." Answer (B) is incorrect since there is no verb after it. Answer (D) does not make sense since perspiration does not occur *for* exercise.

Part 2: Error Identification

16. The surface of the tongue covered with tiny taste
                    A   B   C
    buds.
    D

(B) Verb. The correct answer is "is covered," a passive voice verb. The active voice would be "Taste buds cover the surface of the tongue."

17. Cosmic distance is measured on light-years.
        A   B   C   D

(C) Preposition. The correct answer is "is measured by light-years." The preposition "by" follows the verb "measured."

13. Goddard developed the first rocket to fly faster _____.
    (A) than sound is
    (B) does sound
    (C) sound
    (D) than sound

(D) Comparison. After the *-er* form the word "than" must be used. Answer (A) is incorrect because there is no verb to complete the word "is."

14. Even if the unemployment rate _____ sharply, the drop may still be temporary.
    (A) to drop
    (B) dropping
    (C) have dropped
    (D) drops

(D) Verb. The verb "drops" is the regular present tense verb following the noun "rate."

15. Studies indicate _____ collecting art today than ever before.
    (A) there are that more people
    (B) more people that are
    (C) that there are more people
    (D) people there are more

(C) Word Order. The verb "indicate" must be followed by the word "that" in this sentence. The sentence could also be ". . . there are more people who are collecting art. . . ."

18. A million of tourists from all over the world visit
        A   B   C   D
    New York every year.

(B) Preposition/unnecessary word. The correct answer is "a million tourists." There should be no preposition following the noun "million."

19. Whereas Earth has one moon, the planet call
            A   B   C
    Mars has two small ones.
                       D

(C) Verb. The correct answer is "planet called Mars. . . ." This is a passive verb. A more compete sentence would be ". . . the planet that is called Mars has two small ones."

20. An ardent feminist, Margaret Fuller, through her
   $\overline{}$
   $\underset{A}{}$

   literature, asked that women be given a fairly
   $\overline{B}$ $\overline{C}$ $\overline{D}$

   chance.

(D) Word form. The correct answer is ". . . be given a fair chance." The adjective "fair" modifies the noun "chance."

21. No longer is scientific discovery a matter of one
   $\overline{A}$ $\overline{B}$ $\overline{C}$

   person alone working.
   $\overline{}$
   $\underset{D}{}$

(D) Reversed words. The correct answer is "one person working alone." The adverb "alone" describes the way one person works.

22. The scientific method consists of forming hy-
   $\overline{A}$ $\overline{B}$

   potheses, collect data, and testing results.
   $\overline{C}$ $\overline{D}$

(C) Parallel construction. The correct answer is "collecting data." The series of verbs are "forming. . . , collecting. . . , and testing. . . ."

23. All data in computer are changed into electronic
   $\overline{A}$ $\overline{B}$

   pulses by an input unit.
   $\overline{C}$ $\overline{D}$

(A) Singular/plural noun. The correct answer is "all data in computers are . . . ." The verb "are" is plural, so the noun must also be plural. It would also be possible in this sentence to use the word "computer" as a mass noun referring to all computers. In this case, however, (A) is still wrong since the phrase would have to be "all data in the computer. . . ."

24. The basic law of addition, subtraction, multipli-
   $\overline{A}$

   cation and division are taught to all elementary
   $\overline{B}$ $\overline{C}$

   school students.
   $\overline{D}$

(A) Singular/plural noun. Since the verb is "are," the subject must be plural: "laws."

25. A largely percentage of Canadian export busi-
   $\overline{A}$ $\overline{B}$

   ness is with the United States.
   $\overline{C}$ $\overline{D}$

(A) Word form. The correct phrase is "a large percentage. . . ." The word "large" is an adjective that means "big," or "great." The word "largely" is an adverb that means "much" or "mainly." The adjective in this sentence describes the noun "percentage."

26. The famous Jim Thorpe won both the pentathlon
   $\overline{A}$ $\overline{B}$

   or decathlon in the 1912 Olympic Games.
   $\overline{C}$ $\overline{D}$

(C) Conjunction. The correct word is "and." Since the sentence says that Jim Thorpe won both events, the word "and " is necessary.

27. Acute pharyngitis pain is most often caused by a
   $\overline{A}$ $\overline{B}$

   viral infection, for who antibiotics are ineffective.
   $\overline{C}$ $\overline{D}$

(C) Pronoun. The correct word is "which," a pronoun that stands for the noun "pain." The word "who" stands for people, not things.

28. Knowledges about cultures provides insights into
   $\overline{A}$ $\overline{B}$

   the learned behaviors of groups.
   $\overline{C}$ $\overline{D}$

(A) Singular/plural noun. The correct word is "knowledge," a mass noun that does not have a plural -s form.

29. A fiber-optic cable across the Pacific went into
   $\overline{A}$ $\overline{B}$

   service in April 1989, link the United States and
   $\overline{C}$ $\overline{D}$

   Japan.

(D) Word form. The correct answer is "linking," a participle that begins an adjective phrase that describes the cable.

30. Dislike the gorilla, the male adult chimpanzee
    ‾A‾   ‾B‾

    weighs under 200 pounds.
    ‾C‾   ‾D‾

(A) Verb/adjective. The correct answer is "Unlike the gorilla . . . ." The word "dislike" is a verb that means "do not like." The word "unlike" is an adjective that means "having little resemblance" or "not alike" or "different."

31. Before lumberjacks had mechanical equipments,
    ‾A‾   ‾B‾

    they used horses and ropes to drag logs.
    ‾C‾   ‾D‾

(B) Singular/plural noun. The correct answer is "equipment," a mass noun that does not have a plural -s form.

32. George Gershwin not only composed popular
                              ‾A‾

    songs for musicals, also wrote more serious
    ‾B‾   ‾C‾   ‾D‾
    concerts.

(C) Omitted word. The correct answer is either "he also wrote" or "but also wrote" or "but he also wrote." The phrase "not only" in the beginning of the sentence is a clue. After "not only" you will usually find "but also."

33. Among the world's 44 richest countries there has
    ‾A‾   ‾B‾   ‾C‾

    been not war since 1945.
    ‾D‾

(D) Adverb. The correct answer is "there has been no war since. . . ." It would also be possible to say, "There has not been war since. . . ." The word "not" is part of the verb, and must be put between "has" and "been." The word "no" refers to an absense of the noun; in this sentence, it refers to the absense of war, and it is put just before the noun it modifies.

34. Caricature, a type of comic exaggeration, is
                  ‾A‾   ‾B‾

    common used in political cartoons.
    ‾C‾   ‾D‾

(C) Word form. The correct answer is "commonly," an adverb that describes how often caricature is used.

35. One and more sentences related to the same topic
    ‾A‾   ‾B‾   ‾C‾

    form a paragraph.
    ‾D‾

(A) Conjunction. The correct word is "or." The phrase "one or more" is used with the plural noun in this sentence to mean one sentence or more sentences.

36. Mirrors done of shiny metal were used by the
            ‾A‾   ‾B‾

    Egyptians in ancient times.
    ‾C‾   ‾D‾

(A) Verb. The correct answer is "made of . . . metal. . . ." The word "made of" refers to the material that is used in the mirror.

37. Mark Twain's *Adventures of Huckleberry Finn*
    are one of America's national treasures.
    ‾A‾ ‾B‾   ‾C‾   ‾D‾

(A) Verb. The correct answer is "is." The subject of this sentence is the name of one book, so the verb must be singular.

38. In his early days as a direct, Charlie Chaplin
        ‾A‾   ‾B‾

    produced 62 short silent comedy films in four
                  ‾C‾   ‾D‾
    years.

(B) Word form. The correct answer is "director," a noun that describes a person.

39. Some studies show that young babies prefer the
                              ‾A‾

    smell of milk to those of other liquids.
    ‾B‾   ‾C‾   ‾D‾

(C) Pronoun. The correct phrase is "to that of other liquids." Since "that" refers to "milk," a singular noun, the pronoun must also be singular.

40. Plants absorb water and nutrients and
            ‾A‾

    anchoring themselves in the soil with their roots.
    ‾B‾   ‾C‾   ‾D‾

(B) Verb/parallel construction. The correct phrase is "anchor themselves." This sentence is describing two things that plants do: (1) absorb water, and (2) anchor themselves in the soil. The verbs must both be simple present tense.

SECTION 3

Reading Comprehension

1. What does the passage mainly discuss?
  (A) twentieth-century music of the South
  (B) a change in the role of the blues harp
  (C) good harpmen of the traditional blues harp
  (D) the variety of instruments in jug bands

(B) This is a main idea question. The main topic is the evolution of the blues harp into a lead instrument. The final sentences of the passage emphasize the change from a support to a lead instrument.

2. The blues harp is another name for the
  (A) harpsichord
  (B) guitar
  (C) harmonica
  (D) banjo

(C) In the first sentence the word "or" indicates that the blues harp is the same as the harmonica.

3. The word "flourished" as used in line 1 could best be replaced by which of the following?
  (A) began to burgeon
  (B) was profound
  (C) appeared
  (D) entertained

(A) The verb "to burgeon" means "to thrive," "to grow," or "to put forth new life," which is similar in meaning to "flourish."

4. The author uses the phrase "rural South" in line 1 to refer to the southern
  (A) landscape
  (B) metropolis
  (C) countryside
  (D) nation

(C) The word "rural" means "country" or "country-side." It is the opposite of "urban" or "city."

5. It can be inferred that George "Bullet" Williams
  (A) was the best blues harp player
  (B) became friends with the later harpmen
  (C) played lead guitar in his band
  (D) influenced some of the later harpmen

(D) This is an inference question. The best clue to the answer is the word "followed" in the final sentence. Because they came after Williams, these other men either had heard his music or had heard of it, and they were probably influenced by their knowledge of what Williams did. While it is possible that Williams might have become friends with some of these men, this is not mentioned in the passage. Though the passage infers that Williams was a good player, it does not say that he was the best player (answer A). Answer (C) is incorrect because it refers to Williams as playing a guitar, not a harp.

6. As used in line 5, the word "primarily" could best be replaced by
  (A) chiefly
  (B) peculiarly
  (C) favorably
  (D) advantageously

(A) This is a vocabulary question. The word "primarily" means "mainly" or "chiefly."

7. According to the author, when was the harp first used as a lead instrument?
  (A) 1920–1925
  (B) 1925–1930
  (C) 1930–1935
  (D) 1935–1940

(B) In line 6 the author states that "Bullet" Williams made recordings in the late 1920s, which is closest to 1925–1930.

8. The word "lead" as used in line 6 is closest in meaning to which of the following?
(A) model
(B) only
(C) control
(D) principal

(D) The word "lead" in this sentence refers to the use of the harp as the main instrument for melody, as compared to being used only for support. The word "principal" also refers to being the main or most important thing. Answer (B) is similar to the word "sole," but in this sentence the words "only" and "lead" are not synonymous but give two variations of the role of the blues harp.

9. In line 6, the word "recordings" most likely refers to
(A) readings
(B) tapes
(C) records
(D) movies

(C) Since "recordings" refers to preserving sound, and since the year is sometime in the 1920s, we can infer that this refers to records and not cassette tapes or compact disks.

10. The word "revolutionizing" in line 8 could best be replaced by which of the following?
(A) reforming
(B) fighting
(C) resisting
(D) turning

(A) The words "revolutionizing" and "reforming" both refer to making a change in something.

11. Which of the following would most likely be the topic of the previous paragraph?
(A) the use of instruments for rhythmic support in rural southern music in the 1920s
(B) lead instruments in rural southern music of the 1920s
(C) music in the American rural South before 1920
(D) jug bands and their role in 1920s southern music

(B) This is a question of the previous possible topic. The first sentence implies that the previous topic was also about rural southern music in the 1920s and 1930s, and the last two sentences focus on the role of the blues harp in its change to becoming a lead instrument. By this we can infer that the previous topic was also about rural instruments that were lead instruments.

12. According to the passage, jug bands were likely to perform in all of the following places EXCEPT
(A) on street corners
(B) at country suppers
(C) in concert halls
(D) in saloons

(C) According to the third sentence, jug bands commonly played "on street corners, in saloons, and at country suppers." There is no mention of performing in a concert hall.

13. What is the main topic of this passage?
(A) the number of nonnative users of English
(B) the French influence on the English language
(C) the expansion of English as an international language
(D) the use of English for science and technology

(C) This is a main idea question. Answers (A), (B), and (D) are all mentioned in the passage but are too narrow to be the general idea.

14. The word "emerged" in line 2 could best be replaced by which of the following?
(A) appeared
(B) hailed
(C) frequented
(D) engaged

(A) This is a vocabulary question. The words "emerged" and "appeared" both refer to something gradually coming into view. In this sentence, the meaning is that the English we use today began to be used around the year 1350.

15. As used in line 3, the word "elements" is most similar to
    (A) declarations
    (B) features
    (C) curiosities
    (D) customs

(B) This is a vocabulary question. The words "elements" and "features" both mean "parts" of something. In this sentence, the "parts" may be any part of a language: words, structures, pronunciation, spelling, and so forth.

16. The word "extended" as used in line 4 is most similar to which of the following?
    (A) experienced
    (B) conferred
    (C) spread
    (D) stretched

(C) This is a vocabulary question. The word "extended" usually means "prolonged" or "made longer." In this sentence, however, it is most similar to "spread," which means "extend out" or "move out." Answer (D) is also similar in meaning, but it is more commonly used to mean "extend out fully" or "extend forcibly."

17. Approximately when did English begin to be used beyond England?
    (A) in 1066
    (B) around 1350
    (C) before 1600
    (D) after 1600

(D) This is a restatement question. The passage states that English began to spread beyond England during the two centuries after 1600.

18. According to the passage, all of the following contributed to the spread of English around the world EXCEPT
    (A) the slave trade
    (B) the Norman invasion
    (C) missionaries
    (D) colonization

(B) This is a negative question. The Norman invasion brought French influence to the English language, but it did not contribute to the spread of English worldwide, as did (A), (C), and (D).

19. As used in line 5, which of the following is closest in meaning to the word "course"?
    (A) subject
    (B) policy
    (C) time
    (D) track

(C) This is a vocabulary question. All of the above can mean "course" in some contexts, but in this sentence "course" is similar to the "development of time" or the "progression of time."

20. The word "enclaves" in line 7 could best be replaced by which of the following?
    (A) communities
    (B) organizations
    (C) regions
    (D) countries

(A) This is a vocabulary question. The word "enclaves" refers to small groups or communities that share some commonality.

21. The word "proliferated" in line 8 is closest in meaning to which of the following?
    (A) prospered
    (B) organized
    (C) disbanded
    (D) expanded

(D) This is a vocabulary question. The verb "to proliferate" means "to grow," "to expand," or "to increase in numbers."

22. Which of the following is closest in meaning to the word "stored" as used in line 10?
    (A) bought
    (B) saved
    (C) spent
    (D) valued

(B) This is a vocabulary question. The verb "to store" means "to save" or "to keep for later use."

23. Which of the following is closest in meaning to the word "constituting" in line 13?
    (A) looking over
    (B) setting down
    (C) doing in
    (D) making up

(D) This is a vocabulary question. The verbs "to constitute" and "to make up" both mean "to compose," "to comprise," or "to form the basis of" something.

24. According to the passage, approximately how many nonnative users of English are there in the world today?
    (A) a quarter million
    (B) half a million
    (C) 350 million
    (D) 700 million

(C) This is a restatement/computation question. The passage states that about half of the 700 million speakers of English are nonnative speakers, which is approximately 350 million.

25. What does the passage mainly discuss?
    (A) risk factors in heart attacks
    (B) seasonal and temporal patterns of heart attacks
    (C) cardiology findings in the 1980s
    (D) diet and stress as factors in heart attacks

(A) This is a main idea question. Answers (B) and (D) refer only to portions of the passage, but not the main idea. Answer (C) is too general.

26. In line 2, the word "potential" could best be replaced by which of the following?
    (A) harmful
    (B) primary
    (C) unknown
    (D) possible

(D) This is a vocabulary question. The word "potential" in this context refers to possible, but not yet confirmed, factors.

27. The word "trigger" as used in line 2 is closest in meaning to which of the following?
    (A) involve
    (B) affect
    (C) cause
    (D) encounter

(C) This is a vocabulary question. The word "trigger" means "to set off" or "to cause something to begin."

28. Which of the following could best replace the word "incidence" as used in line 3?
    (A) increase
    (B) rate
    (C) chance
    (D) factor

(B) This is a vocabulary question. The words "incidence" and "rate" both refer to the frequency with which something occurs.

29. The author uses the word "temporal" in line 5 to mean
    (A) affected by
    (B) of a certain date
    (C) expected
    (D) regularly

(A) This is a vocabulary question. In this sentence, the word "temporal" refers to time. Answer (B) is too specific. Answer (C) might be inferred, but it is not the meaning of "temporal." Answer (D) is similar in meaning to "temporal," but it is not as specific.

30. The phrase "susceptible to" in line 7 could best be replaced by
    (A) aware of
    (B) affected by
    (C) accustomed to
    (D) prone to

(D) This is a vocabulary question. The phrases "susceptible to" and "prone to" both mean that one is "vulnerable to" something.

31. According to the passage, which of the following is NOT a possible cause of many heart attacks?
    (A) decreased blood flow to the heart
    (B) increased blood pressure
    (C) lower heart rate
    (D) increase in hormones

(C) This is a negative question. Answers (A), (B), and (D) are all mentioned as possible causes of heart attacks in the early morning.

32. The word "phenomenon" in line 8 refers to which of the following?
    (A) habit
    (B) illness
    (C) occurrence
    (D) activity

(C) This is a vocabulary question. The word "phenomenon" means an event or happening; that is, something that occurs.

33. The word "implicated" in line 12 could best be replaced by which of the following?
    (A) indicated
    (B) disregarded
    (C) investigated
    (D) discovered

(A) This is a vocabulary question. The words "implicate" and "indicate" can both mean "suggest" or "infer."

34. Which of the following is NOT cited as a possible risk factor?
    (A) having a birthday
    (B) getting married
    (C) eating fatty foods
    (D) being under stress

(B) This is a negative question. Answers (A), (C), and (D) are all mentioned as possible factors in the increase of heart attacks. Answer (B) is the opposite of what is stated.

35. Which of the following does the passage infer?
    (A) We now fully understand how risk factors trigger heart attacks.
    (B) We recently began to study how risk factors trigger heart attacks.
    (C) We have not identified many risk factors associated with heart attacks.
    (D) We do not fully understand how risk factors trigger heart attacks.

(D) This is an inference question. The final sentence of the passage indicates that many risk factors have been identified over the years, but how these factors actually trigger heart attacks is not clearly understood and is still being studied.

36. As used in line 13, which of the following could best replace the word "reveal"?
    (A) show
    (B) observe
    (C) mean
    (D) explain

(A) This is a vocabulary question. The words "reveal" and "show" both mean "to disclose" or "to give information about" something. Answer (B) means "to see." Answer (C) means "to imply" or "to suggest." Answer (D) is similar in that it also means "to give information," but the meaning is a bit different. The statistics do not "explain" the heart attacks; instead, they make certain facts known to all.

37. What does this passage mainly discuss?
    (A) the difference between fastballs and curveballs
    (B) America's favorite pastime
    (C) illusions about the movements of pitched balls
    (D) perceptual problems among baseball players

(C) This is a main idea question. The main idea of this passage is that the pitched balls, called "fastballs" and "curves," are not really thrown faster or more curved by the pitcher; rather, it is the batter who sees them that way because of the visual illusion.

38. As used in line 1, the word "contend" could best be replaced by which of the following?
    (A) maintain
    (B) operate
    (C) propose
    (D) suppose

(A) This is a vocabulary question. The verbs "to contend" and "to maintain" in this context both mean "to declare" or "to insist."

39. Which of the following words could best replace the word "thrill" in line 1?
    (A) activity
    (B) excitement
    (C) remedy
    (D) issue

(B) This is a vocabulary question. The word "thrill" refers to a feeling of sudden intense excitement, joy, or sometimes fear.

40. In line 3, the word "exasperating" could best be replaced by which of the following?
    (A) challenging
    (B) exhausting
    (C) exciting
    (D) frustrating

(D) This is a vocabulary question. To be exasperated means to be angry, irritated, or annoyed, generally as a result of frustration.

41. As used in line 5, the word "zooms" is closest in meaning to which of the following?
    (A) falls
    (B) rolls
    (C) speeds
    (D) bounces

(C) This is a vocabulary question. The word "zoom" means to go fast, or "speed."

42. Which of the following words could best replace the word "plunges" as used in line 6?
    (A) drops
    (B) withdraws
    (C) emerges
    (D) tips

(A) This is a vocabulary question. In this context, the words "to plunge" and "to drop" both refer to something falling suddenly or rushing downward.

43. According to the author, why is it difficult for the batter to hit the "rising fastball" and the "breaking curveball"?
    (A) Because the ball approaches too quickly
    (B) Because the ball veers just before reaching home plate
    (C) Because the batter misjudges the pitcher's intention
    (D) Because the batter misjudges the speed and angle of the ball

(D) This is a restatement question. In the second paragraph of the passage the author states that it is the batter's misperception that makes the balls hard to hit. In the first paragraph the author describes what the batter thinks and what many people think they see (answer B), but the second paragraph of this passage states that this is only an optical illusion.

44. In line 10, what does the word "they" refer to?
    (A) the "rising fastball" and the "breaking curveball"
    (B) the engineers and psychologists
    (C) the research studies
    (D) the optical illusions

(A) This is a referent question. The word "they" refers to the closest, previous head noun phrase, which in this sentence is the phrase "the 'rising fastball' and the 'breaking curveball.'"

45. Which of the following is closest in meaning to the word "gaze" as used in line 14?
    (A) to glance quickly
    (B) to blink rapidly
    (C) to look steadily
    (D) to peek briefly

(C) This is a vocabulary question. The word "gaze" refers to a look that is long and steady. Each of the the the others refers to a brief look. Answer (A) refers to a brief glance. Answer (B) refers to the eyes opening and closing quickly. Answer (D) refers to a brief look, often in a shy manner.

46. According to the passage, how is the optical illusion of the "rising fastball" and the "breaking curveball" produced?
    (A) by the pitcher's delivery
    (B) by the batter's failing to track the ball accurately
    (C) by the speed and angle of the ball
    (D) by the studies of engineers and psychologists

(B) This is a restatement question. In the second paragraph, the author states that it is the batter's inability to track the ball accurately that causes the illusion. The batter briefly looks away from the ball and as a result misjudges the angle and speed of the ball. The studies of engineers and psychologists did not produce the illusion; they produced written studies about the illusion.

47. Which of the following words could best replace the word "vehemently" in line 16?
    (A) certainly
    (B) impassively
    (C) socially
    (D) furiously

(D) This is a vocabulary question. The words "vehemently" and "furiously" both mean "passionately," "intensely," and "strongly." Answer (A) means "very sure." Answer (B) is the opposite of (D). Answer (C) refers to social relations in a group; it might refer to "friendliness."

48. The word "imbue" in line 18 is closest in meaning to which of the following?
    (A) fill
    (B) spoil
    (C) affect
    (D) change

(A) This is a vocabulary question. The verb "to imbue" means "to penetrate," "to inspire," or "to fill with ideas or feelings."

49. What is the main topic of the passage?
    (A) why Timber rattlesnakes hibernate
    (B) how Timber rattlesnakes are surviving
    (C) how Timber rattlesnakes adapted to northern climates
    (D) why Timber rattlesnakes are endangered

(D) This is a main idea question. The first paragraph introduces the topic of the Timber rattlesnake as an endangered species. The following paragraphs explain why they are endangered, what they have done to adapt to cold weather, and how their behavior contributes to their being endangered. Answers (A), (B), and (C) are too narrow; they are specific issues discussed in the passage but are not the main topic.

50. Which of the following is closest in meaning to the word "vulnerable" in line 3?
    (A) unprotected
    (B) impervious
    (C) insensitive
    (D) deprived

(A) This is a vocabulary question. The word "vulnerable" refers to be subject to danger, injury, or attack. The word "unprotected" is the closest synonym. Answer (B) means "incapable of being penetrated or affected." Answer (C) means "not capable of intense feelings." Answer (D) means "not having" or "not able to have."

51. Which of the following is true about Timber rattlesnakes?
    (A) They migrated to the eastern states.
    (B) They migrated northward during a warming period.
    (C) They migrated to escape a cold climate.
    (D) They migrated to the South to seek a warmer climate.

(B) This is an inference question. The passage states that Timber rattlesnakes migrated northward as glaciers retreated or melted, which can only happen during a warming period.

52. In line 11, the word "crevices" could be replaced by which of the following?
    (A) tombs
    (B) rocks
    (C) cracks
    (D) tunnels

(C) This is a vocabulary question. The words "crevice" and "crack" both refer to a narrow separation between two things or fracture of a hard substance. The snakes climb inside the crevices to be protected.

53. Which of the following could best replace the word "emerge" in line 12?
    (A) come out
    (B) set off
    (C) get up
    (D) see through

(A) This is a vocabulary question. The words "emerge" and "come out" both mean "to rise into view" or "to appear." Answer (B) means "to start" or "to begin" something. Answer (C) means "to stand up." Answer (D) has many meanings, including "to perceive."

54. In which of the following places might a person be most likely to find Timber rattlesnakes in the spring?
    (A) in the woods
    (B) in meadows
    (C) in bushy areas
    (D) in canyons

(B) This is an inference question. The passage states that the rattlesnakes lie on rocks in open areas, which means areas that get direct sun. Of the above answers, the most open area would be a meadow. In woods, bushes, and canyons, there would most likely be more shade.

55. Which of the following could best replace the phrase "coupled with" in line 13?
    (A) compared with
    (B) combined with
    (C) controlled with
    (D) supported with

(B) This is a vocabulary question. The word "coupled" means joined or combined, the bringing together of two or more factors (ideas, people, etc.).

56. The phrase "easy prey" in line 14 could best be replaced by which of the following?
- **(A)** relaxed
- **(B)** protective
- **(C)** victims
- **(D)** sociable

(C) This is a vocabulary question. In this sentence, the word "prey" refers to an animal that is killed by another animal. The phrase "easy prey" refers to the fact that it is easy for an animal to find and kill the snakes while they are lying in the sun in large numbers. The best synonym is "victim."

57. Which of the following words can best replace the word "basking" in line 15?
- **(A)** washing
- **(B)** eating
- **(C)** sleeping
- **(D)** lying

(D) This is a vocabulary question. The word "to bask" means "to relax in the warmth of the sun." The word "basking" does not mean "sleeping," even though one may fall asleep while basking. The best choice is "lying," since the snakes must be lying while basking.

58. According to the passage, which of the following does NOT contribute to the rattlesnake being an endangered animal?
- **(A)** hibernating for eight months
- **(B)** basking in the sun
- **(C)** congregating together
- **(D)** long intervals between births

(A) This is a negative question. Of all the above, answers (B), (C), and (D) are reasons given that make the snake vulnerable. The only protective measure is (A), since the snakes are hidden in the rocks when they hibernate.

59. Which of the following could best replace the word "depredation" in line 20?
- **(A)** fear
- **(B)** habitation
- **(C)** destruction
- **(D)** depression

(C) This is a vocabulary question. The word "depredation" refers to complete destruction.

60. What is the author's attitude toward the topic?
- **(A)** accusative
- **(B)** nostalgic
- **(C)** regretful
- **(D)** humorous

(C) This is an author's-attitude question. In this passage, the author projects a feeling of regret for the demise of the Timber rattlesnake. This is evident in the final sentence, where the author states that it is already too late to save the rattlesnake. The author does not seem to accuse people of killing rattlesnakes (answer A), to yearn for the past (answer B), or to be funny (answer D).

Test 6 • Answers

FOUR

Tapescripts for Practice Tests

C O N T E N T S

Practice Test 1

SECTION 1

Listening Comprehension

Part A

Directions: In Part A you will hear short conversations between two people. After each conversation a third person will ask a question about what was said. You will hear the conversation only one time, so you must listen carefully to what each speaker says. After you hear the conversation and the question, read the four possible answers in your test booklet and pick the one which best answers the question. Then look on the answer sheet for the number of the question and fill in the oval that corresponds to the letter of your answer choice.

Listen to an example.

> *You will hear:*
>
> > Woman: Have you called Pete?
> > > Man: I'll call him as soon as I get home.
>
> > What does the man mean?

> *You will read:*
> (A) He will call Pete before he goes home.
> (B) He will call Pete after he gets home.
> (C) He called Pete at home.
> (D) He will call Pete tomorrow.

You learn from the conversation that the man will call Pete as soon as he gets home. The best answer to the question "What does the man mean?" is (B), "He will call Pete after he gets home." Therefore, the correct answer is (B).

Now continue listening to the tape.

[To the Reader: Pause 12 seconds after the third person asks each question.]

1. Woman: Didn't Kathleen go traveling with you last summer?
   Man: Are you kidding? Even if it didn't cost anything, she'd rather stay home.

   What does the man imply about Kathleen?

2. Woman: You bought another book on architecture?
   Man: This book has some details I need.

   What does the man mean?

3. Man: Professor Benson is working in his lab this afternoon.
   Woman: But his vacation isn't over until next week.

   What did Professor Benson probably do?

4. Man: I was surprised when you told me that Connie and David have become good friends.
   Woman: I know. They didn't used to get along well, did they?

   What does the woman mean?

5. Man: Have you been to the city museum?

    Woman: Twice, I believe.

    What does the woman mean?

6. Man: Excuse me, Amy, is it possible for us to switch our shifts this week?

    Woman: Which day do you want to switch to?

    What does the woman imply?

7. Woman: Greg says he's going to take three extra classes.

    Man: He's got to be kidding.

    What does the man mean?

8. Woman: I need to advertise for another roommate for next semester.

    Man: Why bother? Sandy is interested.

    What does the man mean?

9. Man: How did the movie end?

    Woman: I don't know; it'll be continued tonight.

    What does the woman mean?

10. Man: Do you want to see if I can get tickets to the football game next week?

    Woman: I don't think we stand a chance, but try anyway.

    What does the woman mean?

11. Woman: Do you really mean you want to quit this job?

    Man: Well, maybe I'd better give it a second thought.

    What is the man going to do?

12. Man: You should persuade Alex to change his major.

    Woman: Why? He's mature enough to make up his own mind.

    What does the woman mean?

13. Woman: Are you going to the group meeting tonight?

    Man: I can't, I have another commitment.

    What does the man mean?

14. Woman: Hey, Jim, how was your vacation?

    Man: Oh, I did nothing but study.

    What does the man mean?

15. Woman: Do you think Laura will accept this proposal?

    Man: No way.

    What does the man mean?

16. Man: Why did Sue change her schedule?

    Woman: So she could leave from a closer airport.

    What does the woman imply about Sue?

17. Man: Can I eat this fruit as it is?

    Woman: No, you have to peel it first.

    What does the woman mean?

18. Woman: Marcus didn't get the score he wanted.

    Man: But he did pass the test.

    What are they saying about Marcus?

19. Woman: I feel like it's only been a few weeks since school started.

    Man: And it's already almost time for our final exams!

    What do the speakers imply?

20. Woman: What does Rich want?

    Man: He wants some ice for his sore shoulder.

    What does the man imply about Rich?

Part B

Directions: In Part B you will hear longer conversations between two people. After each conversation you will be asked some questions. You will hear the conversations and the questions only once, so listen carefully to what is said. After you hear a question, read the four possible answers in your test book and decide which one is the best answer to the question you heard. Then, on your answer sheet, find the number of the question and fill in the oval that corresponds to the letter of the answer you have chosen. Answer all questions based on what is stated or implied by the speakers.

Listen to the example.

You will hear:

Questions 1 and 2 are based on the following conversation between two friends at school.

Man: Hi, Joanie. Where are you going?
Woman: Oh, hi Paul. I'm on my way to the library.
Man: I just wondered if you wanted to go to a movie with me.
Woman: I'd love to, but I can't. I can't believe all the work I have this semester. I only have three classes, but in all of them I have lots of reading, term papers, reports, and essay exams. It's incredible! I feel like I'll never get through everything.
Man: That's terrible. I felt that way last year when I had term papers to write, but this semester seems much easier. I spend a lot of time in class, but most of it is in labs doing experiments. I hated writing all those term papers. Can't I talk you into going to the show anyway? I've heard that the movie over at the East Auditorium is really good. It's a murder mystery.
Woman: Oh, now I'm sure I won't go. I might go to a comedy, but I hate murder mysteries.

Now listen to sample question number 1.

Where is the woman going?

In your test booklet you will read:

    (A) to the cafeteria
    (B) to the movie theater
    (C) to her dorm room
    (D) to the library

The best answer to the question "Where is the woman going?" is (D), "to the library." Therefore, the correct choice is (D).

Now listen to sample question number 2.

Which best describes the man's feelings about his classes?

You will read:

    (A) Term papers are easy for him.
    (B) He has a lot of essay exams.
    (C) He finds lab experiments easier than writing term papers.
    (D) He is busier this semester than last semester.

The best answer to the question "Which best describes the man's feelings about his classes?" is (C), "He finds lab experiments easier than writing term papers." Therefore, the correct answer is (C).

Now listen to the test. Remember, you are not allowed to take any notes or write in your test book.

Questions 21 to 24. Listen to the following conversation between an instructor and a student:

Woman: Hi, Jack. Come in. As you know, I'm meeting with all the students to talk about their class research projects. Can you tell me what you're planning to write about?

Man: Yes. At this point I'm thinking about investigating the Anasazi Indian civilization in the Southwest desert states. When I traveled there last summer, I got really interested in these people, and I've found some good sources of information about them. Maybe I will focus on why their civilization suddenly ended in about the year 1400.

Woman: That sounds very interesting, and it looks like you've got a good start. I think Eddy in our class is also writing about the Anasazi, but he's taking a different focus. Maybe you could call him to see if you could share some information. Are you finding enough books and articles?

Man: Yes, I think I'm OK so far.

Woman: Good. If you need any help, come in and let's talk about it. At any rate, I'm going to make appointments with everyone again in three weeks to look at your rough draft.

Man: All right, Dr. Fisher. Thanks.

Woman: Sure. See you in class tomorrow.

[To the Reader: Pause 12 seconds after each question.]

21. What is this conversation mainly about?

22. Where was the Anasazi civilization located in the United States?

23. What subject is the student going to focus on?

24. Which of the following things does the woman say?

Questions 25 to 27. The following conversation takes place in a train station:

Man: Next, please.

Woman: Yes, how much does a ticket to New York cost?

Man: $30.50.

Woman: That's really expensive. Are there any other trains going to New York?

Man: Well, there's the late train that arrives in New York at midnight and then continues on to Boston the next morning.

Woman: How much is that?

Man: The ticket for the late train to New York is $22.

Woman: That sounds better. I'd like one ticket please.

Man: $22 exactly.

Woman: Thanks.

Man: Thank you and have a nice trip.

[To the Reader: Pause 12 seconds after each question.]

25. Where is the woman interested in going?

26. What is the woman's response to the first train mentioned?

27. Why is one ticket cheaper?

Questions 28 to 31. Listen to the following conversation between two students:

Man:	Hey Jane, where are you going this weekend?
Woman:	Hi, Bob. I'm going to the beach with some friends. Do you want to come, too?
Man:	Yeah, that sounds like fun. Which beach are you going to?
Woman:	We were thinking about driving north to Grover's Beach. I like to watch the sea birds and wildlife there.
Man:	That sounds great! When do you plan to leave?
Woman:	Well, I think at about four o'clock on Friday.
Man:	Do you have space for me in one of the cars?
Woman:	Sure, we'll fit you into a car.
Man:	Great. Where should we meet?
Woman:	Meet me on Friday in front of my house.
Man:	OK, I'll see you then. Bye.

[To the Reader: Pause 12 seconds after each question.]

28. What is the main topic of this conversation?

29. What can you infer about these two speakers?

30. Why does the woman like going to Grover's Beach?

31. When do they plan to meet again?

Questions 32 to 35. Listen to the following conversation between two friends:

Man:	We need to take a vacation.
Woman:	Well, we both have two weeks of vacation time. Why don't we drive north to Canada?
Man:	I'd like to go camping, maybe in the mountains.
Woman:	That sounds good to me. I'm so tired of city living. New York is so congested and full of traffic all the time. We need to get away from that.
Man:	Ahh, just us and the mountains. Do you want to leave tomorrow?
Woman:	Sure, of course. Hey, why don't we leave tonight? Why wait?
Man:	Well, we haven't packed our backpacks and the car needs an oil change. I need to check the engine tonight if we're going to leave in the morning.
Woman:	OK, well, why don't you go fix the car while I go up to the attic and get out the camping things.
Man:	Sounds great. I'll be out in the garage, so just yell if you need me for anything.
Woman:	OK.

[To the Reader: Pause 12 seconds after each question.]

32. What are the two speakers talking about doing?

33. Where is this conversation most likely taking place?

34. Why does the woman want to spend her vacation camping?

35. Why can't they leave that night for their vacation?

Part C

Directions: In this part of the test, you will hear talks by a single person. After each talk, you will be asked some questions. You will hear the talks and the questions only once, so listen carefully to what is said. After you hear a question, read the four possible answers in your test book and decide which one is the best answer to the question you heard. Then, find the number of the question on your answer sheet, and fill in the oval that corresponds to the letter of the answer you have chosen. Answer all questions based on what is stated or implied in the talk.

Listen to this sample talk.

You will hear:

Questions 1-4 are based on the following announcement:

[FEMALE SPEAKER]

At this university we offer three different programs for students who have children. For those of you with very young children, we have a day care program that takes infants from 3 months to 30 months. We have another program for children between two and five years of age. And we also have an after-school program for school-aged children. This program offers sports, crafts, outings, and tutoring during after-school hours. Enrollment in these child care programs is limited and early application is essential, since our programs often have waiting lists. The fees are on an hourly basis. If any of you new students need these services, please let me know right away so I can get you an application form.

Now listen to sample question number 1.

What is the main purpose of this announcement?

You will read:

       (A) to demonstrate tutoring techniques
       (B) to explain school policies
       (C) to recruit childcare workers
       (D) to explain a service

The best answer to the question "What is the purpose of this announcement?" is (D), "to explain a service." Therefore, the correct choice is (D).

Now listen to sample question number 2.

What does the speaker recommend?

You will read:

       (A) Give your child extra tutoring.
       (B) Take your child to the program today.
       (C) Apply as soon as you can.
       (D) Pay next month.

The best answer to the question "What does the speaker recommend?" is (C), "Apply as soon as you can." Therefore the correct choice is (C).

Now listen to the talks. Remember, you are not allowed to write any notes in your test book.

Questions 36 to 39. Listen to the following lecture by a professor:

[MALE SPEAKER]

While we're talking about the media, let me tell you about a little known magazine that was printed in New York City before World War I. This magazine with its strong socialist political views published articles on such topics as free love, feminism, and peace that wouldn't really become popular again in this country until the late 1960s. It was very influential in some circles in this country. The magazine was called *The Masses,* and was especially popular in Greenwich Village, a neighborhood in New York famous for its unusual cultural life. The students and artists who populated Greenwich Village in those days had a lifestyle that was unique for their time. People would go there to discuss political ideas such as the growing movements for peace during World War I and women's right to vote. *The Masses* covered not only the people and life of Greenwich Village, but also hot political topics that were rarely spoken of by most Americans during these prewar years.

[To the Reader: Pause 12 seconds after each question.]

36. What is the main topic of this lecture?

37. When was *The Masses* first published?

38. Which of the following topics would most likely be printed in *The Masses*?

39. What class would this lecture most likely be a part of?

Questions 40 to 43. Listen to the following announcement at a zoo:

[FEMALE SPEAKER]

Ladies and gentlemen, may I have your attention please. There will be three animal shows this afternoon at the City Zoo. The first show will begin at three o'clock in the marine arena. There, Flipper, the dolphin, and Orca, the killer whale, will dazzle the audience with jumps and flips and other funny antics. The second show will be a feeding of the monkeys and apes at four o'clock in the primate center. Visitors can assist the staff in feeding the apes and playing with the monkeys. The last show will be at 4:30 in the giant bird cage, where Dr. Smith will give a guided tour, pointing out more than 300 species of birds from Central and South America. If you have any questions about these shows or other upcoming events at the zoo, please ask at the information booth at the main entrance next to the gift shop. Thank you.

[To the Reader: Pause 12 seconds after each question.]

40. What is the purpose of this announcement?

41. Which of the following kinds of animals is one of the shows featuring?

42. What will Dr. Smith give a guided tour of?

43. Where does the announcer say that a person can get information about the animal show times?

Questions 44 to 46. Listen to the following introduction to a class:

[MALE SPEAKER]

Good morning. My name is John Smith, and I will be the main instructor for this semester's history class, The American South after the Civil War. We'll read books covering the years after 1865, when the Union defeated the Confederate forces of the southern states. There will be three midterms and one final exam at the end of the semester. In addition, there will also be one paper that is due on December 15th, at the end of this school term.

The first topic we'll be discussing is the famous speech made by Abraham Lincoln after the decisive battle at Gettysburg in the state of Pennsylvania. This speech is one of the most famous in American history, and I think it appropriately describes the feelings of many people at that time during this war between American states.

[To the Reader: Pause 12 seconds after each question.]

  44. What subject is this introduction mainly about?

  45. What is the significance of December 15th?

  46. What will the speaker probably discuss next?

Questions 47 to 50. Listen to the following introduction given by a lecturer:

[FEMALE SPEAKER]

Today we are going to listen to one of the greatest musical pieces ever composed. But before we begin listening to the *Messiah* by Handel, I would like to mention that there is no original version of the *Messiah*. Handel was a practical man and he altered the symphony depending on the instruments he could use and the special conditions at a specific performance. The version you are going to hear today is a collection of different performances by the London Philharmonic of the version that Handel wrote in 1750. There are only 50 instruments and 70 voices. In later years, conductors would often add more instruments. At one performance called "The Grand National Celebration of Peace," given in Boston in 1869, there were at least 10,000 voices and 500 instruments. It has not been until recent years that conductors have begun to study Handel's original arrangements of the *Messiah* and have performed the piece with much smaller ensembles. One final note to consider is that most people associate the *Messiah* with Christmas; but, this was not what Handel intended. He wrote the *Messiah* to be performed in the spring, just before Easter.

[To the Reader: Pause 12 seconds after each question.]

  47. What is this lecture about?

  48. What is the name of the musical piece the speaker describes?

  49. How have the versions of this work varied throughout the years?

  50. What celebration was this work intended for?

This is the end of Section 1, Listening Comprehension. Turn off the tape and continue with Section 2, Structure and Written Expression.

Practice Test 2
SECTION 1
Listening Comprehension

Part A

Directions: In Part A you will hear short conversations between two people. After each conversation a third person will ask a question about what was said. You will hear the conversation only one time, so you must listen carefully to what each speaker says. After you hear the conversation and the question, read the four possible answers in your test booklet and pick the one which best answers the question. Then look on the answer sheet for the number of the question and fill in the oval that corresponds to the letter of your answer choice.

Listen to an example.

You will hear:

> Woman: Have you called Pete?
> Man: I'll call him as soon as I get home.

What does the man mean?

You will read:

> (A) He will call Pete before he goes home.
> (B) He will call Pete after he gets home.
> (C) He called Pete at home.
> (D) He will call Pete tomorrow.

You learn from the conversation that the man will call Pete as soon as he gets home. The best answer to the question "What does the man mean?" is (B), "He will call Pete after he gets home." Therefore, the correct answer is (B).

Now continue listening to the tape.

[To the Reader: Pause 12 seconds after the third person asks each question.]

1. Man: These gloves look good as a gift for my nephew, but I don't know if they will fit.
   Woman: Look, it says one size fits all.

   What does the woman mean?

2. Man: Oh no, I can't use the computer to test my experiment; I'll never get my paper finished in time.
   Woman: Why don't you begin with the library research part?

   What does the woman suggest the man do?

3. Woman: Come on, what are we waiting for?
   Man: I can't start until you put your seat belt on.

   What does the man mean?

4. Woman: Oh, this line is for tickets to the wrong show.
   Man: We'd better move to the other line.

   What are the people going to do?

5. Man: I was really worried about doing well at my presentation this afternoon.

    Woman: But it turned out well, didn't it?

    What does the woman mean?

6. Woman: Dan, how would you like your egg cooked?

    Man: Medium please.

    What is the woman probably going to do?

7. Woman: I'm glad I called to check on the time for picking Sue up.

    Man: Was the plane delayed again?

    What does the man imply about Sue?

8. Woman: Do you know Jack?

    Man: Yes, I do; in fact he's my cousin.

    What does the man mean?

9. Man: I can't stand living in this place anymore.

    Woman: Well, why don't you move then?

    What does the woman suggest the man do?

10. Woman: It's really rocky here.

    Man: Yes, watch your step so you don't trip.

    What does the man mean?

11. Woman: I have so much to do!

    Man: Take it easy, school doesn't start until next week.

    What does the man mean?

12. Man: I feel like taking a walk; it's so nice outside.

    Woman: Great, let's walk around the lake in the park.

    What does the woman mean?

13. Woman: I happened to find the book you were looking for when I was in the bookstore.

    Man: Oh, which one?

    What does the man mean?

14. Man: Is that it for today?

    Woman: That's it.

    What does the woman mean?

15. Man: Here's our telephone bill.

    Woman: Good, why don't you figure out your calls, and I'll pay the rest.

    What does the woman mean?

16. Man: Can I eat one of these bananas?

    Woman: They're not ready to eat yet.

    What does the woman mean?

17. Man: We were on vacation for two weeks.

    Woman: And half the time it was rainy.

    What does the woman imply?

18. Man: Kathleen, how did you like your organic chemistry class?

    Woman: The more I learned, the better it got.

    What does the woman mean?

19. Man: You made a reservation for ten, right?

    Woman: I sure did.

    What does the woman mean?

20. Man: Penny's still going to Smith College, isn't she?

    Woman: No, she transferred to Yale.

    What do they say about Penny?

Part B

Directions: In Part B you will hear longer conversations between two people. After each conversation you will be asked some questions. You will hear the conversations and the questions only once, so listen carefully to what is said. After you hear a question, read the four possible answers in your test book and decide which one is the best answer to the question you heard. Then, on your answer sheet, find the number of the question and fill in the oval that corresponds to the letter of the answer you have chosen. Answer all questions based on what is stated or implied by the speakers.

Listen to the example.

You will hear:

Questions 1 and 2 are based on the following conversation between two friends at school.

> Man: Hi, Joanie. Where are you going?
> Woman: Oh, hi Paul. I'm on my way to the library.
> Man: I just wondered if you wanted to go to a movie with me.
> Woman: I'd love to, but I can't. I can't believe all the work I have this semester. I only have three classes, but in all of them I have lots of reading, term papers, reports, and essay exams. It's incredible! I feel like I'll never get through everything.
> Man: That's terrible. I felt that way last year when I had term papers to write, but this semester seems much easier. I spend a lot of time in class, but most of it is in labs doing experiments. I hated writing all those term papers. Can't I talk you into going to the show anyway? I've heard that the movie over at the East Auditorium is really good. It's a murder mystery.
> Woman: Oh, now I'm sure I won't go. I might go to a comedy, but I hate murder mysteries.

Now listen to sample question number 1.

Where is the woman going?

In your test booklet you will read:

> **(A)** to the cafeteria
> **(B)** to the movie theater
> **(C)** to her dorm room
> **(D)** to the library

The best answer to the question "Where is the woman going?" is (D), "to the library." Therefore, the correct choice is (D).

Now listen to sample question number 2.

Which best describes the man's feelings about his classes?

You will read:

> **(A)** Term papers are easy for him.
> **(B)** He has a lot of essay exams.
> **(C)** He finds lab experiments easier than writing term papers.
> **(D)** He is busier this semester than last semester.

The best answer to the question "Which best describes the man's feelings about his classes?" is (C), "He finds lab experiments easier than writing term papers." Therefore, the correct answer is (C).

Now listen to the test. Remember, you are not allowed to take any notes or write in your test book.

Questions 21 to 23: Listen to the following talk between two teachers:

Man: Good morning, Susan. How's it going?

Woman: Pretty good, Bill. How about you?

Man: Oh, I'm OK. I have to teach five classes today, so I'm really busy. How is that English class you're teaching?

Woman: It's going really well. I have a great class this year. I've got 30 students, and most of them are putting a lot of time into their work.

Man: That's great. I love to teach English. Right now I'm only teaching history, but I hope I can teach English next year.

Woman: Well, it can be a lot of fun when the students want to learn.

Man: Oh, I've got a class in a few minutes. I've got to get going. Have a good morning.

Woman: All right, you too. Bye.

[To the Reader: Pause 12 seconds after each question.]

21. What is this conversation mainly about?

22. How many classes does the man say he is teaching?

23. What subject does the man teach now?

Questions 24 to 27: Listen to the following conversation between two people in a restaurant:

Man: Have you ever eaten here before?

Woman: Only in the evenings. I didn't know until now that they served breakfast, too.

Man: That's what the Carolina Coffee Shop is famous for. People have been coming here for over 60 years for breakfast before going to the university football and basketball games. It's a tradition.

Woman: Oh. What's good here?

Man: The best is their French toast. They take stale pieces of French bread and dip them in eggs. Then they bake them, and when it's done they sprinkle the toast with powdered sugar and top everything with fresh fruit. It's delicious.

Woman: I think I'll try it.

Man: OK. Since this is your first visit to the Carolina Coffee Shop in the morning, I'll buy your breakfast.

Woman: Thanks!

[To the Reader: Pause 12 seconds after each question.]

24. What time of day is this conversation taking place?

25. What is the name of the restaurant?

26. What does the man recommend the woman get?

27. About how long has the restaurant been open?

Questions 28 to 31. Listen to the following conversation between two travelers.

Man:	Do you see any signs for San Francisco?
Woman:	No. According to the map we should be close to the city, but the highway signs don't say anything about San Francisco.
Man:	What city names do the signs show?
Woman:	I see road signs for San Jose and Los Angeles. Do you think we're lost?
Man:	Yeah, I think we're going the wrong direction. I'm going to stop at the next gas station and ask the attendant for directions. I hope we can reach San Francisco before it gets dark.
Woman:	Is San Francisco the capital of California?
Man:	No, it's Sacramento.
Woman:	Oh. I think I see a gas station up there on the right.
Man:	Great. I hope we haven't gone too far out of our way.

[To the Reader: Pause 12 seconds after each question.]

28. How are the two speakers traveling?

29. What is the destination of the two travelers?

30. What are the man and woman mainly concerned about?

31. Why are the speakers going to the gas station?

Questions 32 to 35. Listen to the following conversation between two students.

Woman:	Hey Bobby, how long have you been here?
Man:	Oh hi, Judy. I started swimming this morning at 5:00.
Woman:	Goodness! That's early! I got here at 6:00. How many laps have you done?
Man:	I swam 50 laps before 6:00, but I can't remember how many laps I've done since then.
Woman:	I have 10 more to do and I'll be done.
Man:	I'm almost finished too. Do you have any classes right after you finish?
Woman:	No, I don't go to class until 11:00. How about you?
Man:	No, I don't have to go to class until 10:00. I usually go out for breakfast after I swim. Would you like to join me today?
Woman:	Sure, that sounds like fun. Let me finish and I'll meet you outside of the locker room.
Man:	OK, see you then.

[To the Reader: Pause 12 seconds after each question.]

32. Where is this conversation taking place?

33. How many laps had the man completed by 6 A.M.?

34. Where will the speakers probably go after they meet outside the locker rooms?

35. What time of day is the conversation taking place?

Part C

Directions: In this part of the test, you will hear talks by a single person. After each talk, you will be asked some questions. You will hear the talks and the questions only once, so listen carefully to what is said. After you hear a question, read the four possible answers in your test book and decide which one is the best answer to the question you heard. Then, find the number of the question on your answer sheet, and fill in the oval that corresponds to the letter of the answer you have chosen. Answer all questions based on what is stated or implied in the talk.

Listen to this sample talk.

You will hear:

> Questions 1-4 are based on the following announcement:
>
> [FEMALE SPEAKER]
>
> At this university we offer three different programs for students who have children. For those of you with very young children, we have a day care program that takes infants from 3 months to 30 months. We have another program for children between two and five years of age. And we also have an after-school program for school-aged children. This program offers sports, crafts, outings, and tutoring during after-school hours. Enrollment in these child care programs is limited and early application is essential, since our programs often have waiting lists. The fees are on an hourly basis. If any of you new students need these services, please let me know right away so I can get you an application form.

Now listen to sample question number 1.

What is the main purpose of this announcement?

You will read:

> (A) to demonstrate tutoring techniques
> (B) to explain school policies
> (C) to recruit childcare workers
> (D) to explain a service

The best answer to the question "What is the purpose of this announcement?" is (D), "to explain a service." Therefore, the correct choice is (D).

Now listen to sample question number 2.

What does the speaker recommend?

You will read:

> (A) Give your child extra tutoring.
> (B) Take your child to the program today.
> (C) Apply as soon as you can.
> (D) Pay next month.

The best answer to the question "What does the speaker recommend?" is (C), "Apply as soon as you can." Therefore the correct choice is (C).

Now listen to the talks. Remember, you are not allowed to write any notes in your test book.

Questions 36 to 39. Listen to the following announcement:

[FEMALE SPEAKER]

Good afternoon, folks. I'm sorry to tell you that today's showing of the movie *To Be or Not to Be?* is canceled because of a leak in the ceiling of the movie theater. We are sorry about this inconvenience. If you have already bought your tickets, your money will be refunded. The movie will be shown again at its regular times of 2, 4, and 8 P.M. beginning Saturday. *To Be or Not to Be?* is a humorous film about England's greatest poet and playwright, William Shakespeare. It's the story of Shakespeare's life, and, though it's mostly a comedy, the film does probe into more serious questions about the origins of the plays Shakespeare is said to have written. The movie is interesting and thought provoking. Again, we apologize for the inconvenience and hope you'll return. Thank you for coming.

[To the Reader: Pause 12 seconds after each question.]

36. What is the purpose of the announcement?

37. What is the problem?

38. What famous person is the subject of *To Be or Not to Be?*

39. How could *To Be or Not to Be?* best be described?

Questions 40 to 42. Listen to the following announcement by a member of a campus club:

[MALE SPEAKER]

Attention everyone. The university dance club is going to begin offering weekend classes in stilt walking. If you've never tried walking on stilts, this is your chance. You will suddenly be transformed into a nine-foot tall giant, and you'll feel like you are walking among the trees and the clouds. The art of walking on stilts comes from Kenya, where some tribes used stilts in festival performances, giving the dancers the appearance of being giants. Walking on stilts can be an empowering experience, especially for those of us who have always been shorter than the rest. And for the beginners there is no need to fear the heights, for there will be experienced stilters to help you by holding your hands and supporting you.

The first class will be held on the fieldhouse lawn this Saturday. In case it rains, it will be held in the gym. You should wear athletic clothes and sport shoes. After this first Saturday, classes will be held every other Saturday. There will be a total of seven classes this semester. There is no cost to students but there is a $75 fee for anyone else who wishes to participate. For more information, contact Sue Higgins, president of the university dance club, at the physical education department.

[To the Reader: Pause 12 seconds after each question.]

40. What is the main topic of this announcement?

41. What organization is offering the event?

42. On what day of the week is the event to be held?

Questions 43 to 46. Listen to the following argument by a speaker in a public forum:

[FEMALE SPEAKER]

At a time when our legislature has cut millions of dollars from health and education programs, it is continuing to allow the state to pay out over $50 million each year for retirement pensions for judges. The Judicial Retirement System is the only one in the state that does not pay for itself. Instead, judges pay for only about 15 percent of their retirement benefits, while the state is left to cover the rest. After only 10 years of employment, a judge over 60 can receive 50 percent of his or her salary at retirement. By contrast, the average state employee over 60 would only receive 20 percent of his or her salary. Our state is paying for an extremely generous judge's retirement system while the governor is cutting money for health and education services. It's time for a change in the laws. Act now. Call your state representative and ask that the Judicial Retirement System be reformed.

[To the Reader: Pause 12 seconds after each question.]

43. What issue is the speaker talking about?

44. What is the speaker's opinion?

45. According to the speaker, how much money can a judge get when he or she retires?

46. What does the speaker urge listeners to do?

Questions 47 to 50. Listen to the following lecture by a professor.

[MALE SPEAKER]

The first book we'll be reading in this class will be *One Hundred Years of Solitude* by Gabriel García Márquez. Márquez was the winner of the 1982 Nobel Peace Prize and this is his most famous novel. The story is set in the 1700s in South America. It's a story of the successes and failures of the Buendia family, and it covers it all—love and death, war and peace, youth and age. The story begins with one man and one woman, Jose Arcadio and Ursula, setting off in the jungles to start a new life in a new town. What follows is a chronicle of their lives. You can find copies of the book at most bookstores downtown, and I think the school bookstore has some used copies, too. We'll be reading the English translation, but I encourage you to read the Spanish edition, too. The novel has been translated into 15 different languages, though the most common editions are in either Spanish or English.

[To the Reader: Pause 12 seconds after each question.]

47. In what department would this class most likely be offered?

48. What was Gabriel Garcia Márquez awarded?

49. During what period of time does the novel take place?

50. The novel is most commonly published in which two languages?

This is the end of Section 1, Listening Comprehension. Turn off the tape and continue with Section 2, Structure and Written Expression.

Practice Test 3
SECTION 1
Listening Comprehension

Part A

Directions: In Part A you will hear short conversations between two people. After each conversation a third person will ask a question about what was said. You will hear the conversation only one time, so you must listen carefully to what each speaker says. After you hear the conversation and the question, read the four possible answers in your test booklet and pick the one which best answers the question. Then look on the answer sheet for the number of the question and fill in the oval that corresponds to the letter of your answer choice.

Listen to an example.

> *You will hear:*
>> Woman: Have you called Pete?
>> Man: I'll call him as soon as I get home.
>
> What does the man mean?
>
> *You will read:*
>> **(A)** He will call Pete before he goes home.
>> **(B)** He will call Pete after he gets home.
>> **(C)** He called Pete at home.
>> **(D)** He will call Pete tomorrow.

You learn from the conversation that the man will call Pete as soon as he gets home. The best answer to the question "What does the man mean?" is (B), "He will call Pete after he gets home." Therefore, the correct answer is (B).

Now continue listening to the tape.

[To the Reader: Pause 12 seconds after the third person asks each question.]

1. Woman: Barbara sure found a nice job!
    Man: So you know about it too?

    What can we assume about the man?

2. Man: Victor's always willing to help me.
    Woman: What a good buddy!

    What does the woman mean?

3. Woman: Simon, the vegetables at the farmers' market are fresher and cheaper than these.
    Man: Really? I guess I'd better try going there.

    What does the man mean?

4. Man: I feel great today; shall we go to the beach?
    Woman: After the plumber finishes his work; he's coming shortly.

    What does the woman mean?

5. Woman: None of us enjoyed the movie very much.
    Man: I did.

    What does the man mean?

6. Man: Do you mind if I open the window?
    Woman: Not a bad idea, we need some fresh air.

    What does the woman mean?

7. Woman: The health clinic was so swamped with people that it took me three hours to get in.
    Man: Yeah, the clinic is always busy this time of year.

What does the man imply?

8. Woman: Hi, Roger, good to see you again. So you're back at school now?
    Man: I'm still recovering, so I'm taking only two classes for the time being.

What does the man mean?

9. Man: Sarah, you're one of the speakers for today's presentation, aren't you?
    Woman: That's what I'm preparing for.

What does the woman mean?

10. Woman: I just learned something really exciting!
    Man: What, Sylvia?

What does the man want to know?

11. Woman: Can you give me a driving lesson this afternoon, Will?
    Man: Yes, I guess I can, but I'm afraid I don't have much time.

What will the man probably do?

12. Woman: You didn't stay up late last night, did you?
    Man: Not late, just all night.

What does the man imply?

13. Man: Why isn't Dr. Byron teaching art history again this semester?
    Woman: No time. He just became department chair.

What does the woman mean?

14. Woman: How did your first exam go?
    Man: I thought I did poorly, but I ended up with eighty percent, the highest grade in the class.

What does the man mean?

15. Woman: At least I've learned one thing at this university.
    Man: To manage your time, right?

What does the man mean?

16. Man: Is this coupon still good?
    Woman: Till the end of this week.

What does the woman mean?

17. Man: May I park here?
    Woman: You can normally, but today is street cleaning day.

What does the woman mean?

18. Woman: Do you have to go to the meeting tonight?
    Man: I don't have to, but I'd like to know more about the university.

What does the man imply?

19. Man: I finally finished all my interviews.
    Woman: And now you need to write them up.

What does the woman mean?

20. Man: Aren't you ready yet?
    Woman: Almost. Hang on a bit.

What does the woman mean?

Part B

Directions: In Part B you will hear longer conversations between two people. After each conversation you will be asked some questions. You will hear the conversations and the questions only once, so listen carefully to what is said. After you hear a question, read the four possible answers in your test book and decide which one is the best answer to the question you heard. Then, on your answer sheet, find the number of the question and fill in the oval that corresponds to the letter of the answer you have chosen. Answer all questions based on what is stated or implied by the speakers.

Listen to the example.

You will hear:

Questions 1 and 2 are based on the following conversation between two friends at school.

Man: Hi, Joanie. Where are you going?
Woman: Oh, hi Paul. I'm on my way to the library.
Man: I just wondered if you wanted to go to a movie with me.
Woman: I'd love to, but I can't. I can't believe all the work I have this semester. I only have three classes, but in all of them I have lots of reading, term papers, reports, and essay exams. It's incredible! I feel like I'll never get through everything.
Man: That's terrible. I felt that way last year when I had term papers to write, but this semester seems much easier. I spend a lot of time in class, but most of it is in labs doing experiments. I hated writing all those term papers. Can't I talk you into going to the show anyway? I've heard that the movie over at the East Auditorium is really good. It's a murder mystery.
Woman: Oh, now I'm sure I won't go. I might go to a comedy, but I hate murder mysteries.

Now listen to sample question number 1.

Where is the woman going?

In your test booklet you will read:

(A) to the cafeteria
(B) to the movie theater
(C) to her dorm room
(D) to the library

The best answer to the question "Where is the woman going?" is (D), "to the library." Therefore, the correct choice is (D).

Now listen to sample question number 2.

Which best describes the man's feelings about his classes?

You will read:

(A) Term papers are easy for him.
(B) He has a lot of essay exams.
(C) He finds lab experiments easier than writing term papers.
(D) He is busier this semester than last semester.

The best answer to the question "Which best describes the man's feelings about his classes?" is (C), "He finds lab experiments easier than writing term papers." Therefore, the correct answer is (C).

Now listen to the test. Remember, you are not allowed to take any notes or write in your test book.

Questions 21 to 24. Listen to the following conversation between a coach and a player.

Woman: Derek, how is your knee today? Is it still giving you trouble?

Man: No. It feels a lot better today. I went to the doctor and he told me it was only a pulled ligament. I should be fine for Saturday's game.

Woman: Great. But why don't you take it easy today. Maybe just practice throwing. Don't do any running.

Man: OK. Do you have any news about Michigan and what we can expect in Saturday's game?

Woman: Yes, I have some films showing Michigan in the last three games. They're in my office. If you want to see them after practice, you can.

Man: Oh, that would be great. I'd like to see what we're up against.

Woman: Michigan has a strong team. We're in for a tough one. They're one of the top football teams in the country now since they beat Iowa last weekend. Come to think of it, why don't you go ahead and check out the game films right now. And just rest that knee this afternoon. I want you to be well in three days.

Man: All right. I'll be back tomorrow afternoon for full practice.

Woman: OK. Here's the key to my office. The films are on my desk, and the projector is all set up.

[To the Reader: Pause 12 seconds after each question.]

21. What is the main subject of this conversation?

22. What sport are the coach and player talking about?

23. Where does this conversation most likely take place?

24. Where does the woman tell the man to go?

Questions 25 to 28. Listen to the following conversation between two students:

Man:	How did you do on the exam?
Woman:	I passed, but I didn't do so well. The essay question was the worst part for me. How about you?
Man:	I did all right on everything except the essay question, too. I wasn't really prepared to write about the tribes in the rainforests of Brazil. We studied the rainforests for only a few days. I didn't think it would be on the test.
Woman:	Me either. I thought for sure he would ask us something about the Incas in Peru or maybe the mountain peoples in Chile. I studied most of the material on these groups and didn't spend much time on the people of the rainforest. Do you know how much the exam counts towards our final grade?
Man:	I think it's 30 percent.
Woman:	Thirty percent! Oh no, I'm in deep trouble this time! That means I'll have to get A's on everything else to get a decent grade.
Man:	That may not be too hard. We've already gone through most of the readings the class is supposed to cover. After next week it will just be review. But then there is the final paper, of course.
Woman:	Yes. I was hoping to do well on this test so I could relax when writing my paper, but now it looks like I'll have to spend more time preparing to write that paper.
Man:	Well, I will too. Hey, I'm kind of hungry. I think I'll go get some lunch. Do you feel like joining me?
Woman:	I'd love to, but I have to go home and study. I'll call you later.
Man:	OK, see you later.

[To the Reader: Pause 12 seconds after each question.]

25. What is the main topic of this conversation?

26. What topic did the essay question cover?

27. What is the woman upset about?

28. Where is the man going after they finish talking?

Questions 29 to 32. Listen to the following conversation between two students:

> Man: That looks good. What is it?
>
> Woman: A grilled chicken sandwich with extra lettuce and tomato.
>
> Man: Mmmm. Where did you get it?
>
> Woman: Over there at the counter. There's a long line there right now, but the sandwich is worth the wait.
>
> Man: Maybe I'll get one too. Say, how did you like the guest speaker this morning?
>
> Woman: He was OK, but I don't really see why we had a doctor come to our anthropology class to talk about ancient medicine.
>
> Man: You don't? I thought it was relevant to our discussion of ancient societies since medicine is such an important part of any culture. I really liked his discussion of ancient Chinese herbal treatments and of surgery in ancient Egypt.
>
> Woman: That was interesting. I guess the speaker wasn't so bad after all. Did you take any notes during his lecture? I didn't, and I was just thinking that the information might be on our next test.
>
> Man: I sure did. Here. You can look at them while I get in line for a sandwich. I'll be back in a few minutes.

[To the Reader: Pause 12 seconds after each question.]

29. What two topics does this conversation focus on?

30. What was the occupation of the guest lecturer?

31. What did the guest lecturer speak about?

32. Where would this conversation most likely take place?

Questions 33 to 35. Listen to the following conversation between two friends on vacation.

> Woman: OK, Jim, are you ready to dive?
>
> Man: No. Hold on a second. I still need to get my airtanks. Are we already over the dive site?
>
> Woman: Yeah. Look in the water there. You can see the dark shadow of the wreck below us. It's supposed to be about 50 feet deep here.
>
> Man: Boy, I wouldn't want to run out of air 50 feet below the surface. Where are my tanks?
>
> Woman: Oh, I think I put them near the back of the boat.
>
> Man: There they are! Great! I'm so ready to get into the water. It seemed that those scuba diving classes would never end. I'm glad the weather is warm, too. Everyone else is probably spending Christmas break freezing in the snow somewhere.
>
> Woman: This was a great idea. Hurry up so we can get down there.
>
> Man: OK, all ready. Let's dive.

[To the Reader: Pause 12 seconds after each question.]

33. Where are the woman and man talking?

34. What is the man doing?

35. During what vacation is this conversation taking place?

Part C

Directions: In this part of the test, you will hear talks by a single person. After each talk, you will be asked some questions. You will hear the talks and the questions only once, so listen carefully to what is said. After you hear a question, read the four possible answers in your test book and decide which one is the best answer to the question you heard. Then, find the number of the question on your answer sheet, and fill in the oval that corresponds to the letter of the answer you have chosen. Answer all questions based on what is stated or implied in the talk.

Listen to this sample talk.

You will hear:

Questions 1–4 are based on the following announcement:

[FEMALE SPEAKER]

At this university we offer three different programs for students who have children. For those of you with very young children, we have a day care program that takes infants from 3 months to 30 months. We have another program for children between two and five years of age. And we also have an after-school program for school-aged children. This program offers sports, crafts, outings, and tutoring during after-school hours. Enrollment in these child care programs is limited and early application is essential, since our programs often have waiting lists. The fees are on an hourly basis. If any of you new students need these services, please let me know right away so I can get you an application form.

Now listen to sample question number 1.

What is the main purpose of this announcement?

You will read:

     (A) to demonstrate tutoring techniques
     (B) to explain school policies
     (C) to recruit childcare workers
     (D) to explain a service

The best answer to the question "What is the purpose of this announcement?" is (D), "to explain a service." Therefore, the correct choice is (D).

Now listen to sample question number 2.

What does the speaker recommend?

You will read:

     (A) Give your child extra tutoring.
     (B) Take your child to the program today.
     (C) Apply as soon as you can.
     (D) Pay next month.

The best answer to the question "What does the speaker recommend?" is (C), "Apply as soon as you can." Therefore the correct choice is (C).

Now listen to the talks. Remember, you are not allowed to write any notes in your test book.

Questions 36 to 39. Listen to the following discussion by a recreation teacher:

[FEMALE SPEAKER]

Since I know that many of you are interested in buying a bicycle, I'd like to explain some things about different frames. The two I'll talk about today are the diamond frame and the mixte frame. The most common bicycle frame is the diamond frame, which is shaped like a diamond. But another common design is the mixte frame, which is sometimes called the women's frame. One advantage of the mixte frame is that it's easier to mount since it doesn't have a top bar connecting the handlebar to the seat. That makes it easier if a woman is wearing a skirt. But it's not as strong and rigid as the diamond frame. Rigidity is important in a frame because it makes the most of your pedaling energy. The manufacturers of mixte frames compensate for the lack of rigidity by using heavier metal tubing in the rest of the frame. In the past, since most bikes were made of heavy steel alloys, the heavier weight of the mixte frame was not a concern. But bike materials have changed a lot in the last decade. Modern technology has developed much lighter materials, and the demand for lighter-weight bikes has increased. The extra weight in the mixte frame is not that important if you're mainly interested in riding around town. However if you're planning to do some long-distance cycling it probably will make a difference. For a more versatile bike, the diamond frame, which is stronger, more rigid, and lighter, is probably a better choice.

[To the Reader: Pause 12 seconds after each question.]

36. What is the main topic of this discussion?

37. What is one advantage of the mixte frame?

38. Which of the following statements most likely characterizes the speaker's opinion?

39. What recent development has increased the demand for diamond frames?

Questions 40 to 43. Listen to the following announcement by a park ranger:

[FEMALE SPEAKER]

The hunting of walruses for their ivory tusks is illegal in the United States. Such hunting is cruel and wasteful, since most ivory hunters do not make use of the carcasses at all. But in Alaska, the coastal native residents are allowed to hunt the walruses for food, clothing, traditional carvings, and skin boats. Currently, though, the Fish and Wildlife Service is investigating many cases of illegal hunting. Both natives and nonnatives have been found with supplies of tusks, and many have been found to be trading the ivory for illegal drugs. Most residents in the coastal communities are law abiding citizens who support the ban, but still want to allow the legal hunting of walruses. However, many residents fear they will be blamed for the unlawful killing of the walruses.

[To the Reader: Pause 12 seconds after each question.]

40. Why do some people want to hunt walruses illegally?

41. What group of people are allowed to hunt the walrus for food and basic needs?

42. According to the speaker, what are the tusks being traded for?

43. What are some coastal residents afraid of?

Questions 44 to 47. Listen to the following announcement:

[MALE SPEAKER]

The university child care center offers three different programs for parents in family student housing. In order to qualify for the programs, the following requirements need to be met: at least one of the parents must be a full-time student at the university, the family must reside in university housing, and eligible children must be between the ages of two and six. The first program is the nursery for infants and toddlers. The nursery is open from 8 A.M. to 6 P.M., and parents must schedule in advance the times at which they plan to drop off children. There is no cost for the nursery as long as the total hours for each child per week does not exceed 30 hours.

The second program is the university kindergarten, which is available to parents with children between the ages of five and six years. This kindergarten is fully accredited by the public school system. Teachers are all state certified, and the curriculum either meets or surpasses the curriculum of public kindergartens. The kindergarten is open from 8 A.M. to 4 P.M.

The third program is an after-school day care program, open until 6 P.M. at a cost of $100 per school term. The after-school day care program is also fully accredited by the public school system.

In addition to the nursery, the kindergarten, and the after-school day care program, the university child care center provides a list of available babysitters from a qualified, experienced pool of college students. If you would like more information about our programs, please see the director of family student housing or make an appointment with me at the school.

[To the Reader: Pause 12 seconds after each question.]

  44. What is the purpose of this announcement?

  45. How many programs does the child care center offer?

  46. Which of the following is a requirement for having children qualify for the programs?

  47. How much does the after-school day care program cost per school term?

Questions 48 to 50. Listen to the following discussion by a musician performing at a college:

[MALE SPEAKER]

Many students ask me about who was my greatest influence in jazz. And by far I have to say the late Duke Ellington. If you will bear with me I'll give you a little biography of the man. "The Duke," as he was called, was born Edward Kennedy Ellington, on April 29, 1899, right here in Washington, D.C. He started studying the piano in 1906 with his elementary school music teacher, and from there he took off to become one of jazz's greatest legends. He played the Washington clubs in high school, and he became the regular pianist at the Poodle Dog Cafe. It was there that he wrote his first song, *Soda Fountain Rag*. But it wasn't until Duke hit the road with his band, the Washingtonians, that he made it big. From 1927 to 1930 he was based at the famous Cotton Club in New York, the place where all jazz musicians stopped. And this was where I met the great Duke Ellington. I toured with him for 30 years playing saxophone. The musicians who played saxophone along with me certainly had a lot to do with the changes in my style of music, but at the heart and soul of it there was Duke Ellington, band leader and a master composer.

[To the Reader: Pause 12 seconds after each question.]

  48. What is the significance of Duke Ellington to this speaker?

  49. What place was considered to be the center for all great jazz musicians in New York City?

  50. What instrument does the speaker play?

This is the end of Section 1, Listening Comprehension. Turn off the tape and continue with Section 2, Structure and Written Expression.

Practice Test 4
SECTION 1
Listening Comprehension

Part A

Directions: In Part A you will hear short conversations between two people. After each conversation a third person will ask a question about what was said. You will hear the conversation only one time, so you must listen carefully to what each speaker says. After you hear the conversation and the question, read the four possible answers in your test booklet and pick the one which best answers the question. Then look on the answer sheet for the number of the question and fill in the oval that corresponds to the letter of your answer choice.

Listen to an example.

You will hear:

      Woman: Have you called Pete?

         Man: I'll call him as soon as I get home.

What does the man mean?

You will read:

  (A) He will call Pete before he goes home.
  (B) He will call Pete after he gets home.
  (C) He called Pete at home.
  (D) He will call Pete tomorrow.

You learn from the conversation that the man will call Pete as soon as he gets home. The best answer to the question "What does the man mean?" is (B), "He will call Pete after he gets home." Therefore, the correct answer is (B).

Now continue listening to the tape.

[To The Reader: Pause 12 seconds after the third person asks each question.]

1.   Man: I didn't expect Lisa to spend so much of her time helping me.
  Woman: She really has a tight schedule this semester, doesn't she?

What are the speakers saying about Lisa?

2.   Woman: Guess what? I'll be a teaching assistant for Chemistry 1B.
  Man: I thought your major was computer science.

What had the man assumed about the woman?

3.   Woman: Mark sure smokes a lot when he studies hard.
  Man: Not any more he doesn't.

What does the man mean?

4.   Woman: Dozens of people signed up for the workshop.
  Man: But only a few showed up, didn't they?

What does the man imply?

5. Man: Steve won't graduate until this summer, but did you know that he has already started his own computer consulting company?

    Woman: Boy, he's really using what he's learned.

    What does the woman say about Steve?

6. Man: I need to take a break.

    Woman: Let's go to the movies tonight.

    What are the speakers going to do?

7. Man: Would you please drop this book at the library for me when you go to school?

    Woman: I would if I were going, but I have to work today.

    What does the woman imply?

8. Man: Excuse me, but is this seat taken?

    Woman: No, somebody just left.

    What is the man probably going to do?

9. Woman: The professor seems exhausted after that long lecture he gave.

    Man: So am I.

    What does the man mean?

10. Man: You don't want to start graduate school right after graduation, do you?

    Woman: Well, actually I do.

    What does the woman mean?

11. Man: Two of the classes I want to take have conflicting schedules.

    Woman: Then you need to make a decision.

    What does the woman suggest the man do?

12. Woman: You've already read this book, haven't you?

    Man: I wish I had.

    What does the man mean?

13. Woman: Bill, I think I'll ride my bike to school today; do you want to go with me?

    Man: Sure, the exercise will do me good.

    What does the man mean?

14. Man: Uh-oh, these two books are due tomorrow.

    Woman: Already?

    What does the woman mean?

15. Man: This is the second time my machine has broken since I started working five minutes ago.

    Woman: Let me try to fix it for you, it's probably a bad connection.

    What does the woman mean?

16. Man: Excuse me. Did you drop this?

    Woman: Oh, thanks.

    What does the woman mean?

17. Man: Do you know how to get there?

    Woman: I think so, but give me the directions, just in case.

    What is the man probably going to do?

18. Woman: Mark, the university library is hiring now; are you still looking for a job?

    Man: I've found one, but thank you anyway.

    What does the man mean?

19. Woman: Jack, do you work on weekends too?

    Man: Yes, but the hours are different.

    What does the man mean?

20. Woman: Jill is very excited about her new project.

    Man: But is it feasible for her to complete it within a year?

    What is the man's concern about Jill's project?

21. Man: If only Laura would come back!

    Woman: I know; I feel the same.

    What does the woman mean?

22. Man: Barbara should have mailed the check a week ago.

    Woman: I wonder what happened?

    What are the man and woman talking about?

23. Woman: You'd better hang on to your present job.

    Man: At least for a while.

    What does the man mean?

24. Woman: Peter would be better now if he hadn't gone back to work so soon.

    Man: Yes, but we couldn't force him to stay home.

    What do the man and woman think?

25. Woman: The recreation room is open four nights a week, isn't it?

    Man: Let's find out.

    What does the man mean?

26. Man: Hey, Linda, how long are you staying this time?

    Woman: Oh, I'm here for good now.

    What does the woman mean?

27. Man: Sue, are you sure this is the right way to get there?

    Woman: Sure. This is a shortcut; we'll be there in no time.

    What does the woman mean?

28. Woman: What took you so long?

    Man: I didn't think it would be so complicated.

    What does the man mean?

29. Man: Boy, that was a close call.

    Woman: Yeah, I was really scared.

    What do the man and woman mean?

30. Man: Have you gone shopping for Jimmy's present yet?

    Woman: I'm waiting for the sale to begin.

    What does the woman mean?

Part B

Directions: In Part B you will hear longer conversations between two people. After each conversation you will be asked some questions. You will hear the conversations and the questions only once, so listen carefully to what is said. After you hear a question, read the four possible answers in your test book and decide which one is the best answer to the question you heard. Then, on your answer sheet, find the number of the question and fill in the oval that corresponds to the letter of the answer you have chosen. Answer all questions based on what is stated or implied by the speakers.

Listen to the example.

You will hear:

Questions 1 and 2 are based on the following conversation between two friends at school.

    Man: Hi, Joanie. Where are you going?
    Woman: Oh, hi Paul. I'm on my way to the library.
    Man: I just wondered if you wanted to go to a movie with me.
    Woman: I'd love to, but I can't. I can't believe all the work I have this semester. I only have three
            classes, but in all of them I have lots of reading, term papers, reports, and essay exams. It's
            incredible! I feel like I'll never get through everything.
    Man: That's terrible. I felt that way last year when I had term papers to write, but this semester
            seems much easier. I spend a lot of time in class, but most of it is in labs doing experiments.
            I hated writing all those term papers. Can't I talk you into going to the show anyway? I've
            heard that the movie over at the East Auditorium is really good. It's a murder mystery.
    Woman: Oh, now I'm sure I won't go. I might go to a comedy, but I hate murder mysteries.

Now listen to sample question number 1.

Where is the woman going?

In your test booklet you will read:

> (A) to the cafeteria
> (B) to the movie theater
> (C) to her dorm room
> (D) to the library

The best answer to the question "Where is the woman going?" is (D), "to the library." Therefore, the correct choice is (D).

Now listen to sample question number 2.

Which best describes the man's feelings about his classes?

You will read:

> (A) Term papers are easy for him.
> (B) He has a lot of essay exams.
> (C) He finds lab experiments easier than writing term papers.
> (D) He is busier this semester than last semester.

The best answer to the question "Which best describes the man's feelings about his classes?" is (C), "He finds lab experiments easier than writing term papers." Therefore, the correct answer is (C).

Now listen to the test. Remember, you are not allowed to take any notes or write in your test book.

Questions 31 to 34. Listen to the following conversation between two friends:

Woman: Hi Sid. I loved your concert last night! How are you?

Man: I'm a little bit tired. We didn't go to bed until five o'clock in the morning. And I injured my ankle before the show. But I feel better this afternoon. I slept all morning. How did you like the show?

Woman: I loved it. Your singing was great. When are you playing next?

Man: We have our next show here in New York at the Roxie Theater this Thursday.

Woman: I would love to go, but I have to stay and work here at the store.

Man: Well maybe you can see us next week when we play in Washington.

Woman: Yeah, maybe. I'm planning to go to San Francisco on vacation in April, so I may not be able to travel to Washington.

Man: Really! We were invited to play at the Rock Music Festival in San Francisco in April, but we don't have a way of getting there. It's a long way from New York.

Woman: Well, a friend and I are driving across the country in a big van, and we might have room for you and the band.

Man: That would be great! Let me talk to the band members and I'll call you later this week.

Woman: OK. I'll look forward to hearing from you. Do you need help looking for any records in the store today?

Man: Yeah, I was looking for an album featuring John Coltrane and Miles Davis. Do you have any in stock?

Woman: No, I'm sorry, we don't. We can order one for you, or you might try down the street at one of the other record stores.

Man: OK, I'll just try down the street. I'll give you a call later this week.

Woman: Good, see you later.

[To the Reader: Pause 12 seconds after each question.]

31. What was the man doing the previous night?

32. Where will the man play next week?

33. Where is the woman working?

34. Where is the woman going for her vacation?

Questions 35 to 38. Listen to the following conversation between two students:

Woman: Hey, Tom.

Man: How's it going, Mary?

Woman: Great, I just finished my last exam for the semester, and now I'm going home to get ready for summer break. What about you?

Man: I'll finish my last exam this afternoon. I'm on my way to the library now to finish studying for it. Where are you going this summer?

Woman: I'm planning to work in Woods Hole, Massachusetts, at the Woods Hole Oceanographic Institute. I'll be studying whales.

Man: That sounds like a great job. I'll be working nearby on the coast at Nantucket.

Woman: What are you planning to do on the coast?

Man: My uncle owns a restaurant there, so I'll be working as a waiter at night and then helping him do some accounting a few days each week. I have to save a lot of money for the next school year. Maybe we can get together and go to the beach this summer since we'll be living near each other.

Woman: That sounds good. I'll be working on a boat during July, and I won't return to shore for the entire month. But in June and later in August I'll be working in the laboratories and I could drive up and see you in Nantucket.

Man: OK. My uncle tells me June is the best time to go there before the town gets too crowded with tourists. Call me before you leave tomorrow and I'll give you a phone number where I can be reached this summer.

Woman: All right. I'll talk to you later. Good luck with your exam!

Man: Thanks!

[To the Reader: Pause 12 seconds after each question.]

35. Where is the woman going to work for the summer?

36. Where will the man be working during the summer?

37. What is the woman going to study?

38. Why can't the woman visit the man in the month of July?

Questions 39 to 41. Listen to the following conversation between two teachers:

Man: Hey Jean. How's it going?

Woman: Oh, the same old thing, I guess. I have to go to Washington next week to meet with my publisher and I don't know how I'll manage with exams coming up. I'm looking forward to the break this summer.

Man: Yeah, me too. How's the book coming?

Woman: Pretty well I think. I just have to meet with the publishers to talk about the format for my last chapter. It's almost done.

Man: What's the last chapter about?

Woman: Well, the book is about the poetry of Edgar Allan Poe, and the last chapter just focuses on "The Raven" as one of his most significant poems.

Man: If you weren't so busy with going to Washington and all, I'd love to have you come and discuss Poe with my American literature class. We've been studying poetry and prose of the nineteenth century.

Woman: I'd love to, Jim, but I don't know what my schedule is going to be like when I get back next Thursday. When does your class meet?

Man: Tuesdays and Thursdays at 3:00.

Woman: I might be able to do it. Let's talk when I get back next Thursday and I'll let you know.

Man: Thanks, it would be great if you could come.

[To the Reader: Pause 12 seconds after each question.]

39. What field of study are these two speakers most likely teaching?

40. Why is the woman going to Washington next week?

41. What favor does the man ask of the woman?

Questions 42 to 45. Listen to the following conversation between two students:

Woman: Mark, are you going to be driving down to the beach for class tomorrow?

Man: Yeah, I need to get down there really early, though, to help set up the tanks and the gear in the boat.

Woman: What time do you think you'll be leaving?

Man: I need to leave about 4 A.M. You're welcome to ride with me. I have plenty of space.

Woman: That's a little earlier than I had planned to wake up, but I guess since you're the only ride I'll do it. Should I meet you at your place?

Man: Sure. I'll give you a wakeup call if I don't see you here by about 4:15.

Woman: OK. Do you know what we're supposed to be looking at tomorrow? I missed class yesterday.

Man: Yeah, we're supposed to be observing blue sharks and great white sharks, if we see any of them.

Woman: Sounds super. I'm really ready to get out of the shallow water dives and into deeper waters. Well, I'm going to get my stuff together and get some sleep. I'll see you tomorrow morning at 4:00.

Man: All right. See you.

[To the Reader: Pause 12 seconds after each question.]

42. What is the main topic of this conversation?

43. What is the most likely subject of the class the students are taking?

44. What is the woman asking for from the man?

45. What time is the man planning to leave the next day?

Questions 46 to 48. Listen to this conversation between two friends:

Woman: Hi, Ed. Are you in town for another job interview?

Man: Yes, I'm pretty hopeful this time. I've just finished my second interview with this company.

Woman: That sounds great. I hope it works out for you. But wasn't it expensive just getting here?

Man: No, in fact the company is paying all my expenses. They've put me up in a hotel downtown.

Woman: How nice! How many people are they interviewing?

Man: Well, they interviewed 16 the first time, and now four of us were chosen to come back for this interview.

Woman: It sounds like you have a good chance to be selected then.

Man: I hope so. The manager told me he would call us on Monday.

Woman: Well, I hope it goes well. John and I would love it if you came to this area to work.

Man: I would too. But my girlfriend doesn't want to leave her family. She hopes I find a job close to home.

Woman: Oh dear, what a decision.

Man: I'm trying to convince her of how good it is to live here. But anyway, I've got to wait until Monday to find out whether I even have the chance.

Woman: Good luck!

[To the Reader: Pause 12 seconds after each question.]

46. How does the man seem to feel after this interview?

47. How many people have been asked for a second interview?

48. What does the man's girlfriend want?

Questions 49 to 52. Listen to this conversation between two students:

Man: Hi, Sandy. How are your finals going?

Woman: Oh hi, Michael. I finished my last exam this morning, and I finished my two term papers. I finally feel like I can see the light.

Man: Great. Now, how about a change? I've got two tickets for the new modern art exhibit downtown. Do you want to go with me?

Woman: Oh, I don't know. I don't know anything about modern art, and I'm no artist.

Man: You don't have to be an artist to enjoy a good art show! Besides, at least it's something different from studying.

Woman: You're right. Have you seen this exhibit yet?

Man: No, but I've heard that it's great. The exhibit was in New York last summer, and in Chicago after that. And next week it goes to Los Angeles.

Woman: Oh. Well, it ought to be good then.

Man: And, besides, next door to the modern art museum is a new Asian art museum. So we could hit both of them if you're up for it.

Woman: OK. You've talked me into it. Did you want to go this afternoon?

Man: If you have time. I'm ready.

Woman: OK. Let's meet after lunch. I'm starving now. I've got to go back home and get something to eat. Shall we meet at 1:30 right here?

Man: Sounds good to me. See you then.

[To the Reader: Pause 12 seconds after each question.]

49. How does the woman feel at the beginning of the conversation?

50. What was the woman's first response to the man's suggestion?

51. Which city will the art exhibit go to next?

52. What does the man suggest they do after going to the art museum?

Questions 53 to 55. Listen to this conversation between two students.

Woman: I'm really upset.

Man: Why, what's going on?

Woman: I just finished trying to use the new telephone system to enroll in my classes.

Man: And...what's wrong?

Woman: I couldn't get anything I wanted. First I had to wait 15 minutes before getting through on the phone. Then the classes I wanted were all full.

Man: So what are you going to do?

Woman: I don't know. I'm on the waiting list for two classes, but who knows if I'll ever get in. I don't know what to do.

Man: Maybe you should see your counselor.

Woman: I guess I could try that. She might be able to suggest some other classes that would fit my major requirements. I only have a few left to take. It's really frustrating. Have you enrolled yet?

Man: No, and after hearing you, I'm not sure if I want to. But I really don't think I'll have any trouble. Last semester it was easy. I got most of my first choices.

Woman: Well, you're lucky.

[To the Reader: Pause 12 seconds after each question.]

53. What is the woman trying to do?

54. What does the man suggest?

55. How does the man seem to feel?

Part C

Directions: In this part of the test, you will hear talks by a single person. After each talk, you will be asked some questions. You will hear the talks and the questions only once, so listen carefully to what is said. After you hear a question, read the four possible answers in your test book and decide which one is the best answer to the question you heard. Then, find the number of the question on your answer sheet, and fill in the oval that corresponds to the letter of the answer you have chosen. Answer all questions based on what is stated or implied in the talk.

Listen to this sample talk.

You will hear:

Questions 1-4 are based on the following announcement:

[FEMALE SPEAKER]

At this university we offer three different programs for students who have children. For those of you with very young children, we have a day care program that takes infants from 3 months to 30 months. We have another program for children between two and five years of age. And we also have an after-school program for school-aged children. This program offers sports, crafts, outings, and tutoring during after-school hours. Enrollment in these child care programs is limited and early application is essential, since our programs often have waiting lists. The fees are on an hourly basis. If any of you new students need these services, please let me know right away so I can get you an application form.

Now listen to sample question number 1.

What is the main purpose of this announcement?

You will read:

    (A) to demonstrate tutoring techniques
    (B) to explain school policies
    (C) to recruit childcare workers
    (D) to explain a service

The best answer to the question "What is the purpose of this announcement?" is (D), "to explain a service." Therefore, the correct choice is (D).

Now listen to sample question number 2.

What does the speaker recommend?

You will read:

    (A) Give your child extra tutoring.
    (B) Take your child to the program today.
    (C) Apply as soon as you can.
    (D) Pay next month.

The best answer to the question "What does the speaker recommend?" is (C), "Apply as soon as you can." Therefore the correct choice is (C).

Now listen to the talks. Remember, you are not allowed to write any notes in your test book.

Questions 56 to 59. Listen to the following lecture given by a professor and then answer the questions that follow:

[FEMALE SPEAKER]

James Joyce was born on February 2, 1882, in Dublin. He grew up in a large family of 17 children and attended Clongowes Wood College and later Belvedere College in Dublin. A very good student at college, Joyce went on to study languages and philosophy at the Dublin college of the Royal University. He spent a good part of his early life in Ireland, tending to his dying mother. In 1904 Joyce married, and he and his wife later left for Zurich and Trieste, where Joyce taught languages in the Berlitz school. Joyce's first attempt to publish *Dubliners* in 1912 was unsuccessful, and he spent the next several years living in poverty in Zurich. He spent the later years of his life in Paris, where he published such works as *Ulysses* and, in 1939, *Finnegan's Wake*. Joyce died in 1941. The first book I would like us to discuss is *Dubliners*. By next class I would like you to have read *Dubliners*.

[To the Reader: Pause 12 seconds after each question.]

   56. What is the main topic of this lecture?

   57. What was James Joyce's occupation?

   58. Where did James Joyce attend college?

   59. Where did Joyce live in his later years?

Questions 60 to 63. Listen to the following discussion about natural history:

[FEMALE SPEAKER]

I am pleased to welcome you to the Institute of Natural History for today's conference on the origins of insects. The Institute has been involved in the past in the study of dinosaurs that once lived in the southwestern region of the United States. For the past five years, however, a group of researchers here have turned from studying dinosaurs to investigating fossil remains of an animal we believe might be the parent of all insects. The Institute's team of researchers is working with an Australian group that discovered an animal called euthycarcinoid, or the "straight crab." The Australians have been working at a site in Murchison Gorge, Australia, and they have uncovered several fossils that predate the earliest known fossils of insects by more than 50 million years. This candidate for the earliest insect, the "straight crab," has a similar structure to insects, with six legs and hard shells.

    The American team has been investigating several sites in the southwestern United States, and we believe they might have found a fossil of the straight crab that could be older than the one found at Murchison Gorge. With us today is Dr. Sawyer, the lead researcher with the Institute's field crew to explain what the American team has found.

[To the Reader: Pause 12 seconds after each question.]

   60. What is the main purpose of the discussion?

   61. What kinds of people are most likely to be listening to this conversation?

   62. Which does the speaker say might be descendents of the "straight crab."

   63. What will probably be discussed next?

Questions 64 to 66. Listen to the following announcement by a university official:

[MALE SPEAKER]

On behalf of the university and the town, I would like to welcome all of you to the University of North Carolina. This is the oldest public university in the United States, and we are proud to say that we offer one of the best public education opportunities anywhere in the nation. The school started in 1792, and has been going strong ever since, with the exception of having been closed for two years in the 1860s because so many young men left to fight in the Civil War. Following the war, the university opened its doors again and has been open ever since. In this century, the university has expanded its enrollment to include women and other minority groups. Now we are looking forward to a bright future where students from all backgrounds attend this university.

[To the Reader: Pause 12 seconds after each question.]

    64. What is the name of the university where the speech is taking place?

    65. According to the speaker, which of the following facts is true of the university?

    66. What once caused the university to close?

Questions 67 to 70. Listen to the following announcement by a teacher:

[MALE SPEAKER]

Before I start with today's lecture on Einstein's theory of quantum mechanics, I'd like to invite anyone who is interested in making a bit of money this summer to see me about working at a summer camp for high school students. The camps will be science camps, one each month, focusing on introducing students to cutting edge technologies such as particle accelerators, microwave communications, and electron microscopes. The science camps need college students to help as camp counselors, and to live with the students in dormitories. Each counselor will be assigned 10 campers, but counselors will have their own rooms. Counselors will also get the chance to use some of the equipment and meet internationally known scientists who will be visiting the camp over the course of the summer. In addition, the entire group will travel to Washington for a week in July. If you are interested please see me after class.

[To the Reader: Pause 12 seconds after each question.]

    67. What type of summer camp is announced?

    68. Where is this discussion most likely taking place?

    69. Why does the camp need college students?

    70. Where will all campers travel in July?

Questions 71 to 74. Listen to this lecture about crocodiles:

[FEMALE SPEAKER]

Today we begin a new topic in our course on the survival of young animals, and I'd like to start with an explanation of a common misconception. Many people have heard that crocodiles eat their babies. Well, in fact they don't. What happens is that the mother crocodiles take all their newly hatched youngsters into their mouths in order to carry them to the safety of the water. The reason this is necessary is that the female crocodile must leave the water in order to hatch her eggs. She goes to the beach and digs a hole approximately 10 inches deep. She then lays her eggs in the hole and covers them with soil, using her body and tail to pat down the earth. While she guards her nest during the day and night for about 12 weeks, the sun heats the soil and hardens it. Then, when the baby crocodiles hatch, they find it almost impossible to get out, and they begin yelping and croaking. The mother hears them and rips open the nest. Then she takes the young into a pouch of skin in her lower jaw, and carries them to the safety of the ocean water before she releases them.

[To the Reader: Pause 12 seconds after each question.]

71. What does the speaker say is the common misconception about crocodile mothers?

72. Where do the young hatch?

73. Why does the crocodile put her babies in her mouth?

74. How long does the mother wait for the young to hatch?

Questions 75 to 77. Listen to this lecture about a winner of the Nobel Peace Prize:

[MALE SPEAKER]

Norman E. Borlaug was the first agricultural scientist to receive the Nobel Peace Prize, and the fifteenth American to do so. He was born in 1914 in Iowa, the son of a farming family. In 1940, Borlaug earned his doctorate degree in plant pathology, and a few years later he was chosen by the Rockefeller Foundation to go abroad to help introduce new agricultural technology to farmers who were growing wheat. Borlaug's goal was to improve the quality of low-yielding wheat that some farmers had been growing for centuries, and he accomplished his goal. He developed new dwarf and semidwarf wheat that had stronger stems and could hold heavier heads of grain. In Mexico, for instance, the new methods resulted in doubled wheat yields. As a result Mexico changed from a country with a wheat shortage to one that was a wheat exporter. For the introduction of these new wheat growing methods Borlaug was dubbed "father of the green revolution."

[To the Reader: Pause 12 seconds after each question.]

75. Which of the following was Borlaug's goal?

76. What helped finance Borlaug's trip abroad?

77. What did Borlaug do when he left the United States?

Questions 78 to 80. Listen to this lecture about a river:

[FEMALE SPEAKER]

This week we're going to begin a new topic in our geography class. We'll focus on the great rivers of the world. And we'll start today with the St. Lawrence River, a major waterway linking the Great Lakes of the United States with the Atlantic Ocean, a distance of about 750 miles. Not all portions of this waterway, which divides Canada and the United States, have been open to large ships, and, in fact, it's only been since 1959 that a series of canals, locks, and dams have made the river navigable up to the inland cities of Detroit and Duluth.

The St. Lawrence is quite a busy river. Each year it handles some 50 million metric tons of cargo; mostly grain, coal, and iron ore. And it's not only cargo boats that you see on the river. There are pleasure boats and ocean-going freighters as well, especially in the area of the Thousand Islands, near Lake Ontario. If you'd like a beautiful place to vacation, this is one of them. The Thousand Islands is an area of the river that is dotted with tree-covered islands. In fact there are probably more nearly 2,000 islands there. Known as a millionaire's retreat since the 1860s, the small islands are covered with beautiful homes and castles covering the small islands. Well, this has been just a short introduction to the St. Lawrence River. We'll be talking more about it next week.

[To the Reader: Pause 12 seconds after each question.]

78. What can you best infer about the speaker's attitude toward the St. Lawrence River?

79. What happened in 1959?

80. Which of the following best describes the Thousand Islands?

This is the end of Section 1, Listening Comprehension. Turn off the tape and continue with Section 2, Structure and Written Expression.

Practice Test 5
SECTION 1
Listening Comprehension

Part A

Directions: In Part A you will hear short conversations between two people. After each conversation a third person will ask a question about what was said. You will hear the conversation only one time, so you must listen carefully to what each speaker says. After you hear the conversation and the question, read the four possible answers in your test booklet and pick the one which best answers the question. Then look on the answer sheet for the number of the question and fill in the oval that corresponds to the letter of your answer choice.

Listen to an example.

> *You will hear:*
> > Woman: Have you called Pete?
> > Man: I'll call him as soon as I get home.
>
> What does the man mean?
>
> *You will read:*
> **(A)** He will call Pete before he goes home.
> **(B)** He will call Pete after he gets home.
> **(C)** He called Pete at home.
> **(D)** He will call Pete tomorrow.

You learn from the conversation that the man will call Pete as soon as he gets home. The best answer to the question "What does the man mean?" is (B), "He will call Pete after he gets home." Therefore, the correct answer is (B).

Now continue listening to the tape.

[To the Reader: Pause 12 seconds after the third person asks each question.]

1. Man: I really like this shirt, but I'm afraid it's not my size.
    Woman: Don't worry, we can exchange it.

    What is the problem?

2. Man: It's usually crowded here at lunch time.
    Woman: Usually. I know; I wonder why it's not today.

    What does the woman imply about the restaurant?

3. Woman: Next customer please.
    Man: Hi, I would like to cash this check.

    What does the man mean?

4. Man: Have you finished? We're going to have some dessert.
    Woman: I'm done.

    What does the woman mean?

5. Woman: I'm worried about the speech I'm going to give tonight.
    Man: You'll be just fine. Everyone was really impressed with your last one.

    What does the man mean?

6. Woman: How long will it take this package to get to New York?

Man: How do you want to send it?

What probably is the man's occupation?

7. Man: I was hoping to take this class last fall.

Woman: Me too, but we're lucky to get in now.

What does the woman mean?

8. Man: Would you like some chicken?

Woman: No, thanks, I'm a vegetarian.

What does the woman mean?

9. Woman: Do you still have time for fishing?

Man: Only once in a while now, but I still consider it my hobby.

What does the man mean?

10. Man: I'd like to send a card to my mother for Mother's Day.

Woman: Oh, I didn't know you had that tradition in your country.

What does the woman imply?

11. Woman: Bob, you'd better get down to the museum tomorrow if you want to see the exhibit.

Man: Yeah, I don't want to miss it again!

What is the man probably going to do?

12. Woman: Do you usually drink so much water?

Man: Only after this much exercise.

What does the man mean?

13. Man: What are you going to cook tonight?

Woman: Nothing. The Johnsons invited us over.

What does the woman mean?

14. Woman: Hi, how's it going?

Man: OK, but I can't stand all the homework.

What does the man mean?

15. Man: Mary, did you wash the car yourself?

Woman: No, I got Don to do it.

What happened to the car?

16. Woman: Do you carry containers for a microwave oven?

Man: Umm . . . check the grocery store next to the gas station to see if they have any.

What does the man imply?

17. Woman: Mr. Blake misread the bus schedule.

Man: So he wasn't able to get there in time.

What do they imply about Mr. Blake?

18. Woman: John has his hair cut every two weeks.

Man: But Peter has his cut every month.

What do they say about John and Peter?

19. Man: Pat, are your parents still supporting you?

Woman: I'm on my own now.

What does the woman mean?

20. Woman: I'm supposed to turn left at the second stop sign, right?

Man: Right.

What does the man mean?

Part B

Directions: In Part B you will hear longer conversations between two people. After each conversation you will be asked some questions. You will hear the conversations and the questions only once, so listen carefully to what is said. After you hear a question, read the four possible answers in your test book and decide which one is the best answer to the question you heard. Then, on your answer sheet, find the number of the question and fill in the oval that corresponds to the letter of the answer you have chosen. Answer all questions based on what is stated or implied by the speakers.

Listen to the example.

You will hear:

Questions 1 and 2 are based on the following conversation between two friends at school:

      Man: Hi, Joanie. Where are you going?

Woman: Oh, hi Paul. I'm on my way to the library.

      Man: I just wondered if you wanted to go to a movie with me.

Woman: I'd love to, but I can't. I can't believe all the work I have this semester. I only have three classes, but in all of them I have lots of reading, term papers, reports, and essay exams. It's incredible! I feel like I'll never get through everything.

      Man: That's terrible. I felt that way last year when I had term papers to write, but this semester seems much easier. I spend a lot of time in class, but most of it is in labs doing experiments. I hated writing all those term papers. Can't I talk you into going to the show anyway? I've heard that the movie over at the East Auditorium is really good. It's a murder mystery.

Woman: Oh, now I'm sure I won't go. I might go to a comedy, but I hate murder mysteries.

Now listen to sample question number 1.

Where is the woman going?

In your test booklet you will read:

      (A) to the cafeteria
      (B) to the movie theater
      (C) to her dorm room
      (D) to the library

The best answer to the question "Where is the woman going?" is (D), "to the library." Therefore, the correct choice is (D).

Now listen to sample question number 2.

Which best describes the man's feelings about his classes?

You will read:

      (A) Term papers are easy for him.
      (B) He has a lot of essay exams.
      (C) He finds lab experiments easier than writing term papers.
      (D) He is busier this semester than last semester.

The best answer to the question "Which best describes the man's feelings about his classes?" is (C), "He finds lab experiments easier than writing term papers." Therefore, the correct answer is (C).

Now listen to the test. Remember, you are not allowed to take any notes or write in your test book.

Questions 21 to 24. Listen to this conversation between two friends at school:

Man: Hey, Nicole! I haven't seen you for awhile. What've you been doing with yourself?

Woman: Oh, hi John. I've been studying a lot lately. All of my classes seem to have exams during the same week.

Man: Oh, that's awful. Where are you going now?

Woman: I'm headed to the gym. I've been sitting at my desk all day and I need some exercise. Do you want to walk out there with me?

Man: Actually, I'm on my way back from the gym. I just had swim practice and I'm going to dinner.

Woman: Well, I guess I'll see you around.

Man: Hey, why don't we meet at the dining hall tomorrow for lunch? Maybe we'll be able to relax and talk.

Woman: OK. What time?

Man: How about one o'clock?

Woman: Sounds great. I'll see you there.

[To the Reader: Pause 12 seconds after each question.]

21. Why has the woman been studying a lot recently?

22. Where is the woman going?

23. What has the man just finished doing?

24. What will happen tomorrow?

Questions 25 to 28. Listen to this conversation between two students:

Man: Excuse me. Do you know where Davies Auditorium is?

Woman: I'm not sure. I'm looking for it too because I have a class there at 10:30. I think it's this way.

Man: Do you mind if I walk with you?

Woman: No. What class do you have in Davies?

Man: I'm taking the introductory economics class. I hear it's a big class.

Woman: Yeah. My roommate took the class last semester and he said there were over 400 people in the lecture hall.

Man: Wow. I hope the lecturer is good, because, if he isn't, the class will be boring. I hate boring classes!

Woman: Oh look. Here's Davies. I hope you have a good class. Hope it's not too boring!

Man: Yeah, me too. Thanks for your help.

[To the Reader: Pause 12 seconds after each question.]

25. What class is the man trying to find?

26. Where does this conversation most probably take place?

27. Approximately how many students were in the economics class last semester?

28. How does the woman know that the economics class had a lot of students?

Questions 29 to 32. Listen to the following conversation between two students in a dormitory room:

> Man: Hi, Katrina. What are you up to?
>
> Woman: Not much, Greg. How are things with you?
>
> Man: Pretty decent. I wanted to know if you could do me a favor.
>
> Woman: What do you need?
>
> Man: I finished my exams and I have to catch a flight early tomorrow morning. I was wondering if you could give me a ride to the airport.
>
> Woman: No problem. I'll be driving right by there. What time do you need to be there?
>
> Man: My flight leaves at 7:00 A.M. and I should get there 30 minutes before it leaves.
>
> Woman: I guess we should leave at about 6:00 then.
>
> Man: Thanks, Katrina. I really appreciate it.
>
> Woman: I'll see you tomorrow morning at 6:00 in front of the dorm.

[To the Reader: Pause 12 seconds after each question.]

29. Why did the man want to talk to the woman?

30. At what time does the man's flight leave?

31. Where will the two students meet tomorrow morning?

32. Why is the man leaving tomorrow morning?

Questions 33 to 35. Listen to the following conversation between two students:

> Man: Are you going to the game tonight?
>
> Woman: What game?
>
> Man: The lacrosse game for the league championship. It starts at 7:30.
>
> Woman: Oh. I didn't realize that was tonight! I was planning to go out to dinner with my roommate and her parents. But maybe I can come if dinner doesn't run too late.
>
> Man: Good. I hope you can make it. I'll be sitting in Section C with some friends. Join us if you can.
>
> Woman: OK, I'll try. See you later, I hope.

[To the Reader: Pause 12 seconds after each question.]

33. What are the students talking about?

34. What would prevent the woman from seeing the game?

35. Where will the man be sitting?

Part C

Directions: In this part of the test, you will hear talks by a single person. After each talk, you will be asked some questions. You will hear the talks and the questions only once, so listen carefully to what is said. After you hear a question, read the four possible answers in your test book and decide which one is the best answer to the question you heard. Then, find the number of the question on your answer sheet, and fill in the oval that corresponds to the letter of the answer you have chosen. Answer all questions based on what is stated or implied in the talk.

Listen to this sample talk.

You will hear:

Questions 1–4 are based on the following announcement:

[FEMALE SPEAKER]

At this university we offer three different programs for students who have children. For those of you with very young children, we have a day care program that takes infants from 3 months to 30 months. We have another program for children between two and five years of age. And we also have an after-school program for school-aged children. This program offers sports, crafts, outings, and tutoring during after-school hours. Enrollment in these child care programs is limited and early application is essential, since our programs often have waiting lists. The fees are on an hourly basis. If any of you new students need these services, please let me know right away so I can get you an application form.

Now listen to sample question number 1.

What is the main purpose of this announcement?

You will read:

    (A) to demonstrate tutoring techniques
    (B) to explain school policies
    (C) to recruit childcare workers
    (D) to explain a service

The best answer to the question "What is the purpose of this announcement?" is (D), "to explain a service." Therefore, the correct choice is (D).

Now listen to sample question number 2.

What does the speaker recommend?

You will read:

    (A) Give your child extra tutoring.
    (B) Take your child to the program today.
    (C) Apply as soon as you can.
    (D) Pay next month.

The best answer to the question "What does the speaker recommend?" is (C), "Apply as soon as you can." Therefore the correct choice is (C).

Now listen to the talks. Remember, you are not allowed to write any notes in your test book.

Questions 36 to 39. Listen to the following information about a class assignment:

[MALE SPEAKER]

The writing assignment for this class is a 10- to 12-page research paper. I want you to imagine that you are low-level officials in the United States State Department who have been asked to research a policy issue for the government so that others can make a decision on it. You must do your research, write your argument, and conclude the paper with your recommendations for the policy the United States should adopt. By the middle of the term, I expect all of you to have discussed a potential topic with your teaching assistant. There are two possible ways to complete this assignment. The first way, and the one I recommend for first-year students, is to hand in a rough draft of the paper to your teaching assistant during the week of April 6th. She will give you advice on how to improve that first draft. The papers will be returned the following week and your final draft will be collected the week of April 20th. For those of you who do not want to write a rough draft, the paper is due the week of April 13th. Your teaching assistant will be explaining more about these final assignments in your next section meeting.

[To the Reader: Pause 12 seconds after each question.]

36. How long does the paper have to be?

37. By when must the students discuss a potential topic with their teaching assistants?

38. Why are first-year students advised to write a rough draft?

39. When is the paper due for those not writing a rough draft?

Questions 40 to 43. Listen to the following announcement:

[FEMALE SPEAKER]

Let me be the first to welcome you to Middletown. I hope you've had a pleasant journey. If you are connecting to another flight, an attendant at the gate will give you the departure gate number for your next flight. If Middletown is your destination, we thank you for traveling with us. As you exit the plane, walk to your right towards the baggage claim area. Your baggage will be arriving on Carousel B in about 10 minutes. Be sure to have your baggage claim slip with you when you pick up your luggage. Airport transportation is available under the green signs as you depart the baggage claim area. There are buses there that will take you into the center of Middletown. Taxis are also available in the blue parking area. As we taxi to the gate, please stay in your seats until the captain has turned off the seat belt sign.

[To the Reader: Pause 12 seconds after each question.]

40. To whom is this announcement most likely directed?

41. When the passengers exit, what should they do?

42. Where will the baggage arrive?

43. Where can the passengers find airport transportation?

Questions 44 to 46. Listen to the following class lecture:

[MALE SPEAKER]

I always like to begin the first day of class with some English literature that is less serious and somewhat playful. *Winnie-the-Pooh*, a book of tales about a happy little bear named Pooh and his friends, captures what is at the heart of all good literature: the story. It was written by A. A. Milne in the finest of storytelling traditions. The author wrote these stories over 60 years ago for his son Christopher Robin, who served as the model for the little boy in the tales. The tales of Pooh, his best friend Piglet, and the other animals are treasures for children of all ages.

The story of how Milne came up with the name Winnie-the-Pooh is interesting, and is worth discussing before we try our hand at reading these stories aloud. Milne and his son would visit the polar bears at the London Zoo. Young Christopher would talk to the gatekeeper, and the gatekeeper would then unlock a series of doors allowing Milne and his son to see a small furry bear named Winnie. The real Christopher Robin loved Winnie so much that his father made him the main character of this collection of tales.

[To the Reader: Pause 12 seconds after each question.]

44. What general subject is this lecture most likely a part of?

45. Who is Milne?

46. Where did the author get the idea for the main character of his book?

Questions 47 to 50. Listen to the following lecture.

[FEMALE SPEAKER]

I wonder how many of you would want to work in a tall building such as the Empire State Building if you had to climb 102 flights of stairs to reach the top? Not many, I imagine. If it were not for the invention of elevators, or lifts, tall buildings would be unusable. The first lift was just a box suspended on a rope. Using a series of pulleys, a group of oxen or strong men would pull the rope and lift the box to a higher point. Lifts were used only for heavy materials, not passengers. Even in the nineteenth century, when steam power was used to operate the lifts, people didn't ride them. They didn't trust the rope that held the box.

In 1853, Elisha G. Otis invented the first safe lift. He showed his invention in New York at the Crystal Palace Exhibition. At the exhibition, Otis was hauled up in an open box that was attached to two guide rails. When he was lifted far above the spectators, he gave the order to cut the rope. To the amazement of the crowd, the lift did not plummet to the floor. Instead, it clamped fast to the guide rails. He had built powerful metal clamps on the carriage as a safety device. The demonstration worked, and people have been riding as passengers in elevators ever since.

[To the Reader: Pause 12 seconds after each question.]

47. What is the main topic of this lecture?

48. Where was the Crystal Palace Exhibition in 1853?

49. What was special about Otis' elevator?

50. Which of the following topics is the lecturer most likely to discuss next?

This is the end of Section 1, Listening Comprehension. Turn off the tape and continue with Section 2, Structure and Written Expression.

Practice Test 6
SECTION 1
Listening Comprehension

Part A

Directions: In Part A you will hear short conversations between two people. After each conversation a third person will ask a question about what was said. You will hear the conversation only one time, so you must listen carefully to what each speaker says. After you hear the conversation and the question, read the four possible answers in your test booklet and pick the one which best answers the question. Then look on the answer sheet for the number of the question and fill in the oval that corresponds to the letter of your answer choice.

Listen to an example.

> *You will hear:*
> > Woman: Have you called Pete?
> > Man: I'll call him as soon as I get home.
>
> What does the man mean?
>
> *You will read:*
> > **(A)** He will call Pete before he goes home.
> > **(B)** He will call Pete after he gets home.
> > **(C)** He called Pete at home.
> > **(D)** He will call Pete tomorrow.

You learn from the conversation that the man will call Pete as soon as he gets home. The best answer to the question "What does the man mean?" is (B), "He will call Pete after he gets home." Therefore, the correct answer is (B).

Now continue listening to the tape.

[To the Reader: Pause 12 seconds after the third person asks each question.]

1. Woman: Fred, have you done anything about that strange noise in the car?
   Man: Oh, I'll have Adam fix it.

   What does the man mean?

2. Woman: Did you hear that Jeff has passed his oral exam?
   Man: Finally.

   What does the man imply?

3. Woman: How do you like the new librarian at the information desk?
   Man: You mean Ron? He's been here as long as I have!

   What does the man imply?

4. Woman: Would you like me to type your paper this time?
   Man: Would I? Please do.

   What does the man mean?

5. Man: I have to go back to the classroom again.
   Woman: What's up?

   What does the woman want to know?

6. Woman: Mary is going to give me a ride to the party.
   Man: How could she? She doesn't have her license yet.

   What does the man mean?

7. Man: Would you like me to call a night escort?

    Woman: If possible.

    What does the woman mean?

8. Man: Do you accept credit cards?

    Woman: Only if the charge is more than $15.

    What does the woman mean?

9. Woman: I hope I still can register for the speech class.

    Man: I heard there was a waiting list.

    What does the man mean?

10. Man: Dr. Jones, is it possible for the exam to be an open-book exam?

    Woman: Well it would be OK with me, but we have to follow the department regulations.

    What does the woman mean?

11. Woman: Could you take my phone calls for me while I am away?

    Man: Sure, when will you be back?

    What does the man mean?

12. Man: You really shouldn't take any more.

    Woman: Well, one more, and then no more.

    What does the woman mean?

13. Woman: How are you and your roommates getting along?

    Man: So far, so good.

    What does the man mean?

14. Woman: The university policy has changed a lot since I've been here.

    Man: Hasn't it.

    What does the man mean?

15. Man: You weren't scared, were you?

    Woman: Not much, I wasn't! My heart was beating fast and tears were running down my face, that's all.

    What does the woman mean?

16. Woman: Shall we sit here and talk?

    Man: There is no better place than here.

    What does the man mean?

17. Woman: What would you like for your present?

    Man: A racing bike; that's what I've always wanted.

    What does the man mean?

18. Man: Why didn't you buy it?

    Woman: If it had been only two dollars cheaper, I would have.

    What does the woman mean?

19. Man: Marie, why did you get up so early today?

    Woman: I thought someone was coming over.

    What does the woman mean?

20. Woman: Usually Jim washes his car himself.

    Man: Yeah, but this time he took it to the carwash.

    What do they say about Jim?

Part B

Directions: In Part B you will hear longer conversations between two people. After each conversation you will be asked some questions. You will hear the conversations and the questions only once, so listen carefully to what is said. After you hear a question, read the four possible answers in your test book and decide which one is the best answer to the question you heard. Then, on your answer sheet, find the number of the question and fill in the oval that corresponds to the letter of the answer you have chosen. Answer all questions based on what is stated or implied by the speakers.

Listen to the example.

You will hear:

Questions 1 and 2 are based on the following conversation between two friends at school.

Man:	Hi, Joanie. Where are you going?
Woman:	Oh, hi Paul. I'm on my way to the library.
Man:	I just wondered if you wanted to go to a movie with me.
Woman:	I'd love to, but I can't. I can't believe all the work I have this semester. I only have three classes, but in all of them I have lots of reading, term papers, reports, and essay exams. It's incredible! I feel like I'll never get through everything.
Man:	That's terrible. I felt that way last year when I had papers to write, but this semester seems much easier. I spend a lot of time in class, but most of it is in labs doing experiments. I hated writing all those term papers. Can't I talk you into going to the show anyway? I've heard that the movie over at the East Auditorium is really good. It's a murder mystery.
Woman:	Oh, now I'm sure I won't go. I might go to a comedy, but I hate murder mysteries.

Now listen to sample question number 1.

Where is the woman going?

In your test booklet you will read:

> **(A)** to the cafeteria
> **(B)** to the movie theater
> **(C)** to her dorm room
> **(D)** to the library

The best answer to the question "Where is the woman going?" is (D), "to the library." Therefore, the correct choice is (D).

Now listen to sample question number 2.

Which best describes the man's feelings about his classes?

You will read:

> **(A)** Term papers are easy for him.
> **(B)** He has a lot of essay exams.
> **(C)** He finds lab experiments easier than writing term papers.
> **(D)** He is busier this semester than last semester.

The best answer to the question "Which best describes the man's feelings about his classes?" is (C), "He finds lab experiments easier than writing term papers." Therefore, the correct answer is (C).

Now listen to the test. Remember, you are not allowed to take any notes or write in your test book.

Questions 21 to 24. Listen to this conversation between two friends:

Woman: Hi Tim. Where're you headed?

Man: Oh, I'm going downtown to the auction.

Woman: What auction?

Man: The radio auction. It begins today at noon. Have you heard about this kind of auction?

Woman: No, what happens?

Man: Well, people and businesses donate all kinds of things. You can get some great deals. Once I got a $50 gift certificate for the downtown bookstore for only $30. So I saved $20 on books.

Woman: Sounds pretty good. How do you get the things?

Man: Well, you can just listen to the radio and call in the amount you want to pay for something. Or you can come downtown with me if you want. I'm going to the park, where they're broadcasting the auction. If you're there you can call out your bid. The highest bidder wins. Look at my auction booklet. Here's a gift certificate for a dinner for two people at that fancy restaurant called the Ocean Palace. And here are four passes to any show at the Central Cinema.

Woman: OK. You talked me into it. Let's go.

[To the Reader: Pause 12 seconds after each question.]

21. Where is the man going?

22. What did the man previously get at an auction?

23. How can a person get an item at the auction?

24. What is the woman going to do?

Questions 25 to 28. Listen to the following conversation between two people in a restaurant:

Woman: Excuse me, waiter, but I think there is something in my soup.

Man: What's wrong?

Woman: Well, I think I saw an insect or something when I was spooning out the noodles. Could you please bring me another bowl?

Man: Oh, I'm very sorry. I'll get you another bowl.

Woman: Thank you.

Man: Here you are, a fresh bowl of soup.

Woman: Thanks a lot.

Man: I'm very sorry this happened. I'll tell you what; I won't charge you for the soup today.

Woman: That's great. I can use a free lunch.

Man: Good. I hope you come again.

Woman: I'll do that. Thanks.

[To the Reader: Pause 12 seconds after each question.]

25. What is this conversation mainly about?

26. What is the man's occupation?

27. Why did the woman get the attention of the man?

28. At the end of the conversation, how does the woman feel?

Questions 29 to 32. Listen to the following conversation between two friends:

Man: Hi, Marsha. When are you going home today?

Woman: Oh hi, Greg, I have to stay here at the library and study until at least eleven o'clock tonight. Are you studying here, too?

Man: No, I'm not studying; I'm working. I work at the circulation desk until eleven o'clock tonight. Do you want to meet me then?

Woman: OK. Are you working full time now?

Man: Yeah. I work 40 hours a week. And I'm taking three classes.

Woman: Wow! When do you have time to study?

Man: In the mornings usually. Some days all I do is eat, study, work, and sleep.

Woman: That sounds terrible. If you ever get some free time, maybe we could get together and watch a movie or go dancing or something.

Man: That would be great. I'll check my work schedule. Why don't we talk about it when we meet later on.

Woman: OK, see you then.

[To the Reader: Pause 12 seconds after each question.]

29. Where does this conversation take place?

30. What is the woman going to do until eleven o'clock?

31. What is the man doing?

32. What seems to be the main purpose of this conversation?

Questions 33 to 35. Listen to the following conversation between two students in a class:

Man: Caroline, do you know where Tuskegee is?

Woman: Sure, it's in Alabama.

Man: Oh, no. I thought it was somewhere in a foreign country.

Woman: It's a Native American name. Do you know what Tuskegee is famous for?

Man: No.

Woman: It's the home of the Tuskegee Institute, where George Washington Carver worked.

Man: Who was he?

Woman: He was a great scientist who invented over 200 uses for peanuts, sweet potatoes, and other agricultural products.

Man: Really? That's interesting. I like peanuts.

[To the Reader: Pause 12 seconds after each question.]

33. Where is Tuskegee located?

34. What does the woman say about George Washington Carver?

35. What quality most clearly describes the man?

Part C

Directions: In this part of the test, you will hear talks by a single speaker. After each talk, you will be asked some questions. You will hear the talks and the questions only once, so listen carefully to what is said. After you hear a question, read the four possible answers in your test book and decide which one is the best answer to the question you heard. Then, find the number of the question on your answer sheet, and fill in the oval that corresponds to the letter of the answer you have chosen. Answer all questions based on what is stated or implied in the talk.

Listen to this sample talk.

You will hear:

Questions 1–4 are based on the following announcement:

[FEMALE SPEAKER]

At this university we offer three different programs for students who have children. For those of you with very young children, we have a day care program that takes infants from 3 months to 30 months. We have another program for children between two and five years of age. And we also have an after-school program for school-aged children. This program offers sports, crafts, outings, and tutoring during after-school hours. Enrollment in these child care programs is limited and early application is essential, since our programs often have waiting lists. The fees are on an hourly basis. If any of you new students need these services, please let me know right away so I can get you an application form.

Now listen to sample question number 1.

What is the main purpose of this announcement?

You will read:

        (A) to demonstrate tutoring techniques
        (B) to explain school policies
        (C) to recruit childcare workers
        (D) to explain a service

The best answer to the question "What is the purpose of this announcement?" is (D), "to explain a service." Therefore, the correct choice is (D).

Now listen to sample question number 2.

What does the speaker recommend?

You will read:

        (A) Give your child extra tutoring.
        (B) Take your child to the program today.
        (C) Apply as soon as you can.
        (D) Pay next month.

The best answer to the question "What does the speaker recommend?" is (C), "Apply as soon as you can." Therefore the correct choice is (C).

Now listen to the talks. Remember, you are not allowed to write any notes in your test book.

Questions 36 to 39. Listen to the following announcement given by a professor at the beginning of a class:

[FEMALE SPEAKER]

Before we get started with the lecture today, I want to share some information I received in the mail yesterday. This letter is announcing a program called "Paleontology with the Smithsonian." It says that Smithsonian Research Expeditions is offering a study trip for volunteer field workers. The volunteers will help explore some current archeological digs in Wyoming. The trip will last from May 22 to June 5, and the participants will learn about the animals and plants that existed about 150 million years ago near the town of Cody, Wyoming. Volunteers will search for remains of plants and animals while living in tents near the dig sites. Smithsonian paleontologists will teach field skills such as prospecting, mapping and labeling, and excavation techniques. During the evenings, they will give informal lectures and lead discussions. You need to bring your own sleeping bag. The cost of the expedition is $1,500, and you get class credit from our department here. It sounds like a good opportunity to learn a lot about archeology, and have a good time. If you'd like more information, come see me after class.

[To the Reader: Pause 12 seconds after each question.]

36. What class are the students most likely taking?

37. Where will the volunteers go?

38. What will the field workers be doing?

39. How much does the trip cost?

Questions 40 to 43. Listen to the following announcement by an announcer on a local radio station:

[MALE SPEAKER]

KKED radio is pleased to announce the opening of our annual festival of animation. This year's festival will include the Oscar-winning film *Mona Lisa Descending a Staircase*. The movie is an animated journey through several hundred years of art history. It includes some particularly scary images of Francis Bacon. Other highlights of the festival include some beautiful cut-out animation in the French movie *The Prince and the Princess*. The festival begins April 16 and will run through May 9th at the Palace of Fine Arts. For more information you can call us here at KKED radio, or call the Palace of Fine Arts.

[To the Reader: Pause 12 seconds after each question.]

40. What is the main topic of this announcement?

41. What academic subject is expressed in the film *Mona Lisa Descending a Staircase?*

42. What is featured at the festival?

43. Where is the festival being held?

Questions 44 to 46. Listen to the following talk given by a tour guide:

[MALE SPEAKER]

Los Angeles today is the second largest city in America, sprawling over 464 square miles along the southern California coast. It is the center of the entertainment industry, and it has a balmy climate of mostly sunny days. But there was a time when Los Angeles was nothing more than a tiny Indian village. The Spanish expedition searching for Monterey Bay camped there the night of August 1, 1769. Twelve years later, other Spaniards started a settlement at the village, which remained unchanged for decades. Yankee sea traders used the settlement as a port, and the California gold rush brought some new economic life to the village, but the town remained quite small. It was not until the completion of the transcontinental railroads in 1869, and the discovery of oil in the 1890s, that the population began to grow. Later, during the two world wars, Los Angeles experienced more growth, in part because of the new airplane industry. At about the same time, the arrival of two New York motion picture producers in search of sunny weather marked the beginning of an entertainment industry that has become a multibillion-dollar industry today. In just the past 100 years, this tiny sea village has grown into the sprawling metropolis that we know today.

[To the Reader: Pause 12 seconds after each question.]

44. What is this talk about?

45. What two factors caused the town to begin to grow?

46. Approximately how many years ago did Los Angeles begin growing into a large city?

Questions 47 to 50. Listen to the following presentation given by a student in her class:

[FEMALE SPEAKER]

Last summer I was working in Washington, D.C., as an intern at the Armed Forces Institute of Pathology. In one way it was an awful job because the purpose was to figure out ways to identify dead people, like identifying the remains of soldiers in wars, or bodies after disasters such as plane crashes or earthquakes. But the exciting part was that I was working with a scientist who heads a program that is identifying bodies by their DNA structures. As you know, DNA is the name for the genetic material in our bodies. In the past, all soldiers had to wear a necklace and a metal tag with their names and identification numbers on the tag. But this method of identification was not very accurate because the tags could be lost or switched around. So in my job I worked at helping the Institute to set up a DNA file to store the genetic information for new soldiers. The armed forces will get a blood sample from each person, and they'll use the samples to create a DNA file for each person in the military. Then, if the body of a military person cannot be identified by its tag, fingerprints, or dental records, the body tissue can be analyzed and matched with DNA records at the Institute.

[To the Reader: Pause 12 seconds after each question.]

47. Where did the woman work the previous summer?

48. What is the purpose of the program the woman is discussing?

49. What did the speaker say was exciting about her work?

50. In what class would the student most likely be making this presentation?

This is the end of Section 1, Listening Comprehension. Turn off the tape and continue with Section 2, Structure and Written Expression.